KEROUAC

KEROUAC

A BIOGRAPHY
BY
ANN CHARTERS

St. Martin's Press
New York

Library of Congress Cataloging-in-Publication Data

Charters, Ann.
    Kerouac : a biography / Ann Charters.
      p.   cm.
    Originally published: San Francisco : Straight Arrow Books, 1973. With new introd.
    ISBN 0-312-11347-1 (paperback)
    1. Kerouac, Jack, 1922–1969.   2. Authors, American—20th century—Biography.   3. Beat generation—Biography.   I. Title.
PS3521.E735Z63   1994
813'.54—dc20
[B]   94-13082
                                            CIP

10 9 8 7 6 5 4

To Allen Ginsberg

"Why, even I myself, I often think,
know little of my real life; only a few
hints, a few diffuse faint clues and
indirections I seek for my own use
to trace out here." —*Walt Whitman*

Contents

Foreword

by Allen Ginsberg

Ann Charters loved Kerouac's art, did his first Bibliography with/for him while alive, cherished his scripture and literary soul-might, researched with dignity the interior of his novels and family, spoke many years with his friends, and applied her vast tactful scholarship as a master musician-archivist of jazz to the understanding of his musical sound as American lonely Prose Trumpeter of drunken Buddha Sacred Heart.

Preface

I am grateful for the opportunity to write a preface to this edition of *Kerouac,* since I'd like to thank certain people again for helping me write the biography twenty and more years ago. When I wrote to Kerouac's mother in 1966 and asked for help in compiling his bibliography, Jack was surprised that anyone was serious enough about his work to take on the job. While Kerouac was alive, he was ridiculed by reviewers and critics for his desire to be regarded as a great writer and for his insistence that the scope of his work was a giant epic in the tradition of Balzac and Proust.

Now that Kerouac's major novel, *On the Road* is accepted as an American classic, academic critics are slowly beginning to catch up with his experimental literary methods and examine the dozen books comprising what he called "the legend of Duluoz." Nearly all of his books have been in print internationally since his death in 1969, and his writing has been discovered and enjoyed by new readers throughout the world. Kerouac's view of the promise of America, the seductive and lovely vision of the beckoning open spaces of our continent, has never been expressed better by subsequent writers, perhaps because Kerouac was our last writer to believe in America's promise—and essential innocence—as the legacy he would explore in his autobiographical fiction.

In retrospect, I feel this biography of Kerouac seems to capture something of the spirit of its time, since it was researched in the 1960s, written in the first years of the 1970s, published by Straight Arrow in January 1973, and last revised for a paperback edition in 1974. Since then there have been several biographies of Kerouac, adding much information to our knowledge of his life. The passage of time itself has also brought posthumous developments important to a biographer. For example, in 1971 I wrote that Kerouac's grave in the Lowell cemetery had no marker. Some years later his wife, Stella, designed a stone marker to commemorate Jack's memory, eloquently engraved, "He Honored Life." You can see a photograph of it in my book *Beats & Company*, published in 1986.

A reader desiring the most personal account of Kerouac's life would be best served by the edition of his selected letters that I have been editing for the past several years. This early biography is less factually detailed, but I think it is useful as a record of the response to Kerouac by a contemporary scholar fortunate enough to be the recipient of generous help from Kerouac and many of his friends. I began my research on Kerouac's life and work a few months after completing my doctorate at Columbia University. At the start I had no intention of writing a biography of a living author, but working with Kerouac in 1966 to compile his bibliography, I discovered I was just as interested in asking him questions about *how* he wrote his books as I was in recording the details of the publication of the books themselves. After Kerouac's death, this biography couldn't have been written or found its publisher without the help of certain key people. It most certainly wasn't the result of my effort and thought alone, even if at the time I was apparently the person most obsessed with telling a coherent story about Kerouac's life.

As I said in an earlier preface to the biography, my most crucial assistance in writing the book came from my husband, Samuel Charters. In his years researching black music in the American South in the 1950s, he had lived the life on the road that Kerouac described. Sam knew firsthand what it felt like to hitchhike back and forth between the East and West coasts, ride cross-country buses, live in noisy hotels next to the railroad tracks, and—at the end of each trip—drop his worn traveling bag on somebody's bedroom floor.

Also, like Kerouac, Sam was a poet and novelist, so he knew firsthand the creative process that was central to Jack's life. Sam wrote the biography with me in the isolation of our rented house by a lake in the country outside Stockholm, Sweden, after we left New York City with our young daughter Mallay at the end of 1970 as a protest against the Vietnam War. We wrote and revised in nighttime, morning, and afternoon shifts. This was after I had completed the primary research and the first rough draft of the book, a difficult job since I was the first person attempting to link the scattered evidence of Kerouac's life and work.

Sam filled in the gaps, recognizing that a sense of Kerouac's America was essential to the spirit of the biography. So on his trips back to the United States to record music for the Swedish company that employed him, Sam rode subways to Brooklyn, walked the streets of Ozone Park, drank beer at the West End Bar near Columbia University, ordered a hamburger and a milk shake and listened to the local people in the Textile Lunch cafe in Kerouac's old French-Canadian neighborhood in Lowell... and returned to Stockholm to add his sense of the essential geography to the book in progress.

I particularly remember one small detail Sam put into the biography that delighted me when I found it in his revision of Chapter Seven: his idea of how Kerouac, after hours of sitting at the typewriter, might kick back his chair and get up to take a beer from the refrigerator. When I read this passage early one morning after Sam had written it in the late hours the night before, I thought to myself, "So that's what Sam does while I'm sleeping and he's at the typewriter." If Jack comes alive on the pages of this biography, it's because Sam put him there.

Allen Ginsberg, of course, was the other key person after Sam Charters whose generous gifts of time, ideas, and research materials were invaluable for the creation of *Kerouac*. When I wrote the introduction to the earlier editions of the book, I described how Allen helped me. Gary Snyder and Michael McClure also gave me much needed encouragement during the final stages of the book when they visited us in Stockholm. McClure went back to San Francisco and interested Straight Arrow in publishing the biography.

But to set the record straight, the Beats weren't the only well-known writers of the 1960s who were my inspiration: the poet Charles Olson was another vital source. I'd worked with Olson on two books, and we talked and corresponded by letter and telegram for two years before his death from cancer in

1970. Olson gave me a sense of history that helped shape my view of Kerouac's life.

Olson believed that history and mythology were central to the human experience. He insisted that we view history not as some abstract phenomenon divorced from us in space and time, but as actual energy and active forces that involve our imagination. To Olson, history is "the function of any one of us." A life is "the historical function of the individual."

Thanks to Olson, I understood that the value of Kerouac's life was what he did, how he acted. And what he did, was that he wrote. I tried to arrange the incidents of his life to show that he was a writer first, and a mythologized figure afterward. Kerouac's writing counts as much as his life.

So how do Kerouac, Ginsberg, Snyder, McClure, Olson, and Charters give a sense of the 1960s? It was a time in the cultural life of America when we possessed a feeling for what we called "the openheart." We believed in dreams and possibilities, in an America that belonged to all of us. We admired, as I've said, those whom Ginsberg called our "secret heroes"—blues and jazz musicians, starving artists and poets, people of various backgrounds and occupations throughout America who thought for themselves about the possibilities of a better world and then were blacklisted during the McCarthy era or jailed or killed protesting our country's intervention in Vietnam. We lived by our ideas and created poetry, fiction, biography, and history out of them. His-story. Her-story. Our story.

—ANN CHARTERS
Connecticut, 1994

Introduction

I first met Jack Kerouac in the spring of 1956 at a poetry reading in Berkeley. Peter Orlovsky took me there to hear his friend Allen Ginsberg recite "Howl." I remember Jack as a darkly intense, handsome young man in rumpled clothes who got to the theater early and stood up near the stage, holding high his own bottle of wine, loudly advising Kenneth Rexroth how to run the show.

When crowds of people had gathered, he passed a hat for contributions and rushed out to buy gallons of wine so everybody in the audience could drink too. I was impressed by his strong will and his wild energy. He waved his bottle of wine and shouted encouragement as Allen rhapsodically chanted his poem. He passed love notes up to Rexroth for poets on the stage throughout the reading, and at the end leaped on stage to congratulate and embrace his friends.

I didn't get to talk to him much that night. I only remember disagreeing with Peter that Ginsberg was as good a poet as Whitman. At the time I was a junior at the University of California majoring in English, and my literary opinions were at least as strongly held as Peter's. I remember as he walked me home that night we argued the length of Dwight Way.

The next time Kerouac came into my life was three years later, when I was a graduate student at Columbia. William York Tindall, lecturing on some modern English writer, paused to make an aside about Kerouac, whose book *The Dharma Bums* was then selling very well and getting a lot of attention. This was the period when *Time* Magazine was needling the beatniks. Tindall referred to Kerouac as a Columbia alumnus, and then went on to put him down as a writer, saying at Columbia he hadn't even been successful enough at football to make the team, and he wasn't doing any better as he got older. Instead of nodding with the class and making a note of Tindall's judgment for a future exam question, I found I didn't agree. Perhaps it was my prejudice as a Californian, but I had liked Jack's picture of Berkeley life in *The Dharma Bums,* feeling it had captured something of my own experience there. In the three years since the Berkeley reading, I'd put myself on Kerouac's side.

My involvement in what has since been called America's counter-culture began with a response to two of the underground poets. In 1957 Kerouac and Ginsberg were the first contemporaries I'd read whose writing seemed true in some essential way to my own thoughts and feelings about America. I went on from *Howl* and *On The Road* to discover that Kerouac and Ginsberg were just two in a larger group of writers whose work was very different from that of Establishment poets and novelists. The underground writers differed not only in their literary style and their political attitudes, but also in their concern for the intuitive as well as the rational bases of human knowledge. The more I read the poetry of Gary Snyder, Gregory Corso, Michael McClure, Lawrence Ferlinghetti, Larry Eigner, Robert Creeley and Charles Olson, the more I responded to them. They were all speaking in different voices as individual poets, but they were also all speaking the same language, my language. As I began to search out their poems in little magazines and small press books, everything I found confirmed my feeling that these writers were speaking for me, expressing my own deepest concerns and interests.

At the same time, in the late 1950s and early 1960s, I was helping my husband, Sam Charters, record and research black music in the South and the Bahamas. The books and records we produced were, as Allen Ginsberg later described them to me, our "chronicles of America's secret heroes." During the years in which this other work was being done, I continued to read Kerouac. He was becoming, through his books, another of my "secret heroes."

It must have been in 1962 that I decided to become

12

a collector of Kerouac's works. I was teaching college in New Hampshire and walked into the Dartmouth Library one day to find an exhibit of Erskine Caldwell's books filling the corridors. The variety of dustwrapper illustrations and foreign editions in the library's glass cases was so impressive, that I decided to make a similar collection of Kerouac works. I started to buy each book I saw, and since he was publishing new titles every year in hard and softcover editions, my collection grew rapidly and became an absorbing interest. I soon realized I wanted to read every word he'd ever published and that I was waiting for new Kerouac titles with the same passion that Jack had waited for the *Shadow* Magazine every other Friday when he was a boy in Lowell.

In 1963, I moved back to New York to complete my doctorate in nineteenth-century American literature, and we lived in the East Village while I studied and taught at Columbia. I scouted Kerouac's books and magazine articles in the used bookstores along Fourth Avenue and in the back-issue and pornographic magazine shops off Times Square. When my husband made a trip around the world in 1966, he sent back all the Kerouac translations in foreign editions he could find.

In 1966, my doctorate completed, the Phoenix Bookshop asked me to compile a Kerouac bibliography for their modern writers series. I'd heard that Jack was moody and uncooperative, an alcoholic who was completely disinterested in strangers who came to his door wanting to meet him. I'd also heard that he had kept a nearly complete collection of his books and articles in his house, and realized that his help was essential. The Phoenix Series had included a Gregory Corso bibliography, and so I decided to use it as a gambit. Instead of contacting Jack directly, I sent the Corso bibliography to his mother, Gabrielle Ange Kerouac, with a letter explaining that I'd like to come to their house to make an annotated and scholarly list of Kerouac's books for his bibliography.

The plan worked. Jack wrote me saying that if I was a "scholar and a gentlewoman," I could come to visit him in Hyannis in August. I set off in my car with my Irish setter, a stack of 3x5 index cards and a carton of Kerouac's books for him to sign from my own collection.

The night before leaving for Hyannis I was so excited I had the first of what was to be many dreams about Kerouac. I dreamed that I arrived to find Kerouac's living room dark and shadowy and filled with scholars who'd come there before me to do research for their own books and articles. The room looked like a library, the sofa and the TV pushed back against the wall to make space for long desks and chairs for the researchers, something like the British Museum Reading Room in miniature. At the center was a desk where mémêre presided over the card catalogue, handing out Jack's books. I joined the line and shuffled forward to present my written request for Kerouac material. Jack's mother disappeared to get it, and as I waited for her to come back I noticed Jack himself sitting alone on the sofa in a dark corner of the room. He was almost concealed by the heavy drapes at the window, ignored by everyone in the room, looking sad and lonely. I went over and sat down beside him. He didn't look up, but I felt I had to talk with him. Leaning toward him, I heard myself say, "Hello, Jack. It seems to me with all these people here working on your books, and you so silent, you're already dead." He didn't even turn toward me but just sat on the sofa and looked straight ahead of him at nothing. I was so horrified at my own words that I woke up.

I never told him the dream. When we compiled the bibliography together our meeting was totally unlike my dream and we worked well together. Our days in Hyannis are described in a final chapter of this biography. When the bibliography was published by Phoenix in 1967, the dreams didn't stop. They came every year or so, in different circumstances, and were usually made up of images or brief conversations that I'd had with Kerouac.

In 1967, I began two books about the poet Charles Olson and started the research for another project that was originally conceived as a history of the underground poetry scene since the 1950s. I collected material, interviewing and corresponding with the poets, and when Kerouac died on 21 October, 1969 I had a trunk full of tapes and books and notes. I went up to Lowell for Kerouac's funeral, saw his body lying in the open casket at the Archambault Funeral Home and steeled myself to touch his forehead. Allen Ginsberg told me I had to do it, so I wouldn't be afraid and would know he was really dead. Standing in the cold, windy cemetery after the church service the following day, I dropped a flower into the grave before leaving with Kerouac's close friends for the wake at the house of his wife's family in Lowell.

When I returned to New York after Kerouac's funeral, I began writing my book on all the underground poets, but the work never found a focus. Then, in 1970 my husband, daughter and I left the United States after the Cambodia invasion to move to Sweden as a personal protest against the Vietnam War. In Stockholm I realized I wanted to write a biographical work specifically about Kerouac. All the material I needed had been shipped in black trunks from Brooklyn Heights. I began the Kerouac biography in Stockholm in February 1971 and finished it in San Francisco in October 1972.

The last dream about Kerouac recently was while I was in Paris, just before coming to San Francisco. I'd walked the streets all day looking for French editions of his books and had found a new, inexpensive reprint of *On The Road* in French translation. The bookseller told me he was selling lots of copies and that "That man Kerouac is a model for the young." Passing Notre Dame, I went inside and on a sudden impulse lit a candle for Jack, remembering from his book *Satori in Paris* how strongly he felt France was his spiritual birthplace. That night, after I'd lit the candle, my husband dreamt about Kerouac. He told me he dreamt he'd met Jack on the street and had said to him, "Come on home and drink a beer with Annie." Jack came home and drank beer all afternoon and wrote a poem. He also said something that summed up his life in a single phrase. I asked my husband urgently what the phrase was. He told me the poem, but the phrase he couldn't remember.

The factual material in this biography was based on several primary sources. Interviews with people who knew Kerouac helped to fill out the story of his life as he wrote about it in his eighteen published books; everything he ever wrote was to some extent autobiographical. Gary Snyder once told me that Jack, in his books, was "a very accurate reporter" of events, but that he changed certain details to protect himself legally as well as to fictionalize what he wrote about himself and his friends. Names, for example, would be changed (Jack renamed himself "Ray Smith," "Leo Percepied," "Sal Paradise," "Jack Duluoz"), locations of friends' houses might be shifted over a block and a mistress might be said to have had a son, not a daughter. Kerouac was often interviewed, and I have made use of these interviews, but toward the end of his life Jack's statements to interviewers sometimes contradicted earlier things he said.

The most reliable source of information about Kerouac's life were the letters exchanged with his friends, a large number of which are now on deposit at various university libraries. Kerouac's letters were often written five minutes after the action they describe, full of details about the most important—and the most trivial—events in his life. The description of his life in his books has been checked against these letters and his journals whenever possible. The interviews with his friends fill out the story. The friends who were with him at different times in his life often have different impressions of what happened and vary their emphasis and emotional interpretation of events. Memories often differ also on straightforward factual details. I have tried to recheck these discrepancies as far as humanly possible.

A list of sources for each chapter appears at the end of the book, to verify information and indicate passages in Kerouac's writing so interested readers can follow the story of Jack's life as he wrote it in the *Legend of Duluoz,* his "fictional" autobiography. Kerouac, of course, is his own best biographer. For the full force of his energy and the dimensions of his spirit, you must read the *Legend* as he wrote it.

Kerouac couldn't have been written without the help of many people. First and most important, of course, was Jack Kerouac himself, who patiently answered my questions and allowed me access to his journals, notes and manuscripts, and corresponded with me for the last three years of his life. His mother Gabrielle Ange Kerouac in Hyannis and his wife Stella Sampas Kerouac at the funeral in Lowell were also both extremely helpful during our informal interviews.

Without doubt the second most important source for the writing of this biography after Kerouac and his family was Allen Ginsberg. I began asking Allen questions about Jack in 1966 when I recorded Ginsberg at a war protest benefit reading in New York at St. Mark's in the Bowery, a record released by Portents and Folkways as *Poems For Peace.* After the business of the record was finished, Allen and I sat down together in his apartment on East 10th Street and had a long exchange about Kerouac's *Legend of Duluoz.*

Ginsberg was of inestimable assistance throughout the years I collected material for this book. Besides our interviews in New York, Brooklyn Heights, Cherry Valley, New York and Lowell, Masschusetts, he gave me unlimited access to the material in his archives on deposit at Columbia University. My work with his photographs there resulted in another book, *Scenes Along The Road,* in 1969, and it was Ginsberg who suggested the title for the collection of Kerouac poems I edited for City Lights, *Scattered Poems,* in 1970.

Kerouac is dedicated to Allen Ginsberg, because like Jack I have felt the full force of his encouragement. Without Ginsberg's help I wouldn't have had the information or the insight necessary to write this book.

Other writers who have been generous with their time and assistance have been William Burroughs, John Clellon Holmes, Gary Snyder, Lawrence Ferlinghetti, Gregory Corso, Robert and Bobbie Creeley, Charles Olson, Kenneth Rexroth, David Meltzer, Peter Orlovsky, Ray and Bonnie Bremser, John Montgomery, Carl Solomon, Herbert Huncke and Michael McClure, who also first interested Alan Rinzler at Straight Arrow in publishing the manuscript.

Friends of Kerouac's in Lowell who helped were Charles Sampas, James Curtis and Charles Jarvis. Marshall Clements and David Stivender in New York City were of great assistance with photographs, manuscripts, xeroxed material and their extensive knowledge of the Duluoz Legend.

Others who contributed information were Robert La-

Vigne, Alene and Lucien Carr, Walter Gibson, Donald Allen, Herb Caen, Joanna McClure, Joan McIntyre, Hal Chase, Hugo Weber, Bill Sanders, Peter Martin, Diana Hansen, David Markson, Arlene Donovan, Andreas Brown, Robert A. Wilson, Robert Hawley, Peter Howard, Shigeyoshi Murao, Gunnar Harding, Kenneth Lohf at the Columbia University Library and the library staff at the University of Texas and the University of California at Berkeley and Los Angeles. Malcolm Cowley, Robert Giroux at Farrar, Straus and Giroux, Edwin Kennebeck at Viking Press and Joyce Glassman at McGraw-Hill made available to me their editorial files and personal memories of Kerouac.

For help with this revised edition, I thank Stella Kerouac, Allen Ginsberg, Tom Parkinson, David Diamond, Robert Giroux, Alfred Kazin, John Montgomery, Joseph Le-Sueur, Jeff Weinberg, Martin Swanson, Marshall Clements, Lawrence Ferlinghetti, William Burroughs, John Clellon Holmes, Barbara Burgower, Bob Abel, and Arthur Knight.

I also wish to thank the many friends in New York, Los Angeles, San Francisco, Berkeley, Stockholm and London who helped watch my young daughter Mallay while I worked on the book: Mary Forte, Roz & Edward Danberg, Kate Danberg, Susan & Bart Ferris, Dorothy Hawley, Alison Howard, Hortense Clyne, Lotta Harding, Vivica Haegqvist, Ingrid Goffe, June Svensk, Git Sandstrom, Betty Colyer and Fiona & Hilary Stoll. My friends Rao Roegiers, Reva Brown and Marshall Clements generously shared their homes with me while I did the final revision on the manuscript.

Finally I thank my daughter Mallay for her limitless patience with my work on the book, and my husband Samuel Charters, who personally encouraged and assisted me beyond limit or measure. He began reading the underground poets and Kerouac's books years before I did. He criticized every stage of the manuscript and helped in the rewriting of some of the revised chapters. This biography couldn't have been written without him, but its errors and omissions are my own. With Samuel Charters, as with Kerouac and Ginsberg, it's love that animates the poetry and sustains every word.　　　　　　Stockholm
1971–1974

KEROUAC

Part One

1922–1951

Chapter One

In 1954, when Jack Kerouac was thirty-two years old, he tried to define, for a friend, what it was he wanted out of life. The friend suggested that what he really wanted was a thatched hut like Thoreau's, not at Walden Pond, but in Lowell, the town where Jack was born, near Walden, in Massachusetts.

Kerouac agreed. He had left Lowell after high school, but, emotionally, he never left it at all, and whatever it was that held him there was always with him.

No one completely outgrows his childhood and everyone tends to sentimentalize the place where he grew up, but Lowell is not a town that's easy to feel sentimental about. It is an old Massachusetts mill-town, not Thoreau's Concord or Walden Pond. Yet Kerouac's attachment to Lowell, like so many other things in his life, was dominated by fantasy, as much as by anything real.

Through most of his life Kerouac played games with himself, giving himself new roles and identities, vanities as he called them in his last years. His belief in himself as a writer was his main identity, and in an essential way after he left Lowell it was the only identity that held him fast.

Neal Cassady once imagined a mutual friend saying of Jack: "Where is this guy, Kerouac, anyway?" Kerouac himself never knew. His essence lay in a romantic vision of himself. It lay in his fantasies: as a child, the fantasy of living with a saintly older brother Gerard; as an adolescent, of fighting evil alongside the mysterious Doctor Sax, of going with a football scholarship from a small high school to All-America fame at an Ivy League college; then, as an adult, the fantasy of being the greatest writer in the English language since Shakespeare and James Joyce, and when that success didn't come, in desperation, successive fantasies of being a drifter, a railroad brakeman, a Zen mountaineer, a holy mystic living on simple foods cooked along lonely streams; and through everything returning again and again to the only fantasy that always held him, the vision of being a child permanently cut adrift in a darkening universe.

This stream of fantasies, visions, myths, dreams, vanities—Kerouac used all these words for them—made up his life. They were the legend that he felt his life became. And they became more than this. In the intensity of the vision he had of his confused life he caught the dreams of a generation: the feeling that at some point something had been together, that there was a special vision they all shared, a romantic ideal that called on the road just ahead.

To this generation Jack Kerouac became a romantic hero, an archetypal rebel, the symbol of their own vanities, the symbol of their own romantic legend. He never understood this. He was a man whose life was dominated by a deeply felt sense of mortality, not the actual circumstances of what happened to him. His real life lay in his "vanities" and the legend he made out of them. Until, as he wrote it down, the legend became, finally, the only reality his life had.

Lowell is a small textile manufacturing center, a milltown, on the Merrimack River in northeastern Massachusetts, about thirty miles north of downtown Boston. It's poor, dirty and rundown, both working-class and obstinately bourgeois, belligerently provincial.

If you go back to the Lowell main streets looking for traces of Kerouac there isn't much to find. New buildings, housing projects and modern store fronts have obliterated much of what he can have remembered from the twenties and thirties. But in the old French-Canadian neighborhoods on the other side of the river you can still turn a corner, or walk down a street and feel that nothing has changed. You can still get coffee and a hamburger in the Textile Lunch where Kerouac lived in the wooden building upstairs. On a winter afternoon in Lowell not long ago I heard a young French-Canadian high school boy at the narrow lunch counter tell the lady cooking in the back about the injury to his left knee that he'd gotten in a football game. Standing there, short, thin, with shining eyes, in a T-shirt and wash pants under his mackinaw, he could have been Kerouac after a game for 'Lowell High on an afternoon over thirty years before.

The houses Kerouac lived in are still there down Beaulieu Street, or Lupine Road, or Sarah Avenue, the same cracks he jumped in the sidewalks, the same scrubby brush alongside the Merrimack River where his imaginary friend Doctor Sax waited in the gloom of misty November evenings. Kerouac grew up mostly in the shabby French-Canadian neighborhood of Pawtucketville, and he never made much of an impression on downtown Lowell. If you ask today at a florist's shop in which of the city's two Catholic cemeteries he's buried, you'll probably be sent to the wrong one.

It is difficult to be sure if Jack loved Lowell itself, or if he was only attached to a romantic picture of the childhood he'd spent there. He was proud of having come from Lowell and went back even when his family had left. He couldn't stay there but he did always remain aware of the part of Lowell that was in him. His life centered there. He had memories of it all, from the textile mills along the river to the main business center where his father had a printing shop, to the rundown neighborhoods across the river where he grew up.

The raw outline of the legend which he made out of his life in Lowell is simple and uncomplicated. He was born at 9 Lupine Road, a simple, yellow-brown, wooden house on a back street almost out of Lowell in the hilly woods to the northeast, on 12 March, 1922, at 5 o'clock in the evening. He was the third child of Leo Alcide Kerouac, a job printer born in New Hampshire, who'd worked in the mills as a boy, and Gabrielle Ange Levesque Kerouac. Both were French Canadians whose families had emigrated to New England from Quebec.

Writing about his childhood in an "Author's Introduction" written in 1960 for his book, *Lonesome Traveler*, Kerouac described his family's origins in Breton, France. He said that around 1750 Baron Alexandre Louis Lebris

22

de Kerouac of Cornwall, Brittany received a land grant in Canada where various descendants married Mohawk and Caughnawaga Indians and went into potato farming. His grandfather, Jean-Baptiste, was the first Kerouac to settle in the United States. He was a carpenter in Nashua, New Hampshire. His mother's ancestors, the L'Evesques, came from Normandy.

Jack was proud of this background. His father told him the family were aristocratic descendants of Cornish Celts who had come to Cornwall from Ireland "in the olden days long before Jesus." Their name itself was an ancient Gaelic name, "Kerouac'h," meaning, according to Jack's father, "Language of the House." After moving from Cornwall to Brittany, Jack was told, the family acquired an ancestral shield, "blue with gold stripes accompanied by three silver nails" and the motto *"Aimer, Travailler et Souffrir"*—Love, Work and Suffer.

Jack was baptized Jean Louis Lebris de Kerouac, supposedly after the French baron who had been his first North American ancestor. At home Jack was called "Ti Jean," Little Jack. He continued to use it in signing his letters to close friends until the last years of his life.

Jack had a brother, Gerard, who was five years older, and a sister, Caroline, nicknamed "Nin," who was three years older. His first memory was of sitting in his mother's arms. She was wearing the old brown bathrobe that members of the family always put on when they were sick. After that, brown was always associated with the color of life, the color of Jack's family, the comfort and security he felt there.

But Jack's strongest memories were of his brother Gerard's illness and death. Shortly after Jack's birth the family left their home on Lupine Road and moved to a house on Beaulieu Street in a quiet residential neighborhood called Centralville. Gerard died at the age of nine at home on Beaulieu Street, and Jack, then four years old, remembered that he was too nervous to sleep alone for years afterwards, so he slept in his mother's bed.

His sister Caroline was an early playmate. When she was eight years old and Jack was five, they went to the Saturday matinee movies together in downtown Lowell. They got in free because their father used to print the theater's programs. They used to arrive nearly an hour early and wait for Tim McCoy, Hoot Gibson or their favorite, Tom Mix, to appear on the screen, as they sat restlessly in their balcony seats close to the Moorish plaster cherubim in the ceiling, blowing bubble gum and ducking the usher.

The language spoken at home was French-Canadian. This was Kerouac's first language, and learning English in first grade from the nuns at St. Joseph's Brothers School was a struggle. On Sundays Jack walked to church with his mother and his sister. Later he was allowed to attend Sunday religious classes and go to confession by himself. Like most children, Kerouac made at least one attempt to run away from home. When he was eight, he left Lowell with a couple of small friends on a twenty-mile hike, heading for Pelham, New Hampshire, and adventures in the open country. The next day they were found cold and wet after a dismal night spent on the banks of the Merrimack River.

Centralville was the first neighborhood Kerouac remembered well. The family moved around a lot in Lowell, so Jack did not grow up with any one place which he cherished in particular. In 1932, when Jack was ten years old, after having changed houses a couple of times in Centralville, the family moved out to the French-Canadian neighborhood of Pawtucketville. This was the neighborhood where Jack felt most comfortable, the one he remembered as his childhood home more than any of the others.

Jack's mother Gabrielle—everyone called her mémêre —was fiercely devoted to her family and never made any close friends among their neighbors in Pawtucketville. She was a deeply religious Catholic. After Gerard's death she was very protective of her only son Jack, yet held the memory of Gerard up to him as a nearly saintly ideal of human perfection. She was always at home cleaning, washing, cooking. He never forgot her cooking—pancakes and maple syrup and sausages for breakfast, for lunch hamburgers and pork chops, or porkball stews, lots of fluffy mashed potatoes, buttered pieces of bread to dip in the gravy, desserts of cherry pie with whipped cream or vanilla pudding and for supper liver paté sandwiches

24

followed by warm peach cake or Leo's favorite dessert, date pie with whipped cream.

Mémère was intensely practical. She spent no money on herself, dressing in shabby housedresses and clean aprons, her face round and serene under her glasses. Leo Kerouac was much more sociable. He'd been, in turn, an insurance salesman, a job printer and then manager of a bowling alley. In Jack's words, he was "a popular fellow around Lowell." He took Ti Jean with him to the horse races in Boston one fall day when he was twelve, and shortly afterwards, absorbing his father's taste for the races (they both had the same memory for racing percentages and batting averages), Jack began his own involved horse racing games with marbles in his bedroom. He wiped the linoleum floor meticulously with a damp mop before every race and afterwards recorded the results for imaginary racing fans who followed the series in his own turf paper.

When his mother heard the mournful strains of the old 78 record "Dardenella" on Jack's wind-up phonograph coming from upstairs, she knew that the race was about to begin. Mémère was less enthusiastic about horse racing than Leo and tried to stop Jack from hanging around his stuffy room, telling him instead to play outside in the fresh air. She hung the nursery picture "Jack be nimble, Jack be quick" on his bedroom wall.

After the family moved to Phebe Avenue, Jack went to Bartlett Junior High School and, between the ages of twelve and thirteen, began to spend hours playing in the Pawtucket neighborhood or exploring the banks of the nearby Merrimack River. Kerouac remembered that when he was little he got all his boyhood "in vanilla winter waves around the kitchen stove," but after he began junior high school his mother took a job in the mills downtown so Jack stayed out on the streets instead of coming straight home from school. His first and favorite game was a fantasy baseball game he played by himself with a steel ball bearing, hitting it into different parts of his backyard. One day, on a lucky hit, the "ball" sailed over into the next block, and was lost for good.

Jack also clowned away the long afternoons before suppertime with friends from junior high school. Textile

Avenue, Riverside Street, Sarah Avenue and Gershom were the streets of the neighborhood where they played. Moody Street was the main street running from downtown Lowell, lined with nondescript insurance offices, cigar stores, lunch stands and five and dime stores. It crossed the river into Pawtucketville and ended in what was then high open country at the last stop of the trolley line. The district was called Dracut. It contained woods and farms owned primarily by Greek immigrants. Kerouac played baseball there as the pitcher of his team, the Dracut Tigers.

Jack liked team games but essentially he was a loner. Once during a Dracut football game he was tackled hard and someone shouted to him, "Little Christ." The name stung so that he never forgot it. The summer of 1935, when Jack was thirteen, he invented a timing clock out of an old phonograph turntable and used it for his friends' track meets at the Lowell Textile Institute, a redbrick college on Textile Avenue in Pawtucketville. A cinder track circled the playing field, and Jack began to work out on it regularly, discovering he was the fastest runner among his friends. He wasn't particularly tall, but he was strong and sturdy, with short muscular legs. Later, in his novel *Doctor Sax,* he wrote about the summer evenings on the track at the Textile Institute, remembering the arduous hours of running against his own timing clock, keeping records of his improvement, running until it was dark and time to go home to supper.

As a young boy Jack was also deep into the radio serials, the Saturday movies and the pulp magazines of the 1930s. When he was very young he drew his own comic strips, and by the time he was eleven he was filling nickel notebooks with "novels" as well as writing his horse racing newspaper, which he printed by hand.

His favorite reading was the pulp weeklies, especially the *Shadow* Magazine published every other Friday afternoon by Smith and Street. The magazine, with its stories of Evil lurking behind lamp posts vanquished speedily by the urbane Shadow, probably highlighted all of Jack's feelings about what lurked in the shadows of his own neighborhood. He bought the magazine in a newspaper and candy store he called Destouches' in *Doctor Sax,* and he fantasized that he could see the ghost of a playmate who had died accidently in Pawtucketville, called Zap Plouffe in *Doctor Sax,* whenever he tucked the *Shadow* Magazine under his arm and walked quickly toward home.

In his imagination Jack was always sliding into fantasies like this from the pulp magazines and movies. A walk in a snowstorm a few days before Christmas, starting from his house at Phebe Avenue and circling three miles up and around through the woods to the top of Textile Avenue, was dramatized as an heroic exploit. When he and his friends made errors in their sandlot baseball games, they said "Drat it," in imitation of B-movie English noblemen.

But Kerouac's childhood was still often a dark and gloomy time. In Pawtucketville the houses and tenements would be lit and noisy for holidays like Christmas and on most Saturday nights, but the rest of the time they were dark and stuffy, their bare windows suggesting the hard times within during the Depression years.

For the first ten years of his life, Kerouac associated the gloom and darkness with the confusion and un-happiness he felt after Gerard's death. He thought he had licked the fear when unexpectedly it nudged him again on a warm summer evening in 1934, while he was crossing the Moody Street bridge with his mother. A man carrying a watermelon suddenly dropped dead right in front of them. Mémère saw at a glance what had happened, but Jack, twelve years old, was terrified. He followed the staring eyes of the dead man into the water of the Merrimack below the bridge, and it seemed to him that the August moon shining on the river and rocks was death itself, beside them on the bridge. Jack was completely devastated.

That night he refused to sleep alone, and crawled in between his mother and sister (Leo Kerouac slept in a bed by himself) until his sister got fed up with the crowd and moved to Jack's bed. It was only huddled against the warm back of his mother that he felt the shadows of the night pressed against the dark screened window of the bedroom couldn't hurt him. He felt ashamed at first about returning to his mother's bed. He thought he was over the nervousness which followed Gerard's death, but as time went on this physical and emotional intimacy seemed a blessing.

Kerouac's fear of death was with him his entire life, and intensified his private fantasies. The long movies he created by himself to music as a child became, when he got older, his novels. He was always adopting roles, always an outsider, a spectator peering through the window like the Shadow. It began, perhaps, at Gerard's funeral in the Catholic church where Jack remembered the service as a big movie, with Gerard the star, Jack in a supporting role and God the director.

When he was fourteen, the Merrimack River flooded parts of Lowell, the biggest event in the city in years, ruining his father's printing business, but Jack saw it as something in "The News of the Day" on the screen of the Royal Theater.

None of what happened to him in Lowell was material for a legend, but Kerouac knew, despite all the hazy confusions and defeats he suffered, that any life can be epic in its own way. In a way even his friends were legendary to him. The boys he played with as they went on to Lowell High School after Bartlett Junior High, walking the same route to school, meeting one another racing down the street past the Textile Institute, over the bridge and down the hill into the city, in his novels later became mythic heroes.

His memory lingered on the school lunches his mother would make him the night before, slices of bread and butter and ten cents to buy hot mashed potatoes in the lunchroom and a chocolate-covered ice cream stick. The family had no money, mémère was working in the shoe factory at a skiving machine, holding shoe leathers to a blade, her fingertips blackened. Leo left Lowell to find work as a job printer in Andover, and the family moved out of the house on Sarah Avenue to a tenement apartment above the Textile Lunch at 736 Moody Street. Times were hard, but they were the best times Jack knew. In Lowell High School he developed into a track and football star, and he fell in love for the first time. This happened, like a technicolor dream come true, in his senior year, 1938.

28

Chapter Two

Kerouac matured physically the summer of his senior year when he was just sixteen. He began to shave and started slicking back his hair with cold water to make a little wave. His sister Nin laughed at these exaggerated preparations for his dates with Mary Carney, the Irish girl he fell in love with that winter. His mother thought the girl was pretty, but she worried Jack would be trapped into an early marriage. Later in life he wondered if he would have been happier married to Mary Carney at the end of high school. Instead he left behind both Lowell and her to go to Horace Mann Prep School on a football scholarship the next autumn.

Jack hadn't played much varsity football for Lowell High until his senior year. At sixteen he was short and stocky but by no means the heaviest on the team which had Greeks, Canucks, Fighting Irish, Polish kids, sons of mill workers. By the big game of the season between Lowell and Lawrence High School at Thanksgiving in 1938, Kerouac had played enough football for scouts to be watching him. He had running skill and a certain dare-devil exhibitionism, even if his coach didn't feel he could quite trust Jack on the field. In the second half of the Thanksgiving game, Kerouac scored a brilliant touchdown, winning the game for Lowell High, and he was offered an athletic scholarship to either Boston College or Columbia. His father wanted Boston College, his mother Columbia. Jack had a little trouble making up his mind, because Boston College was also offering his father a job as a printer for the school. His friend Freddy Bertrand was in the Kerouac apartment the day the letter came from the Boston College coach and years later he could still remember Jack's mother saying, "Never mind us. Go to Columbia." Jack chose Columbia, with a year before at Horace Mann in New York. It was the first time he had left Lowell, and it was his last permanent sense of home.

While attending prep school on a scholarship, Jack lived with his mother's step-sister in Brooklyn, a one-and-a-half-hour ride on the subway to the Bronx and Horace Mann. He ate the big suppers his aunt cooked him at night, wrote a little in a diary before going to bed early, made himself a lunch of bread and butter sandwiches to take to school the next day, did his studying on the subway, dozed through his classes and came awake in the games after school, where he worked out with the team to the point of stumbling exhaustion. Then back on the subway to Brooklyn and, after meat and potatoes for supper, right to sleep.

At Horace Mann the team was made up of athletes like himself on scholarship making up credits for college. Kerouac played good football but he also had time to write for the school newspaper and literary magazine. Except for the football team, the students at Horace Mann (at least as Kerouac saw them) were Jewish rich kids from New York City and the suburbs. To Ti Jean, who had grown up in Lowell in a French-Canadian working-class neighborhood, they were exotic. One of Jack's friends at Horace Mann, Alan Temko, later remembered he was very much the poor country boy at prep school. Jack's clothes were too small, his big hands hanging from the short sleeves of his blue serge suit. At the Sixth Form prom, the girl he invited from Lowell—his sweetheart Mary Carney—took one look at the expensive gowns of the rich New York girls, burst into tears and asked to leave. His buddies on the football team were scornful of the interest Jack paid to the other students during school hours. They accused him of wanting to make friends with the rich kids just to get an occasional handout. They had chicken sandwiches for lunch while Jack had to eat dry bread and butter sandwiches.

The fall 1939 issue of the *Horace Mann Quarterly* printed a mystery story called "The Brothers," which Jack wrote for the literary magazine a few months after he entered school. Later the school yearbook proudly announced that "Brain and brawn found a happy combination in Jack, a newcomer to school this year. A brilliant back in football, he also won his spurs as a *Record* reporter and a leading *Quarterly* contributor."

Throughout the winter and spring of his year at Horace Mann he wrote music notes for the school paper, mostly about popular swing bands like Glenn Miller. He amused his young literary friends by writing what they considered pornographic love stories, and in the spring of 1940, Jack remembered, "I scored all the winning touchdowns in the fall so they put me at the top of the literary magazine in the spring" with a story about Jesus, "Une Veille de Noel." He had done well at Horace Mann, but the next year as a freshman at Columbia, he found the situation very different.

Kerouac was to write about Columbia over and over. His time there was the turning point in his legendary drama. What happened was simple, yet he never came to terms with it. He broke his leg early in his freshman season and never played on the varsity team. For one reason or another most of the boys who try to play football don't make the team, but for Kerouac, with his heroic view of himself, it remained always a crushing personal defeat.

The Columbia College newspaper covered the highlights of his brief career. Although Kerouac was not named in the paper as a member of the starting line-up of the freshman football team, he was put into play as a substitute in the first game against Rutgers early in October 1940, and the paper reported the coach was very satisfied with him. Jack "was probably the best back on the field." After the second game, which Columbia tied 13-13 against St. Benedict's Prep School, Kerouac was called a "star back." But luck was against him. It was the last game he played with the team. On 31 October, 1940, the *Spectator* reported:

Their hopes darkened by the news that Jack Kerouac, star back, will be out with a leg injury for the rest of the season, Coach Ralph Furey's gridiron charges practiced in the rain yesterday afternoon, preparing for Saturday's game with Cheshire Academy.

The loss of Kerouac, fleet-footed backfield ace, is a blow to the Yearlings' chances of breaking into the victory column for the first time on Saturday.

Hurt in the game against St. Benedict's Prep two weeks ago, after having run the opening kick-off back to St. Benedict's 12-yard line, Kerouac was helped off the field and was unable to see action in last week's engagement with Princeton.

It had been believed, however, that he would break into the line-up this Saturday, until an x-ray taken Tuesday revealed that the injury is a split bone and is more serious than originally thought.

Later Kerouac blamed the coach for making him run on the leg and not listening to his complaints that he was seriously injured or letting him get an x-ray at the hospital.

After the leg was put into a cast, Jack hobbled around campus on crutches, playing the part of an honorably wounded football hero for the rest of the winter. He wrote a sports article about the track team for the *Spectator* in December 1940, but most of his writings at the time were private journals and stories inspired by a new enthusiasm for the novels of Thomas Wolfe.

Before going to college he had romantic dreams of campus life out of the Depression fantasy movies of the 1930s, smoking a pipe in a button-down sweater like Bing Crosby, serenading a pretty co-ed in the moonlight outside the fraternity house. He tried to make the dream come true at Columbia by pledging a fraternity, but he stubbornly refused to wear the dinky cap and preferred to sit alone in the cafeteria with his crutches beside him, every inch the tragically martyred football hero, eating steak dinners and hot fudge sundaes in his sports jacket.

In some ways being injured was better for his dream image of college life than being on the football team, at least at the time it was all happening. Before Jack broke his leg he had no time to pose beside the fraternity fireplace. He was too worn out from the long hours of football practice, too harrassed finding time to read the long list of books for his courses and maintaining the

B average for his athletic scholarship. Besides, before he had broken his leg, he had had to work as a dishwasher in the dining room cafeteria to pay for his meals. Years later when he looked back at it, not making the team was a major blow in the legend of his life, but in the spring semester of his freshman year, his leg better, he thought he was doing all right.

He wasn't working hard enough in his classes, however, and at the end of the year he failed chemistry. At home in Lowell that summer he had to make up the course, or lose his football scholarship. Instead of sudying chemistry, Jack spent "a nutty summer at home." He swam and played baseball and drank beer with his Lowell friends, especially young Alex Sampas, who also loved Thomas Wolfe and, like Kerouac, wanted to write poetry. Sampas was a Greek boy in a large family in Lowell living close to Kerouac's house. His older brother Charlie had a job on the Lowell newspaper. With "Sabby," as his friend Alex was called, Jack could talk about the books he was reading at college, and Sabby enthusiastically harangued him about political idealism, the Brotherhood of Man. Jack laughed at him for these "big Leninist speeches." Sabby had wild black hair and was full of Romantic idealism.

At the end of summer 1941, Jack's family moved from Lowell to New Haven, where Leo had a new job as a linotypist. Jack felt lost as they broke up the apartment and he had a dream which he later claimed was the key to the story of the first part of his life. As mémère and a cousin sat in the kitchen talking among the crates and cartons, Jack fell asleep on the porch after staring at the stars a long time. He dreamed that he actually was the hero of a legend, going back to his sophomore year at Columbia and taking the football team on to glory in the Rose Bowl, following this with an A in Chemistry, running the fastest mile ever run at Madison Square Garden, being scouted by the Yankees for their baseball team, becoming a great actor playing King Lear, impressing Madison Avenue by writing "a book so golden and so purchased with magic that everybody smacks their brows," and ending up with knocking out Joe Louis and becoming the world's heavyweight boxing champion. Waking up to reality, Jack wondered if he were crazy, then decided the world was crazy; "the war must have been getting in my bones."

However strong his private fantasies, and whatever the growing sense of confusion in his life, Kerouac went back to Columbia in September 1941. He began fall training with the varsity team under Coach Lou Little. The *Spectator* reported the previous spring that sophomore students would play on the team because many of the upper classmen athletes were enlisting in the armed services. Jack hadn't included the possibility of becoming a war hero in his Lowell dream, but back at college in New York it suddenly appeared to him that it was a waste of time playing football when the stars of the varsity team, like fullback Len Will, were being drafted into the Air Corps.

On the hot September day when Roosevelt's famous "I hate war" speech was coming over every radio in the city, Kerouac walked out of the training house at Baker Field without saying goodbye to the coach. He "joyed like a maniac," sure that it was the most important decision of his life.

Confused about what he was doing, however, Kerouac didn't enlist right away. The Columbia paper reported that Jack had returned to a job in Lowell, but before going back he took a short joyride on a Greyhound bus to Washington, D.C., wishing he had enough money to go on to Virginia to see the South described by Thomas Wolfe. He had only enough cash to catch the return bus to New York and go straight on to his parents' cottage in New Haven. Mémère and Leo were furious that he'd left Columbia, insisting that he get a job immediately. His father told him, "It isn't that we don't want you in the house . . . but I have to walk a mile to that printing plant every morning, your mother remember was wiping tables in the Waldorf Cafeteria in New Haven last week while you were s'posed to be making the football team. Here we whack along in the same pickle as ever. Why don't you people ever do right?"

Jack moved out of the cottage and into a furnished room in New Haven, working as a grease-monkey in a gas station, then pumping gas and wiping windshields when the boss discovered he didn't know anything about cars. On Thanksgiving Day, Alex Sampas come down from Lowell to visit him, curious about why Jack had quit Columbia. Jack didn't have a clear answer, but he thought he was living like a character in a Burgess Meredith movie.

He was proud of having been on his own for the first time in his life, and told Sampas that what he had to show for it was a collection of short stories he'd just written in the style of Hemingway and Saroyan. Alex advised him to move back to Lowell and let his brother Charlie get him a job writing sports articles for the Lowell paper, so when Jack's parents moved back to Lowell two weeks later, he went too. After a couple of months Jack quit the job on the Lowell *Sun*, much to his father's disgust, and rode a bus back to Washington, D.C., too restless to stay at home. He lived briefly with a Lowell friend in Washington who got him a job on the Pentagon construction project, then quit to work as a short-order cook and soda jerk at a lunchcart.

He had just turned twenty years old and was completely unsettled. He showed up again in Lowell, fought with his parents about enlisting in the service, and then belligerently left home once again, this time for Boston. Acting wildly on the impulse that he had to make something heroic happen in his life, Jack walked into the U.S. Marine Recruiting Center there and was officially sworn in. He'd had the notion that he'd be in uniform at once, but when he found himself back on the street a few hours later with nothing to do for the rest of the afternoon, he turned around and joined the Coast Guard. After being fingerprinted and photographed the second time that day, Jack panicked. There was nothing to do but get drunk as quickly as possible. Night came in blurs of nausea before he finally passed out in a men's toilet in downtown Boston.

The next morning, terribly hung over, his first thought was to get out of town. Confronting his parents in Lowell was clearly impossible, and the only thing he could think of was looking up the address of the National Maritime Union Hall. He begged them for a seaman's job, any job, and he was lucky. He signed aboard as a scullion on the *S.S. Dorchester* sailing that afternoon to Greenland with a gang of airport construction workers. Before leaving Boston harbor, Jack telephoned his parents to say he'd be a little late getting home. It was early in the spring of 1942, and he came back in October.

Kerouac's life as a seaman during World War II was as confused as his actions in Boston before first shipping out. He later described being on the *S.S. Dorchester* (it was the ship's last run before being torpedoed) as a kind of holiday. He got $470 for the voyage, sailing "with a bunch of drunks" among the icebergs, teased by the crew for his inexperience on his first ship. During a submarine attack at sea one morning in which the destroyer escort of the *Dorchester* sank a German ship, Kerouac fried bacon crisp for the entire crew's breakfast and thought of his German counterpart drowning in the scullion of the submarine. The image of death in his family crest came to his mind, three silver nails in a blue field turned gray by the sea, and from that moment he believed that "the Germans should not have been our 'enemies.' I say this and stake my life on it."

In October 1942, the *Dorchester* returned to Boston and Kerouac went back to his parents in Lowell to find that his buddy Alex Sampas had enlisted in the Army. They had made vague plans to go into the Coast Guard together, but Sampas had given up on Jack after he'd left for Greenland.

Leo Kerouac wasn't angry about the *Dorchester*. He had a quick temper, but there'd been months to cool off while Jack had been away, and besides he was excited about a telegram from Lou Little saying the Columbia football team needed his son for the fall scrimmage. Jack went straight back to New York, enrolled in all his classes, but walked out again after the first game because Little kept him on the bench.

Shipping out to Greenland, Jack had lost weight and was out of shape. At 155 pounds he didn't make much of an impression. After fighting with the coach, Kerouac decided that football at Columbia "was just a great big bunch of horseshit where they don't let you prove yourself." Leo was upset enough to come to New York to argue with Lou Little about Jack's getting back on the team, but it was no good. The Columbia Sports Publicity Office issued a statement by Lou Little, "Jack has left the team because he is tired," and his football career was over. Jack went back to Lowell once more, began neatly handprinting a novel he titled *The Sea Is My Brother* and convinced his parents that the best plan for him was enlisting in the U.S. Navy and going to Officers' Training School.

He wasn't any more ready for the Navy than he'd been for anything else. Kerouac lasted barely six months, most of the time under observation in the hospital, and he was never clear afterward about what happened. Insisting he had the highest I.Q. in the history of the Newport Naval Base, he nevertheless managed to flunk the exam for the Naval Air Training School, and was assigned instead to bootcamp at Newport with "a bunch of bores."

He later gave several explanations for what was wrong with Navy life. The other recruits were eighteen and Jack was twenty-one, and they bored him to death. It was impossible to sleep in the hammocks. Smoking was not allowed. A visiting admiral insisted the ship's deck had to be clean enough to eat an egg off it. The dentists were fussy lieutenants who hurt his teeth. He was ordered to wash garbage pails, "as if they couldn't hire shits to do that." One afternoon when he'd had enough field drill, Kerouac put down his gun and walked off to peaceful soltitude in the base library. He was reading when the guards came to take him to the hospital for psychiatric observation.

Jack was moved to Bethesda, Maryland, where doctors pondered his handprinted novel about the sea being his brother, and he was kept in the hospital with other "psychopathic maniacs" until a sympathetic psychiatrist finally got around to his case. The Navy psychiatrist asked Kerouac who he really thought he was. Jack replied, "I'm only old Samuel Johnson." He meant he was "a man of letters" and "a man of letters is a man of independence." It all came down to the simple matter of Navy discipline, he told his doctor, not that Jack wouldn't take it, but that he *couldn't*. He kept insisting he was "too much of a nut, and a man of letters." The authorities agreed with part of what he said at least. A few weeks later Kerouac was honorably discharged with an "indifferent character."

As a kid in Lowell, Jack described himself at the end of high school cutting classes to go to the movies, cocky with his Columbia scholarship, as "independent, nutty with independence in fact." In the Navy he was four years older, but he had still acted like a wiseguy kid. He felt later that the legend of his life pivoted here. In fact, after what happened to him at Columbia and in the Navy, his dreams began increasingly to take hold of him.

From the window of the Navy hospital Jack could see a road leading westward into the woods of Maryland. In his fantasy, he imagined it traveling west miles across country, but it was a road forever closed to him. It was the saddest dream he ever had, because he saw it recede with absolute finality, almost as helpless against it as a child being denied paradise. As he wrote years later in *Vanity of Duluoz,* it was his "lost dream of being a real American Man."

Chapter Three

After leaving the Navy in June 1943, Kerouac again went back to live with his mother and father. While he'd been away they'd left Lowell and were living in a small apartment on Cross Bay Boulevard in Ozone Park, a neighborhood just beyond Brooklyn on Long Island. They were upstairs over a drugstore in a redbrick two-storey building on a corner, with the boulevard traffic rushing by, and the rest of the neighborhood sprawling around them in undistinguished monotony. For Leo and mèmère it meant a chance to pick up a new life, to start something for themselves after their failures in Lowell and New Haven. For Jack it meant the end of everything he had associated with his past. His boyhood was over.

As soon as he could, he signed up to work as an ordinary merchant seaman again, this time on the *S.S. George Weems,* bound for Liverpool with 500-pound bombs in the hold, flying the red dynamite flag. He'd told the Navy psychiatrists about his preference for service in the Merchant Marine, with its looser discipline, but Jack didn't try to fit in with the other seamen aboard the *Weems.*

Writing about the Liverpool voyage years later in *Vanity of Duluoz,* Kerouac described himself as a recluse aboard ship, speaking only ten words to the rest of the crew the entire time at sea, spending his hours off duty sleeping or reading Galsworthy's *Forsyte Saga.* They called him "the Sleeping Beauty." Jack was still trying to finish his first novel, *The Sea Is My Brother,* but reading Galsworthy suggested a different approach to what he wanted to do as a writer. Enthusiastically, he imagined writing based on "an idea about sagas, or legends, novels connecting into one grand tale," and he lost interest in *The Sea Is My Brother,* seeing it half-jokingly as more an example of handwriting than of a novel.

Most of the time in Liverpool Jack was confined to duty aboard the ship, but he was free for one weekend and he caught a train to London, sleeping overnight in a mailcar crowded with Australian soldiers. In London he was just another young seaman on shore leave. He went straight to Trafalgar Square to see the pigeons and the statue of Nelson, then to Piccadilly Circus and later to a concert at the Royal Albert Hall—Sir John Barbirolli conducting Tchaikovsky. In the middle of the concert, the sirens announced an air raid by the German Luftwaffe, but the music continued anyway. He spent the night in a room with a girl called Lillian, and after a few more beers in Piccadilly, he borrowed money for the train back to his ship in Liverpool from an American shipping office, since "Lillian or something or somebody took most of my money away."

In September 1943, the *Weems* lifted anchor and sailed out of Liverpool bound for New York, empty of bombs and riding high in the water. German ships made a brief torpedo attack in the middle of a storm in the Irish Sea and Jack saw a little action. But there was no further trouble on the way back to New York. Kerouac regretted that he had never seen a heavy bombing raid either on the *Weems* or earlier while he was in Greenland aboard the *Dorchester*, but he wasn't eager enough to see action during the war to continue work as a merchant seaman. Instead of signing aboard another ship, he spent the winter of 1943-44 at home, working odd jobs for pocket money, including a stint as switchboard operator in a hotel near Columbia University. His sister Nin was away in the WACs and his parents didn't push him to go back into the service, especially after the family heard that his friend Alex Sampas had been killed in action overseas. Jack took it easy over the winter, planning to ship out again in the spring, this time from New Orleans.

It was comfortable at home for him. Both his parents had steady jobs. Leo was working as a linotypist in Brooklyn and mémère as a skiver in a factory making Army shoes, and they were making more money than they had in a long time. What Jack would do was entirely unsettled, except that he began to talk about himself as a serious writer, not thinking any longer about a career as a journalist or sports writer.

Leo argued with him, insisting that Jack had to find a way to make a living first, snorting derisively when Jack talked about his grandiose plans for "a lifetime of writing about what I'd seen with my own eyes, told in my own words, according to the style I decided on at whether twenty-one years old or thirty or forty or whatever later age, and put it all together as a contemporary history record for future times to see what really happened and what people really thought." None of it meant anything to Leo, and the argument raged between them about Jack's refusal to go to work. He insisted that he wanted to write, shouting, "I'm an artist," and Leo would shout back at him, "Artist shmartist, ya can't be supported all ya life."

Nine months before, in October 1942, while still at Columbia, Jack had met a girl named Edie Parker through a prep school buddy, Henri Cru. Before he sailed to Liverpool on the *Weems*, he visited her in Asbury Park,

New Jersey, where she was living for the summer with her grandmother. Her background was almost completely different from his. She was from a wealthy family in Grosse Pointe, Michigan. But she was alive and she was pretty, as he described her, with an "almost buck-toothed grin, that eagering grin and laugh and eagerness entire that makes the eyes slit but at the same time makes the cheeks fuller and endows the lady with the promise that she will look good all her life." In Asbury Park they had one long day together, Edie putting earrings on Jack when they went to the beach so her girlfriends would think he was a gypsy, and he promised to come back from England in the fall and live with her in her apartment near the Columbia campus.

Jack went to her straight from the Brooklyn docks the day the *Weems* got back, and he put his black leather jacket over a chair in her bedroom with a new sense of possession. Edie's roommate, Joan Vollner, liked him, so it was no problem spending a lot of time in the apartment, until finally Jack's mother began to worry about him. Jack had never been so serious about any girl since falling in love four years before with Mary Carney in his senior year at Lowell High School, and while mémêre hadn't liked the idea of Jack marrying so young, at least Mary had been a good girl.

Jack brought Edie to Brooklyn to meet his parents and they all drank beer together in the tavern on Liberty Avenue and Cross Bay Boulevard. They walked back to the apartment down the street as two couples arm in arm in the mild October night, but mémêre had never met anyone like Edie Parker and she was confused. In mémêre's morality, a girl didn't really respect the man when she let him live with her, and so Jack's mother tried to discourage him from living with Edie. There were arguments and Jack stayed away from home more and more.

Restless as the winter ended, Jack took a train with Edie to Grosse Pointe to meet her family. Back in New York in the middle of spring 1944, he again felt he had to get out, so he rode the bus to New Orleans, had no luck signing aboard a ship and, after hanging around the N.M.U. hall and getting drunk, walking up and down

41

Magazine Street trying to make a lunchcart waitress, he ran out of money. He wrote home to his parents and to Edie saying he was starving and needed the bus-fare back to New York. When he got home, mémère told him the trip had been foolish, and Jack agreed, but it was beyond his parents to point out directions for him in his life anymore. Instead, it was with Edie and the people around her that his new life began.

Back from New Orleans, Jack once more hung his black leather jacket over the back of the chair in Edie's bedroom, sleeping in the afternoons while Edie took painting classes with George Grosz at Columbia. One night Jack went with her to drink beer at the West End Bar on Broadway and 114th Street, across from the Columbia campus, and there he met the first of the people who were to change him and his life, a friend of Edie's called Lucien Carr.

Edie had met Lucien while Jack was out of town. He was slender, good looking, from a wealthy family, but he'd been expelled from prep school by the time he was eighteen as a "wild kid." He managed to enroll at Columbia College and was in his first year there when he met Edie at the West End. After he had become her friend, he used her apartment to take showers and to sleep on the couch with his girl friend Cecily. After hearing Edie's stories about Lucien, Jack was jealous, but his impression on meeting him was that he looked "like a mischievous little prick." They bantered together in the West End that first night and almost immediately were friends.

Jack had never met anyone like Lucien in Lowell or at Horace Mann, where the rich boys he had known had been for the most part from New York Jewish families. Lucien Carr was, if anything, more impulsive than Kerouac. The first night they got drunk together, Lucien told Jack to get into an empty barrel and then he rolled the barrel down the sidewalks of upper Broadway. Lucien was smaller and slighter and three years younger, and Jack felt as protective toward him as he would have toward a younger brother, but Jack didn't have his poise and social arrogance, so Lucien kept the upper hand. They exchanged insults with the familiarity of blood brothers,

Lucien telling Jack, "Trouble with you Duluoz is, you're a hardhearted mean old tightfisted shitass no good Canuck who shoulda had his ass froze in the hearts of Manitoba where you and your bad blood belong, you Indian no-good bully." Weakly Jack would insist, "I'm no bully," and Lucien, who didn't want to fight, would shift ground and say, "Well bully for you, give me a drink."

Lucien told Jack he also wanted to be a writer, but he was much more intellectual about it than Kerouac, spending more time talking about aesthetics and philosophy than he did writing. Jack thought Lucien's conversation was more inspired than his writing. To prove it Jack wrote a paper for Lucien's English class about his trip to Piccadilly Circus as a merchant seaman, and Lucien got an A for the story. Jack was exactly the type of friend Lucien wanted at this point because, despite his family background and his intelligence, Lucien had problems of his own. With his blonde hair, classic features and slight wiry build, he exuded an indefinite but strong impression of homosexuality, and although Kerouac saw at once he "was no fairy," Carr had been followed for years by a man called Dave Kammerer, who was in love with him. According to Kerouac, it wasn't only Kammerer. Lucien had "absolute physical male and spiritual, too, beauty. Slant-eyed, green eyes, complete intelligence, language pouring out of him, Shakespeare reborn almost, golden hair with a halo around it, old queens when they saw him in Greenwich Village bars wrote odes to him starting 'O fair-haired Grecian lad.' "

Dave Kammerer had met Lucien before Lucien went to prep school and then followed him on to Columbia. While Lucien hadn't exactly encouraged Kammerer, he also, as Kerouac saw it, hadn't turned him away—"it's just a lot of fun." Jack met Kammerer at the West End Bar and disliked him on sight, but it was through Kammerer that he met William Burroughs, who the following year was to be the strongest influence on Kerouac's life at that time. Burroughs and Kammerer had been friends at Harvard ten years before, had gone separate ways and then found themselves living close to each other in Greenwich Village.

One warm afternoon in July 1944, Jack was in Edie's

apartment taking a shower while she and Lucien were on campus at a life drawing class. Jack heard a knock on the door. He opened it to find Kammerer standing behind "a tall thin fella in a seersucker jacket," Burroughs, who had dropped around ostensibly to talk with Jack about shipping out in the Merchant Marine. Jack suspected they had come only on the chance of finding Lucien at the apartment. He didn't like Kammerer and he sensed Burroughs was also a homosexual "but didn't admit in those days."

Kerouac wasn't put off by Burroughs as he was by Kammerer, although he had an uneasy sense that Burroughs was patronizing him, perhaps having heard from Kammerer that Jack was an interesting "seaman type." He let them into the apartment and lounged in the easy chair answering Burroughs' practical questions about how to get sea papers, not quite trusting them, studying Burroughs' enigmatic appearance.

Beneath his skepticism, Jack was flattered that Burroughs wanted to meet him. Burroughs struck him as "Tall, 6 foot 1, strange, inscrutable because ordinary-looking (scrutable), like a shy bank clerk with a patrician thinlipped cold bluelipped face, blue eyes saying nothing behind steel rims and glass, sandy hair, a little wispy, a little of the wistful German Nazi youth as his soft hair fluffles in the breeze—So unobtrusive as he sat on the hassock" in the middle of Edie's livingroom.

Once he had met Burroughs, Jack would take the subway down to the Village with Lucien to drink in Burroughs' apartment on Bedford Street. Mostly he sat back and watched Burroughs, Carr and Kammerer as they talked. The more Kerouac watched, the more he admired their "terrible intelligence and style." Burroughs enjoyed bizarre jokes. One afternoon he excused himself from the room, disappeared into the kitchen and reappeared with a plate of razor blades and lightbulbs, passing it around saying, "I've something real nice in the way of delicacies my mother sent me this week, hmf hmf hmf."

William Burroughs' grandfather had started the Burroughs business machine company in St. Louis, and Bill had inherited money from his family. He was living on his trust fund, making extra money from a series of odd jobs in New York. In 1936 Burroughs had left Harvard after doing some graduate work in anthropology, and he spent a year as a copy writer in a small advertising agency in New York. He was "in the Army for a bit, honorably discharged, and then the usual strange wartime jabs—bartender, exterminator, reporter, and factory and office jobs."

When Jack met him, he was working as a bartender in the Village. Although Burroughs had done a little writing at Harvard, he didn't think of himself as a writer. He had no dreams like Lucien and Jack about the great books they were going to write, but he tolerated their belief in themselves as romantic geniuses.

Kerouac was so awed by Burroughs' style that he didn't stop to wonder too much why he had been picked up by Lucien and his friends. Years later Jack felt "my saving grace in their eyes (Bill's, Lucien's especially) was the materialistic Canuck taciturn cold skepticism all the picked-up Idealism in the world of books couldn't hide." Instead of trying to imitate their style, Kerouac hung on to his own, a mixture of pugnacious working-class seaman, college football athlete and apprentice novelist (Jack had already started his second novel, which he never finished and eventually lost in a taxicab).

Burroughs and Carr responded also to Kerouac's directness and honesty. In *The Vanity of Duluoz,* Jack described the hot summer night in 1944 they all sat talking on a bench on Riverside Drive and they asked him why he didn't wear a merchant seaman's uniform and "get a lot of soft entries into things" in New York City during wartime. Kerouac, dressed as always in a T-shirt and chino pants, startled everyone with his quick and vehement hostility to the idea, telling Burroughs that dressing in uniform would be a "finkish thing to do." "It's a finkish world," Burroughs answered drily.

After knowing Kerouac a couple of months, Lucien began spending more of his time with him and Kammerer soon became jealous. One night Kammerer went over to Edie's apartment with Burroughs while Edie and Jack were out. He took a kitten Jack had adopted and tried to hang it from the lamp with Burroughs' tie. Burroughs took it down at once before it was hurt, and nobody told

Jack until long afterwards. Kammerer was afraid of what Jack would do to him when he found out. He pretended to be Jack's great friend, buying him beers in the West End, but he only wanted to talk endlessly of Lucien. Sensing Kammerer's desperation, Burroughs tried to talk him into leaving New York and finding someone who would love him someplace else, but Kammerer refused.

When the Columbia term ended in July 1944, Lucien and Jack decided to sneak out of New York themselves without telling Kammerer. They both had seaman's papers, so they began to wait at the N.M.U. Hall for a turn to come up for a ship, preferably to France. They talked wildly of jumping ship in France and walking to Paris to live as poets together, Lucien pretending to be a deaf mute and Jack speaking his country French so they wouldn't be caught and sent back to their ship.

Kammerer heard about their plans and decided to join them. The situation became worse than ever. Lucien and Jack tried to lose him whenever they could. One night on the way to a party on MacDougal Street, Kammerer went around the corner first, letting Jack and Lucien out of his sight for a minute, and they slipped away, thinking he'd never track them down since he didn't know where the party was. Hours later, they heard somebody climbing up the marquee of the bar downstairs on MacDougal Street. It was Kammerer coming to join the party.

The atmosphere began to get tense. Eating steak together in Burrough's apartment—since he was the only one with a job and got money from his trust fund every month, he often fed his friends dinner—Lucien suddenly grabbed the meat before Bill could divide it into four and began chewing on it. When nobody got angry, being used to what Jack called Lucien's *actes gratuites* (doing something just for the hell of it), Lucien started growling like a tiger. Kammerer jumped up and started wrestling the steak from his fingers, and they ripped it apart until Jack protested, "Hey, . . . My steak!" They they turned on Kerouac: "Ah, The Louse, all you think about is food, you beefy clout!"

Another evening, Lucien saw a tear in the sleeve of Bill's seersucker jacket. He stuck his finger in it and ripped a big hole. Kammerer grabbed the other sleeve, yanked it off and wrapped it around Burroughs' head while Bill just sat there making contemptuous "thfunk" sounds down his nose, watching with Jack while Carr and Kammerer ripped the coat into strips which they tied together to decorate Bill's bookcases and lamps. Jack felt it was nothing to them that they destroyed a perfectly good coat. As he wrote later in *Vanity of Duluoz,* "they all came from well-to-do families," but as a Lowell boy, he didn't know what to make of it.

As the weeks passed, Kammerer began to lose control. One night in August he climbed the fire escape in back of the residential hotel near Columbia where Lucien lived, got through the open window of Lucien's room and watched him sleeping in his bed for a half hour without waking him up. Leaving the hotel, Kammerer was caught by the guard and taken to the foyer at gunpoint. He explained to the police that he'd been drinking in Carr's room all night. Lucien was awakened to corroborate the story, but it was obvious to everyone the situation was becoming difficult.

The tragedy finally came on the night of 13 August, 1944. Kerouac was sleeping in Edie's apartment when Lucien awakened him at dawn, saying he needed help. They had been together all through the previous day and had almost succeeded in getting aboard a ship bound for the Second Front on war bonus pay, but at the last minute, after stowing their gear aboard, they were thrown off by the chief mate in a union dispute before they could sign on for the voyage. Discouraged after waiting so long for the ship and coming so close to sailing, Lucien and Jack had returned at the end of the hot afternoon to Edie's apartment where they'd napped and eaten and then gone back down in the evening to the West End for a few beers. Jack had returned alone, leaving Lucien with friends. As he was crossing the campus headed for Amsterdam Avenue and the apartment, he'd met Kammerer, who asked for Lucien. Jack had told him to look in the West End.

Lucien Carr told Jack how the evening had finished. He and Kammerer had had a few drinks in the bar and then had gone down to Riverside Park below the West End Bar to sit on the grass near the Hudson River and drink some more. Kammerer had gotten excited and said he'd kill Lucien if they didn't make love. In self-defense, Lucien had pulled out his boyscout knife and in the struggle, Kammerer had been stabbed. Losing control, Carr had stabbed him twice more in the heart, and then he had thrown Kammerer's body into the Hudson River.

Not knowing what to do next, Carr had gone down to the Village to ask Burroughs' advice. Burroughs had told him to contact his family, get a good lawyer and turn himself in to the police. Instead he had gone back uptown to 118th Street to wake up Jack. He had five dollars he'd borrowed from Burroughs and wanted to have a final drink before he went to his family.

Jack was frightened, but he dressed, kissed Edie goodbye and went out to help Lucien. On their way to a bar in Harlem, they dropped the knife down a subway grate. After a few beers, they went to the movies, looked at some paintings at the Museum of Modern Art, ate hot dogs and then, in the afternoon, Lucien was ready to turn himself in. That evening the police came to Edie's apartment looking for Jack. Because he had spent the day with a confessed homicide and helped dispose of the murder weapon, he was an accessory after the fact. A plainclothesman drove Jack to the precinct house on 98th Street, where he stayed overnight in a cell.

The next day Jack was booked as a material witness to a homicide. Kammerer's body had been recovered and the newspapers were calling the crime an "honor slaying." Lucien's defense rested on proving that Kammerer was a known homosexual and that he had only been protecting himself in the struggle in Riverside Park. Like Kerouac, Burroughs was also booked as a material witness, but Burroughs' family posted his bail right away. Jack's parents wouldn't help him. When he telephoned his father from jail to ask for bail money, Leo told him that no Kerouac had ever been involved in a murder, and that Jack could go to hell. Jack then called Edie, who was willing to help him any way she could. They decided to get married so that she could borrow the bail money from her family. Jack was let out of jail for an afternoon to marry Edie in City Hall.

A police detective was one witness and Lucien's girl friend Cecily was Edie's maid of honor.

He wrote later that as soon as he felt his father had abandoned him, his first thought was to get married. But his parents were less angry with him after he had told them he had married Edie. They visited him before he left jail, sitting at a long table in front of a guard in a scene Jack visualized as being out of a John Garfield movie. In *Vanity of Duluoz* Jack wrote that they looked on him "as an errant but innocent son victimized by decadent friendships in the evil city," but they hoped that marriage would settle him down.

Jack went with Edie to live in Michigan, where he took a factory job counting ballbearings. He saved $100 in a month to pay back her family for posting the bail bond for his $5,000 bail, but instead of settling down, Jack was if anything more restless than before. He was twenty-two years old and totally uninterested in marriage. Living in Edie's house made him feel "slightly guilty." The social differences got him down. Her mother sat with him in the parlor before Jack went off to work and tried to make polite conversation about the "writing game," telling Jack that at her club she had heard of some people who made money writing books, like Pearl Buck.

It was obvious to everyone that he and Edie came from two different worlds, and Jack felt that he couldn't accept her family's financial help. He clung doggedly to a study schedule while he lived in Edie's house, reading books on American literary criticism and taking notes, working harder at being an apprentice writer than he did at being a young husband. He was very proud (and fortunate that Edie understood him) that, as he wrote later, he had to go his own way. He was "a gypsy who doesn't eat up others as he goes along."

In October 1944, Jack said goodbye to Edie and got a truck ride back to New York. His first marriage had lasted less than two months. The plan was for him to ship out to Europe again, and he went straight to the N.M.U. Hall to sign on as a seaman. This time Kerouac had no trouble getting a ship the first day he applied. In fact, the Merchant Marine was so short of seamen that he was designated an acting able-bodied seaman by the union although he didn't know enough for the job. He had a day before he was due to sail, so he rode the subway uptown to Columbia to find out about Lucien's trial from any of Lucien's friends who might still be on campus.

Lucien was in the state reformatory in Elmira, New York. He had been found guilty of manslaughter. The stabbing in Riverside Park and the trial had been covered in the Columbia *Spectator* as well as the New York daily papers, and Kerouac found himself something of a minor campus celebrity because of his association with Lucien Carr. The *Spectator* had even reported Jack's marriage to Edie: "Jack had been held at the Bronx City Jail in default of $5,000 bail. Last Tuesday, 22 August, he was escorted by police down to the Municipal Building for his marriage, and then returned to the prison."

His friends had expected Lucien to receive a suspended sentence, so the court's decision to send him to Elmira for two years came as a shock. Jack found Lucien's nineteen-year-old girl friend, Cecily, on campus, and they went out together for a beer at the West End. Cecily was with another of Lucien's friends whom Jack had met earlier in the summer, a "spindly Jewish kid with horn-rimmed glasses and tremendous ears sticking out," a boy who, like Kerouac, had felt very close to Carr, Allen Ginsberg.

Ginsberg had met Lucien Carr a year before when they roomed down the hall from each other as Columbia freshmen in the Union Theological Seminary close to campus. When he entered Columbia, Allen had been fired with enthusiasm about becoming a labor organizer, helping the poor and struggling masses of the world, but after he met Lucien he became more involved in aesthetic philosophy and literature. Their friendship began with a common interest in the French symbolist poets and Dostoyevsky, and they spent hours in their dormitory rooms working out a concept of a "post-human post-intelligence" which they called their "New Vision," hoping it would help them compose great poetry as college freshmen. Ginsberg had come to Columbia from a middle-class home in Paterson, New Jersey where his childhood and adolescence had been scarred by the insanity

50

of his mother, Naomi. His father had published poetry and taught English in high school for years. Like Kerouac, Ginsberg had never met anyone like Lucien before.

Jack had not felt particularly close to Allen when they first met in the summer. If anything, he'd been jealous of Allen for being Lucien's friend. He'd first heard about Allen from Edie Parker. When Jack went home on his periodical visits with his parents, Allen would take Edie out on dates with Lucien and Cecily, and Allen and Lucien would try to make the girls laugh by causing a commotion in the theater or in the subway, something Jack sneered at as "all such Joe College stuff."

Kerouac had made such a deliberate effort to snub Ginsberg when they first met that Jack felt it took Allen years to get over it. Their first meeting was in Edie's apartment in the summer of 1944, when Allen had just turned eighteen. Allen walked into the living room to find Jack sprawling in the armchair, and trying to make an impression, looked at him with shining black eyes and confided in a deep voice, "Discretion is the better part of valor." Instead of finding this funny, Jack replied, "Aw, shut up, you little twitch," turning away to yell at Edie, "Aw, where's my food!" Jack felt after this that Allen regarded him as a "brooding football artist yelling for his supper in big daddy chair," but Ginsberg was as little taken in by Kerouac's strongman pose as Carr or Burroughs had been.

According to Ginsberg, his friendship with Kerouac was already firmly established when Jack helped him move his things out of the university dormitory at the end of term in July 1944. Standing together ·in the corridor, Allen had suddenly become absolutely still, before putting his hand to his lips in a gesture of farewell. When Jack looked at him curiously, Allen pointed to an empty room and explained it had been Lucien Carr's. Allen had roomed across the hall, and he'd first made friends with Lucien one night when he'd heard Lucien playing a Brahms trio on his phonograph and had gone across to listen. The dormitory would always have nostalgic memories for him, because it was where he first saw Lucien.

Jack nodded and, much to Allen's surprise, described

how he'd felt the same way moving out of his bedroom in Lowell when his parents had left that city for New Haven. At that moment, standing in the corridor with Jack, Allen sensed what he later called a special affinity between them, an emotional reverence for life and its impermanence he felt he shared with Kerouac as with nobody else.

Jack spent his first night back in New York that fall with Allen and Cecily in Allen's room in Livingston Hall on the Columbia campus. Jack remembered that he necked with Cecily all night and, years later, he still thought it was "the rattiest thing" of his life, not because he'd been unfaithful to Edie, but rather because Lucien would have hated him, since Cecily was still Lucien's girl. The next day Jack went down to the docks to ship out to sea, but by the time the ship pulled into its first port, he was ready to get back to New York. Totally confused about what he was doing, Kerouac jumped ship, put his merchant seaman's uniform in a duffel bag, changed to his chinos and black leather jacket and caught a bus back to New York. He moved into Ginsberg's dormitory room. After a few more nights with Cecily, she moved out and Jack and Allen settled down together to become great writers.

Chapter Four

Kerouac's mood in October 1944 had changed completely from that of two months before, when Edie had snapped a picture of him and Lucien standing together in the bright August sunshine on the Columbia campus, smiling at her in what was intended as a souvenir photograph before they sailed off to France.

Now Jack saw himself as "a picture of despair in bone and flesh." He had ruined his chances of ever signing aboard another ship in New York, he was stuck without money and Ginsberg was his only friend. He didn't even think about the problem of trying to explain to his parents why he'd jumped ship after leaving his wife.

Ginsberg tried to cheer him up, asking his advice about such matters as whether Allen should change his name as a writer to "Allen Renard." Jack told him no, or he'd kick Allen "right in the balls." It was also Jack who was the first person to learn about Allen's "social anxieties" about homosexuality. Ginsberg trusted him with the knowledge because Allen also felt, as he said later, that "nostalgia dominated Jack's soul."

Kerouac hid out in Ginsberg's room for a few weeks in the fall of 1944, not telling Edie or his parents he was in New York. Allen brought him books from the Columbia Library, especially Rimbaud, who was Allen's favorite poet at the time, as well as Yeats, Huxley, Nietzche and *Maldoror.* When he wasn't reading, Jack spent his time writing, even lighting a candle and cutting his finger so he could write in blood "The Blood of the Poet" as proof of his calling as a creative artist.

Later he called this part of life his "Self-ultimate" period, because he burned all that he wrote, but some of his notes survived in copies that Ginsberg made. Jack and Allen were both trying to write novels about Lucien Carr and Dave Kammerer, and Ginsberg was so impressed with Kerouac's notes about Lucien, that Jack let Allen copy them out.

Kerouac, of course, was not a Columbia student at this time, and it was against campus rules for him to be living in Ginsberg's room at Livingston Hall. For the few weeks that Jack stayed with Allen it was passed off as a kind of literary stunt to the other students who knew about it.

Allen was at this time an editor of the campus humor magazine, *Jester of Columbia,* and he explained that he and Jack were working on a literary collaboration. He admired Jack very much as an older and more experienced writer. Writing to his brother Eugene Ginsberg, who was in the Army, Allen described Jack as the most interesting friend he'd met at Columbia. Jack had "left college when he couldn't take the philistinism of Lou Little, the piggish priggishness of the football players, and the restrictions of academic life. He went into the Navy, was discharged as a psychoneurotic, sailed to England in the Merchant Marine (he's 21 or 22), came back . . . ."

The literary collaboration between Kerouac and Ginsberg resulted in a poem published by the *Jester* in January 1945. Jack called it a "literary joke, or lark," because it was a poem that he had written in French and that Allen had translated into English for the magazine. They called it "A Translation from the French of Jean-Louis Incognito by Allen Ginsberg."

Shortly after the poem appeared, Ginsberg was suspended from the college. Word had reached the Dean of Columbia that Kerouac had stayed overnight with Ginsberg in Livingston Hall. That wasn't all. Jack moved out to live with Burroughs and, once alone in his room again, Allen had decided to annoy an unfriendly Irish cleaning lady who hadn't washed his windows in months. He'd drawn a skull and crossbones on the dirty windowpane and scrawled the words "Butler has no balls" and "Fuck the Jews."

It was the slogans that finally did it. In the official letter that Dean MacKnight wrote Allen's father, Louis Ginsberg, Allen was suspended from Columbia College for an indefinite period for "obscene writings on his window and giving overnight housing to a person who is not a member of the College and whose presence on the Campus is unwelcome." Allen thought the Dean had been particularly hard on Kerouac because Jack hadn't bothered to pay his bills before he'd dropped out of Columbia. Kerouac's involvement in the Lucien Carr incident hadn't helped his reputation with the college authorities either.

Later, in a *Paris Review* interview, Jack insisted that he had nothing to do with Allen's getting "kicked out" of Columbia. "He let me sleep in his room. He was not kicked out of Columbia for that. The first time he let me sleep in his room . . . a guy came in . . . the guy that ran the floor and he thought that I was trying to make Allen . . . . But we were just actually sleeping." Allen moved to a room on West 92nd Street and took a job as a bus boy at Bickford's Cafeteria. He decided to join the Merchant Marine, and he also told his brother

Eugene that he was going "to consult with a physician," because Dean MacKnight was requiring a letter of recommendation from a psychiatrist before Allen could be readmitted to the College.

After Jack left Allen's room, he moved into Burroughs' apartment on Riverside Drive. Burroughs had come back to New York late in 1944, after Lucien's trial. As Jack remembered, Bill "showed up early that December after much candle-writing and bleeding on my part. 'My God, Jack, stop this nonsense and let's go out and have a drink.' " Jack told him he'd been sharing Allen's bowls of potato soup at the West End, and Burroughs said he could offer something better in his apartment—as Jack described it, "a bang of morphine." This was the first time Burroughs was involved with morphine in New York, and he described the addiction in the opening pages of his novel *Junkie*.

Jack declined the morphine, but he stayed with Burroughs until Edie came back to her old apartment near campus with Joan Vollner. After Jack moved in with her, they persuaded Burroughs to move in too, and he began staying with Joan Vollner. The apartment became, as Ginsberg remembered it, a commune.

As in the previous winter, Kerouac split his time between Edie's place and his parents' in Ozone Park. Mémêre and Leo were completely unable to understand what was happening to him or how he was living, and the arguments began again between Jack and his father about how Jack was throwing his life away. To complicate matters, Jack had begun taking benzedrine and he had to keep his parents from knowing about it.

The first time he tried bennies was with a friend of Burroughs named Vicki Russell, who lived at that time in the Village on Henry Street. She was a tall, attractive redhead, and she took a liking to Kerouac. She showed him how to break open benzedrine inhalers they bought in the drugstore, remove the soaked paper and roll it into little balls that they swallowed with coffee or coca-cola.

Jack spent three days on bennies the first time he tried them and he got sick. When he went home to his parents they exclaimed over his thin, drawn face, but Jack just told them he'd been sick at Edie's apartment. He was afraid to try morphine—he "turned it down"—but he was fascinated watching Burroughs take it, and he enjoyed the kick from bennies so much he got high as often as he could.

The more Jack saw of Burroughs the more impressed he was. Bill became his literary mentor, his trusted and experienced advisor. He haunted Burroughs' apartment and, like Ginsberg, thought Burroughs his "greatest teacher," who educated him more than his courses at Columbia.

Allen was so excited by Burroughs' apartment on Riverside Drive that he listed the memorabilia in the room: the needles, the alcohol and the morphine in the drawer, the books that Burroughs was reading, always for some specific purpose—Charles Jackson's *Lost Weekend* "to see what alcoholism is like," Jean Cocteau on opium, Spengler's *Decline of the West,* the poems of Blake, Rimbaud, and Baudelaire, Gogol's *Deal Souls* and Nabokov's study of Gogol, Abrahmson's *Crime and the Human Mind,* as well as lighter reading—Raymond Chandler, John O'Hara, James M. Cain and books on card tricks and ju-jitsu.

Burroughs had also annotated lists of bars along Eighth Avenue in Manhattan from 40th to 60th Streets, which fascinated Ginsberg with their cryptic notes about gamblers' bars, fag bars, old men's bars and bars with cheap liquor or quiet lounges. Burroughs introduced Jack and Allen to the "characters of the underworld" as Jack described them, whom Burroughs had begun to meet after his addiction to heroin. One of them was Vicki Russell who supplied them with benzedrine and marijuana. Others were thieves like Bill Garver and Phil White, who had shot a man robbing a liquor store, and Herbert Huncke, another heroin addict who became Burroughs' close friend.

They were all older than Jack and Allen. Burroughs was thirty, and he began taking drugs, he later told the *Paris Review* interviewer, because he was bored. He didn't have much interest in "living the kind of life Harvard designs for you." Burroughs became involved with the carny world of thieves, pickpockets and short-change artists he met in the Eighth Avenue bars around

Times Square, and he took copious notes on his experiences, material he used later in *Junkie* and *Naked Lunch*.

Kerouac regarded the people he met with Burroughs as an extension of the romantic self-torture of "Self-ultimacy" he had begun in Ginsberg's room at Columbia. He and Allen were still troubled with what had happened between Carr and Kammerer and they were both writing novels about it. Allen made several attempts to write a fictional treatment of what had happened. In one of these efforts Lucien committed suicide after the stabbing by rushing into Burroughs' apartment to take all the morphine in his drawer.

Burroughs and Kerouac, more as a joke than anything else, collaborated on a novel about the event. They titled it *And the Hippos Were Boiled in Their Tanks*. He and Bill had been sitting in a bar one night listening to the news. The newscaster ended his program saying in a rush that there had been a great fire in the London zoo: "the fire raced across the fields and the hippos were boiled in their tanks! Goodnight everyone!" The title was Burroughs' idea, but they each took alternate chapters of the novel, writing in the hard-boiled detective style of Dashiell Hammett, another one of Burroughs' favorite writers at the time. Burroughs read Jack's chapters and always returned them without comment.

As Kerouac remembered in *Vanity of Duluoz,* when he pressed Burroughs for a critical judgment, his friend would always peer over his joined fingertips and answer, "Good, good."

"But what do you specifically think of it?" Jack would insist.

"Why . . ." Burroughs would answer carefully, "why, I don't specifically *think* of it. I just rather like it, is all."

When Burroughs left New York City at the beginning of summer 1945—he describes in *Junkie* how his addiction got him in trouble with the law—Kerouac moved back to live with his parents in Ozone Park. Although he'd been with Edie in the apartment on 118th Street, they decided to end the marriage. As Jack later remembered, he let Edie "handle the annulment papers in Detroit, I was of no more use to her as a husband, I sent her home."

They'd been so poor that they'd been living on mayonnaise sandwiches and Jack told her to go back to her parents and get fed properly.

Allen was working in a shipyard, enrolled in the Maritime Service Training Station in New York. After graduating as a seaman in November 1945, he shipped out as a messboy on a tanker. The group of friends living in the 118th Street "commune" really lasted only during the first half of 1945. Kerouac was vague about the time later, exaggerating it into "a year of low, evil decadence," a time when everybody at the apartment got high together on bennies and sprawled on beds, discussing skepticism and decadence. One of Burroughs' friends came in to stash a gun and later hanged himself in the Tombs. Vicki Russell applied pancake makeup to Jack's face during a benzedrine depression when he insisted he looked too terrible to ride the subway.

In *Vanity of Duluoz* Jack called this "joining in with the despairists of my time." He took so much benzedrine that his parents realized something was happening to him, and he watched himself deteriorate with morbid fascination, getting soft and flabby around the middle, fancying that his hair was beginning to recede. He kept a photograph of himself taken after leaving Columbia in 1941, "a melancholy sort of picture" showing him gazing emptily into space and looking completely lost. It was as though Jack took a perverse pleasure in watching himself go completely to hell.

His mother tried to talk some sense into him, but Leo just got angry with him, saying that Jack was hanging around with a bunch of "dope fiends and crooks." Kerouac defended what he was doing by insisting that he was storing up information he'd use later as a writer. He swore to his parents that he wasn't using drugs himself, but they suspected the truth. Bad feelings mounted between them and Leo Kerouac began to shout that the way Jack was headed, he'd end up a dope fiend and a bum "no better than the ones you hang around with." In turn, Jack would get so angry himself having to defend what he was doing, that he'd say anything that would make his father mad.

Finally in July 1945, when the commune had broken

up and Jack went back to live in Ozone Park, his parents insisted he find a job to straighten himself out, at least give it a try for the summer. Jack was happy to leave the apartment to get away from the arguments. First he tried to ship out on a freighter sailing to Europe, but after having jumped his last ship the year before, he couldn't get a job as a merchant seaman. Instead, Jack worked a month as a busboy at a summer camp, returning home when his parents found him a job as a soda jerk in the drugstore under their apartment in Ozone Park.

There were other troubles in the family now. Leo Kerouac had begun to develop Banti's disease, cancer of the stomach. He became unable to keep his job as linotypist because the fluid swelling up in his stomach had to be drained every two or three weeks. The family decided that mémêre would keep working at the shoe factory, supporting them, and Jack would stay home to nurse his father. Suddenly everything had changed. Up to this point, Jack had felt he "had goofed throughout the entire wartime," but the party came to an abrupt end as he began to watch his father dying before his eyes.

The only thing that didn't stop was the benzedrine. Confined to the apartment most of the time, Jack took bennies late at night when his parents were in bed and he had the kitchen to himself. He told them he had to write at night, that, looking after Leo, he couldn't concentrate during the day. First, as he wrote to Allen in August 1945, he wanted to write a batch of magazine love stories, but two weeks later he'd abandoned the magazine stories for a diary and rough drafts of three novels.

The benzedrine made him feel stronger, more self-confident than when he was straight, and he took pride in himself for being able to take such massive doses. Jack felt he was blasting so high that he was experiencing real insights and facing real fears. With benzedrine he felt he was embarking on a journey of self-discovery, climbing up from one level to the next, following his insights. As he told Allen, benzedrine intensified his awareness and made him feel more clever.

But by early December 1945, Kerouac had taken so much benzedrine that he became sick, developing thrombophlebitis in his legs. He went into the Veterans'

Administration Hospital in Queens and lay in bed with his legs up on pillows swathed in hot compresses. When he remembered the time later in *Vanity of Duluoz,* he said that he first began to think in the hospital and understand "that the city intellectuals of the world were divorced from the folkbody blood of the land and were just rootless fools." He "began to get a new vision of my own of a truer darkness" overshadowing "all this overlaid mental garbage of 'existentialism' and 'hipsterism' and 'bourgeois decadence' . . . ."

The month before entering the hospital Jack had written Allen a letter hinting that he had begun to think of a new way to write that was less neurotic than the work he had done before. Jack had been brooding for months about a new novel and the rest in the hospital helped him get on track of his ideas. He put out of his mind all the New Vision talk he'd heard with Allen and Lucien, he bypassed Allen's beloved Rimbaud and Burroughs' Dashiell Hammett and he returned to his original and instinctive response to the novelist he'd admired at Columbia before listening to any of his New York friends, Thomas Wolfe.

When Jack told Allen about his plans to write a great novel modeled after Thomas Wolfe, Ginsberg was so impressed by the force of Jack's conviction that he wrote his own story incorporating Jack's arguments for this literary approach. In Ginsberg's story, he described Kerouac as working on a novel called *Galloway,* the name Jack actually gave his fictional birthplace when he began the novel he had planned in the hospital, later titled *The Town and the City.*

As the young writer in Ginsberg's story, Jack was named "Bill Ducasse." Allen named himself "Leon Bliestein." The two friends sat drinking in what Allen called "The Radical Cafe," modeled on the West End Bar, sitting in the dim red booths over beers, arguing their aesthetic philosophies. In the story, Ducasse tells Bliestein, "The trouble with you, Bliestein, is that you don't write about your own environment—In *Galloway* I'm going to throw away all this damned decadence. All you can write about is Rimbaud and Lautreamont. Look at you—a Jew from Jersey City, and you don't have a feeling for your country . . . . You have no sense of the present, of land."

Kerouac later told an interviewer that at the time he "was determined to be a 'great writer,' in quotes, like Thomas Wolfe. . . ." He'd learned from Burroughs and Ginsberg, but his instinctive response had been to model his writing on Wolfe, Hemingway and Saroyan. The novels of Thomas Wolfe especially had affected Kerouac like "a torrent of American heaven and hell that opened my eyes to America as a subject in itself."

Ginsberg sensed something else in this influence. From what Jack told him about his response to Thomas Wolfe, Allen understood that Wolfe's novels strengthened Jack's wish to base his art on personal relationships. Ginsberg felt that Kerouac wanted to write books celebrating a "tender consciousness, a realization of mortal companions whose presence together makes the event sacramental." Allen had seen this in Jack's response to Allen's farewell to the Divinity Dormitory the summer they first met, and he felt that Kerouac's books were the expression of the theme of "mortal souls wandering earth in time that is vanishing under our feet."

Thomas Wolfe was a dominating figure also partly because Kerouac came of age as a young writer in the early 1940s, when Wolfe seemed like the only writer to imitate. So when Jack came out of the V.A. Hospital at the end of December 1945, he began to make notes and outlines for what he envisioned as a great American novel, a "huge novel explaining everything to everybody."

Leo Kerouac was sicker than ever and it was apparent to Jack and mémère that he wouldn't live long. He was in pain, irritable and cantankerous. Every two weeks the doctor climbed the stairs to the apartment to drain his stomach of fluids, and Jack would hear his father in the kitchen wincing and groaning, and then weeping as the doctor left. There was no more talk about Jack throwing his life away. Leo made him promise he'd always take care of mémère whatever else he did, and Jack promised.

Leo Kerouac died in the spring of 1946. Jack and his mother followed his hearse to the family cemetery in Nashua, New Hampshire, where he was buried. When they returned to the still apartment in Ozone Park, mémère did her spring house cleaning and went back to work at the shoe factory. As before with the death of his older brother Gerard, Jack was overcome with grief and a sense of personal loss. It seemed to him, as he forced himself to pick up the outlines for his projected novel, that death was the greatest mystery, the greatest theme for literature. Grimly he settled down to write the novel he had planned earlier in the year. He had taken Thomas Wolfe as his model, but his book was really written for his father, to prove to the memory of Leo Kerouac that Jack could write a book that would sell, that he could be a creative writer.

Jack had failed to fulfill his father's dreams of seeing him a football champion, a success at college and a hero in the Navy. At each one of Jack's failures, Leo Kerouac had supported him, confronting the Columbia football coach and the Navy psychiatrists as though his Ti Jean could do no wrong. But privately, at home, the arguments had raged between father and son. Jack felt that Leo had never believed in his promise as a creative writer, so he would prove himself there where everything else had gone awry.

Before beginning *The Town and the City,* Jack had seemed incapable of disciplined, sustained effort. But mémère believed in him, because for the first time since leaving Lowell for Horace Mann, her son Jackie really seemed to know what he wanted to do. It was a long and grueling two-year stretch for Kerouac to finish his first long novel; before he was through he had piled up 1,183 pages of manuscript. It was the most disciplined act of his life, because he was held fast to the book by the strength of his belief that "When this book is finished, which is going to be the sum and substance and crap of everything I've been thru throughout this whole goddam life, I shall be redeemed."

What also seemed clear within the first few months of work on the novel was that he possessed the necessary talent, as well as the sense of purpose, for the job. Whatever feelings of guilt or stubborn will brought him to start *The Town and the City,* he used the book to romanticize his past. The book was like a shield between the life that had disappointed Leo and the life that would come for Jack and mémêre when he had been "redeemed" as a creative writer.

Sitting at his typewriter on the kitchen table in his mother's apartment in Ozone Park, Kerouac imagined a home and a childhood in Lowell modeled on his own life but changed significantly so that his novel would read like the romantic fiction of Thomas Wolfe. He later said that he wrote his first published book "according to what they told me at Columbia University. Fiction." And fiction, to Kerouac, was written so that "you put in it all your dreams."

The Town and the City was autobiographical, like nearly everything Kerouac ever wrote. From his earliest writing he preferred to stay close to things that had actually happened to him. His talent as a writer was not his inventiveness with new characters and plots, but rather his power to dramatize the spirit of his own life into romantic fantasy.

One of his natural talents was the possession of a very accurate, very detailed memory. As a child he was proud of the nickname "Memory Babe" that his friends gave him in school. He could visualize scenes, people and conversations in his past so closely that his memory became his stock in trade as a writer. He began using the talent in *The Town and the City* by describing the changes that face the various members of a large New England family, called Martin, as they leave the town where they were born and raised and move to the city to encounter the restlessness and confusion of World War II. The novel follows an American literary tradition of contrasting the innocence of country and small town life with the destructive experience of a big city. But because his own boyhood in Lowell had actually been darkened and restricted by his brother Gerard's death, the economic depression of the 1930s and his father's financial failures, Kerouac had to imagine a more bucolic setting for the first half of his book. What he did was combine details from his own boyhood in Lowell with memories of his friends' lives, specifically the large family of his high school friend Alex Sampas.

In his novel, Kerouac divided himself into five characters

who are all sons of George Martin. He put most of himself into Peter Martin, the central character of the sprawling narrative, who is thirteen years old when the novel begins in 1935, the same age as Kerouac himself was in that year. Like Kerouac, Peter Martin is ambitious, though confused. He is athletic and gets a football scholarship to an Ivy League School (the University of Pennsylvania instead of Columbia). Peter, too, is troubled by his relationship with his father, yet believes that "the most beautiful idea on the face of the earth is the idea the child has that his father knows everything."

Jack's method was always to soften character and to smooth out edges so that a romantic nostalgia, rather than social realism, flooded the page. His parents were models for George and Marge Martin in the novel, but George Martin was a more prosperous businessman than Leo had ever been. In real life Leo Kerouac had been a strong, brusque man who once knocked a rabbi off the sidewalk in New York when the rabbi refused to get out of his way, but the fictional George Martin was more of an earnest, perhaps confused, but always well-meaning man. By changing the background of the family in the novel from French-Canadian immigrant to vaguely Irish-Catholic, Kerouac suggested a blander stereotype of the American family, more centered within the framework of his romantic fiction.

Sitting in the small kitchen in the flat and featureless neighborhood of Ozone Park, hearing the rattle of traffic on Cross Bay Boulevard, the drab, dingy Lowell of Jack's childhood became romanticized into "Galloway," where the Martin family lived near woods and fields in an old frame house that bulged with the life within it. Even his brief high school football career was romanticized in a passage he was so proud of that he showed it to Ginsberg, with the comment that it was the best writing in the novel:

... The roaring of the crowd surged and grew thunderous, the Martin mother jumped up on her seat to see, and she saw a figure racing down the sidelines, shaking off tacklers with a squirming motion, plunging through others with a striding determination, tripping, stumbling, staggering on

64

half fallen and half running, straightening out once more, plodding, faking, yet suddenly approaching the goal line in a drunken weary run, staggered aside by another lunging figure, momentarily stopping, then carrying on again, striding to the line falling, with a dark figure smashing into it, now wavering on bent knees, now finally diving over and rolling in the end zone triumphantly.

As Jack went on with the manuscript it became more and more a projection of his own life. Midway through the novel, after Peter Martin has won his scholarship to college, he sits on the porch of his house, just like Kerouac before leaving Lowell, and dreams prophetically of the disappointments in his life ahead. The book darkens at this point; ". . . strange melancholy forebodings were in him, and a heaviness of heart, a dark sense of loss and dull ruin, as though he had grown old at nineteen."

When the family moved to New York, George Martin, like Leo Kerouac, is unable to understand his son's new friends. Jack took whole into the novel all the people he had met at Columbia: Lucien Carr (named "Kenneth Wood"), Allen Ginsberg ("Leon Levinsky"), William Burroughs ("Will Dennison"), Dave Kammerer ("Waldo Meister"), as well as several of the people he had met through Burroughs hanging around Times Square. They lead Peter Martin into a life totally unknown to his parents.

After smoking marijuana in Dennison's apartment, listening to a young heroin addict describe how he'd blown marijuana smoke at the cockroaches "so they wouldn't mess around" with his bread and jam, Peter Martin goes home to dinners of pork chops and chocolate cake with his family, who can only wonder about how little he tells them of what he is doing. Peter never resolves the conflict between his family's values and those of his friends, brooding only that while "all his friends were engaged in their morbid demonisms, these people were working gravely and living earnestly and enjoying their evenings with quaint and homely gladness. He felt humble and strangely glad."

Kerouac kept Kammerer's stabbing out of *The Town and the City*, romanticizing it as a suicide. He incorporated some of Ginsberg's literary ideas into the novel, attempting to widen his picture of social disintegration after the war. Allen had written a prose sketch of Times Square for a projected story that Jack used in the novel as a conversation between Peter Martin and Leon Levinsky while they sat talking in a Times Square cafeteria over coffee with "Junky" (Burroughs' friend Herbert Huncke) and "Jack the Hoodlum" (Phil White).

Allen's original prose sketch was titled "A Vision of the Apocalypse," which he wrote after walking through Times Square with Huncke one winter day. Huncke pointed out to Allen a place called the Pokerino that used to be the All-American Bus Terminal where Huncke sometimes stole suitcases. The Pokerino was filled with men who had been asked to leave Bickford's Cafeteria or the Automat on Times Square, and junkies who'd drifted in from the bars on Eighth Avenue. As Allen described the scene in his early sketch, the Pokerino was filled with

. . . beat, absolutely beat, characters . . . . Teaheads from everywhere, hustlers with pimples, queens with pompadours, lushes with green faces, fat dicks with clubs, cherubs with sycophants, wolves with adenoids, faces with blotches, noses with holes, eyebrows with spangles, old men with the horrors, bums with the stumbles, and some squares with curiosity or just passing through to catch a bus . . . .

Jack developed Allen's image of the Pokerino by enlarging its symbolic suggestion of a larger cultural malaise affecting every one of his friends and ultimately threatening the entire world. Huncke had told Ginsberg to look for an "unclassifiable skin mortification" that everyone on Times Square was concealing. Allen later thought that the "peeling skin" Huncke described was the physical result of the benzedrine everyone was breaking out of inhalors and swallowing. But it was also, according to Ginsberg, the "first psychical revelation of the ecological disturbance" of the atomic bomb, exploded at Hiroshima shortly after everyone began taking benzedrine in the apartment on 118th Street.

At the end of *The Town and the City,* the novel turns again to Jack and his own lost unhappiness. In the final scene, Peter Martin is left alone on a rainy night on a highway traveling west, his mind filled with the memory of his dead father, hearing the promise of his father's dream of America still calling after him, "Peter, Peter! Where are you going, Peter?" But Peter—and Jack—had been left alone. Leo was dead, and the life that Jack so painfully described in his novel was over.

The book he had forced himself to complete represented the end of the life he'd known up till then. But a new life was beginning for Kerouac, when it seemed to him for a while at least that he wasn't alone.

Chapter Five

Almost a year after his father's death, while he was still writing *The Town and the City,* Kerouac met Neal Cassady for the first time and like almost everything that happened to him during these years he included the meeting as part of a book. Jack described "Dean" in the first paragraph of a manuscript that was later published as *On The Road*:

I first met Dean not long after my wife and I split up. I had just gotten over a serious illness that I won't bother to talk about, except that it had something to do with the miserably weary split-up and my feeling that everything was dead. With the coming of Dean Moriarty began the part of my life you could call my life on the road . . . .

One day I was hanging around the campus and Chad and Tim Gray told me Dean was staying in a cold-water pad in East Harlem, the Spanish Harlem. Dean had arrived the night before, the first time in New York, with his beautiful little sharp chick Marylou; they got off the Greyhound bus at 50th Street and cut around the corner looking for a place to eat and went right in Hector's, and since then Hector's cafeteria has always been a big symbol of New York for

Dean. They spent money on beautiful big glazed cakes and creampuffs . . . .

I went to the cold-water flat with the boys, and Dean came to the door in shorts. Marylou was jumping off the couch; Dean had dispatched the occupant of the apartment to the kitchen, probably to make coffee, while he proceeded with his loveproblems, for to him sex was the one and only holy and important thing in life, although he had to sweat and curse to make a living and so on . . . . My first impression of Dean was of a young Gene Autry—trim, thin-hipped, blue-eyed, with a real Oklahoma accent—a sideburned hero of the snowy West.

In this opening paragraph Jack changed the scene a little from how he originally remembered it. When he told his friend Carl Solomon about meeting Neal in 1947, there weren't any shorts. Then he remembered Neal standing naked in the doorway of the tenement, as a kind of Nietzschean hero.

Neal Cassady quickly became a dominant influence in Kerouac's life. As Dean Moriarty he was the central figure in *On The Road,* the book that made Cassady a legend. He was also the center of an even longer novel, *Visions of Cody.* He appears in *The Dharma Bums, Big Sur* and *Desolation Angels.* Neal became almost an extension of Jack's personality, a part of his own life.

It is almost impossible to fully understand Neal Cassady or get more than a glimpse of him and his frantic, chaotic life in the years that Kerouac knew him. Neal told his friends that he'd been born while his parents were passing through Salt Lake City in a jalopy on 8 February, 1926, and nobody ever had any reason to question it. It hadn't been jails for him yet when Jack first saw him, but it had been three stretches in reform school, and that was close enough to jail for the friends who told Jack about him. Neal's mother had been married before, and her marriage to his father only lasted until he was six years old. He remembered a time in early childhood when his parents lived together. His father worked as a barber. Then they split up, his mother took her younger children and Neal went with his alcoholic father into a series of wino hotels and flophouses in Denver. He didn't attend school any oftener than he had to. He was restless and began to hitchhike around out of Denver, and hung out in the pool halls in the poor sections of town.

Neal was fourteen when he discovered that what he liked to do best in life was to drive cars. From then until he was eighteen, he "borrowed" cars off the streets, casing blocks of parked cars until he spotted one with the key left in the ignition, or hot-wiring them so that he could roar off for joyrides in the mountains. Neal had no intention of destroying the cars or selling their parts or doing anything in them more illegal than driving without a license, although if he could pick up a girl to ride around with him and park in the mountains for a few hours, so much the better. By his own count he took 500 cars between 1940 and 1944 and was caught by the police only three times, and each time he was caught he was sent to reform school.

It was while Cassady was in reform school that Jack first heard about him from his Columbia friend Hal Chase. Cassady had known Chase in Denver before Chase went off to New York. When Chase came back to Denver from Columbia, he impressed Cassady with stories about the people he had met in New York and the things, especially philosophy, he was studying in college.

Before knowing Chase, Cassady's ideal had been his older half-brother Jack, his mother's son by her first marriage, who was part Indian and a tough guy. Neal remembered that when he was ten, his brother Jack let him throw darts at him, trying to teach Neal to come as close as possible under his arms. When some of Neal's wilder throws landed in his brother's chest, Jack Cassady told him it felt like the initiation ordeals of the Cheyennes, and Neal was proud of him.

Neal had done some reading in the reformatory. How much or how intensely is difficult to tell. He told a Denver friend, Justin Brierly, that "I see Philip Wylie had written another book, *Night Unto Night* supposedly as good as *Generation of Vipers.* Peter Arno also had a new collection of cartoons out. *Man in a Shower* it's called. They had the Harvard Classics up here, the five foot shelf of books, I've read about two feet of it, very nice, I especially enjoy Voltaire and Bacon (Francis)."

The philosophy came some time later. Neal, with his

intensities and enthusiasms, burst in and out of ideas, coming to them, throwing them in the air, dropping them behind him and hurrying on to the next one. He made Kerouac feel thick and heavy, just as Burroughs and Ginsberg had made him feel stupid, and in the encounter between them Kerouac's life was permanently changed. Neal had the same effect on almost everyone he met in this first rush of his life when he came East with his confused, sixteen-year-old-bride, Luanne (called "Marylou" in *On The Road*).

Neal was almost as complete an experience for Allen as he was for Jack, and it was Allen whom he met first, though they didn't have much to say to each other at their first meeting. In 1950 Cassady wrote an "autobiographical fragment" describing what happened when he first got to New York. The high point was Chase's introducing him to Ginsberg in the West End. In Denver, Hal Chase had told him about Allen's poetry, and Neal had what he called "an extreme, abstract portrait of a young college Jew, whose amazing mind had the germ of decay in it and whose sterility had produced a blasé, yet fascinating mask." Face to face with Allen over a booth in the West End, Neal was most taken with the eyes. "They were dark, large and brooding; I was not quite sure how much of the brooding was there as such; and how much he was putting there for us to read into." On his part, Ginsberg saw a roughly handsome boy his own age, twenty years old, with a strong forehead, deeply set eyes, a broken nose that had healed slightly Roman and a wide Western smile. In his features and his muscular, stocky build, he resembled Kerouac enough to be taken for Jack's brother.

But since Allen couldn't help Neal and Luanne find a place to stay, they got no further into friendship, and it was Jack who was first close to him, although they had different memories of when it had been. Neal said he came to New York in October 1946; Jack said he met Neal a few days after Cassady came to New York in 1947. Hal Chase, the man who introduced them, remembered it was shortly before Christmas in 1946. Jack was as curious as he was impressed the first night with Neal and Luanne, but the quality in Neal that fascinated him was Neal's wild excitment. Just a few months before meeting Cassady, Kerouac had complained to Ginsberg that he was tired of the emotional excesses that Ginsberg, Burroughs and Lucien Carr had indulged in. What Jack wanted was the kind of ebullient enthusiasm he got from Cassady.

A few days after arriving, Neal had found a job parking cars in a Manhattan lot, moved into a furnished room with Luanne and begun to see more of Kerouac. He sensed immediately that he had to cultivate Jack's mother, but although Neal was as polite to mémère as he knew how to be when Jack brought him home to dinner, Cassady failed to impress her. She didn't like him at all. Neal had been born a Catholic so, in her eyes, that made him better than Jack's Jewish friend Ginsberg, but even though Jack had not told her about Neal's stretches in reform school, she saw Cassady as a wild kid who talked too much and mistrusted him instinctively. Jack didn't pay too much attention to her criticism, because by this time Neal had invited him around to the lot to watch him park cars. Jack was knocked over by Neal's skill as a driver. He was "the most fantastic parking-lot attendant in the world." Jack couldn't drive a car too well himself and didn't have a license, but after listening to Cassady and watching him move cars, Kerouac was convinced that he could get a job parking cars in New York if he ever needed to make quick money to finish his book.

Neal understood immediately how to make Kerouac his friend, almost too well, Jack felt. He simply asked Jack to teach him how to write. Hal Chase may have repeated what Jack had told his friends at the West End about writing being more important to him than anything else. But Neal could have seen that for himself. Once when he went over to Ozone Park for dinner, Jack was still at the typewriter, clattering away furiously, working on the chapter in *The Town and the City* which describes the football game in Galloway that won Peter Martin his scholarship to college.

It didn't take much encouragement from Neal for Jack to begin telling the story of how he himself had scored the winning touchdown for Lowell High in the

71

Thanksgiving game of 1938 and won the football scholarship to Horace Mann and Columbia. Jack got so carried away by his own enthusiasm for the story and by Neal's sympathetic and close attention, nodding his head, shrugging his shoulders, "throwing in a thousand 'Yeses' and 'That's rights' " that the chapter became Kerouac's virtuoso performance in the novel. Jack showed it to Neal when it was finished and Neal agreed with him that the description of the football game was the best prose Jack had ever written, with sentences Kerouac was so proud of that he'd copied them out for Ginsberg too.

Kerouac was taking a lot of benzedrine to write the novel, and Neal liked the benny high too. He told Jack that he had been introduced to it by Hal Chase. But Neal was able to match Jack's energy level effortlessly with or without bennies. When they rode the subway together from Ozone Park to find girls in New York (Luanne was being left alone in the furnished room more and more), Jack saw people looking at him and Neal as if they were both what his mother called "overexcited nuts." They would sit together talking ferociously, torrentially, with Neal waving his fingers in the air and wiping his sweating face with a handkerchief.

One night in January 1947, when they had no money for girls, Jack suggested going up to Vicki Russell's apartment to smoke marijuana, and he learned to his great surprise that Cassady had never tried it. When they got to the small apartment, furnished only with a bed, a dresser, a small stool and a radio, they found Ginsberg already there, sitting on the stool smoking pot in a water pipe. There hadn't been much to Neal's first talk with Allen in the West End, but after they turned on they began talking nonstop to each other. Finally they just left Jack to Vicki Russell and went home together. Jack and Neal had been slowly, cautiously getting to know each other. As Jack described it in *On The Road,* they "tiptoed around each other like heartbreaking new friends." But when Jack saw Neal again, two weeks had passed and Cassady and Ginsberg had become lovers.

Jack never said whether he thought Neal was more or less of a friend after he became Allen's lover. Kerouac's attitude toward homosexuality was complex and ambivalent. He couldn't accept it in Ginsberg as anything but a weakness, but if he was ill at ease with Cassady's homosexuality, he never put it down as he did with Ginsberg. Kerouac's own sexuality was confused. Before Jack met Neal, he had once joined Ginsberg and Burroughs in a homosexual romp at the Everard Baths on 28th Street, but he had no real involvement in that scene. He was still living with his mother when he met Cassady, and his love for his mother was the strongest emotion he ever felt for another person. Despite his brief marriage to Edie, he had not resolved his sexual conflicts. Coming from a working-class French-Canadian Catholic background, he believed fundamentally that there were two kinds of women: those who were Good and whom you idolized, and those who were Bad and with whom you had sex. He preferred whores or masturbation to marriage, and in his sexual timidity he admired Neal for being so apparently uninhibited, for sweeping into New York and taking anyone he wanted.

Neal became more highly charged sexually to Jack after he saw Allen fall so desperately in love with him. Kerouac never doubted Cassady's interest in women. As the poet Charles Olson later ironically remarked, Cassady really had two interests, cars and girls. Neal always had something going with a girl. He married three times, he fathered several children and if he had any money he always did his confused best to support his households. All of this masculinity reassured Jack and helped him accept Neal as his best friend. He also knew that Neal's attitudes toward homosexuality had to be fairly open after three stretches in the reform school even if his lack of inhibition was matched by an inability to become totally committed to any lover.

At first, almost despite himself, Jack was so impressed by the way Allen and Neal came together it was almost as though he regretted he'd been left out of something important. He wrote in *On The Road*:

. . . A tremendous thing happened when Dean met Carlo Marx. Two keen minds that they are, they took to each other at the drop of a hat. Two piercing eyes glancing into two piercing eyes—the holy con-man with the shining mind, and the sorrowful poetic con-man with the dark mind that is Carlo Marx. From that moment on I saw little of Dean, and I was a little sorry too. Their energies met head-on, I was a lout compared, I couldn't keep up with them.

When Cassady and Ginsberg finally rejoined Kerouac, Jack noticed that Neal had gotten Allen to teach him about poetry and philosophy, which in a way was what had brought Cassady from Denver to New York, via Hal Chase's stories about Ginsberg, in the first place. Together in Ginsberg's room, Allen and Neal had sat on the bed and had "fiendish allday-allnight-talk" marathons, and the result as Jack saw it was that Neal had "become completely *in there* with all the terms and jargon."

Allen later remembered that Cassady worked out a schedule for himself so that he could continue his lessons with both Ginsberg and Kerouac as his tutors. He spent two days a week with Allen writing poetry and making love, two days with Jack learning about prose writing and two days with his wife Luanne making love and fighting. The schedule lasted barely a week, because Luanne wasn't having any of it. She told Neal that the police were looking for him because he was buying so much marijuana, then she abruptly left for Denver by herself. As Ginsberg saw it, Luanne had no real cause for complaint. Cassady was willing to give her a fair share of his time, but she was jealous because "Neal was a lot more alert than she was and more sociable."

A short time later during the first week of March 1947, Cassady left New York aboard a Greyhound bus headed west. He'd had to work long hours to save enough money, but from what he'd made at the parking lot he was able to go into Chinatown before he left and buy his first suit, a dark pinstriped business suit that he wanted to wear back in Denver to impress his friends at the pool-hall. Jack and Allen both went with him to the Greyhound station to see him off. As a gesture of undying friendship, they posed for photographs in the quarter machine at the bus station, trying to look like gangsters. Allen took off his glasses so he'd look more sinister. Neal first made a profile shot holding a half-smoked cigarette; then he looked straight at the camera, smiling self-consciously.

Finally Jack took what he called a photo that made him "look like a thirty-year-old Italian who'd kill anybody who said anything against his mother." When the strip came out of the machine, both Allen and Neal wanted Jack's picture, so they compromised and cut it neatly down the middle, each taking half for his wallet.

Allen told Neal he would take the bus to Denver as soon as his semester was over at Columbia. Their plan was to spend the summer together in Denver. Neal could introduce Allen as his big poet friend from New York, while Allen would take Neal to meet Burroughs, who had married Joan Vollner and moved to a citrus fruit ranch in New Waverly, Texas. Jack had no money and he could not make any definite plans until he had gotten further along on his novel, but watching Cassady's bus roar out of the terminal into the night, the sign on the front reading Chicago, a place Jack had never seen, he promised himself that he'd make it west as soon as he could.

New York suddenly seemed tight and cramped, everybody on the streets bent and huddled against the bitter March winds. In the West, Kerouac knew it had to be warmer. It could not be anything else, because through Cassady Jack had caught a glimpse of the West that captivated him. He was sure that the horizon spanned adventures that would be "too fantastic not to tell."

As though Cassady were introducing Kerouac to the pleasures of the road before Jack actually went west for the first time himself, Neal began writing him long, detailed letters before his bus got back to Denver. The letters were meant to encourage Jack to hurry on with *The Town and the City* and to convince Jack that Neal was an undying, admiring friend. Cassady was still talking as though he were in Jack's living room in Ozone Park. Neal loved to talk, and once out of New York he missed the excited exchanges with Jack and Allen, so he wrote them letters as though they were still having their marathon talk sessions. He asked Jack to read the first letters as "a continuous chain of undisciplined thought," and in the second letter a week later he told Jack he hoped they could "fall into a spontaneous groove in not only our correspondence, but letter writing in general."

75

When Kerouac answered the first letter with a description of how badly he had done taking over Cassady's job at the parking lot (Jack did not last long), Neal did not comment on Jack's lack of skill with cars, but encouraged him with a remark about Jack's personality. He felt the letter expressed the Jack Kerouac he felt closest to.

Kerouac was supposed to be flattered with Cassady's analysis of their friendship, but he was mostly taken with the letters for another reason. The first one on 7 March, 1947 was unlike anything Jack had ever read before. When he showed it to Allen, Jack called it "the great sex letter." Cassady had written it in a Kansas City bar shortly after the experience, and he later apologized to Jack for the drunken rambling of the story, but actually it was one of the most succinct narratives Neal ever put down on paper:

I was sitting on the bus when it took on more passengers at Indianapolis, Indiana—a perfectly proportioned, beautiful, intellectual, passionate, personification of Venus De Milo asked me if the seat beside me was taken!!! I gulped, (I'm drunk) gargled & stammered NO! . . . She sat—I sweated— She started to speak, I knew it would be generalities so to tempt her I remained silent.

She . . . got on the bus at 8PM (Dark!) I didn't speak until 10 PM—in the intervening 2 hours I not only of course, determined to make her, but, how to DO IT.

I naturally can't quote the conversation verbally, however, I shall attempt to give you the gist of it from 10 PM to 2 AM.

Without the slightest preliminaries of objective remarks (what's your name? where are you going? etc.) I plunged into a completely knowing, completely subjective, personal & so to speak "penetrating her core" way of speech . . . by 2 AM I had her swearing eternal love, complete subjectivity to me & immediate satisfaction. I, anticipating even more pleasure, wouldn't allow her to blow me on the bus, instead we played, as they say, with each other.

Knowing her supremely perfect being was completely mine (when I'm more coherent, I'll tell you her complete history & psychological reason for loving me) I could conceive of no obstacle to my satisfaction, well, "the best laid plans of mice & men go astray," and my nemisis was her sister, the bitch.

The sister appeared in the St. Louis depot and took the girl home. Frustrated but undaunted, Cassady got back on the bus and tried again:

In complete (try & share my feeling) dejection, I sat, as the bus progressed toward Kansas City. At Columbia, Mo. a young (19) completely passive (my meat) *virgin* got on & shared my seat . . . In my dejection over losing Pat, the perfect, I decided to sit on the bus (behind the driver) in broad daylight & seduce her, from 10:30 AM to 2:30 PM I talked. When I was done, she (confused, her entire life upset, metaphysically amazed at me, passionate in her immaturity) called her folks in Kansas City, & went with me to a park (it was just getting dark) & I banged her; I screwed as never before; all my pent up emotion finding release in this young virgin (& she was) who is, by the way, a *school teacher*! Imagine, she's had 2 years of Mo. St. Teacher's College & now teaches Jr. High School . . . .

If Jack had any lingering doubts about Neal's heterosexuality after his affair with Allen, they disappeared after "the great sex letter." Once back in Denver, Neal rejoined his wife Luanne, but he also began a new affair with a girl studying at the University of Denver named Carolyn Robinson. She was a Bennington graduate, a very pretty blonde who was soon deeply in love with Cassady. Otherwise things did not go that well for him in Denver. He lived in a six-dollar-a-week basement room and found a job in a gasoline station, but he could not keep it. Broke, he hocked the suit he had bought in Chinatown but when the money from that ran out, he jokingly wrote Jack that he went down to the "nearby newsstand" to steal the change on the papers so he could buy some "bowery beefstew."

A few months later, Allen took the Greyhound to Denver and tried to resume their love affair in Neal's basement room. Sharing Neal with Luanne and Carolyn was hard on Allen. It gave him what he called the "Denver Doldrums." But Cassady seemed capable of endless emotional complications. It made no difference

77

to him if he loved one person or three. In fact he thrived on rushing to his various loves, making schedules to meet later, endlessly analyzing the relationships in long "raps," unfocused rambling philosophical monologues that he continued in letters. His friends took Neal's marathon monologues as proof of how much he loved them. They felt he had a brilliant mind, although what he said usually lacked any clearly defined content. Carolyn, who became Cassady's wife after he divorced Luanne, later remembered:

He could talk and would talk with anybody and instantly they felt that he really cared about them. How many people do you know who give of their selves when you first meet them? And it was a powerful thing because he was so perceptive and intelligent that he could meet them right where they were. Now part of that became conning, he learned how to use that to con. He was a master at getting you to think that he knew exactly where you were and what you needed and he could always supply it.

By the time Jack was ready to go west in July 1947, the scene between Allen, Neal and the women in Denver was so confused that Kerouac decided not to get involved. Besides, he really wanted to make some money. He hadn't worked a job since his father had died more than a year before, and although he'd written over half a novel, he wanted to help mémère out a little.

His friend Henri Cru from Horace Mann School had gone to San Francisco and become a seaman, and he wrote Jack that they'd have no trouble getting a ship together out of San Francisco. Cru painted a rosy picture of the pleasures of a seaman's life in the West. When Jack came to San Francisco, he and Cru could sign aboard a ship together as Chief (Cru) and Assistant (Kerouac) Electricians, pulling down good wages. It sounded good to Jack. Getting to San Francisco he could spend a few days in Denver with Neal and Allen, and make a side trip to see Burroughs' ranch in Texas. Coming back to New York in the fall, he wrote Burroughs he'd stop at the ranch again, and he'd try to time the trip so he could see the Texas-Rice football game.

All spring while Jack was trying to push his novel to the halfway point, he'd been preparing himself for his first trip across country. Filled with the spirit of the West, he hit upon what seemed to him the most poetic and cheapest way to travel. He pored over his maps of the United States and planned a route hitchhiking all the way to San Francisco via Denver from New York, something he knew neither Neal nor Allen had ever done. Allen had been so impatient to be with Neal again that he'd taken the Greyhound too. Jack thought he'd just show up suddenly in Denver and impress Cassady and Ginsberg, having hitchhiked all the way. Jack pictured himself walking across the land, strange and raggedly like a prophet.

But first he had to get on the road. In July 1947, he started the hard way, in the Bronx, trying to get rides north to Bear Mountain so he could get to Route 6, which he figured would take him west. If he'd talked more to Cassady about hitchhiking, he would have found out that the quickest way to head west was to get over to New Jersey and try to thumb a ride on the major highways, not head north to a nowhere traffic circle in upstate New York to put himself on an out-of-the-way highway that never got cross-country traffic. But Jack was an idealist. He hadn't been on the road very much, just short distances on the East Coast, and his vision of how he wanted to travel west the first time couldn't have been any simpler. As he wrote in *On The Road*:

I'd been pouring over maps of the United States . . . for months, even reading books about the pioneers and savoring names like Platte and Cimarron and so on, and on the road-map was one long red line called Route 6 that led from the tip of Cape Cod clear to Ely, Nevada, and there dipped down to Los Angeles. I'll just stay on 6 all the way to Ely, I said to myself and confidently started.

Jack was too late to join the covered wagon trains, but he wanted to come as close as possible to their style and their experience of the West. In his imagination the "one long red line" of Route 6 heading to California without a break was the trail of the American pioneers a hundred years before. Like the adventurous American settlers before him, Kerouac wanted the long red line of the setting sun in his eyes as he covered ground heading for California.

Chapter Six

Kerouac began his first cross-country trip by dropping a subway token into the slot on the Seventh Avenue I.R.T., riding to the end of the line at 242nd Street and taking trolley cars to the city limit in Yonkers on the east bank of the Hudson. Then he began hitchhiking. It took him five different rides to get the forty miles to the Bear Mountain Bridge, where Route 6 comes in from New England, but his troubles were only beginning. It began to rain heavily while he stood under a tree at the traffic circle on the highway, looking down the quiet stretch of Route 6. There were very few cars on the road. He was angry that he'd been hours out his first day and he wasn't any farther west than when he'd left New York in the morning.

Finally he gave up on Route 6 and accepted a ride to Newburgh, where he could get a bus back to New York. The only smart thing to do was go through the Holland Tunnel and head for Pittsburgh on the truckers' route: ". . . there's no traffic passes through 6." Grimly determined Jack rode the bus back to New York City with a bunch of noisy schoolteachers coming home from a holiday weekend in the mountains. He was so discouraged that he went straight to the Greyhound Terminal off Times Square where Cassady had taken his bus for Denver. Jack only had fifty dollars and he didn't want to blow it all on a bus ticket to San Francisco, but he compromised with his finances and his principles. He bought a ticket to Chicago, just to get out of New York.

Once west of Chicago, Jack began hitchhiking. He'd learned not to fight the complexities of big city traffic, so he took a bus to Joliet, Illinois, walked to the outskirts of town and held up his thumb. More than half his money was gone, and if he were going to get into the West, he'd have to find rides. For sentimental reasons he had put himself on Route 6 again. In Illinois the trucks were roaring down the highway and he had no trouble stopping one for his first ride. Twenty-four hours and six rides later, Kerouac was in Des Moines, Iowa. He hadn't covered that much ground, but he'd crossed the Mississippi River and he felt he was somewhere at last.

That afternoon in Des Moines he spent in a hotel room, the first of the long series of rooms in ramshackle hotels by the railroad tracks he was to sleep in the next ten years of his life. He fell asleep on the big clean hard bed, the yellow windowshades pulled against the daylight, and he slept so soundly, despite the sounds of the locomotives in the railroad yard across the way, that he only woke up as the sky reddened into dawn the next day. Kerouac's sleep had been so profound, his exhaustion from the exhilarating day hitchhiking so complete, that when he first opened his eyes in the dim light of his hotel room, he didn't know who he was. He felt like a person reborn. He lay still in bed, barely conscious of the dawn in the sky outside the window, and for about fifteen seconds he was just a body, just some nameless somebody in a strange bed far from home. The experience didn't threaten him, and when his sense returned of being Jack Kerouac, his mother's "Ti Jean" gone on the road, he felt that he had marked some turning point in his life.

He was, as he wrote in *On The Road*, ". . . halfway across America, at the dividing line between the East of my youth and the West of my future . . ." He lay in bed thinking about what had happened, and then he rolled over to make notes about the six rides the previous day that had taken him as far as the hotel room. When the morning had turned into afternoon, it was check-out time, time to get out on the road again.

Breakfast was pie and ice cream, which he told himself was good for him. ". . . that's practically all I ate all the way across the country. I knew it was nutritious and it was delicious, of course." That day the first ride came from a man driving a "toolshack on wheels," standing up to drive it like a milkman. Then on top of a long hill, Jack was picked up by a farmer and his son. There was a short wait in Adel, Iowa, but Jack was into the rhythm of the midwest, and he loafed under a big elm tree near a gas station, talking to another hitchhiker. The next ride only went as far as Stuart, Iowa, where Jack and the other hitchhiker were stranded until three o'clock the next morning in front of the railroad ticket office. He heard the freights slamming around in the yard, and he thought about hopping a train west, but he didn't know anything about doing that, how to tell whether a boxcar was going east or west, or even what kind of freight car to pick to jump on. Just before dawn he gave up on the road and took a bus as far as Council Bluffs. This was a place he'd read about when he was making out his route cross-country, and he'd looked forward to seeing it because it had been the place the wagon parties met a hundred years ago before hitting the Oregon and Santa Fe trails. From the window of the bus all he could see were little suburban houses, and the dawn seemed "dismal gray" to him.

Rides came again west of Council Bluffs. Everybody who stopped for Jack was a "cowboy" or "rancher" now, but from one of the drivers he learned a little about hopping freights. This "cowboy" had been out of work in the Depression and joined the hundreds of men all over the West wandering from town to town, looking for jobs. For a few hours in the early morning Jack was a little closer to the reality of the West in 1947 with its new suburban bungalows beginning to creep along the highway on the outskirts of big towns, the men who had been forced on the road ten and fifteen years before through economic necessity.

But Jack hadn't come west to find out these things. He was hurrying on to Denver and San Francisco and he thought he could still find his dream of the adventurous spirit of the pioneers in other encounters on the road. In a Nebraska diner where he stopped for cherry pie and ice cream, a great burst of laughter made him turn around. An old farmer came in and called out to the waitress, "Maw, rustle me up some grub before I have to start eating myself raw or some damn silly idee like that." The old man's vitality so charmed Kerouac that he could hear the laughter and yells echoing outside clear across the Nebraska plains, and he told himself, "Wham, listen to that man laugh. That's the West, here I am in the West."

Jack was still with the other hitchhiker he'd joined the day before in Adel, Iowa, a man about five years older than he who'd begun to bore Kerouac with his stories about New York. When they'd first met, Jack had been feeling a little lonely. It was right after the Des Moines hotel room. But the other hitchhiker had no money, so Jack had to pay his bus-fare to Council Bluffs, and when he said he was cold, Jack thought he had to loan him a heavy woolen shirt. Jack was new to the road, and he felt very foolish when the other man, called "Eddie" in *On The Road*, jumped onto a home-made trailer driven by an old man who said he only had room for one person. Alone once again at the side of the highway, Jack watched his plaid shirt disappear into the trailer; his friend hadn't even said goodbye.

But Jack didn't have much time to think about it. Soon afterwards, in Gothenburg, Nebraska, he got what he thought was the greatest ride in his life from a flatboard truck with half a dozen boys hanging onto the back of it. The two drivers, young blond farmers from Minnesota, had been bumping along nonstop from Des Moines, picking up any hitchhiker who looked right to them. After jumping aboard, Jack was passed a bottle of rotgut, nearly empty. He took a deep swallow and suddenly the air became "the wild, lyrical, drizzling air of Nebraska" as the truck lurched into 70 miles an hour and passed everything on the road. They were headed for Los Angeles, and Jack was tempted to stick with them and bypass Denver, but he had to see his "gang" in Denver, show up before them and hear Neal say, "You old sonumbitch you finally got on that old road."

The stretch from Chicago to Denver in July 1947 was the longest distance Kerouac ever hitchhiked. From then on he always took the bus to cover long distances, or got Cassady to drive him or, after be became a brakeman, used his pass on the railroads. But it was exhilarating to have come west the first time by himself thumbing rides and he kept thinking with fierce pride, "Damn! damn! damn! I'm making it!"

Once in Denver, Kerouac couldn't find Cassady or Ginsberg right away. He had Hal Chase's address, and after calling his house, Jack was invited over to spend the night. Chase and another Denver friend, Ed White, (they're called "Chad King" and "Tim Gray" in *On The Road*) were seeing less of Cassady that summer. Jack described the mood as "some kind of conspiracy," even "a war with social overtones," because Neal was the son of a wino bum and Chase and White were college students from respectable homes.

But Chase and his friends didn't stress the social differences when they objected to Cassady. They told Jack they thought Neal was "a moron and a fool" for rushing around Denver making love to any willing girl: his wife Luanne, the new girl Carolyn or a lunchroom waitress. He was still acting like an irresponsible kid, even joyriding again, picking up occasional cars to ride in the mountains. Since he didn't have a job or even any place of his own to stay, he just floated around different rooming houses with his girls, spending a few hours in the basement room with Allen, rushing from one person to another.

But Jack visualized the scene his own way. He looked at Chase's comfortable home, and he compared the quiet way Chase was living with what Cassady and Ginsberg were doing in Denver, meeting in the basement room after Allen finished his job downtown to make love and take benzedrine, talk and write poetry. There was never any question in Jack's mind which he preferred. In his eyes, Neal was "a new kind of American saint." The basement room where Neal, high on bennies, talked excitedly until dawn and where Allen scribbled his journals and composed the "Denver Doldrums" poems, symbolized for Kerouac the rumbling that he was hearing in what he called the "underground." Yet some small part of him stood back and he also saw Neal and Allen as "underground monsters."

When Kerouac described the Denver scene later in *On The Road,* he wrote it as a comedy, with Cassady a confused, ragged, down-at-the-heels hero scattering confusion behind him like a mountain avalanche. Jack had enough sense to leave when his fifty dollars ran out. He wrote home to his mother for another fifty dollars for the bus-fare to San Francisco and enough to tide him over until he shipped out with Henri Cru. Neal had offered to find him a job in Denver, and he actually brought Jack around to talk to a man who wanted to hire laborers to work a fourteen-hour day unpacking crates in the markets, but Jack backed out fast at the thought of so much work.

In his own peculiar way Cassady always tried to keep his word. He delivered a job for Jack, even if it was an impossible one. If he told one of his girls he'd be back in her room at the hotel to make love at 3:14, he'd nearly break his neck trying to be there exactly on time, or a few hours or days late, if something else really important interfered. When Jack's bus left Denver, the situation between Cassady, Ginsberg and the girls seemed precarious, but Neal made vague, if enthusiastic, promises to follow Jack to San Francisco with Allen later so they'd have more time to be together.

The grand reunion in San Francisco never took place. Instead, as he wrote Jack in September 1947, Neal went with Ginsberg to Texas to meet Burroughs and his wife Joan and Herbert Huncke on Bill's ranch in New Waverly, Texas. A few months before, Joan Burroughs had had a son, whom they named William Burroughs III. Joan and the baby and her older daughter were living on the ranch while Burroughs and a Harvard friend, Kells Elvins, grew marijuana and tried to start a citrus farm. The ranch was close enough to Houston to drive into the city regularly to buy benzedrine and fill prescriptions for morphine.

At the ranch during the first week of September, Neal told Allen they had to go their separate ways. Ginsberg desperately thought of returning to New York for the fall semester at Columbia, but he was hoping to go back the long way as a messman on a merchant freighter.

Cassady promised him a last night together in a Houston hotel before Allen shipped out to sea. Huncke went with them when they left New Waverly, and they spent the early part of the evening in bars getting high on what Neal told Jack was assorted stuff. Suddenly Cassady cut off in the jeep by himself and found what he called "a mad woman." He brought her back to the hotel, where Allen waited alone outside while Huncke was with a boy in the room they had rented for the night. Neal burst in with the girl, and in a moment the girl was bewildered and hysterical, Huncke was angry at being interrupted and Ginsberg was furious at Cassady's betrayal. In the middle of the long argument, Neal passed out. He told Jack later he didn't wake up until nine o'clock the next morning.

Allen was terribly upset. When he shipped out the following week, he was on a ship bound for Dakar, Africa, and he was still so unhappy that he didn't care when he got back to New York. He traded the "Denver Doldrums" for the "Dakar Doldrums," but the poetry he wrote in Africa was just as lachrymose as the stanzas he copied out for Jack in his basement room in Denver earlier that summer:

> Art is illusion, for I do not act
> —Dwell or Depart—with Faithful merriment,
> My thoughts, though skeptic, are in sacrament,
> Holy prayer for knowledge of pure fact.
>
> So I enact the Hope I can create
> A lively world around my deadly eyes.
> Sad paradise it is I imitate,
> And fallen angels whose lost wings are sighs.
>
> In this unworldly state wherein I move
> My Faith and Hope are hellish currency:
> In counterfeit worlds, I coin small charity
> About myself, and trade my soul for Love.

In Allen's tight handwriting scrawl, the words "Sad paradise" looked like "Sal paradise," and it became the name Kerouac gave himself almost four years later in *On The Road*.

After staying in Denver, Jack was a little late getting to San Francisco. He worried that he had messed up the plans his friend Henri Cru had made for them to ship out together. But Cru was very relaxed when he finally arrived, because there'd be a delay before they could get work as seamen. When Jack pinned him down, he really didn't know when they could ship out, so Jack took a job as a night watchman in the same place as Cru. Jack felt that he should send money back to his mother as he'd promised since it was the pretext he'd given her for the trip cross-country. Besides, the uniform he had to wear, with a badge and a gun, amused Jack, who thought of the way Cassady, Burroughs and Ginsberg would laugh if he showed up on the ranch dressed as a guard.

At first he got a kick out of living with Henri Cru in a little one-room shack in Mill Valley, going to work at night pretending he was a character out of a cops and robbers movie. Jack got on well with Henri Cru, who was an old friend. Cru's attitude toward Kerouac had been the same since their prep school days, a mixture of goodhumored condescension and mild contempt for what he considered Jack's unbelievable naiveté. Possibly because Cru had been born in France, Jack, as a French Canadian, was admiring and respectful of him and played up to his expectations of simplicity.

Jack's first comment to Cru in wide-eyed response to California, reported in *On The Road,* was "There must be a lot of Italians in Sausalito." Cru repeated his words over and over, laughing explosively each time, never explaining why they were so funny, and Jack accepted the laughter without protest or self-defense. Cru also had a notion that he could teach Kerouac how to write, so when they went over to San Francisco together to eat in Chinatown, he pointed out eccentric people on the streets like the "Banana King" selling fruit on the corner. Cru insisted that until Jack learned "to realize the importance of the Banana King," he would know "absolutely nothing about the human-interest things of the world."

Jack, of course, was bored by his friend's presumptuous advice about how to write novels. The vague plans they made for Cru to act as the Hollywood agent for a movie script Jack would write never came to anything. In the end the friendship became a little strained. Jack was sleeping on a cot in the same room as Cru and his girl and got tired of listening to them fight. Cru started hinting that Kerouac wasn't contributing his fair share of the household expenses by taping the long white slips of the grocery store receipts up in the bathroom, where Jack couldn't miss seeing them.

Kerouac stubbornly continued sending almost everything he earned back to his mother in Ozone Park. He rationalized what he was doing by telling himself that Cru was just gambling the money away at the Golden Gate Racetrack .across the bay from San Francisco. The situation resolved itself when Jack was fired from the job as night watchman. He had worn out his welcome at Cru's shack, and there was no reason to hang around Mill Valley. Jack took a couple of hours to go off by himself and climb the road up to Mount Tamalpais, and then he got back on the highway. Nothing much had come of his great dream of good times in California. As he wrote in *On The Road*, "Here I was at the end of America—no more land—and now there was nowhere to go but back."

But California wasn't quite finished with Kerouac. He hitchhiked from Oakland to Bakersfield, got stranded on the highway short of Los Angeles and went back to the bus station for a ticket. All Jack wanted was a little sightseeing in Hollywood before he went back to see Burroughs in Texas. He was resting on a bench in the bus station, as he described it in *On The Road,* when a pretty girl caught his eye:

. . . all of a sudden I saw the cutest little Mexican girl in slacks come cutting across my sight. She was in one of the buses that had just pulled in with a big sigh of airbrakes; it was discharging passengers for a rest stop. Her breasts stuck out straight and true; her little flanks looked delicious; her hair was long and lustrous black; and her eyes were great big blue things with timidities inside. I wished I was on her bus. A pain stabbed my heart, as it did everytime I saw a girl I loved who was going the opposite direction in this too-big world . . .

When Jack got on the bus, the Mexican girl was there, sitting next to an empty seat. What happened next was strangely reminiscent of Neal Cassady's bus pick-up in the "great sex letter" to Kerouac six months before:

. . . I dropped right opposite her and began scheming right off. I was so lonely, so sad, so tired, so quivering, so broken, so beat, that I got up my courage, the courage necessary to approach a strange girl, and acted. Even then I spent five minutes beating my thighs in the dark as the bus rolled down the road.

Kerouac offered her his raincoat for a pillow. The girl declined but allowed him to sit beside her. They began to talk, and Jack learned she had left her husband and child and was going to Los Angeles to live with her sister. It was a classic bus pick-up:

Without coming to any particular agreement we began holding hands, and in the same way it was mutely and beautifully and purely decided that when I got to my hotel room in LA she would be beside me. I ached all over for her; I leaned my head in her beautiful hair. Her little shoulders drove me mad; I hugged her and hugged her. And she loved it . . . .
It was as simple as that. You could have all your Peaches and Bettys and Marylous and Ritas and Camilles and Inezes in this world; this was my girl and my kind of girlsoul, and I told her that. She confessed she saw me watching her in the bus station. "I thought you was a nice college boy."
"Oh, I'm a college boy!" I assured her . . . .

Jack and his girl (he called her "Terry" in *On The Road*) stayed together fifteen days. After living together in a cheap hotel room near the downtown Los Angeles bus station, Jack's money was nearly gone. They hitch-hiked and rode a bus back to the girl's family outside Selma, California in the Central Valley, where they lived in a tent with her little boy, picking cotton to pay for the groceries. From Kerouac's description those were two of the happiest weeks of his life.
The dollar and a half they earned picking cotton every day bought their food and paid for the tent they slept in.

As the days rolled by, Jack "forgot all about the East and all about Dean and Carlo and the bloody road." But it was October, the nights were getting colder and the money from the cotton each day didn't stretch for fuel for the woodstove. Jack thought he should go home to his mother in Ozone Park.

The Mexican girl didn't want him to leave. She told him she'd go back to live in her family's house and get a job picking grapes, making enough money for both of them. Jack could sleep in a barn down the road from her family, and she'd watch him sit in the grass all day and eat the grapes she brought him. But after one cold night in the barn, with her father yelling at her about creeping off to bring Jack a plate of tortillas and beans, Kerouac thought it was time to leave. Waiting for him at the telegraph office in town was the bus-fare mémêre had wired him, and although Jack felt a little sheepish about accepting it, he started back home. As he wrote in *On The Road,* his "lazy butt" had been saved again.

Getting back to New York was more of a struggle than he expected. He rode the bus from Los Angeles to Pittsburgh nonstop with a stack of salami sandwiches in his tattered canvas seaman's bag, figuring it would be easy to hitchhike the last leg of the trip home. But the nonstop bus ride left him exhausted, starving and sexually strung out after necking with a girl all the way from Indianapolis to Columbus, Ohio.

Once off the Greyhound, he stretched his legs with a five-mile walk out of downtown Pittsburgh, but two rides got him only to Harrisburg. He had 365 miles left to go to New York and only a dime in his pocket. It was nighttime and beginning to rain and all Jack wanted was to get back home. The weather was in his favor. Although it was late October, nearly Halloween, the night was warm. Jack began to walk along the highway outside Harrisburg, hoping for a lift, not even sure he was on the right road to New York.

The highway led Jack along the banks of the Susquehanna River, where he met a shriveled old man with a paper suitcase who told Jack he was headed for "Canady." They walked together for seven miles along the river, the old man urging Jack to hurry along, and walking erratically in the middle of the road where the walking was faster. Jack was worried that the old man would get hit by the traffic going the opposite way, and plodded along himself in the ditch. In the rainy mountain blackness, the Susquehanna seemed like something out of a nightmare.

It began to seem to Jack as if he were trapped in some nightmare of his own, hurrying after the old man, who mumbled continuously about the meals he'd eaten in charity homes. Jack was sweating and exhausted by the time he decided he had enough. The old man was probably a senile fool, he thought, leading him completely astray. It began to rain harder, getting darker and darker, and in desperation, Jack stopped a car headed the way he had walked and asked for a ride back to Harrisburg. Once in the car, the driver told him he'd been turned around on a road leading west for Chicago.

Jack spent the night sleeping on a bench in the Harrisburg railroad station. He was thrown out at dawn, his stomach so painfully empty he felt he might not make it home. He finally got a ride all the way back to New York, but the driver was an anxious and skinny man who believed in strict dieting. Kerouac laughed until he was nearly hysterical. At the end of the ride, starved and exhausted, he was back in New York.

Chapter Seven

Someone can wander from city to city, as Kerouac was doing, if he has a strong sense of himself and knows the reasons for his being in all those lonely rooms and for riding on all those endless buses. But Jack's desperate flights back and forth across the country during the next six years only mirrored his own confusion.

On his return to New York toward the end of October 1947, he was almost twenty-six and still didn't have a life he could call his. He had the room at his mother's. He could stay there, he had a bed and clothes there and there was always something to eat in the refrigerator. He was still dependent but he could write there, and the only thing that gave his life any kind of direction was his struggle to become a writer. All of the chaos that he described in his books, the feverish excitement, the meetings and partings, the travels, usually didn't last long. A few weeks, a few months, and he was back with his mother writing it all down.

For a time Cassady was out of his life. He'd driven to New York with Burroughs after Ginsberg had shipped out to Africa, and during the weeks that Jack was still in California Neal hung around New York waiting for him to get back. Mémêre even let him stay at the apartment in Ozone Park, but only for a few days and so he moved in with Allen's brother. He tried unsuccessfully to get his old job back at the parking lot and didn't have enough money to stay on. By the time Jack had limped in from his last lift and dropped his battered traveling bag on the floor of his bedroom in Ozone Park, Neal was back in San Francisco, living with Carolyn. She had completed her Master of Fine Arts degree at Denver and was trying to get a job in California.

Back home with mémêre working at the shoe factory, Jack began again on *The Town and the City,* still trying to give it shape, still trying to finish it. Through November and early December Neal kept in touch. He also was trying to be a writer, working on a daily journal and an autobiography.

Jack went on with his writing and finally, after more than two years, the book was finished, in May. Jack sent the manuscript of *The Town and the City* off to Scribners, the publishers of Thomas Wolfe, that same month and sat around in a kind of tired suspension waiting for a reply. When Scribners rejected the book in June, Jack was utterly crushed.

By this time Ginsberg had returned from Africa and was back at Columbia as a student again. He did what he could to help. He was genuinely excited by the manuscript.

It was fiercely independent, romantically sentimental and of epic length. There were over 1,000 pages of manuscript totaling more than 380,000 words. It was what every young writer in the late forties thought of as a great novel, and that was what Allen called it in a letter to one of his professors, the critic and writer, Mark Van Doren. He asked Van Doren's help in getting this "Great American Novel" published.

When nothing immediately came of this, he got Jack to give him copies of some of the chapters and circulated them among friends, trying to spread the word about what Jack had achieved. After the Scribners rejection Jack had agreed that the ending was still a little "messed up," and he went back to it over the summer, struggling to provide more intellectual substance.

Shortly after the Scribners rejection, Jack got a letter from Neal saying that his life had become even more difficult since he'd written last. In early spring Jack had received a letter from Neal saying he'd been in trouble. It hadn't been anything serious but he'd wanted Jack to write a letter of recommendation, so that Neal could get a job training to be a brakeman on the Southern Pacific Railroad. Kerouac had been surprised but had sent off the letter.

Now, in June, Neal wrote more fully about the winter he'd had in San Francisco since seeing Kerouac, fighting off suicide. He tried it a couple of times before in his teens, hiding under a bridge getting up the courage to jump. In San Francisco he had tried it again, speeding across intersections through stop signs at fifty miles an hour hoping to get hit. When this didn't work he stole a 38-caliber pistol, but couldn't bring himself to pull the trigger, and Carolyn took the gun away from him.

At the beginning of March he made a sudden effort to break out of his life again. He drove to Denver, going round trip from San Francisco, nonstop, driving 2894 miles in thirty-three hours, spending an extra seven hours by the side of the road in a last futile attempt to commit suicide. Crossing the Continental Divide he stopped the car in the bitter cold and sat waiting to freeze to death. In his usual impatience he found that it took too long. There was no anti-freeze in the car, so the radiator froze instead. He stopped a bus which pushed him as far as a gas station where the radiator was fixed and he went on with the journey.

In his letter to Kerouac he told Jack how he had started his apprentice trips on the Southern Pacific in the late spring. He'd got into the training program with the help of an old Denver friend, Ed Hinckle, who'd worked as a brakeman. By June, Neal was working on a job at Pixley, California on a local freight run that picked up at the potato sheds. He got to the job at eight-thirty in the morning and worked until seven at night, sleeping in the outfit car and eating at cafes along the railroad yards. He'd only been working two weeks, but there seemed to be enough time to write and think and smoke and he was finally making a little money.

Jack was so taken by Neal's new life as a brakeman, he wrote back suggesting that they should buy a ranch together when he sold the novel. They'd all live together, Neal and Carolyn and the baby they were expecting in September, with Jack and his mother.

Cassady, with his usual impetuosity, began collecting real estate pamphlets about buying property, but for Jack it was only a fantasy. He was beginning to have doubts about how good the novel was or whether he could sell the manuscript. He was spending more and more time with Allen Ginsberg, who'd gotten his own apartment at 1401 York Avenue and was meeting new friends. When Jack described them to Neal in a second letter, Neal enthusiastically invited all of them to come to the ranch and work as ranch hands.

Allen's apartment was near Seventh Avenue, a dark and narrow cold water flat in a slum tenement, the dirty bricks of the adjoining building facing the rusted fire escape outside his bedroom window. It was hot in the summertime and endless Latin music came in through the open windows, mingled with the sounds of children crying and adults fighting. But the noise was often drowned out with the high, shrill sound of bop coming from a late night radio station. Herbert Gold, one of Ginsberg's Columbia friends, remembered the scene, the empty quart beer bottles piled in the hallway after a party or thrown

94

from the fire escape into the open garbage cans on the sidewalk below.

To get a response out of dark clusters of people sitting against the wall listening to music or warily talking to each other Allen sometimes lit firecrackers in the ashtrays. If he thought somebody could help him sell Jack's book he tried to act like Jack's agent. "Have you read *The Town and the City* yet? . . . Oh, you must . . . . I'll see if I can locate the other copy . . . . It's full of these crazy poems, it's really a big hymn, you see . . . . And *I'm* in it."

Allen had become noisily extroverted, trying to lose his deep unhappiness over Cassady and his anguished concern about Naomi, his mother, who was then in the Pilgrim State Mental Hospital. Herbert Gold brought his wife with him to a party, and he sat next to her as she tried to make polite conversation with Ginsberg about his trip to Africa. Allen barely made an effort to answer and when she insisted on asking precisely where he'd been and what he'd done there, Allen suddenly hurled the glass he was holding at the map of Africa on the wall, the wine splashing all over the girl's dark hair, and he turned away without an apology as the glass smashed to the floor.

At the same party on a hot night in July, Jack met another young novelist, John Clellon Holmes, who was to be drawn into the chaos of Jack's New York life. Almost twenty years later, writing about it, Holmes could still remember the night they met:

The midtown avenues, emptied by the holiday and the heat, gradually gave way to the guitars, crowded stoops, damp undershirts and quick angers of those thronging streets (under their haze of frying beans) that no one escapes simply because it is hot, and we threaded our way down the chalked pavements of a particularly active block, wondering if we were on the right one.

"This must be it, all right," [Alan] Harrington said. "There's Kerouac."

I knew about Kerouac. He had written a thousand-page novel that was being passed around "our" crowd just then in a battered doctor's bag . . . . I surveyed the people moving in and out of the sleazy little grocery up ahead (dark, good-looking men in sport shirts, most of them, with bagsfull of beer), but saw no one I would have identified as the author of a novel, weighing twenty pounds in the hand, that was being seriously touted to publishers by people I respected.

But Kerouac *was* one of those men—the one who looked like the serious tee-shirted younger brother of the others . . . He was making the run for more beer, he said with a hesitant smile, and, while Harrington bought a contribution of big, brown quarts, he and I talked a little there on the sidewalk.

Holmes responded to Kerouac immediately, as another fumbling writer suspended in the void between casting off everything to get the writing somehow finished and getting it published. But he also liked things he could see under the surface, the tenderness, the naive persistence of belief, the clenched commitment of Kerouac, and he liked them from the beginning. By the end of the summer they were close enough friends that Jack left his work journals for *The Town and the City* with Holmes, who took Jack's shabby leather doctor's bag bulging with different size cheap student notebooks filled to the margins with handwriting, and read them through in Alan Harrington's room on East 60th Street. He read them for hours, startled both by their rushing energy and their meticulous concern for word counts and progress reports.

I responded instinctively to the Kerouac I encountered there: the Kerouac who noted down each day's hoard of completed words, and then figured up his overall batting average; who zealously recorded his slumps along with his streaks, and just as zealously pep-talked or remonstrated with himself; the Kerouac . . . who, in those doldrums of midpassage, those horse latitudes that one reaches in the second half of a long, exhausting project, wondered pensively whether his book was "intellectually substantial," after all, but who, nevertheless, could write at the end: "Sept. 9. Tonight I finished and typed the last chapter. Last sentence of the novel: 'There were whoops and greetings and kisses and then everybody had supper in the kitchen.' Do you mean that the folks of this country won't like this last chapter? —or would it have been better if I had said, 'Everybody had dinner in the dining room . . .' But the work is finished."

But the weeks were slipping by, and Jack's confidence in himself as a writer was ebbing. He went on questioning himself about revisions of *The Town and the City*. Until he sold it to a publisher the novel wasn't proof to him that he was a writer, despite the two years that he'd put into it, or the physical evidence of a thousand pages of manuscript. Driving himself compulsively, he began another novel a few weeks after sending the manuscript off to Little, Brown. They read *The Town and the City* and like Scribners turned it down.

He thought of the new book as "A Novella of Children and Evil," and titled the notebook where he started the story, *Doctor Sax*. The new book was to be a continuation of Goethe's *Faust,* a poetic fantasy based on a "great sax dream" he had in the fall, which he'd interpreted to mean that "Faust thought he was fighting evil. But there is no evil, t'was but a husk of doves." In October 1948, in the first glow of enthusiasm over the idea, he filled the pages of the notebook with the opening passages of the novella, but he soon began to have doubts about what he was doing. He crossed out his first subtitle, "A Novella of Children and Evil," substituting "The Myth of the Rainy Night," and then finally put aside the notebook to pursue another idea for a totally different book.

This new book was *On The Road*, which he actually began writing early in November 1948. When *On The Road* became a best-selling book ten years later Jack preferred not to remember that he'd tried to write it years before. Once it was published he fostered the image of himself tossing it off in an inspired three-week rush in 1951, on a 120-foot roll of teletype paper.

The earliest version of *On The Road* he began in 1948 wasn't the version of the book that was finally published. That was a different *On The Road* of 1951, edited and revised several times before it finally appeared in 1957. But he had actually been trying to write the book for over two years before he finally succeeded in finding a form and a language for it. He described his first attempts at *On The Road* in a journal like the one he kept for

97

The Town and the City (Kerouac wrote journals for all his books), still keeping rough score for himself, trying to gauge where he was in the book, how he was doing with it, and, at this point even more importantly, how he was doing with himself. For the first few weeks he was encouraged because the book seemed to be moving. It had more promise than his short-lived enthusiasm for continuing Goethe's *Faust* and he drove himself at a rate of 1,500 words per day.

By the middle of December, however, he was beginning to get discouraged with the new book. Only a month before he'd been bragging to Ginsberg, to wait till he told Allen what "Levinsky" did in his new novel. ("Levinsky" was Jack's pseudonym for Allen in *The Town and the City*.) In his sudden, tired discouragement he even began to lose confidence in all the work he'd put into the finished manuscript he couldn't sell.

He thought he might be getting stale, that a stretch away from the writing might be a good idea, but the only job he could think of looking for was in a gas station. The only thing he could do was somehow to go doggedly on with it, sitting at the typewriter, anxiously counting up his score when he kicked back the chair and went to stare out the window or turned to get a beer from the refrigerator.

Jack was still in touch with Burroughs, and for a few weeks he thought Burroughs could help him out of the corner he'd written himself into. Burroughs had told him of a new style of writing that he was calling "Factualism." In his depressed mood Jack decided he'd begin again. Allen remembered that by "Factualism" Jack didn't mean Naturalism, but rather that he accepted the fact that he would die like everyone else.

John Clellon Holmes read some of the early fumbling attempts Kerouac made to write *On The Road* in the traditional "novelistic" form of *The Town and the City,* and he remembered that Jack began his story by trying to describe his characters first in a "many-layered New York milieu." In the first versions the book could never open out, could never finish, because Jack hadn't lived enough of the story. The long trip to the West Coast had lasted only a little more than three months, and his

98

hitchhiking had only covered two stretches, from Chicago west, and from Harrisburg east. Out of the two weeks in Denver he later estimated that he'd in fact spent only about five minutes talking to Cassady.

He had enough of a novelistic sense to know he had a story somewhere in everything that was happening to him, but not enough had happened. He was still caught in the tangle of describing his friends in New York, almost in a kind of repetitive sequel to the last half of *The Town and the City*. Ginsberg was still "Levinsky." Jack's desperate creative energy expressed itself, not in plot or in new characters, but instead in long, intricate sentences, in rushes of words and near-torrents of language. Holmes and Ginsberg were swept away in the flood of energy.

Later Holmes remembered that Jack wrote "long, intricate Melvillian sentences that unwound adroitly through a dense maze of clauses; astonishing sentences that were obsessed with simultaneously depicting the crumb on the plate, the plate on the table, the table in the house, and the house in the world, but which (to him) always got stalled in the traffic jam of their own rhetoric." But then they were in their twenties, and the words were almost enough in themselves. Holmes told Jack he'd give anything he owned to write prose like it, but Jack "threw it out, and began again, and failed again, and grew moody and perplexed."

Chapter Eight

The life that Kerouac was living through this period was a jumble of creative brilliance and personal chaos. When his writing was going well, or when his emotional life was less disturbed, he could keep all the pieces in a kind of balance with each other. When any part of the clumsy structure started to slip, the rest of him fell apart with it.

By the beginning of the winter of 1948 everything began to crumble. He hadn't been able to find a publisher for his manuscript, he hadn't been able to get past the opening chapters of two new novels, and he wasn't even able to make enough money to support himself. He was still living with his mother, still dependent on her, still using her money when he had to buy a drink or buy a notebook to make his journal entries.

Cassady realized his desperation when Jack wrote that he was going to try to get a job in a gas station. Neal tried instead to get him to come to San Francisco, saying he could make more money working on the railroad. But Kerouac didn't have enough money to get out to California. He couldn't even hitchhike. It was already winter and he couldn't face the cold and snow. Neal tried his best to get him out of the situation he was in, telling him that even the men running the cable cars were making $1.40 an hour. When this had no effect Cassady tried to rally Kerouac by joking that although they were blood brothers, they'd never done anything together: "stop and think, NEVER have we gone into action as one."

But Neal was too far away, and he'd been away too long. It had been over a year since they'd had their hectic five minutes of talk together in Denver, and Jack's most persistent memories of San Francisco were his weeks in Henri Cru's shack and his dreary job as a night watchman. There was still the scene at Allen's, but Allen was getting closer to his graduation from Columbia (in February 1949). He was involved with student literary magazines and prizes. There were fewer parties, fewer nights to sit all night and talk, rushing each other on from one idea to the next, until they'd gotten out whatever it was that was bothering them.

Jack began to have a recurrent nightmare, and there was no one to take it to but Allen. They sat down facing each other so closely that their knees touched, just as Allen and Neal had done to discuss philosophy. In the nightmare Jack described he was being pursued across a desert by "a strange Arabian figure," who caught up with him just before he reached the safety of "the Protective City." Jack's first response had been that the figure was himself, wearing a shroud, but as he described

100

it to Allen he decided that it was someone else. They decided it might be the spirit of his own death, relentlessly pursuing him, but Jack couldn't bring himself to believe this interpretation.

He was haunted by the images of the dream, and by the feeling that he'd forgotten to make a crucial decision about something important. Whatever it was had slipped completely from his mind. He kept snapping his fingers, trying to remember it. He'd always been "Memory Babe" at Lowell High School, but now something was happening to him he didn't understand and couldn't remember. He didn't know what it was, but something was closing in on him. Even Burroughs, living in New Orleans, was troubled about him, writing Allen that he doubted Jack ". . . will ever get away from Ozone Park at all unless Ma K. decides to move."

It was Neal, finally, who ended the nightmare. On another of his sudden impulses, he called Jack long distance from San Francisco, reaching Jack through the number of the drugstore downstairs (mémère couldn't afford a phone herself). Jack rushed down to the pay phone to hear Neal's wild, excited voice asking him for a loan of fifty dollars.

The money was for Carolyn and their new baby to live on while Cassady himself drove to New York to pick up Jack. Jack had written that he thought he might hitchhike west in the spring, but Neal had a new plan. He would break in his new car by driving it to New York to pick up Jack. They'd go first to San Francisco, then back to Arizona where Neal had lined up railroad jobs.

With all of the money he'd saved from his months on the railroad, Cassady had traded in his old Ford on a brand new 1949 Hudson sedan, which he assured Jack was the greatest car in the country. Kerouac was too desperate to argue with him. He told Neal he'd go with him whenever he showed up. Jack and his mother had planned to go down to Rocky Mount, North Carolina, to spend Christmas with his sister Nin in her new house and he told Neal how to get there.

One December afternoon a muddy car pulled up in front of the house, and it took a minute for Jack to register that it was a new Hudson. Behind the wheel was "a weary young fellow, muscular and ragged in a T-shirt, unshaven, red-eyed." Cassady wasn't alone. He had Luanne and his brakeman friend Ed Hinckle with him. Jack's brother-in-law let them come in to wash up and eat.

Cassady's wild energy filled the rooms. He was himself again, pushing, going, seeing, listening. Mémère had said she wanted to bring some furniture back to Ozone Park. Neal could take it up the next day. He offered the services of the new car, piled the furniture in the back, squeezed Jack beside him up in front and promised mémère he'd return for her, so she'd be back at her job at the shoe factory on time. With Neal's frenzy returned there was no time for Jack to worry about nightmares, or whether his novel would find a publisher. Neal had arranged it so they were finally on the road together and going "into action as one." It was Jack's first in a succession of trips with Cassady that drove them both to the edge of raggedy madness.

This one was short and relatively calm. Neal did make it to New York and back to North Carolina in a day and a half. As Jack described it later to Carl Solomon; they raced from North Carolina to New York City, 450 miles, and then back to North Carolina in thirty-six hours. And in all that time Neal just talked and talked and talked.

Mémère had to pay for a speeding ticket of Cassady's so he wouldn't spend a night in jail and when Jack got back to North Carolina she told him he was wasting his time hanging around with Neal. Even Cassady himself admitted to moments of confusion about what he was doing. He'd left his second wife, Carolyn, in San Francisco with their new baby to come across the country. He'd told Carolyn that he was going to drive the Hudson to New York because he could sell it there for a lot of money. He hadn't told Kerouac about this when he'd talked to him on the phone. The plan to sell the Hudson didn't materialize. Even if Neal had intended to sell the car, which is doubtful, he'd burned out the bearings pushing ninety miles an hour on the cross-country run from San Francisco.

Cassady wrote Carolyn from New York that he couldn't send her any money, but that he was hurrying straight home to her instead of getting rid of the car. He *had* tried to sell the Hudson but figured the total profit at only $13.19, "so I'll take care of the car and you too. I wound all the people I love—why?"

Cassady stayed in New York over New Year's in a rush of parties and frantic introductions and it was during this trip that he met new friends that had become part of Jack's New York life, like John Clellon Holmes and Alan Harrington. Many of them were nervously confused by the thin, intense figure who never stopped talking.

There was only one time that Jack remembered Neal silent. Allen, who couldn't go to San Francisco (he was graduating from Columbia the next month), asked Neal one day, "What is the meaning of this voyage to New York?" Neal was silent because he didn't have an answer. Jack remembered that "We sat and didn't know what to say; there was nothing to talk about any more. The only thing to do was go."

Once they'd actually gotten into the car and turned it toward San Francisco, it seemed that everything had new and great promise. Jack put his worries about *The Town and the City* out of his mind and forgot about his recurrent nightmare of the "Shrouded Traveler," which Neal had instantly interpreted as Jack's unhealthy longing for "pure death." Cassady told him to have nothing more to do with that dream because "we're all of us never in life again." Instead of the futility of his last months in his mother's apartment in Ozone Park, instead of his obsession with "the myth of the rainy night," Jack was back on the road. When the Hudson left New York, heading for New Orleans on the first stage of the trip to San Francisco, Jack remembered later:

It was drizzling and mysterious at the beginning of our journey. I could see that it was going to be one big saga of the mist. "Whooee!" yelled Dean. "Here we go!" And he hunched over the wheel and gunned her; he was back in his element, everybody could see that. We were all delighted, we all realized we were leaving confusion and nonsense behind and performing our one and noble function of the time, *move.*

103

No book has ever caught the feel of speeding down the broad highway in a new car, the mindless joyousness of "joyriding" like *On The Road,* and this trip west went into the book almost straight. All the "spats back there" were forgotten as Neal, Luanne and Jack sat in the front seat of the Hudson, and Ed Hinckle sprawled in the back, and they all "had the warmest talk about the goodness and joy of life," listening to bop on the radio with the volume turned up high enough to make the car shudder. Cassady got them to New Orleans in one of his manic bursts of driving.

Hinckle's wife Helen was staying at Burroughs' house in Algiers, a picturesque neighborhood of wooden frame houses across the Mississippi from New Orleans. It was the end of January 1949 when Cassady and Kerouac pulled in, and the talk began in the dark rooms of Bill's house. The talk never stopped. Jack and Neal drove themselves with marijuana, benzedrine, morphine and alcohol. Almost immediately they ran out of money. Neal had driven Bill to New York the year before so they knew each other slightly but the atmosphere cooled perceptibly when Neal asked him for a twenty-five-dollar loan to get all of them to San Francisco.

Burroughs refused, and later wrote Ginsberg that Cassady had taken it hard. Neal ". . . couldn't leave quick enough, and acted as though I had lured him here on false pretenses. He didn't unlock any 'charm' or 'graceful human nature' around here." Jack and Neal talked hazily about getting a job in New Orleans, to work until they had enough money for the rest of the trip, but in the torrents of talk they never slept, or when they did sleep and got up it was too late to go out and look for a newspaper.

To Burroughs the trip was totally without purpose. He wrote Allen that for "sheer compulsive pointlessness," Neal's driving back and forth across America "compares favorably to the mass migrations of the Mayans . . . Neal is, of course, the very soul of this voyage into pure, abstract, meaningless motion. He is the mover, compulsive, dedicated, ready to sacrifice family, friends, even his very car itself to the necessity of moving from one place to another. Wife and child may starve, friends exist only

104

to exploit for gas money. Neal must move." After all the driving was finished Neal was the one who didn't have any place to go home to. The only place for him was his car.

After several days in New Orleans, they could feel themselves losing the sense of moving and in a kind of desperation Jack wired to his mother to dip into their savings account to get him back on the road. Ragged and nearly broke, traveling on the few dollars Jack's mother was able to send to New Orleans, Neal, Luanne and Jack climbed back into the Hudson. The Hinckles had had enough, and they stayed in New Orleans. There might not be enough money for a meal before they got to San Francisco, but Cassady was once more behind a steering wheel, jazz was blowing loud and clear on the car radio, and sitting in the Hudson as it rocked along the highway, it seemed to Jack that the promised land had to be right up the road. They were just about flat broke, reduced to stealing food and cigarettes from little grocery stores when they stopped for gas, but Luanne was promising to sleep with Jack in San Francisco, and Neal's driving still seemed to him to have a kind of ecstasy in it:

Up ahead we saw Tehachapi Pass starting up. Dean took the wheel and carried us clear to the top of the world. We passed a great shroudy cement factory in the canyon. Then we started down. Dean cut off the gas, threw in the clutch, and negotiated every hairpin turn and passed cars and did everything in the books without the benefit of accelerator. I held on tight. Sometimes the road went up again briefly; he merely passed cars without a sound, on pure momentum. He knew every rhythm and every kick of a first-class pass . . . In this way we floated and flapped down to the San Joaquin Valley. It lay spread a mile below, virtually the floor of California, green and wondrous from our aerial shelf. We made thirty miles without using gas.

In San Francisco, when the three of them staggered out of the Hudson, wrinkled and dirty and gritty-eyed and hungry, it was like getting on shore after a long voyage at sea. But there was no lasting sense of kinship after the days together with Cassady in the car. Neal immediately left Jack and Luanne standing on the sidewalk with their bundles at their feet, stone broke, while he drove off "bursting to see" Carolyn and the baby. Kerouac stayed in San Francisco with Luanne, but instead of the love he thought he'd found in her, he found only "hunger and bitterness" in "the beatest time" of his life. He was so strung out after the hours without sleep in the car, the lack of food and the heavy drugs with Burroughs in Algiers, that walking in San Francisco one day he had a vision of heaven. But the reality of his life was a kind of shambling hell. He fought with Luanne, who was sulking because Neal had gone back to Carolyn. Jack himself was almost as angry with Neal. Cassady had got himself all the way to San Francisco, using Jack's mother's money for most of the trip, and then had left him with an old girl friend. As Jack said later, "I lost faith in him that year."

Neal suddenly showed up again and took Jack back with him to Carolyn's. Mémêre had sent Jack enough money for him to take the bus back to New York. Neal immediately borrowed some of it and gave it to Carolyn so they could eat. He then got a short-lived job selling pressure cookers, but his enthusiasm for going out and talking to ladies about pressure cookers died early. There was just enough money for Neal and Jack to have a night out before Jack went back to his mother. They went out and heard Slim Gaillard at a San Francisco jazz club. Neal decided Gaillard was God and out of their thin funds bought Gaillard a drink so he'd sit at the table and talk with them.

There was a short reunion when Jack went to the Greyhound depot to catch his bus back to New York. Luanne and Neal both showed up to see him off, but Neal and Jack were hostile and wary. Just as he'd done on his bus trip from Los Angeles to Pittsburgh, after his weeks picking cotton almost a year and a half before, Jack bought a loaf of bread and a package of salami to make a lapful of sandwiches for the bus trip, and the food smelled so good Neal and Luanne wanted a sandwich. Jack said no. "It was a sullen moment. We were all thinking we'd never see one another again and we didn't care."

Chapter Nine

On 29 March, 1949, two months after he'd stumbled out of the Hudson with Neal and Luanne in San Francisco, Kerouac wrote an exultant letter to one of his Denver friends, Ed White, telling him he had sold *The Town and the City* to Harcourt, Brace for a $1,000 advance. It had previously been rejected by Little, Brown. He was very pleased his editor would be a young man of thirty-five named Robert Giroux, who Kerouac felt really understood his writing. He signed the letter "BET-A-THOUSAND KEROUAC."

Somehow he had done it. Out of all the confusion of his life he had produced a novel that had been bought and was going to be published. The Scribners rejection was forgotten in his excitement. He was so completely "redeemed" in his own sense of himself that he never turned away from it again. Despite whatever happened, he always went on writing.

The Town and the City had been sent to Robert Giroux by Mark Van Doren, who finally read the manuscript at Ginsberg's insistence. Van Doren phoned Giroux, a 1936 Columbia graduate then an editor at Harcourt, Brace, and asked him to consider "John" Kerouac's novel. When Giroux agreed to look at it, Kerouac showed up the next day himself at Harcourt, Brace neatly dressed in a jacket and tie to deliver his manuscript. Giroux was immediately impressed. Although he felt the book was too long—over 1,100 pages—it reminded him of the lyricism and poetry of Thomas Wolfe's *Look Homeward Angel,* and he offered Jack a contract with Harcourt, Brace.

For someone as poor as Jack had been $1,000 was a lot of money. Ed White was in Paris when Jack sent him his news, and he wondered if he should join Ed. He finally decided to go back to Denver on his own while he worked on his new book, *On The Road*. He didn't get away for two more months, cutting and revising *The Town and the City* with his editor Robert Giroux and waiting for his mother to leave for Rocky Mount. Jack's sister Nin had had a complicated Caeserian, and mémêre was going to live with her while Nin recuperated.

Jack left for Denver in late May and rented a small house in the foothills outside of town. He thought of himself as a modern day Thoreau. With a new burst of creative energy he picked up the work he'd been struggling with the previous fall. He started *On The Road* again, but he was actually more interested in picking up *Doctor Sax,* so he worked on both novels again, just as he had done in October and November the winter before.

There was also time for him to write long and frequent letters to Ginsberg, who had run into trouble. In March, after his graduation from Columbia, Allen let a friend of Burroughs, Herbert Huncke, move in with him on York Avenue, despite Burroughs' warning. Huncke was a talented writer himself and the best storyteller Allen had ever heard. Huncke had the same concerns and enthusiasm as the rest of them. But he was also a junkie, and he paid for his habit with a hopeless succession of petty crimes. He'd stayed with Burroughs on the farm in Texas, where Burroughs had taken a picture of him, thin and shirtless, leaning on a shovel. Then he'd moved into Burroughs' house in Algiers, where he'd stolen the only thing of value that Burroughs had in it, the rug. As Bill wrote Allen, every time he looked at the bare floor he was ". . . put in mind of his vile act."

Huncke was on morphine when he moved in with Allen, and within a few days he was using the apartment to store stolen goods until he could find someplace to sell them. Allen was working in a news agency and really didn't have much of an idea what was going on in his apartment all the time. On 22 April, 1949, he went for a ride with two of Huncke's friends, Priscilla Arminger and Jack Melody, in a car that had been stolen in Washington, D. C. the month before. Melody made a wrong turn, and the rest of the story was splashed across New York's newspapers. The New York *Times* reported:

An unwitting turn of a stolen car in the wrong direction along a one-way street in Queens ended yesterday with three young men and a girl being held on burglary charges and a charge of assault against one man.

One of the accused, Allen Ginsberg, 21 years old, of 1401 York Ave., told the police that he was a copy boy for a news service who had 'tied-in' with the gang, all with police records, to obtain 'realism' he needed to write a story.

The *World-Telegram* headline read, "WRONG-WAY AUTO TIPS OFF POLICE TO NARCOTICS-RULED BURGLARY GANG."

They had gone driving in Queens about four in the afternoon, when Melody had made his wrong turn. When a radio car patrolman stopped him for driving against one-way traffic Melody panicked and it seemed to the patrolman that he tried to run him down. There was a frantic six-block chase, that ended when Melody rounded a corner at sixty-five miles an hour and hit a curb, turning the car over twice and stopping upside down. Ginsberg managed to open the doors and get away, but the police captured Melody and Priscilla Arminger. In the wrecked car the police found half of the loot from a $10,000 jewelry theft and furs and clothing from an Astoria contractor's home that had been robbed the week before. Among the papers in the car was the address of Ginsberg's apartment on York Avenue, and the police arrested Ginsberg and Huncke there a short time later. As Allen tells the story, he phoned his apartment after the car accident to warn Huncke the police would be looking for them, and asked Huncke to "clean up" the place. When Allen arrived, Huncke was sweeping the floor.

Huncke and Melody were held without bail because of their previous police records. Melody had been arrested eighteen times and was on parole. Huncke, who was thirty-four at the time—ten years older than Allen—had served sentences on six narcotics charges and one burglar tool charge. Priscilla Arminger, who was twenty-four, had been arrested three times for narcotics addiction.

She and Allen were held in jail in default of $2,500 bail. All of them were charged together with burglary, grand larceny, receiving stolen goods and attempting to run over a policeman.

Despite the evidence in the apartment, the police couldn't implicate Allen in any of the criminal activities of Melody and Huncke, and he managed to get off. They were sent to prison for five years each. While escaping the stolen car, Ginsberg had left behind diaries and poems from his years at Columbia. The police confiscated them and Ginsberg was sent in May to the Columbia University Hospital for psychiatric observation. In the late spring and early summer of 1949 from his house in Denver, Jack wrote what he hoped were encouraging notes to Allen in the hospital, telling him that society was at fault and that men had to do what was right. Jack quoted from the new manuscript he was working on, written in the lofty romantic Thomas Wolfe style of *The Town and the City*.

But in his letters, when he wasn't talking about his writing, there emerged the familiar strain of loneliness. He was desperately lonely in his empty house, and he missed Neal. He ran around miserably in Denver imagining how Neal would pass the time, even hoping by some miracle he might run into Luanne.

> Down in Denver, down in Denver
> All I did was die

In his sad, almost helpless loneliness Kerouac couldn't stay long in Denver. He was still living alone, although he met Robert Giroux, his Harcourt, Brace editor, again. He wrote Allen that Giroux was very sympathetic and advised Allen to show him some poetry. Giroux had hitchhiked with Kerouac, as Jack told Allen, to understand *On The Road*. Kerouac was trying to impress Ginsberg in his letter saying he'd introduced Giroux to hitchhiking. Robert Giroux remembered they only hitchhiked about a half hour that summer, and that it wasn't his first time on the road. Jack could brag more easily about his hitchhiking experience than he could about his work-in-progress to his editor. He only showed Giroux his journal notes for *On The Road*; he wasn't yet confident

110

enough of the novel to let Giroux read the new manuscript.

Jack's plan had been to stay in his house for a year, until he finished *On The Road,* but in less than two months his writing had become snarled and constricted. For Jack, just as at every hard moment in his life, there was one person to turn to.

His mother had gotten back from her stay with Nin in North Carolina and Jack thought of going back to Ozone Park. As Burroughs had said, Jack would never leave Ozone Park unless "Ma K. decided to move." Jack could write in the little apartment, despite the cramped rooms and the noise from the drugstore downstairs, but New York in the summer of 1949 wasn't what he remembered from the summer before. The parties had ended on York Avenue, Allen was still in the psychiatric hospital and other friends were even further away. Neal was in San Francisco again and Burroughs had moved from Louisiana to Mexico City. Even John Clellon Holmes was away, spending the summer in Provincetown, doing research for a novel he would call *Go.*

Mémère was back working at the shoe factory, there was food to eat and a place to write if he went back home, but still Jack couldn't make any coherent plans. He was stuck again on the new books. He'd even started a poem in Denver, titled "The Rose of the Rainy Night," a kind of preparation for the myth section of *Dr. Sax,* "In the Castle," but it was all stifled in the heat and the heaviness of the summer.

Jack felt again the same vague restlessness that had driven him to Denver. He'd left Neal six months before with the feeling that he didn't care if they'd ever see each other again, but he'd spent the months in Denver, where Cassady had spent his childhood, thinking about Neal, slouching through the night streets hoping he'd meet him around the next corner. He suddenly knew he had to go back to Cassady, there was no place else to go. In an abrupt decision that had the sound of Neal's driven desperateness, Jack made plans to get to San Francisco. ". . . there was nothing behind me any more, all my bridges were gone and I didn't give a damn about anything at all."

Was Kerouac in love with Cassady at this point in their lives? For Neal, after his years in reform school and prison, homosexuality didn't threaten him. For Kerouac, despite the closeness of his relationship to Ginsberg, Burroughs and Cassady himself, homosexuality was disturbing, troubling and confusing. He never was able to clearly define for himself what he felt about Neal Cassady. He admired Neal tremendously for all his apparent lack of sexual inhibitions. Yet Jack may also have recognized intuitively that Neal's attitude toward sex was basically the same as his own. They both were emotionally incapable of any sustained sexual relationship. Each of them wanted the other to admire him, so there was a considerable amount of bragging and grandstanding. But they were both Catholics whose narrow upbringing had led them to regard sex as something unclean and unholy. Each felt they were held together by emotional bonds and spiritual affinities higher than anything merely physical.

By some definitions of the word Jack was in love with Neal, by his own definition he wasn't. They were "bloodbrothers." This was as close as Jack could come to the other dimension of their relationship.

Despite everything that had happened, Neal made it easier for Jack to return to San Francisco. While Jack was living in his Denver cabin, Neal had written asking him to come and live with him and Carolyn and learn to be a brakeman on the railroad. He kidded Jack for living alone, staying by himself, thinking of his Denver house as a "Hermitage." When Allen went into the hospital Neal said that writing *The Town and the City* had kept Jack out of similar troubles, besides keeping him in a good relationship with his mother.

But mostly in his letters Neal tried to persuade Jack to come back to San Francisco.

Jack got an $11 ride from Denver to San Francisco in a travel bureau car and was knocking at Cassady's door on Liberty Street at two o'clock in the morning in August 1949, burning with impatience to talk with Neal. It was an even more chaotic scene than Jack had imagined possible, although Neal's letters had prepared him to some extent for what he found in San Francisco. When Kerouac later described the summer of 1949 in *On The*

Road, the confusions of Cassady's life were detailed in passages Jack copied nearly verbatim from Neal's letters to him at the time, like the description Neal wrote about one of his typical schedules shortly before Jack arrived.

Neal had been seeing Luanne again, he'd fought with her, hit her and with typical Cassady helplessness broken his thumb. Consequently Cassady had to take sixty-thousand units of penicillin every day plus an antidote every four hours to fight his allergy to this medication. Moreover he needed leg surgery for an inflamed cyst, had to see a chiropodist twice a week for foot trouble, took cough syrup every night and had to blow his nose constantly due to a cartilage collapse under the bridge from a previous operation.

Even with Jack's need to see Cassady the scene he found in San Francisco was too much for him to deal with. At Neal's apartment he saw Cassady "in idiocy, with infected thumb, surrounded by the battered suitcases of his motherless feverish life across America and back numberless times, an undone bird." Neal's thumb was in a cast with a big traction hook and he was staying at home taking care of the baby while Caroline, pregnant with their second child, went back to work. As Carolyn later remembered the scene:

... I let him take care of Cathy, who was four months old, and I went to work. Well, we had this crummy place on Liberty Street and he had to wash diapers in the sink and he probably wrang them with that hand and got urine in it. Then he went back to changing tires before it was healed, and he always drove himself so hard and fast, he not only had to be the best and the most amazing worker, but it was like flagellation, and the cast was just mash. The bone got infected and I had to give him penicillin shots, but he left for New York and in the end they had to cut off the tip of his thumb.

As usual Cassady's plans had collapsed around him while he stood in the middle of the room talking excitedly about the next idea, holding up his infected thumb, gesturing with hard muscular arms in an old T-shirt. Jack wasn't even sure he was sane, but he went on defending Neal against people in San Francisco who were

113

putting him down. He insisted that Neal's "got the secret that we're all busting to find and its splitting his head wide open and if he goes mad don't worry, it won't be your fault but the fault of God."

But it was all too bewildering for Jack, and within a few days he decided he had to leave. Everything was too unsettled to think of trying to be a brakeman. He hadn't stayed in Denver, and he still had money left from his Harcourt, Brace advance in the bank back at home, so suddenly in a generous burst he told Neal they had to go back to New York together to try to make it over to Europe. Cassady had no money, but by this time the despairing futility of his life in San Francisco was too much for him too. They had another crazy night listening to jazz together, then they got ready to go East. Neal, for a moment, seemed to need Jack almost as much as Jack needed him. There'd be no girls with them. Luanne and Carolyn were left in San Francisco. This was their trip alone, as brothers, on the road together.

Neal didn't have a car anymore, so the two "broken-down heroes of the western night" had to find other transportation, and they started from San Francisco in a "fag Plymouth," helping the owner drive it from San Francisco to Denver. They began the trip sitting together in the back seat of the car, exchanging dreams and reminiscences of their childhood in bursts of excited conversation. It was the first time they'd been alone together to really *talk* since they'd met in New York nearly two years before. Their talk got so wild that the driver of the car complained:

. . . "For God's sakes, you're rocking the boat back there." Actually we were; the car was swaying as Neal and I both swayed to the rhythm and the IT of our final excited joy in talking and living to the blank tranced end of all innumerable riotous angelic particulars that had been lurking in our souls all our lives.

Jack tried his "wildest best" to stay on Cassady's wave length. Neal told him they both knew "what IT is" and what "Time" is and that "everything is really FINE," while the others sitting in the front seat of the car (the owner and the other passengers) we&re on the wrong path:

... They have worries, they're counting the miles, they're thinking about where to sleep tonight, how much money for gas, the weather, how they'll get there—and all the time they'll get there anyway, you see. But they need to worry and betray time with urgencies false and otherwise, purely anxious and whiny, their souls really won't be at peace unless they can latch on to an established and proven worry and having once found it they assume facial expressions to fit and go with it, which is, you see, unhappiness, and all the time it all flies by them and they know it and that *too* worries them no end.

But when Cassady took over the driving his careening rush over the roads of Nevada and Utah was too much for the other passengers, and everyone was relieved to end the chaotic association when they got into Denver. After a couple of days there with Cassady, Kerouac began to lose the rhythm too. They talked with Neal's Denver cousin, who disowned him, and then Neal started to go to pieces, reverting to his old teenage habit of stealing cars for joyrides up into the mountains.

Neal "went mad again with sweats and insanity," and Jack couldn't find anything to cling to in the crazy rush. The police were called in on the stolen cars and Jack feared ". . . the end of my life as I had known it and that it was entering a new and horrible stage of jails and iron sorrows." Hurrying to get out of Denver before the police found Cassady, they arranged with a travel agency to drive a 1947 Cadillac limousine to Chicago. They were desperately on the road again. A few miles out of town Neal detoured to visit one of his guardians, Ed Uhe, who once let Neal live for six months on his ranch during a probationary period after reform school. But the rancher, like Neal's cousin, had lost faith in Cassady. Stiffly apologetic, Neal got back in the car and they started for Chicago.

Back behind the wheel Cassady was his old shouting, exultant self. Driving the Cadillac as fast as he could push it, he saw no end to the trip, telling Jack, ". . .we'd dig the whole world with a car like this because, man, the road must eventually lead to the whole world. Ain't nowhere else it can go—right?" He drove from Denver to Chicago, 1180 miles, in seventeen hours, which Jack thought was "a kind of crazy record," especially on the narrow highways of 1949, but the Cadillac was a ruined, muddy heap when they got it into Chicago.

They heard some bop in Chicago (there was always music to find somewhere in the city nights when they stopped to look for it), and then took a bus to Detroit. By this time, just like on their other trips, they'd run out of money. They couldn't afford a hotel, and to pass the time until they picked up a $4 travel agency ride to New York, they went to an all-night movie.

Sitting up in the shabby, stinking balcony of a thirty-five-cent theater, they sat and slept through the double feature six times. Jack thought it was a "horrible osmotic experience," filling his subconscious with Singing Cowboy Eddie Dean and his gallant white horse during the cowboy feature and with George Raft, Peter Lorre and Sidney Greenstreet during a gangster film about Istanbul. Jack was so worn out that he just fitted his head on the wooden arm of the seat and slept until the attendants came by to sweep up the night's rubbish.

It could have been the effect of the movie, or of the days and nights of meaningless, driven excitement in cars and buses in strange towns and winding highways, but by the next night in the backseat of the car crossing Ohio, Jack had had enough. He was too exhausted to care about what they were doing or why they were doing it. Cassady might have been out of his mind with exhaustion too, but his response was to dig everything even more frantically, in sweating "pious frenzy." But Jack was through. "I realized I was beginning to cross and recross towns in America as though I were a traveling salesman—raggedy travelings, bad stock, rotten beans in the bottom of my bag of tricks, nobody buying."

Neal had become, in Jack's eyes, "that mad Ahab at the wheel" whose soul was "wrapped up in a fast car, a coast to reach, and a woman at the end of the road."

When they finally collapsed in mémêre's apartment Jack was a rumpled shadow, desperate and haggard from crossing the country the hard way twice in a month. His mother, in an outburst, told Neal he could stay a few

116

days to get some rest, but after that he had to get out. Jack didn't argue with her. As far as he was concerned, the trip was over.

Chapter Ten

Cassady managed to get his old job back at the parking lot he'd worked in and stayed on in New York. He met a girl named Diana Hansen at a party just after he got into town, moved in with her and soon she was pregnant. For the first few months Kerouac was still through with seeing him. As Jack told Allen, he refused to be friends anymore with Neal because he was keeping himself together for better things. Cassady was crazy, and when they were together he undermined Jack's reason. It was fall 1949, and *The Town and the City* was scheduled for publication early in the spring. For the last four years Jack had thought of the book as his redemption and his salvation, and it was almost as if renouncing Neal were part of clearing up the loose ends of his past.

When the book came out in February 1950 it got the usual spate of first novel reviews. Generally, the critics were kind. It was praised for being affectionate, intense, high-spirited, and criticized for being foolish, self-centered, overly idyllic and wordy. The New York *Times* thought it was "a rough diamond of a book." The reviewer felt that the arthur grew spiritually and improved technically in writing it. But a first novel has to have something that sets it apart from the year's procession of other first novels. *The Town and the City* had only short passages with an authentic ring to them.

In some other year it would have perhaps received more attention, but there were strong best-sellers out at the same time. Hemingway's *Across the River and Into the*

117

Trees was the "major" book of the year, but there was also John O'Hara's *A Rage to Live* and Joyce Cary's *The Horse's Mouth.* Another of the best-sellers, Nelson Algren's *The Man with the Golden Arm,* was a much more coherent and detailed account of drug addiction than Jack's description of the New York drug scene in his book.

The Town and the City, despite the lyricism and poignance of its finest scenes, wasn't strong enough, and Jack, in the months before it had come out, had begun to have doubts about it himself. Yet it did change his life. It meant that he was a writer. A book of his had been published and he could justify going on. He believed in himself, and he believed that the next novel would be better. With *The Town and the City* finally out he could go back to the new book, *On The Road.*

Once the excitement of the book was over, New York began to pall. He'd been in town since the end of summer 1949, when he'd made the chaotic cross-country odyssey from San Francisco with Neal. It was getting hot in the apartment, and he was restless. He'd been living with his mother for nearly eight months. He decided he had to get back to Denver again, still looking for material for *On The Road.* Later in the summer of 1950, he decided, he'd take some time off and go down to Mexico City and stay with Burroughs.

Allen had been let out of the hospital in March and wanted to go to Mexico City with him, but he was "dead beat" on his family, and didn't have any money to travel. Jack even thought of moving permanently to San Francisco after the summer and getting a newspaper job on the San Francisco *Chronicle.* He told Allen he could earn $100 a week in Hollywood if he wanted it, but he didn't like Hollywood as a town. He was still writing, working at the new manuscript. As it was at the time, the novel was completely imaginary. He had an idea of writing about the obsessive guilt American businessmen felt for their daily sins. At that point Jack thought the best part of the manuscript was his description of a Denver realtor waking up screaming in the middle of the night to pour out his guilt incoherently to someone in the room with him.

Ginsberg had decided he wanted to try a novel and Kerouac advised him to write about Paterson, New York City, Texas and Dakar, not only as autobiography, but as prophecy.

The only one Jack wasn't thinking about at that point was Neal Cassady, who didn't seem to figure at all in Jack's confident plans for his new life. But he did arrange to see Neal and met him on a rainy New York street corner in the early hours of morning before he went off to Denver. Standing and talking in the cold rain he thought Neal sounded defeated by what he had gotten himself into. He began to tell Jack about what would happen to them as their troubles piled up. "You see, man, you get older . . . Someday you and me'll be coming down an alley together at sundown and looking in the cans to see." Jack was incredulous.

Neal at this point was only twenty-four, still rushing around in T-shirts and battered shoes and "belly-hanging pants," turning himself on with a deck of pornographic playing cards, and he was telling Jack that the two of them would wind up as bums together. It didn't seem to bother him. "There's no harm ending that way. You spend a whole life of non-interference with the wishes of others, including politicians and the rich, and nobody bothers you and you cut along and make it your own way."

Jack wouldn't listen to him and tried to shake off the prophecy. "All I hope . . . is someday we'll be able to live on the same street with our families and get to be a couple of oldtimers together."

In May 1950, Jack was on the way to Denver, but once he got there he decided to forget about the novel, to avoid the loneliness he'd felt there the summer before when he'd tried to live like Thoreau. Ed White was back in Denver, the friend he'd written in Paris when he'd sold *The Town and the City*, and Jack just relaxed with him, ". . . an entire week of afternoons in lovely Denver bars." But it couldn't last. The easy pace was short-lived. It was Neal, again, coming after him.

Cassady had decided to divorce Carolyn so he could marry his New York girl and legitimize their baby. Word reached Denver that Cassady had bought a car and was driving west as fast as he could push it, so he'd be able to go down to Mexico City with Jack and get his divorce while they both stayed with Burroughs.

Jack wasn't happy at the news. It seemed to him that Neal was pursuing him like the "Shrouded Traveler" of his dream, bearing down on him, with a death's head and gleaming eyes in an old jalopy with the flames of hell shooting out of it. But there was no more escaping Cassady than there was escaping his nightmare. Cassady was coming to take him back on the road.

If Neal and Jack had stayed on American highways, pushing the car across the miles, desperately trying to get someplace before their money ran out, they would have had another of their "raggedy travelings." But this time it was down across the desert, over the border into Mexico.

Mexico had two things they couldn't get easily on the road in the United States: dope and women. They found marijuana—"a tremendous Corona cigar of tea" —and the whorehouse—"a magnificent establishment of stucco in the golden sun." By the time they got to Mexico City Jack was exhausted and feverish with dysentery, but he made it to Burroughs' apartment, where Bill and Joan took care of him. Neal stayed only long enough to get the Mexican divorce from Carolyn, and was back in the car again, rushing off to New York to marry Diana. Jack was upset with him for leaving, but Neal didn't feel at ease in the scene. He even told Jack, before he left, that he thought Jack was smoking too much marijuana.

Jack had been getting high for years, but the summer of 1950 with Burroughs was one of the heaviest stretches he'd gone through. Allen remembers Neal saying that he'd never seen Jack stoned so high or so often. "He was really stoned consistently for long periods, alone." For Neal the worst part of it was that Jack did it alone. "When one is alone on this stuff the sheer ecstasy of utterly realizing each moment makes it more clear to one than ever how impossibly far one is from the others. . . ."

After two months in Mexico City, Jack made his way back to Ozone Park in October 1950. He was physically and emotionally worn to a ragged thread. John Clellon Holmes remembered that his face looked haggard and he seemed "stretched taut," but he didn't want to talk about what had happened to him.

Instead, he stayed alone in Ozone Park. He told Ginsberg everything after he'd been home a few weeks. Allen was the one person he felt could understand how far he'd gone with drugs in Mexico City. Allen was sure there was no danger of Jack's becoming an addict, that he was only making occasional experiments with morphine, because too much made him throw up and become dizzy. But Burroughs was afraid that if Jack went too far with his interior searching he'd become like the Tibetan Buddhist monks who walled themselves into a small cell with a slot where food was pushed in and stayed there until they died. As Burroughs told Jack, since he didn't have a habit, he was still free to decide what he was going to do.

When Jack recuperated, he came into the city more often, and he ran into a girl named Joan Haverty, who'd been living with one of Ginsberg's friends, a law school graduate named Bill Cannister. Cannister had been an alcoholic, one of the wildest of the group at the parties the previous two years in New York. The month before while drunk he'd put his head out an open subway window when the train was in motion and was at once decapitated.

Joan was still living in his loft on 21st Street off Seventh Avenue. Before Cannister's death Jack had been to parties there. At one party the previous spring before Jack had gone to Denver he'd gotten as drunk as Cannister and they'd run around the city block, Jack wearing only his undershorts, Cannister absolutely naked, in the rain at three o'clock in the morning. Cannister had made a peephole in the bathroom so he could look inside at people. He showed it to Kerouac, but Kerouac drew the line. "I'm not interested in that, Bill," he'd muttered, and Cannister had answered, "You're not interested in anything."

Whatever Cannister thought of Kerouac, they had what Jack called "a couple of collaborations in bed" with girls in the loft, and this memory is what might have led him back there. Jack spent the night with Joan Haverty, and to mémère's dismay they were married two weeks later.

Joan, according to Holmes, who described the wedding to Cassady, was a tall, dark-haired and very self-effacing girl. At the wedding party in the middle of November 1950, all of the crowd came to celebrate: Seymour Krim, Bill Frankell, the Bowmans, Alan Ansen, Lucien Carr, Holmes and Ginsberg. At three A.M. Jack, Lucien and Holmes put their heads together and sang "Wedding bells is breaking apart that old gang of mine," but, as Holmes remembered, they sang "with real sadness, since we knew that anyway we could break into each other's apartment still in the middle of the night."

Kerouac moved his clothes and his typewriter out of his mother's apartment and into the loft. Despite Holmes' shrewd forebodings, it looked as if a new life had begun.

Chapter Eleven

After his marriage, Kerouac lived in the loft with Joan and found a job as a script synopsizer for Twentieth Century-Fox reading novels and making plot outlines. But mostly he worked on *On The Road,* struggling to finish it. Neal Cassady was back in San Francisco. He hadn't stayed long with his wife Diana before rushing once again cross-country to Carolyn, who had had their second child.

For Neal, working again as a brakeman, this began the most settled, creative period of his life. He'd fixed up a room in the attic for himself in a new house at 29 Russell Street and bought a tape recorder. He wanted Jack to get one himself so they could speak to each other every day, sending back and forth the kind of wild talk they'd had on their trips across the United States.

Neal finally seemed to have settled down a little. He told Jack that he finally found the three things he wanted to do with his life: drive cars, learn to play the saxophone and write his autobiography. If his car had been running and he could have left his job, he'd have come to Jack's wedding, but he was going to send on his railroad pass so Jack and Joan could get to Mexico for a honeymoon. Settled in San Francisco, he'd finally started writing seriously and had enough done by December 1950 to be able to tell Kerouac, "If my novel is ever put up for sale the editor's preface will be: 'Seldom has there been a story of a man so balled up. No doubt many readers will not believe the veracity of the author, but I assure these doubting Thomases that every incident, as such, is true.' "

On Jack's recommendation Neal had read Thomas Wolfe's *Time and the River*, and he'd even glanced at Proust. After getting started on his book, Cassady told Kerouac, "I know it's the style to create a fiction of a bunch of characters thrown together in a composite—like Wolfe or Proust did. But, how for one as just straight case-history? I know, none of the characters would stand up—no living one person has all the necessary attributes to hold water in a novel."

As a more experienced and published writer, Kerouac enjoyed advising Cassady on how to write, but Neal, in turn, gave Kerouac support with his books. They began to exchange manuscripts as well as letters. By 8 January, 1951, Jack was able to send Neal a long section of still another version of *On The Road*, and he mailed off a second section at the end of March.

But Jack wasn't satisfied with how the novel was going. Holmes remembered Kerouac still fighting to find a new form, caught in the traditional mould of his first novel. Jack kept complaining that what he was writing wasn't fluid enough to match the looseness and shapelessness of the experience he was describing. He was struggling to find something that went beyond the set of literary patterns he'd been left with by the writers he'd admired when he began his first book. He felt his prose was limited by an inappropriate structure built around the outside of the experience. He wanted a form that was more intensely poetic. "I want *deep* form, poetic form—the way the consciousness *really* digs everything that happens."

At this moment of their two lives, Neal, writing out of his own forlorn need to tell his story in any way he could, was closer to the kind of style Jack was searching for than Jack was himself. In February 1951, as if he were answering Jack's section from *On The Road* sent him the month before, Neal sent the longest letter he'd ever written Kerouac, a detailed account of his second trip hitchhiking from Denver to Los Angeles nearly ten years before. Then in March he sent Jack what Allen later called "The Big Letter," or "The Joan Letter." Neal confessed that he had written the letter on benzedrine but that he was able to write it with a "sense of careless freedom." In his three sessions he'd written 13,000 words, a lot of writing even for someone with experience, but for a clumsy beginner like Cassady, who could barely type, it was a staggering feat. It was part of his autobiographical novel, the story of a girl named Joan Anderson he'd loved and lost a short time before meeting Kerouac and Ginsberg in New York, five years before.

The "Joan Anderson" letter literally overwhelmed Kerouac. He sat down and wrote Neal about it immediately, because in his opinion the letter was almost as good as Dostoyevsky's *Notes From Underground,* and he wanted to rush it off to Robert Giroux, who he thought would be interested in publishing it right away.

Jack was most impressed by what he called "the muscular rush" of Neal's narrative style, the excitement of the prose, even better than Dreiser, Thomas Wolfe and Melville. Neal had discovered a new way of writing that exposed everything in a mad rush of frenzied ecstasy.

Cassady had been writing letters to Jack and Allen for years at this point, since leaving New York for Denver in 1947. If his autobiography went slowly, Cassady had no trouble writing letters, and he had sent hundreds to Jack written high on marijuana and benzedrine. He described long, rambling, excited plans to drive east from San Francisco, or gave weary accounts of how hard he was working on the railroad. There were ecstatic stories of girls he'd "banged" in city parks, and as he settled into his marriage with Carolyn and the children, detailed paragraphs about their apartment on Russian Hill in San

Francisco, his sax lessons, his tape recorder, his painful attempts to write.

As the first installment of his autobiography, the "Joan Anderson" letter actually reads stiffly and self-consciously compared to some of his long "raps" with Kerouac and Ginsberg. What excited Jack in reading the letter wasn't only the way Cassady was writing. Jack had been getting the letters for years and already had a sense of Neal's style. What was new for him was reading an extended narrative about Cassady's adventures. Neal's autobiographical style was exactly what Kerouac had been searching for himself in his grandiose plans to be a writer. Neal had set down the story of his life directly, instead of through the medium of a stylized imitation of Thomas Wolfe.

Instead of Wolfe, Kerouac took Cassady as his model. Ginsberg understood exactly what Jack was doing. "The kind of things that Jack and Neal were talking about, Jack finally discovered were *the* subject matter for what he wanted to write down."

Jack, in his enthusiasm, wanted Neal to send him everything as soon as he finished getting it down on paper, his poolhall musings, details about streets, appointment times, hotel rooms, bar locations, window measurements, smells, heights of trees. Kerouac wanted to read everything. Jack was even getting his wife Joan to write her autobiography, and he encouraged Neal to keep working. In fact, he felt Cassady was the greatest, and that he would have to hustle to catch Neal if he wanted to succeed as a writer himself.

Jack was still together with Joan in the loft, working on a script synopsis for Twentieth Century-Fox, trying to get enough money together to pay the rent and his income taxes as the winter dragged on. He and Joan planned to work until March and save their money for a trip to Mexico. He applied for a Guggenheim Fellowship so he'd have enough money to buy a panel truck. He hoped to live for three years on the $3,000 grant, thinking he could stay in Mexico for a few hundred dollars a year. They would go to San Francisco, so Neal could teach him how to drive a car well enough to get a license.

But the plans didn't come to anything. The phlebitis in Jack's legs acted up again, and in March 1951 he went back to the V.A. Hospital.

Jack's stay in the hospital was painful, but he used his time there as he told the painter, Hugo Weber, to make a plan for the writing he was going to do when he got out. For the first time he began seriously to think of his projected book *On The Road* as a continuous narrative, and, as his legs healed, he outlined a series of books that would be a "legend" about himself, a long autobiography that would hold all the pieces he could remember of his entire life. Jack would use as his model the letters Neal had started writing him. Burroughs would be another influence. In the months that had passed since Jack left Mexico, Burroughs had finished his first novel, *Junkie,* and in December he sent it to Lucien Carr to read. Jack had read the manuscript in the loft and thought it was a great novel. It was written in Burroughs' "Factualist" style, as Burroughs said, to show that arguments about what people should do are irrelevant, and only take a reader away from what people actually do.

Burroughs' flat, structured narrative style was a strong counter to Cassady's rushed enthusiasms, and the mingling of the two influences left a sharp impression on Kerouac's mind as he lay in his hospital bed. He decided to imitate Burroughs' style for his new work, describing his adventures on the road as a first-person narrative, just putting down the facts flatly, without the extravagantly long sentences or philosophical images that were still a hangover from his long infatuation with Thomas Wolfe. He would write the kind of detailed personal history he was getting from Neal, using Burroughs' directness and straight narrative technique.

Instead of making himself the hero of the novel he made Neal the hero of it. He would just write about what happened to them on their four trips on the road. He would keep the title he'd been using for the versions of it he'd done over the past three years. It could still be called *On The Road.* Jack decided to open the book with his first meeting with Neal, telling enough of Neal's Denver childhood and reform school experience to give the necessary background.

As with *Junkie, On The Road* would start at an arbitrary point, and it would go on until it seemed finished, without any sense of social context or dimension. Burroughs' sentences in *Junkie,* "I was born in 1914 in a solid three-story, brick house in a large Midwest City. My parents were comfortable . . ." even suggested to Jack the tone he would use for his own sentences, "I first met Neal not long after my wife and I split up. I had just gotten over a serious illness . . ."

Kerouac decided to use the real names of people like Cassady, Ginsberg, Burroughs, Hal Chase and Ed White to help give a raw frankness to his story, all the details just as they'd happened. He'd mention his life with his mother in Ozone Park while he was writing *The Town and the City,* Neal's job at the Hotel New Yorker parking lot on 34th Street in Manhattan, his attempts to con Jack into teaching him how to write. Kerouac would even include personal details about Ginsberg's homosexuality and tell how he lay in the same room with Allen and Neal and heard them come together. That was something he didn't want to get involved with. Once Kerouac had the idea about how to begin his narrative, he wanted to get right to work on the book. All he had to do when he got out of the hospital and back in the loft was pile up the benzedrine and sit in front of the typewriter.

Holmes saw Jack soon after he got out. He dropped by Holmes' apartment to talk. He was nervous and irritable, but he had to tell somebody about how he was going to write *On The Road.* Holmes remembered that he said, "You know what I'm going to do? I'm going to get me a roll of shelf-paper, feed it into the typewriter, and just write it down as fast as I can, exactly like it happened, all in a rush, the hell with these phony architectures—and worry about it later." Whatever else he thought about it, Holmes thought ". . . this method of composition sounded like good therapy at least, and when I visited him a few days after that, I heard his typewriter (as I came up the stairs) clattering away without pause, and watched, with some incredulity, as he unrolled the manuscript thirty feet beyond the machine in search of a choice passage. Two and a half weeks later, I read the finished book, which had become a scroll three inches thick made up of one single-spaced, unbroken paragraph 120 feet long, and knew immediately it was the best thing he had done."

Lucien Carr continued to live in the loft after Jack and Joan had moved. Carr brought home a roll of teletype paper from his office at the United Press, where he worked as a news editor. Lucien later remembered that he used to hear the sound of the typewriter when he got up in the morning, again when he came back from the offce and by the time he was ready for bed, Jack could still be heard at work at his table.

Kerouac later told an interviewer he wrote *On The Road* for his wife. "She'd come home from her four-hour waitress job and she'd always want to know all about Neal and what we'd done. 'What did you and Neal really do?' she'd ask, and I'd write it for her, and she'd come home and laugh at what I'd written. I'd sit behind a big screen and yell, 'Coffee!' and her hand would come around the corner holding a cup."

A short time after the novel was finished a little cocker spaniel that Lucien had at the loft chewed up the last few feet of the manuscript and Jack retyped it, but it was the only part of *On The Road* that he rewrote there. He didn't think of the novel as finished, and he told Allen he needed an ending. Ginsberg's response was to send a letter to Neal on 5 May, 1951, telling him that *On The Road* was finally written to Jack's satisfaction as a "concise poetic opinion of Neal." Allen added blandly, "the hero is you," but since Jack needed an ending he asked Neal to "write him a serious self-prophetic letter foretelling your fortune in fate."

Robert Giroux remembers that Kerouac phoned him from the loft in great excitement to say he'd just finished *On The Road*. The next day he appeared at Giroux's office with the huge roll of paper under his arm and threw it across the floor shouting, "Here's your novel!" Jack had pasted the sheets of teletype paper together—Giroux said they felt rubbery, like Thermo-fax paper—to make one big roll. Giroux was so startled that he said the wrong thing: "But Jack, how can you make corrections on a manuscript like that?" Later he realized that Jack was in a state of ecstasy and wanted a ceremonial reaction, dancing around the paper carpet of manuscript. Kerouac drew back, obviously hurt at his editor's response. Belligerently insisting he wouldn't change a word for anyone, he rolled up his manuscript and disappeared. Giroux heard nothing more from him for several years.

The sickness, the burst of work to finish the new book, the pressures of trying to work his meaningless job as a script writer had taken their toll. Two nights after he finished his book Kerouac decided his marriage was over. He might have said later that he wrote *On The Road* to explain to his wife Joan all about his adventures with Cassady, but once he'd explained it to her he packed up the typewriter, rolled up the teletype manuscript and moved back into his mother's apartment in Ozone Park. When he told Allen about the move he said that he'd gone back to "the woman that wanted him most," his mother. His wife was bitter and confused, and there were angry scenes between her and Kerouac. She discovered she was pregnant a short time after they separated, and Jack denied that he could possibly have fathered her child. He took a superior tone and told her that he'd known even a week before the wedding that the marriage couldn't work.

The marriage had lasted barely six months, but he'd been struggling to write *On The Road* for two years before he'd met her, and in their months in the loft he'd only been thinking of the manuscript. All he wanted, once it was finished, was to get home, back to his mother's apartment, out of the noise and jumble of the city streets where he was living with Joan, away from the crowds and the smells and the traffic and the rusted fire escapes, back to his own room.

He rested in his mother's apartment, sleeping through the day until she got back from work, drinking beer in the kitchen while she fixed dinner, staying up late to talk, spending time together again. Mémère was going down to North Carolina in July to stay with Nin, and he decided to go with her. The incessant, hectic excitement, the sprawling uncertainties, the exhaustions and agonies of his life with Neal Cassady had finally become *On The Road*.

KEROUAC

Part Two

1951–1957

Chapter Twelve

After what Kerouac had been through, the summer of 1951 was quiet. In Rocky Mount with his mother, his sister and her family, he let the weeks go by with a kind of summer languor. He had the manuscript of *On The Road* with him, but he worked on it only sporadically. He had finished the heavy writing in the three-week burst in the loft, but in Rocky Mount he started cutting the manuscript and inserting new material. He didn't stop writing entirely. There was almost no time in his life during which he wasn't writing. But he spent most of the days that summer resting and thinking about a new novel, still centered on Cassady, but this time about his life in San Francisco and his wild enthusiasm for jazz. Jack wrote a long letter to John Clellon Holmes describing what he was thinking about a jazz novel, stretching out so much in the letter that when he'd sent it off to Holmes he lost interest in writing the book itself. Restlessly he turned to the milieu around him and began a new novel, but the book was put away until the last years of his life, when he was living in the South again, and only finally published in 1971 as *Pic*.

He remained suspended over the long summer, postponing his decision about what he was going to do and how he was going to live now that his second marriage had broken up. When he and Joan were married his mother had moved out of their old apartment on Cross Bay Boulevard into a smaller place in the same building directly below it. New tenants moved in above in the rooms where they had last lived with Leo Kerouac. Coming back to the apartment after the summer at Rocky Mount it seemed even less tolerable to Jack and his mother than when they'd left it. He and mémère felt "exiled to this horrible downstairs," sitting in the evenings listening to the sounds of the new tenants upstairs "as if in hell listening to the upper sounds of heaven."

Mémère was as upset by it as he was, and she finally began to look hard at her own life. She had worked for more than five years in a shoe factory while Jack wrote and published his novel, but he hadn't made enough money out of it to support her. She decided it was time for a change. Nin had offered her a room in the house at Rocky Mount and mémère told Jack she was going to take it. She'd had enough of the shoe factory. He'd have to take care of himself.

Jack's expectations that life would take a new turn for him after *The Town and the City* had disappeared long ago, and his mother's decision to live with Nin came as a shock. His first thought was to go back to San Francisco to live with Neal in the attic of the Cassadys' new house on Liberty Street. He wrote, asking Neal if he could stay, telling him he was his last remaining friend. Cassady didn't answer the letter. Jack thought the silence might have been because he'd been foolish enough to half-jokingly suggest that he'd come to California with a girl he knew Carolyn didn't like, but, whatever the reason, he didn't have the invitation from Neal he had been counting on.

There weren't many other choices open to him. He hadn't been included in the plans for mémère to live permanently in Rocky Mount, and he began to feel a little panicked. Ginsberg was still under psychiatric observation, and when not at the hospital he was living at home in Paterson with his father. Burroughs was in Mexico City with Joan and the two children, but Jack knew he couldn't go down to live with them unless he had a little money. Mémère was leaving for North Carolina in December. Jack was unable to pay the rent in Ozone Park, and had no desire to live there by himself anyway.

Finally one of his old friends, Henri Cru, who'd let him stay in his shack across from San Francisco three years before, came up with a solution. Cru was a seaman on the *S.S. Harding,* a cargo ship going around the world, and he wrote Jack that when the ship docked in New

133

York en route to Panama and California, Jack could join him aboard as a merchant seaman.

Early in December 1951, Kerouac prepared to ship out. He was upset and resentful at this separation from his mother. He felt unsettled to be breaking up what had been his only sense of home, even if it was only a crowded apartment in a nondescript neighborhood of Long Island. He was nearly thirty now, but he still was helplessly dependent on people who would take him in, feed him and let him use a table to write on. As he packed his bag, he tried to give himself courage, imagining a great black bird hovering outside his bedroom window in the dark winter night waiting to grab him when he felt the apartment, "only I'm going to dodge it successfully by sheer animalism and ability and even exhilaration."

Into his old seaman's bag he packed what he thought would be of most use on Cru's ship sailing around the world: a pair of new crepe sole shoes that he'd originally bought to escort his mother to movies at Radio City Music Hall, his reading glasses, a blue Eversharp pencil, new nickel notebooks for his journals, a bundle of letters and papers, his worn French dictionary with the red cover. He also packed a tiny Bible which he'd stolen from a Fourth Avenue shop after he felt the owner had cheated him over an exchange of books. Jack found the print hard to read in his Bible, but he thought he might want it on a stormy night in the Indian Ocean, lying on his bunk on the cargo ship. He'd had the Bible with him the previous summer with Burroughs in Mexico City, and he found that reading it while high on marijuana before dropping off to sleep led to "sleeps that in Mex-City on T were never equaled in sheer sweetness and LOVE . . . ."

After packing his bag, Jack took off at dawn the following day to meet Henri Cru, riding the El from Jamaica to Brooklyn, then crossing to Staten Island and waiting for Cru to disembark from his ship at eight o'clock in the morning. That night they got drunk together in the West End, and the next day Jack dashed out for the nine o'clock call at the Marine Cooks and Stewards Union, hoping there'd be a place open on Cru's ship.

There wasn't anything for him. Jack couldn't believe it and he went almost out of his mind, attending union meetings to badger officials, riding subways back and forth in Brooklyn, getting off at the wrong stops and getting hopelessly lost in the maze of ramps and stations, tokens and refunds. He knew he had to follow Cru to California. He was so positive about getting a seaman's job that he thought he was finally growing up and wanting to work for his living. In his mind, there even seemed to be a spiritual portent involved in his getting on Cru's ship. His friend had told him that the life preservers on the ship were painted red on a white rail and said "San Francisco," and Jack took them as a symbol that he was fated to get aboard.

But nothing helped him get a berth. All the available jobs were given to more experienced seamen, and Cru was sailing to Panama without him. They thought up another plan. Cru said he'd get the chief cook to write a letter to the union agent in San Pedro so Jack could get some kind of berth, no matter what, when the ship docked in California on Christmas Eve. Jack thought it was worth a try, so long as Cru helped him out with money to get to the coast. Borrowing sixty dollars from Cru and thirty dollars more for expenses from mèmère, Jack had enough to get to California without hitchhiking. He left immediately for San Francisco so he could stay a few days with Cassady before going down to meet Cru in San Pedro. He felt so depressed leaving mémère behind just before Christmas, with no home left to come back to, that he took a lot of dexedrine to push the trip as fast as possible.

It was snowing by the time his bus reached Pittsburgh on the turnpike, making Jack feel even more homesick for Christmas than ever. But riding with a wild gang of Air Force men who had "satchels of whiskey," he was soon drunk enough to talk easily and relax with them, "no more brooding or paranoia or nothing, preparing for world." By Toledo, Ohio, he was really into the trip, getting off the bus to stretch his legs, and drinking hot cocoa to keep him from freezing in the streets "in cold downtown red neon night." He wrote down his impressions of the trip so he'd have a record of it to show Cassady when he finally arrived in San Francisco, scribbling in his notebook on the bus and finishing it later in Neal's attic room:

. . . Across Illinois to Davenport, where I woke up just before dawn, dug the Mississippi again, the ninth time, now flowing in winter, walked in cold dawn near oldman bar's street where I slaked my hot thirst in summer 'forty-seven . . . bam, in Omaha it's snowing—a blizzard—dirty old scabrous shithouse character watches me shit, another sells me comb for dime, I eat sandwiches (now down to bread and boiled eggs) . . .

The Cassadys let him stay with them, but it was only a short visit while he waited to go down to Los Angeles to join Henri Cru. Neal got him a job for four days during the Christmas rush as a baggage-handler with the railroad, so Jack would have a little money. Three days before Christmas, Kerouac started south on the Zipper express freight train to Los Angeles with Neal's brakeman's pass. He was going to claim that Neal was his brother when he showed it to conductors on the train.

Choked with a sudden winter virus cold, he tried to get some sleep lying flat on the caboose seat with his face buried in his jacket, but every conductor from San Jose to Los Angeles shook him awake during the night to see his pass, and he was stultified with exhaustion when he signed into a skid-row hotel near the bus terminal at Sixth and Main to wait a day for Cru's ship. Years later when he wrote about the experience in a magazine story, "Piers of the Homeless Night," he was living high and described it exuberantly, but at the time it was no fun at all. Lying in bed on the stiff gray sheets drinking cheap bourbon and lemon juice to chase down the Anacins for his cold, Jack remembered his first trip to Los Angeles in 1947 when he'd stayed in a similar hotel with his Mexican girl. Now four years later he'd turned into a "lonesome traveler," and no girl would mistake him for a college boy anymore.

The day before Christmas 1951, Kerouac waited at the San Pedro pier for Cru to disembark, but when Cru's ship came in, the difficulty of getting a berth started all over again just as it had in New York earlier that month. Jack even made it worse. Cru had asked him to pick up a gun and bring it along with him to the ship, so Cru could have it to settle a dispute with one of the crew, but Jack refused to have anything to do with guns. Cru was disgusted with him, but Jack insisted that he was a loyal and faithful friend, only "old Ti Jean who'll go anywhere follow anyone for adventure."

They left the docks together to take the red streetcar from San Pedro to downtown Los Angeles, but after missing it and chasing it fruitlessly in a cab, they bought six packs of beer and stood drinking at the deserted street-car stop trying not to feel the damp chill of the December night. It was Christmas Eve. Finally they were so cold they went across an empty lot into a bar. At three o'clock in the morning, they'd had enough waiting for the Red Car and gave up on reaching Los Angeles until later Christmas Day. They sneaked back aboard Cru's ship and in a drunken private holiday celebration, shoved a huge tumbleweed up the gangplank into the engine focsle, before they fell into bed.

At the Maritime Union Hall after Christmas, Jack was told there were no free berths aboard and that he definitely couldn't ship out with Cru. He went back to San Francisco, broker than ever, and persuaded the Cassadys to let him move into Neal's attic room. He told them he was ready at last to learn how to be a railroad brakeman, just like Neal, and Neal grinned and told him to help himself to anything he wanted in the house. In January 1952, Jack started his training program on the Southern Pacific Railroad in the Oakland yards. He stayed with Neal and Carolyn through the foggy, rainy San Francisco winter, and did not leave until May 1952.

Later in his life, thinking back to the attic room in Cassady's small house on Russian Hill, Kerouac remembered it as one of the best places he ever lived in, because it was an ideal place to write: "It rained every day, and I had wine, marijuana, and once in a while Neal's wife would sneak in." Neal told Allen that he'd tried to persuade Jack to "make it three ways," but Jack refused, only wanting to make love with Cassady's wife. Carolyn later remembered that it was all Neal's idea:

Neal wanted it that way. He always passed on his girl-friends to Jack, it was a ritual. It happened to me and I had to work it through. I knew about Luanne, Neal's first wife, that they'd shared her . . . . But then when Jack was living with us—Jack who was very, very moral, oddly enough, and so strait-laced about other people's wives—Neal was called to go on a two-week hold-down on the railroad and when he left he said, "My best pal, my best gal" and Jack and I were just perfect all the time he was gone, we hardly dared to be in the same room together. When Neal came back I said, "Did you say that because you were afraid we were going to and you didn't want to be made a fool of, or did you say it because you really wanted it to happen?" He said, "Oh, I thought it would be nice." So I said to myself, "If that's how you are then let's see how nice it is." Be-cause he was really jealous and it was the only way I could keep him home. It worked like a charm. They both stayed home and watched each other. I had two husbands for a long time. It wasn't actually all that great as far as sex was concerned, there was nothing all that exciting in either one of them, but at least it made home life fun and we could do things together where before they'd always gone out and I was left.

For the most part, the new living arrangement suited Jack fine. If anything it confirmed his belief in Cassady's freedom and made him admire Neal even more. Jack loved living in the clutter of Neal's things scattered on the floor of the attic, "his workgloves, dungarees, chino pants, shirts, socks, shoetrees, cardboards, white shirts piled on top of ancient leather belts, ancient railroad overtime papers now stomped with the dust of shoes." When Neal and Jack didn't feel like showing up to work at the railroad yards, they drove around San Francisco in Neal's old car, the Green Hornet, racing around corners to go out to the beach and drink beer, parking on Market Street downtown for movies of the Three Stooges, rushing out for wine and marijuana in "bumclothes that put real bums to shame," sitting up in the attic all night and into the morning putting down on tape parts of their rambl-ing, marathon conversations.

Jack became a special buddy "uncle" to Neal's little

138

girl Cathy, but all those months with the Cassadys, sharing in every part of their lives, even for a while putting in his hours working in the Oakland railroad yards, Jack kept writing. He might be learning how to be a brakeman, but he was still a writer, and in San Francisco, in the spring of 1952, he had three books in varying stages of completion: *On The Road, Visions of Cody* and a third, *Doctor Sax,* which he had begun four years before.

Jack revised and typed *On The Road* while he was at the Cassadys'. Then he sent it to a friend Ginsberg had made at the Columbia Psychiatric Institute in 1949, named Carl Solomon, for whom Allen would later write "Howl." Allen came upon Carl Solomon in the hospital and introduced himself as Prince Myshkin. Recognizing their spiritual affinity, Solomon replied that he was Kirilov, the character in Dostoyevsky's *The Possessed* who thought suicide was the only solution to the tragedy of life. Solomon's uncle, A. A. Wynn, owned Ace Books, a paperback house specializing in drugstore fiction. After leaving the hospital, Solomon had become an editor at his uncle's publishing house, and in 1952 Ace Books was considering Burroughs' *Junkie.* Ginsberg had told Solomon about Burroughs' novel, described the teletype roll manuscript of *On The Road* and Cassady's plans for an autobiography, all of which interested Solomon very much.

Jack was willing to let him read *On The Road,* but he was still rewriting it. It wasn't ready finally until May 1952, when Jack sent it for Allen to read and deliver to Solomon. So a whole year passed between Jack's three-week writing burst in the loft in New York and what he thought was the final version of *On The Road.* Halfway along, in October 1951, six months after the teletype version, Kerouac had found a new way to write. It had been the discovery of his "writing soul at last."

This new way to write was his method of spontaneous composition. The idea had come to him after he and his mother had come back from their summer in Rocky Mount and were still living in Ozone Park. At first he called his new method "sketching," and described it to Allen as coming to him suddenly on 25 October, 1951. As Jack remembered, he was sitting upstairs in the Chinese restaurant on 124th Street and Broadway, near Columbia, with his Denver friend Ed White, who casually suggested that he work like a painter using words instead of paint. Mulling over the idea, Kerouac rode the subway back to Ozone Park, but instead of going straight upstairs to the apartment he stood on Cross Bay Boulevard, took out a notebook and began describing what he saw in front of him in the window of a bakery.

For Jack the appeal of sketching was his excitement letting himself go on paper, just as a jazz musician blew riff after riff of a solo following whatever direction his own mind and immediate emotions led him. As he told Allen, when he sketched, he wrote "with 100% honesty," and sometimes was so inspired he lost consciousness. The original source of sketching, Kerouac was sure, was Yeats' trance writing, and once he had begun to sketch, Jack felt it was the only way to write.

It was a big decision in Kerouac's life to write by sketching and perhaps his only aesthetic one. He later told John Clellon Holmes that he was afraid to give up conventional narrative for spontaneous prose because he felt it meant the end of making his living as a writer. Earlier when he had shown the teletype manuscript of *On The Road* to his Harcourt editor, Robert Giroux, and Giroux had mentioned revisions, Jack backed off angrily.

But after discovering spontaneous prose he wanted to rework it, to sketch in it, to make it more poetic and more profound. Instead of trying to get a large advance for *On The Road,* as Holmes had just done in December 1951 for his novel *Go,* Jack decided to turn to a job as a seaman or railroad brakeman while he went on sketching. The result of sketching, as Ginsberg recognized, was a long sentence page that later at its best in *Doctor Sax* or *October in the Railroad Earth* had "the density of poetry, and the beauty of poetry, but most of all the single elastic rhythm running from beginning to end of the line and ending 'mop!' " In his early revisions of *On The Road* Jack struggled with the images it contained. Writing for example on 18 May, 1952 (his estimate changed all the time) that the greatest line in the novel was the image of "the charging restless mute invoiced road keening in a seizure of tarpaulin power . . . ."

Kerouac continued to work sporadically on the novel until it was published in September 1957, first by himself, sketching, and later with the help of his editor, Malcolm Cowley, after the manuscript finally had been accepted by Viking.

Chapter Thirteen

With his discovery of "sketching," in October 1951, Kerouac had realized that he had found his voice at last. But he still had to face the problem that sketching didn't lead to finished manuscripts with any commercial potential. He was desperately concerned with making money from his writing and as ashamed as ever that he wasn't helping his mother. Yet he had to go on writing. Nothing really mattered to him except sketching everything in sight. The conventional narrative survey of road trips in the teletype *On The Road* seemed flat and uninspired to him after his discovery of sketching, and so, while still at Ozone Park before moving to San Francisco and living with the Cassadys, he had begun another version of the book. It, too, was about Neal, and Jack called it *Visions of Cody* or, sometimes, *Visions of Neal*. When Ginsberg read it, he called it an "in-depth version" of *On The Road*. A selection from the long manuscript was published as *Visions of Cody* by New Directions in 1960, and the complete book was published posthumously in 1973 by McGraw-Hill.

Kerouac never in all his life felt closer to Cassady than when he started writing *Visions of Cody*. It was as though he were trying to merge his personality with Neal. Suddenly what Neal had been telling him all those years about their being blood-brothers finally became real for Jack. They were both Catholics, and in some way Jack felt this gave them a special brotherhood, since his sketching method had its roots in his experience inside the confessionals of the Catholic church. In the confessional it was a sin to hold anything back. Through sketching Kerouac felt he had a method that could perfectly capture Cassady's soul. He had finally learned, as the poet David Meltzer once phrased it to Lew Welch, that language was a way of moving too.

In *Visions of Cody* the language tried to be an image of Cassady, reflecting his sound and his movement, projecting a frame of Cassady as big and as wide as a movie screen:

. . . Everybody got excited this year about Marlon Brando in *Streetcar Named Desire*; why Cody has a thinner waist and bigger arms . . . can run the 100 in less than 10 flat, pass 70 yards, broad jump 23 feet, standing broad jump 11 feet, throw a 12-pound shot 49 feet, throw a 150-pound tire up on a 6-foot rack with just one arm and his knee, plays pinochle at night with the boys in the caboose, wears a slouched black hat sometimes, was walking champ in the Oklahoma State Joint Reformatory, cuts and switches poetic old dirty boxcars from the Maine hills and Arkansas, holds his footing when a 100-car freight slams along in a jawbreaking daisy chain roar to him, drives a '32 Pontiac clunker (the Green Hornet) as well as a '50 Chevy station wagon sharp and fast (I see his head bobbing into sight from the sea of heads in cars on Market Street, girls throng at the bell . . .

Kerouac also used Cassady to project his belief in a kind of poetry that could express hope in America. Jack saw in Neal the living embodiment of his idealistic, romantic dream of the promise of America and his dark sense that this dream had been betrayed.

I'm a fool, the new day rises on the world and on my foolish life; I'm a fool, I loved the blue dawns over racetracks and made a bet Ioway was sweet like its name, my heart went out to lonely sounds in the misty springtime night of wild sweet America in her powers, the wetness on the wire fence bugled me to belief, I stood on sandpiles with an open soul, I not only accept loss forever, I am made of loss—am made of Cody, too . . .

The portrait of Cassady that Jack sketched in *Visions*

of Cody was really Kerouac's dream image of himself. Jack wrote as if he were seeing himself through Neal and dramatizing himself through his friend. The Kerouac who wouldn't take discipline in the Navy or who wouldn't fit into the Columbia varsity team was mirrored in the Cassady who emerged in *Visions of Cody*. In San Francisco, Jack had the manuscript of Neal's unfinished autobiography in the attic room, and he read it, but Jack's book was his own vision of Neal's wildness, not how Neal saw himself.

Cassady was a man haunted by his years of early homelessness. Jack passed over this quickly, but Neal's autobiography dwelled on it obsessively, as if it were the only history he had. Jack saw Neal as a lonely, legendary American hero, adrift in a cold, hostile world where survival depended, as Jack had said about himself when he left mémêre in Ozone Park, on "sheer animalism and ability and even exhilaration."

Visions of Cody was one of Kerouac's favorite books. There was energy and confidence in its prose. Jack had succeeded in sketching sound images in sentences that moved across the page like the way Neal walked, tirelessly on the balls of his feet, always talking, a self-proclaimed captive of his own flowing, infinitely spun-out monologues, wrapping himself in his own talk like a sax player soloing, running up and down the changes, intent on covering himself completely with closely interwoven layers of sound.

The book which New Directions published as *Visions of Cody* in 1960 was a selection from Kerouac's 512-page typescript, giving it a tightness and cohesion the original manuscript lacked. Jack's editor at New Directions shaped the book around the long sketch of Neal's earliest years in Denver, but at the center of the book emerged Jack's fascination with the image of redbrick and neon that appeared over and over in his prose at this time.

The image "drove Cody in his secretest mind as it has myself and most others to further penetrations into the interior streets, the canyons, the ways, so much like the direction music takes in the mind or even the undiscoverable flow of dream images that make dreaming a tragic mystery; and so seeking rushing all dreams into the heart of it, always the redbrick wall behind red neons, waiting." At a deeper level, the neon lights and redbrick were an enigmatic image from his unconscious mind. There were the results of his visionary attempts with drugs to penetrate the center of the universe and reduce it to vibrations. The image also suggested the tragic mystery of Jack's dreams which always ended smack up against the redbrick of everyday reality. He never felt at home on earth, and like Cassady, he longed for death to set him free.

On a less private level, the neon lights implied Kerouac's disillusion with America, "the red neons of our frontward noticeable desperately advertised life." Kerouac was caught by the restless energy of American life, "the joy of the downtown city night," a joyous excitement so much stronger than the dreams of his boyhood that "it was like the man's need for whisky supplanting the boy thirst for orange soda and took as much trouble and years to develop."

In *On The Road* Jack chased the neons with Neal and ended up disillusioned and exhausted. His dreams ran out against the grim, unyielding coldness of the icy brick wall. In *Visions of Cody* there is no story or connected narrative linking the pages together. There is no end to the road. The redbrick always looms ominously behind the excitment of the neons downtown. The redbrick and neon images show up everywhere in *Visions of Cody* because they are what Kerouac had seen himself, first as a boy in Lowell and later everywhere across the country as he looked for a vision of America, helplessly rushing toward its promise, and then repelled by its emptiness.

Jack was so completely involved in *Visions of Cody,* and so tightly knotted in his emotional transference to Cassady when he started it in fall 1951, he did not have the distance to know what he was doing with the book until he left Ozone Park and tried to continue writing in Neal's house in San Francisco. Carl Solomon had heard from Ginsberg that Jack was writing another book about Cassady, and before Jack left for California he had told Solomon that he would send *Visions of Cody* back to New York as soon as it was finished. But first he wanted to type the finished version of *On The Road* in San Francisco because he felt he had to revise its "kind of anxious Dashiell Hammett" style and rewrite it, sketching. But after only a few days with the Cassadys, Jack wrote Solomon that he was abandoning his plans for his big book about "Dean Pomeray" (Cassady). He wanted instead to begin his own downtown redbrick neon book about Lowell, because he realized living with Neal that the things he had been writing about Neal curiously were really about himself.

Living in Cassady's attic room, talking to Neal every day, Jack confronted the original "Dean Pomeray," not the vision he had been writing about in the New York loft and his mother's apartment in Ozone Park. He made an effort to finish *Visions of Cody* with Neal's tape recorder, taping conversations between Neal and Carolyn and himself. Mostly he recorded Cassady's monologues about how difficult he found it to write, or even think, complete sentences, or long rambling stories about his girls and cars, like the time he was in a car kissing a girl and got so excited he smashed into a telephone pole and broke his nose.

After Jack had transcribed the tapes—they comprise a long section of *Visions of Cody*—he gave up trying to finish the book that way. As Jack explained later in an interview, it really didn't come out right using a tape recorder with Neal and himself, since "when all written down and with all the Ahs and Ohs and the Ahums and the fearful fact that the damn thing is turning and you're *forced* not to waste electricity or tape . . . ." Instead of taping conversations with Cassady, Jack decided to let his mind follow its own trains of thought, and, sitting at his typewriter, Jack succeeded in catching the twists of language and looping sentences he was looking for in *Visions of Cody*;

. . . all the goofs he felt in him were justified in the outside world and he had nothing to reproach himself for, bonk, boing, crash, skittely boom, pow, slam, bang, boom, wham, blam, crack, frap, kerplunk, clatter, clap, blap, fap, slapmap, splat, crunch, crowsh, bong, splat, splat, *BONG!*

Jack had composed a poem with Allen when Neal had come to New York in Christmas 1948, in the same zany, rhyming style. They'd called it "Fie My Fum" and Allen had given it to Jay Landesman to publish in a magazine called *Neurotica* in the spring of 1950. It began:

> Pull my daisy,
> Tip my cup
> Cut my thoughts
> For coconuts.

(Jack later used the first line, "Pull my daisy," as the title of a film.) Carl Solomon had liked the poem, but now he was disappointed that Kerouac hadn't sent him the two novels about Neal which he'd been hoping to read. Jack told him that Neal was writing his own magnificent book about his own life, and that Ace Books should publish it. Solomon finally got tired of Kerouac's putting him off about the two books and wrote Cassady to advise him how to be a writer, telling him not to listen to Kerouac's suggestions because Jack would only confuse him. It seemed to Solomon that Jack was using Neal to avoid the problems of his own life. He felt Kerouac was struggling with a problem of personality that had left his writing confused. It was a tangle all the way from the Thomas Wolfe style of *The Town and the City* to the unfinished experiments of *On The Road* and *Visions of Cody*.

Solomon told Cassady that he was a more natural storyteller than Kerouac, possessing clear vision, vital content and a grasp of character and concrete detail. He knew Neal was working a sixteen-hour day as a brakeman, but Neal shouldn't give up writing. He urged Cassady to read Truman's autobiography *Mr. President* to understand the "great confession vogue," and Micky Spillane and Gold Medal Original paperbacks, since they were reaching new audiences in places where books had never gone before. Jack was furious at Solomon's letter and especially angry that he should advise Cassady to read Mickey Spillane. Ginsberg remembers his saying at the time, "What does he think our boy is, an idiot? Would I write a book about a dope?"

Cassady needed all the help anyone could give him about how to write his autobiography, because for Neal writing was a terrible struggle. He told Allen he was incredibly slow selecting words and fitting them into sentences. His weakness was that he tried to crowd too much in, and when he thought of a word, even if it wasn't right, he didn't want to drop it. When he sat down at the typewriter, if he accidently hit the wrong letter to begin a word, he didn't erase the wrong letter, but instead he sat for as long as it took thinking up a word to suit the letter. He could usually come up with something after a while, but the problem was that after he'd strung out a series of such words, he had lost the sense of what he'd started out to say. Cassady had in mind a rough outline of his attempts to recall the confusions in his life, and he was determined to get down his life story, even if he could only write very slowly.

But Allen encouraged him to continue, and Allen's friend Carl Solomon wrote him flattering letters: "Big, new-critic professors are going to be washed away by the flood of honest amateur writers on GI Bills in writing correspondence courses who, until now, have been frightened away from the delights of literary confession and self-justification by the likes of Allen Tate, Partisan Review, my penmanship teacher, and the whole apparatus of stinking old-time capitalists . . . ." Jack lived at the house and read what Neal had written and responded to it with loud enthusiasm, so Cassady struggled on.

Neal gave support to Kerouac too, although Jack didn't have him read *On The Road* and only showed him a few sections of *Visions of Cody*. From what Jack told him, Cassady thought the theme of *On The Road* wasn't important enough to bother with. Instead he felt that Jack should extend what he was doing so *On The Road* would only be the first book. He should go on, as Proust had done, to reach new levels of greatness. Jack should return to his early life, to the dark sidewalks and frame houses of Lowell, and fill in the outlines he'd sketched out in the *Doctor Sax* novella years before. When Jack had begun *Visions of Cody,* he had been worried that it would be shapeless but he hoped somehow that it would achieve the structure of a Proust novel because all his visions were unified by the presence of his own consciousness at their center. He had told Allen once that the value of one's mind is its spontaniety. Now Neal with a single intuitively correct suggestion had given Jack the direction for his writing which it had so badly needed. Kerouac took it from there. In *Visions of Cody,* he had projected himself as fantasy hero through the person of Cassady, but in *Doctor Sax* he alone would emerge as the hero of his own legend. Once more Cassady pointed the way.

Jack sat down in front of the tape recorder with the pages of Neal's autobiography, full of memories of his boyhood in Denver, scattered around the attic room, and began the third book on which he worked in Cassady's house. Into the machine he delivered a two-hour taped monologue about being thirteen years old in Lowell. One hour of the tape was the entire tale of *Doctor Sax.*

Writing about his visions of Neal had loosened Jack and brought him, through his sketching method of free association, to confront his own memories about his own life without fear or evasion. He was open enough to be able to express his deepest dreams and fantasies as dramatically as he could envision them, and the breakthrough of discovering in *Visions of Cody* that the things he had written about Neal were really about himself excited him tremendously.

When he had finished typing *On The Road* at the beginning of May 1952, he suddenly felt he had to move on. He couldn't stay any longer with the Cassadys. Jack hadn't worked in the railroad yards for a long time, and Neal didn't understand why he wasn't pushing through his plan to be a brakeman. Jack kept trying to evade the issue, but as he stayed around the house longer, he decided that living with Neal was becoming difficult. Neal insisted on everything going his way and monopolizing the spotlight. He had to emphasize his place at the center of the lives of the people—women, children, Kerouac—living around him.

Neal did more than merely dominate his household. He made himself the only thing happening in the room whenever he was around, and Jack couldn't take it any more. Jack was used to being the center of attention in his mother's house, and the ménage à trois in Neal's kitchen finally got him down. Jack described himself at the table eating supper, jealously watching as Cassady ". . . continually nudges his wife's thigh and sucks juices from her lips and pats her kindly on the head and slaps applesauce out of a can into his children's (his daughters') plates, drinks milk out of the bottle, won't hardly allow me a glass . . . ."

Having Kerouac in their house for such a long stretch was hard on the Cassadys too. They had decided to save money to buy a house of their own in San Jose, closer to Neal's job with the railroad. The crowded little house on Russian Hill might have seemed perfect for Jack, who loved San Francisco, but Carolyn felt the family would be happier living in San Jose, with a yard for the children and where Neal wouldn't have to commute hours to his job. It suddenly seemed to Jack that Neal was hung up on money, working long hours every day to build up the house down-payment, driving back and forth from San Francisco to the railroad yards in San Jose, just wanting to flop into bed when he got home. He had practically stopped talking to Jack, sullenly saying "Yeah, yeah," when Kerouac tried to make conversation.

Having Jack stay at home all day in the attic room, playing with the tape recorder, typing *On The Road,* reading the *Encyclopedia Britannica* for hours in the rainy afternoons and coming up with odd little facts at suppertime didn't amuse Neal anymore. He kept asking Jack why he didn't get a job on the railroad after working as a yardclerk in Oakland learning about switches and boxcars so he'd qualify as a brakeman. Jack didn't want a job with the Southern Pacific. He just wanted a place to live so he could write his books.

Finally, Cassady began to economize so strictly on the household money, saving for the house in San Jose, that he stopped buying wine and marijuana, and then Jack really began to complain. He loved the roach kit above the kitchen sink so much he described it in *Visions of Cody*—"a dish, glass, deep dish, small, with rolling paper, tweezers, roach pipe (hollow steel tube), roach pipe ramrod came with the tube, attached, an art tool actually, bottles of seeds . . ." Jack had no money to buy mari-

149

juana himself, and he was angry with Cassady when he started to cut down on the smoking at home. Kerouac got really mad when Neal turned down peyote when they visited a poet named Philip Lamantia at a party one night in Berkeley. Jack didn't respond positively to Lamantia, but he was impressed despite himself with Lamantia's knowledge of Indian culture and his experience with peyote. He was sure Lamantia wanted to let him and Neal try it, but Cassady came to life at the party and insisted on boring everybody, Jack thought, with a long egocentric monologue about railroad work. Driving back to San Francisco with Cassady, Jack had a furious argument with him, insulting Neal by saying they were like two louts who bored and offended the local nobles with their peasant talk.

Neal was so angry with Jack that when Jack wanted to go back alone the next day to Lamantia's house and try peyote, Neal refused to drive him there. Carolyn smoothed things over and got Neal to treat Jack to a dinner at his favorite restaurant in Chinatown, but a few days later, Kerouac packed his bag and started south to live with Burroughs in Mexico City.

As a gesture of friendship, and with Carolyn's encouragement, Neal offered to drive Jack as far as Nogales. They packed the 1950 Chevy station wagon for a family trip, taking out the seats in back so Carolyn and the children could rest comfortably. They left San Francisco in high spirits, Jack sitting beside Neal on the front seat, with the family on pillows in the back. But by the time they separated at Nogales Jack felt that there was more hostility between them. They had planned a slow, easy trip, taking the long drive in gradual stages, having picnics beside the road in the Imperial Valley and in Arizona, but once Cassady started to drive, it was another nonstop marathon. Neal hustled Jack to the border in as short a time as possible, planning and scheming how long it would take him to race back to San Francisco.

When they said goodbye in Nogales in May 1952 Jack only had eyes for the road leading through the desert and mountains to Mexico City. From Neal's point of view, as he wrote Allen later, Jack was "with the Indians permanent."

Chapter Fourteen

On the dusty, battered, second-class bus that bumped along the road between Nogales and Mexico City, Kerouac met a Mexican boy named Enrique who had a homemade radio set hollowed out to hold half a pound of green marijuana. They rolled heavy joints when the bus stopped among the cacti of the little Mexican desert towns while passengers milled around, loading chickens and vegetables, then got back on to bounce along another stretch of the rutted dirt roads through the desert, headed south.

Sitting in the back with Enrique, drinking mescal, Jack sang bop for his Mexican friends, "Scrapple from the Apple" and "Israel." In Culiacan, Jack, Enrique and the friend's teenage brother left the bus at midnight to smoke opium and marijuana in a hut outside the village, a night Kerouac described in crowing detail to Ginsberg and later used for a sketch in *Lonesome Traveler*, "Mexico Fellaheen."

Jack kept scribbling in his notebook throughout the evening, much to the amusement of the Indians. He shoved his notebook at the Indians forcing them to read his descriptions of the hut where Enrique had taken him and his sensations lighting up the marijuana and opium cigarettes. He insisted they could understand each other's language because Jack was an Indian too, telling them his great-great-grandmother had been a Canadian Indian who married a French baron. Like the Mexicans, Jack felt he had black heels. He squatted with them on the sod floor of the hut and slept on a junkie's floor nearby with Enrique and his brother. They talked of the revolution to come in North and South America, when the Indians would once again get back their land. Jack agreed with them that *"La tierra está la nostre."* After the months

151

in Cassady's house, once on the bus south in May 1952, Jack let himself go as though Mexico were a loose and wild playground.

The next morning Jack pulled himself together enough to buy more opium and marijuana, about two ounces for three dollars, and got high again. He was a little sick, feeling cold and shaky, so his Mexican friends fed him hot peppers and soup. The morning went by in a blur, but at one point he was vaguely aware of being surrounded by soldiers and policemen in the Indian's hut. Jack panicked, thoughts of Burroughs and filthy Mexican jails came to his mind, but the police only wanted some of his marijuana. After they'd taken what they needed, they waved him goodbye. That afternoon walking with Enrique to the bus, they passed an old Catholic church in the village. Suddenly it seemed miraculous to Kerouac that he and the Mexicans were Catholics together. They sat a while in the cool dark church together, waiting out a few minutes of the afternoon heat, until it was time for their bus for Mazatlan to leave.

Now Jack was anxious to join Burroughs in Mexico City. When he traveled by bus in the United States or in Mexico, he usually followed the bus schedule, getting drunk or stoned as he rode along, going out to take walks at the hour-long rest stops, partly for exercise but also to buy more supplies for the bus. He didn't meander. If his destination was San Francisco or Los Angeles or Mexico City, he got there as directly as he could. When his Mexican friend struck up a conversation on the bus with a woman who offered him and Jack her house in Mazatlan, Jack talked him out of it. He didn't want to stop over for a party in Mazatlan. He knew there were plenty of prostitutes waiting for him in Mexico City.

At dusk in Mazatlan, Enrique and Jack left the bus for an hour to walk along the beach while the sun set over the Pacific. They swam in the surf in their under-wear and dried off on the beach, smoking opium and marijuana, admiring the girls. Enrique asked Jack to live with him in Vera Cruz and gave him a rabbit's foot for luck. Jack was greatly moved by the offer.

The friendship lasted only as long as the bus ride. Enrique was a great buddy to share guavas and mangos with at dawn in the markets of Guadalajara, but the next morning when they pulled into Mexico City, Jack wouldn't give him Burroughs' address. When he was smoking dope with Enrique, Jack was perfectly sincere in everything he said, but he didn't go any further. When Burroughs told him not to meet his Mexican friend in front of the post office as they'd planned on the bus, Kerouac stood him up. Burroughs' friends in Mexico City were all Americans, mostly junkies or ex-G.I. American expatriates he met with his old Harvard friend Kells Elvins. Without hesitation Kerouac gave up Enrique to stay with Bill at his apartment at 212 Orizaba.

Burroughs had his own troubles and he was glad to see an old friend. In March 1952, two months before Jack arrived, Bill had accidentally shot his wife through the head. He and Joan had been playing William Tell in a friend's apartment with a gun and a glass on Joan's head instead of an apple. Burroughs had missed the target and killed his wife. He spent two weeks in a Mexican prison, but he could afford influential lawyers and was out on bail by the time Jack reached Mexico City.

After talking to Burroughs, Jack immediately wrote Allen that the shooting had been completely accidental, and that Joan still lived on in Bill's mind. Their son William Burroughs III was taken to St. Louis to live with Burroughs' parents, and Joan's older child, her daughter Julie, went to her family, so Burroughs was living alone when Kerouac came down to spend the summer with him in May.

Bill's first novel, *Junkie,* had been accepted by A.A. Wynn the month before in April 1952 with a $1,000 advance, and he was busy trying to write a sequel about his homosexual history, called *Queer.* Jack thought the new book was even greater than the first. He told Allen the two books should be published together, since *Queer* would attract the attention of East Coast homosexual literary critics.

The scene in Mexico City had quieted by the time Jack arrived. A few days after he got there the police arrested Burroughs' friend Kells Elvins and several other Americans for possessing drugs, and they were still all in jail.

153

Burroughs, obviously, wished to keep clear of the police. He didn't think there was anybody checking on him, but if he were picked up again for any reason he would certainly go back to jail. He had been filling out papers to apply for Mexican citizenship since 1950, but the shooting ended any of his plans to live there. Charged as a "pernicious foreigner," subject to deportation by the Immigration Department once his case was finally settled, he had his eye on Panama as the country he wanted to try next. As he wrote Allen, he detested limitations of any kind and intended "to establish my ass someplace where I am a virgin on the police blotter."

A month before Kerouac arrived, Burroughs started taking morphine again. He didn't worry about kicking his habit once he left Mexico City, since as he said to Jack, he could always break a habit with codeine to get him through the worst of the withdrawal agony. He'd done it five times in the last two years. He insisted he'd picked up his latest habit for his health. He'd been convalescing from a case of jaundice and had to give up drinking, so he used drugs instead of alcohol.

Once back in Burroughs' cluttered apartment, Jack found it was easier to work than it had been two years before, since Bill was busy working on *Queer*. In 1950, Jack had come back from a summer in Mexico City exhausted, but this time he managed to write one book and plan a couple of others.

As Burroughs had written laconically in *Junkie*, it was an "easy life" in Mexico City. He'd moved there after being run out of Texas and Louisiana for drugs, when he found he could live as he liked in Mexico on his income from his family. "I was supplied with plenty of junk for a cost of thirty dollars a month as compared with about three hundred a month in the United States." In Mexico he had become a "connoisseur of drugs," as one of Burroughs' G.I. friends used to say.

Being a "connoisseur of drugs" meant that Burroughs tried more than heroin and morphine. As he described his experiences in *Junkie,* he went on and off junk, sweating through the withdrawal symptoms with his own "cures" of opium, nembutals, codeine, benzedrine, sanicin and tequila. When he was drinking he left his apartment and hung out in Mexican bars, often at a cantina on Monterey Street called the Bounty, where he read the papers and talked with the American G.I.'s, called "refugee hipsters" in *Junkie*, and Kells Elvins, named "Rollins" in the novel. Burroughs brought them back to his rooms on Orizaba to smoke marijuana or shoot heroin. He called his place their shooting gallery. He tried peyote, washing it down with tea, and described the peyote high as being something like a benzedrine high.

With Burroughs, Jack took little trips around Mexico City to see the ruins of the ancient Aztec capital in Tenochtitlan and to the mountain town of Tenencingo. They walked along the steep roads, then cut back through the jungle so Jack could wash his feet in a river, soothing his blisters. His blue canvas crepe soles were just about worn out, but he had only ten dollars left from the little money he'd brought to Mexico. Burroughs, who'd just gotten $500 from A.A. Wynn as half of his advance for *Junkie,* helped him out. Back in the apartment there were always people wandering through, old friends of Bill's, but he and Jack were living as writers, and somehow with all the coming and going, the big cigars of marijuana and the morphine, Kerouac managed to find time to work on *Doctor Sax*.

When he got to Mexico City Jack wrote Allen that he knew at last exactly where he was headed as a writer. After Allen had sold *Junkie* for Burroughs, Jack encouraged him to think of himself as the New York agent for the whole crowd of them scattered across the country writing. Jack had sent Allen the retyped 530-page manuscript of *On The Road* before either Neal or Bill could read it. He said they hadn't had any time. At last Kerouac was satisfied with the novel, with its language and its energy. He thought it was like Joyce's *Ulysses* and should be accorded the same seriousness. If Wynn or Carl Solomon insisted on cutting it up to make the narrative more intelligible, he'd refuse and offer them something else. He asked Allen about subtitling *On The Road "Modern Novel"* (like modern jazz).

With *Doctor Sax* or *The Shadow of Doctor Sax* (he wasn't sure then of the title), Kerouac planned simply

155

to improvise on his vision of the Shadow from his early adolescense on Sarah Avenue in Lowell and build to a wailing climax with the myth dream he'd had of the "Shroudy Stranger" in 1948. He wasn't going to write only *Doctor Sax*. He told Allen that he hadn't sketched in a long time at the Cassadys', but he was going to start again in Mexico when he'd finished *Doctor Sax* with a new book about Indians and William Burroughs. He didn't want Allen to write Burroughs anything about this, since he might become stiff and self-conscious and not say anything interesting for Jack to write down.

In sketching, Jack felt he got better the more he practiced. After fifteen minutes of it he'd have a crazy chapter and the next day when he'd read it back it was great prose. Finally, before he left Mexico City, Jack planned to write a book about the Civil War, an historical novel, but trying to be a little realistic about what he could do, he guessed he'd better wait until he was back in the States and closer to a good library.

When he had been in Burroughs' apartment a few days, Kerouac decided that the best place to write *Doctor Sax* was in the toilet. Jack was smoking marijuana as he wrote, and Bill was sensitive about the smoke. He didn't want the smell of it hanging in the apartment in case the police dropped by. Jack didn't mind writing in the toilet. As he later recalled, "I had no other place to write. So I wrote on my lap in pencil. He had millions of junkies coming in, and women and guests. I didn't have a cent when I wrote that. Burroughs was supporting me."

Jack was amused years later when his editor Malcolm Cowley read *Doctor Sax* and noticed that the novel ". . . continually mentions urine, and quite naturally it does because I had no other place to write it but on a closed toilet seat in a little tile toilet in Mexico City . . ." Jack also wrote in Burroughs' room when he was out or asleep in the afternoons. Bill himself would drop in from time to time, causing an occasional abrupt chapter ending by his presence. Or Burroughs would complain about the smell of marijuana drifting into his back yard. Most of *Doctor Sax* was written while Kerouac was high on grass.

Starting the novel hunched over his notebook in the toilet, Kerouac imagined Burroughs as the physical model for the character of Doctor Sax. The version of *Doctor Sax* he'd started four years before had never focused because Kerouac had been too close to his "Shroudy Stranger" nightmare and his bewildering walk in 1947 with the "Ghost of the Susquehanna" in Pennsylvania while hitchhiking back to New York. With Burroughs in Mexico in 1952, Kerouac felt more in control of his visions.

He admired Burroughs tremendously and in *On The Road* had pictured him as a teacher. In the novel Burroughs was called "Old Bull Lee" after the pseudonym "William Lee" that Bill had given himself as author of *Junkie*. In *On The Road* Jack wrote that Burroughs "spent all his time talking and teaching others . . . . We'd all learned from him. He was a gray, nondescript-looking fellow you wouldn't notice on the street, unless you looked closer and saw his mad, bony skull with its strange youthfulness—a Kansas minister with exotic, phenomenal fires and mysteries."

In *Doctor Sax* Kerouac concentrated on the "exotic, phenomenal fires and mysteries" he sensed in Burroughs' personality, heightening them melodramatically for his portraits of Doctor Sax. Originally the name derived from an imaginary companion Jack had in his early adolescence in Lowell. The early Doctor Sax had been Jack's shadow, but it only became a fully developed character in his fantasy novel after he lived with Burroughs.

The original character of Doctor Sax was based on Jack's memory of *The Shadow* Magazine he read on Friday nights as a boy. Jack was nine years old when the first *Shadow* Magazine was published in March 1931. "The Shadow" was later a very popular radio program, but Kerouac grew up reading the pulps as they came out twice a month on Fridays with the passion of a young addict. Remembering the pleasure of settling down on his bed with a candy bar and a new *Shadow* throughout his adolescence in Lowell, Jack wrote jokingly in *Doctor Sax* that it was possible "to get high on a good magazine story" in those early days.

The character of "The Shadow" was conceived by

Walter Gibson, who wrote the early stories chronicling the heroic exploits of Lamont Cranston (alias "The Shadow") against the forces of Crime. Jack recalled Walter Gibson's language in the original *Shadow* pulps. Gibson liked to create what he called the "mysterioso" atmosphere in every story with sentences like these: "From the Stygian gloom came a sardonic laugh that cleaved the blackness. Shuddering echoes answered."

Jack took his memories of *The Shadow* pulp magazines and transformed them in *Doctor Sax* into "a kind of gothic fairy tale, a myth of puberty." His fantasy grew from his nostalgia for his boyhood in Lowell, given legendary quality by being dramatized as a mythic struggle between the opposing forces of good and evil. With the marijuana he smoked in Burroughs' apartment he was able to recall his memories of boyhood in Lowell and actively relive in his imagination the fears and fantasies he felt when he was entering adolescence, when he didn't like to go out at night alone because in the darkness he didn't know what or who the shadows were. The sentences in *Doctor Sax* rolled in long orchestrated crescendos, as if Jack were a medium for his subconscious with his mind dictating to the pencil as it traveled over his notebook pages much as he imagined Blake and Yeats had been inspired in writing their poetry.

The reality of Jack's daily life occasionally intruded. His imagination transformed his walk with Burroughs in the mountains on the pages of *Doctor Sax* where Sax led young Jackie, Indian-fashion, through the "brown supperlights stretch on sidewalk" backyards of his neighborhood in Lowell. As Kerouac felt about Burroughs, so young Jackie felt about Sax. "All his statements knock me on the head *Come In* even though I don't understand them. I know that Doctor Sax is speaking to the bottom of my boy problems and they could all be solved if I could fathom his speech."

Like Kerouac's nostalgia for the pulp magazines and popular songs of his youth, he was also deeply affected by the movies he remembered as a kid. Near the end of writing *Doctor Sax* he saw the movie "The Wizard of Oz" in Mexico City, and it helped shape the final pages of his novel. He wrote the last pages the afternoon after

158

seeing the film, the climax of the book when Sax and young Jackie met the Wizard, who pointed out the nightmare vision of the Great World Snake lurking at the bottom of the Parapet of the Pit in the Castle on a hilltop in Jack's old Lowell neighborhood. The Wizard in *Doctor Sax* was a technicolor fake, waving "arms aloft showing incredibily skinny wrists and little waxy stick hands trembling with ague." He was no match for the evil Great World Snake, so Sax tried to help him, like Dorothy with the Wicked Witch of the West in the film. His magic potent destroyed the Castle, but the Snake lived on until suddenly a Great Black Bird appeared, a deus ex machina to raise it up into heaven until both Bird and Snake could no longer be seen.

Sax delivered the final judgment. "I'll be damned, the Universe disposes of its own evil!" But his struggle to vanquish the forces of Evil uncloaked him, stripped him of his Ultimate Mystery for young Jackie. In the final light of morning, Jack saw Sax dressed like Burroughs in old beatup trousers and a worn white shirt, wearing regular brown shoes and socks. "His hair fell over his eyes, he looked a little bit like Bill Burroughs (tall, thin, plain, strange) or like Gary Cooper."

Kerouac ended *Doctor Sax* with a statement that he had written it in Mexico City, Tenochtitlan, 1952, the Ancient Capital of Azteca. Of all his books, he loved *Doctor Sax* the best. In his exurberant three-week burst he felt like he'd written *Faust Part III*, raising his own memories of his Lowell boyhood to legendary heights.

His euphoria was sustained by what he'd taken while writing it. Each of Kerouac's books was written on something and each of the books has some of the feel of what he was on most as he wrote it. *On The Road* has a nervous, tense and benzedrine feel, even with the rewriting he had to put it through. With the drugs he'd used in *Doctor Sax,* Kerouac's hallucinations spilled into the prose. He thought the book was written in "a style truly hallucinated" as he wrote it all on marijuana and morphine. Even the shroudy figure of Doctor Sax was without any menace, only a phantom dressed like something he'd read in an old pulp magazine or seen with his buddies in a movie, reappearing momentarily again in the corner of his eye as he walked up the dark sidewalks beside the shadowy Lowell riverbank.

While Jack was writing in Burroughs' apartment he felt so euphoric that he could have been remembering heaven. Not even the unexpected appearance of Neal Cassady could bring him down from the height he'd reached finishing *Doctor Sax*.

Chapter Fifteen

In a rush of sweats and squabbles Cassady came down to Mexico City in July 1952, just as Kerouac had finished *Doctor Sax*. They were still sullen with each other, despite their rasping band of blood-brotherhood. Neal insisted it was time for Jack to learn how to drive a car, but in the middle of traffic Jack stalled, not knowing when to take his foot off the clutch. Neal refused to believe that he was so uninterested in cars that he couldn't learn how to drive, but Jack swore he hadn't done it on purpose. He shouted that he didn't "know how to drive, just type-write."

As soon as Cassady had gone back to California, Jack spent five days writing a book about him in French-Canadian that was never published. It was a fantasy in the mood of *Doctor Sax*, and as Jack described it later to Neal, the novel took place in 1935 in Chinatown with Uncle Bull Balloon (Burroughs), both of their fathers and some sexy blondes in a bedroom with a French Canadian rake and an old Model-T.

Not yet written out, Jack started still another book about Lowell he first called *Springtime Mary* about his first love in Lowell High School, but he didn't get far with the book because he no longer had a place to stay with Burroughs. Bill was getting out of Mexico City at the end of July 1952, on his way to Central America.

Jack could have found himself a room but he was so broke he had to write his mother in North Carolina for bus-fare home. The life in the apartment at 212 Orizaba was over. Burroughs had heard from his lawyer that he could be acquitted for his wife's death *in absentia*, and since he'd had enough of Mexico City, he decided he'd push on. As he wrote in the final pages of *Junkie*, "I am ready to move on south and look for the uncut kick that opens out instead of narrowing down like junk," the drug the Indians called *yage*, which Burroughs had heard increased telepathic contact.

While Kerouac was still in San Francisco with the Cassadys, he'd told Allen he was going to travel with Bill to Ecuador, but when the time actually came to leave Mexico City, Jack decided to return to Rocky Mount instead. He had no money for a trip after the *yage*, and even a few months later, when he'd saved money working on the railroads, he thought only of using it to make a home for himself with mémêre in New York again. Jack was a "lonesome traveler" who felt guilty when he'd been away from his mother too long, always telling himself that he'd made a deathbed promise to his father to take good care of her forever.

But back in Rocky Mount, Jack found he couldn't move in with mémêre again while she was living in a room at his sister's house. In August, Cassady wrote and told him that there was still such a shortage of brakemen on the Southern Pacific that the railroad was advertising in the newspaper for workers. If Jack wanted to make money fast, there was no better job than the railroad. Cassady himself said that of all the jobs he'd ever had, his favorite had been parking cars, but being a brakeman paid better.

After two weeks of student trips earning only fifty dollars a week, he knew Jack would be earning at least $500 a month after taxes, and since Neal invited him to live in the new house in San Jose, Jack could save all his money and build up a big stake, maybe even $1,500 with overtime before Christmas. Even more helpful than all the advice, Cassady sent him an old 1949 railroad pass so Jack could hop freights from North Carolina to California. When that didn't move him, Neal jumped in his car for a marathon drive to Rocky Mount and brought Jack back to San Jose straight off.

Kerouac began working as a brakeman, and for a while everything went smoothly. He and Neal became friends again after Cassady drove him back to San Jose. Neal and Carolyn had even set up a room for Jack in the new house. As Carolyn remembered, they lived together happily at first.

So Jack'd be out and Neal would be home and Neal would be out and Jack would be home. We had a big house with an extra bedroom and that was Neal's idea, we always had to have a room for Jack . . . . Of course, we were terribly discreet. Whenever Neal was around, Jack and I were perfectly proper. Even though Neal knew and offered this, he'd get fits of jealousy. But he seemed to like the idea, it was his way of showing Jack his love by sharing his women. No matter who it was he always offered her to Jack.

But there were still unresolved tensions, and at the end of September 1952, Kerouac quarreled with Cassady. After Neal hung up on him when Jack phoned from San Francisco to apologize, Jack took all his things out of the house and moved to a skid-row hotel in San Francisco. The room only cost him four dollars a week, and Jack was so happy to be living by himself for the first time in years, that he began a new novel, hoping it would be as big as *The Town and the City.*

He loved being alone in the hotel room, and he immersed himself gleefully setting up housekeeping with a little hot plate and a paper sack full of groceries on the desk next to the Bible—eggs, potatoes, lettuce, peanut butter, raisin bread. He wasn't minding the brakeman's job, enjoying the sense of being on his own as a working man, especially since he knew he wasn't going to stay with it long, only saving his money so he could get back East before Christmas.

The railroad was full of crazy types, something he'd noticed when he was a yardclerk in Oakland the previous January. Of course, Kerouac was just an apprentice, but he made no effort to be friendly with anyone on the railroad. Once, carrying his scuffed black seaman's bag in the freight yards, one of the men laughed and said, "A railroad loot bag if I ever saw one!" but Jack didn't smile and "that was the beginning middle and extent of my social rapport on the railroad with the good old boys who worked it."

Carolyn Cassady later remembered that Jack had been over-sensitive about working with the railroad men: "He grumbled all the time" about the job while he lived at the Cassadys'. Jack was particularly upset when the other brakemen insisted on mispronouncing his name "Kerouay" instead of "Kerouac." Neal tried to get him to laugh about it, but Jack couldn't loosen up. The only men working the railroad that Jack felt friendly toward were the Pomo Indians, who worked as gandy dancers, laborers on section-hand tracks he passed on the freights. Whenever Jack saw them he'd always wave and smile, and he even read a book and learned the Pomo Indian battle-cry, "Ya Ya Henna." He would have yelled it to them as his train rolled by, but as he wrote in *October in the Railroad Earth,* he feared it might cause a derailment.

Since signing aboard the *S.S. Weems* in the summer of 1943, it was the longest time Jack worked a job. He was only a one-year man just starting out, but he was earning $600 a month and he was happy, though he was concerned about the dangers in the yards. Once he narrowly avoided an accident with an iron train wheel when he shoved a block of wood against it to prevent a runaway. In his few months with the Southern Pacific he got to know the run from San Francisco to the Gilroy Sub-Division at Watsonville, a stretch of about a hundred miles. Sticking to the same track came to bore him very quickly, but before he was through he wrote a long prose sketch about what he was doing as a brakeman called *October in the Railroad Earth.*

Living by himself in the small, gritty room in the skid-row hotel, the window curtains so old and dirty he was sure they'd crumble if he touched them, Kerouac let himself go sketching the railroad, trying to "clack along all the way like a steam-engine pulling a 100-car freight with a talky caboose at the end . . ." He thought of the writing as very experimental, mostly because he was sketching on a new high, the same as the bums sitting along the tracks in San Jose, drinking the cheap local sweet wines, like Jack's favorite at that time, sweet tokay.

The speedwriting of *October in the Railroad Earth* came after more tape recorder experiments with Cassady. They'd both done a lot of fast talking the month before when Jack arrived in San Jose, listening to the playbacks instead of trying to transcribe them. Then Jack felt they "both got the secret of LINGO in telling a tale and figured that was the only way to express the speed and tension and ecstatic tomfoolery of the age . . ." It was as if Jack imagined himself in a bar drinking his sweet wine and telling a long, wild tale, his friends listening and shouting and urging him to go higher and higher. Jack would no more go back and correct his phrases on paper than he would revise himself telling a story in a bar. He didn't go back to an earlier sentence, he just rushed on.

Wine was perfect for describing his work on the railroad, not only because it was cheap and readily available in any corner store, but because it wasn't hallucinatory like morphine or leading him back into memory trips like marijuana, both of which he'd wanted to help shape *Doctor Sax* but didn't need with *Railroad Earth*. Instead, wine just made him more excited with his story, like being in a bar with friends, and while he sat at his desk writing in his grimy, old hotel room he centered directly on his daily routine, his actual work on the railroads.

October in the Railroad Earth was one of Kerouac's most eloquent prose sketches. His descriptions of his room in the hotel, his twenty-six-cent egg breakfast at the Public Restaurant on Howard Street (it became the Pubic Restaurant by the end of the story), his mad scrambles to spring after trains which he was always showing up late for, his wary response to the rats scrambling in the darkness of the stockyard platforms in the marshes near the San Francisco airport, his searching the San Jose junkyard to find a piece of chicken-wire for his hot plate so he wouldn't burn his own breakfasts in the hotel, always trying to save a dime, not even buying another pair of thirty-five-cent work-gloves after he'd lost the first pair, just waiting weeks until he picked up a mismatched pair off the ground in the San Jose and Watsonville yards, learning how to kick his first car in the Sunnyvale yard, with the cars full of crates of Del Monte fruit and his instructor Whitey saying to him, "You're the boss do it pull the pin with a will put your hand in there and pull 'cause you're the boss."

The people on the railroad couldn't understand his silences, thinking like Cassady and Henri Cru that Jack was some creep who never said anything and never listened either, but Kerouac's grunts and silences were signs of his intent listening, memorizing the word for word content of conversations he'd write down later in his notebooks. He always carried a notebook and pencil in his black canvas bag, the ten-year old tattered bag he'd bought in Lowell in 1942 and taken with him to Greenland on the *S.S. Dorchester*.

October in the Railroad Earth was full of the talk Jack heard in the yards, from the bums who were constitutionally incapable of saying anything straight, all speech deteriorating immediately to hand-out requests and hard luck stories, to the rambling, detailed and informative raps of the railroad men, shifting the gum in their mouths long enough to spit and deliberate and then pronounce their words with heavy seriousness, usually ending with the common complaints about the railroads.

The wine also turned Jack on sexually, and since he wasn't going to spend five dollars on the prostitutes that Cassady had told him about in the Watsonville whorehouse, in his hotel room he was usually feeling horny and turned on. *October in the Railroad Earth* was consequently a very lusty piece, with wonderfully exuberant images of a Mexican girl getting laid in the dusty, red fruit fields along the railroad track. Words were not enough so Kerouac even scatted bop choruses. As Cassady had said to Ginsberg, "Lyric is supported on bubbles and what is too foolish to be said is sung."

When he got back to the hotel, he'd rest on top of the bed quilt with his bottle of tokay, then turn on the light and begin to write, his mind obsessed, *"attacked by words,"* almost like a tape recorder running his own thoughts and fragments of remembered conversations through his mind, nonstop transcription until he'd driven himself into exhaustion getting down an apparently endless monologue, what Kerouac thought of as his lifelong monologue.

Finally, one night in the San Jose railroad yard, waiting hours for his work assignment, Jack fell asleep on the old, ratty couch in the brakeman's room, and as he told Allen later, he woke up with Neal's face bending over him, laughing and urging him to come home. Jack moved out of his hotel back into Cassady's house in San Jose. He decided to stop caring whether Neal really liked him or not.

It seemed to Jack that Neal had slowed down, that he wasn't excited by life anymore, but Jack had to go on, even without Cassady. The winter before when Jack had been living with Neal in San Francisco and they'd begun to argue after Jack wouldn't take a steady job with the railroad, Allen had written him saying, "What will you care if you faced your responsibilities instead of your mysteries?" Jack thought it was the greatest statement Allen had ever made. He felt that Ginsberg understood him much better than Cassady, that Allen realized that Jack was "at the height of his romantic sense of himself."

Shortly before Christmas, when Jack said goodbye to the Cassadys and started East, it was to live once again with his mother and see if he could find a formal relationship with friends like Ginsberg on the East Coast. He was through with California for a while. It had given him a stake, as well as *Visions of Cody, Doctor Sax* and *October in the Railroad Earth,* but Kerouac's next battle was with New York. He'd been a year out of circulation, and it was time to get back.

Chapter Sixteen

It was winter again when Kerouac got back to New York late in 1952. After the soft mornings and slow rains of California he was back in the grimy, winter streets of New York he'd known all the years he'd lived there. He had a little money. He'd saved over $1,000 from his months on the railroad, and he used some of it to fix up another apartment for his mother, another room he could come back to from the drunks and highs of Manhattan.

This time they moved to Richmond Hill at 94-21 134th Street, a shabby neighborhood of shingle houses and cement driveways and small, still streets a few blocks from the Long Island Railroad embankment. It was a smaller place, a two-storey frame house in a small yard, but his mother had quarreled with the people who'd taken over their old apartment in Ozone Park and she didn't want to go back to the old building, or the old neighborhood.

Jack had a tiny bedroom, but his bed was made, and in the dresser drawer he could find clean underwear anytime he needed it. For a few weeks he'd had enough of railroad bunks, rumpled beds, sleeping bags, hard, smelly floors where he'd slept on lost nights and gritty seats of Greyhound buses. There was some money from the railroad, unemployment compensation, enough to pay the rent. Mémère went back to the shoe factory to pay the rest.

It was a rushed winter for Kerouac. The wild, loose writing jag was still keeping him at his notebooks and his typewriter. In Jaunary 1953 he was back at work on the novel he'd broken off in Mexico. He kept driving on and the most consistent thing in his nervous life was the manuscripts that he kept piling up. But at the edges of his creative life, where he had to meet and deal with people, he was having more and more difficulty. He returned to New York to find everybody moving into new scenes and places, still with him if he wanted to come, but going on without him if he didn't. Uncomfortable, he found Allen tiresome, he thought Lu Carr was looking old and that Alan Ansen was stuffy. He was hard in his wariness of them, not sure in any way if they needed to make a space for him to fit into their lives.

They found him just as difficult to deal with. Allen wrote Neal that Jack seemed "all hung up on noise, noise,

167

music, bands," tea, excitement, organizing and creating artificial excitement. After Jack had made Allen his agent they'd exchanged long, detailed letters about *On The Road, Visions of Cody* and *Doctor Sax*, but when Allen tried to sit down with him to talk about writing he complained "he's too busy flitting from soul to soul like a hornet-bee whenever he comes to Manhattan."

Everything was intensified, rubbed to an even sharper edge over the dragging weeks of winter, by the other reality of his creative life. In his room, at his typewriter, he felt he was writing at a level of intense brilliance that he'd never sustained before, but nothing that he was writing was finding a publisher. Allen, who never wavered in his enthusiasm, responded as he always had to what Jack was doing, and despite Jack's awkward moodiness they were still close. When Jack sent him the manuscript of *Doctor Sax* from San Francisco, Allen liked it immediately, evidence of what Jack thought was their clairvoyance. Allen was touched by the manuscript's emotionalism. The image of Doctor Sax coming out of the shadows at night to peer into the windows of Jack's friends he thought of as a "freeze-frame" movie realization of "visionary tenderness."

But even Allen couldn't always remain in this kind of supportive role. He was also acting as Jack's agent, and he had to consider the manuscripts from their commercial point of view. Jack was painfully sensitive to any criticism, and despite Allen's care he couldn't help touching off outbursts when he tried to make suggestions of any kind. He mentioned that *Doctor Sax* was still a mystery and Jack reminded him that it wasn't the plot but love that gave life to their writing.

Jack was inexpressibly high with his work at this point, writing, he thought, like Shakespeare. If Allen or Lucien couldn't follow him in what he was doing then it had to be because they didn't love him, since what he was writing expressed his own self stripped raw and without barriers. But he had moments when he lost the brilliant sense of control that had given *Doctor Sax* its direction and its poise. His friends would find themselves reading prose passages that had become wild parodies of his style at his best. In the version of *On The Road* that he was reworking at the time a description of Neal began:

Bent over his wheel like a madman, shirtless, hatless, the moon leering on his shoulder, the apex of the night sweeping back in a fast shroud, he unrolled his old Ford . . . poor Crafeen, he made his mew in a churchyard marble pew. The bowl of old Okiah, flung from northern lips of stars, caromed from the baldy temple of the Lazy King; they brought news of a tune.

Of all the people he'd been close to, the one he was having the most difficulty returning to was John Clellon Holmes. Kerouac had come back to New York to find Holmes with a $20,000 advance for his first novel, the novel out to good reviews and Holmes already being used by the New York *Times* for articles on what the whole scene was about. His piece, "This is the Beat Generation," had appeared in the *Times* on 16 November, 1952, a month before Jack arrived in the city. Jack was extremely jealous of Holmes' success, jealous of his money and of all the dinners he was eating in expensive restaurants. As Jack described him, Holmes was spending all his time chasing and hailing cabs with his coat sleeves flailing around him.

The New York publishing industry finally catches up with everything that attracts any attention. There was already some tentative interest in the scene of pads, benzedrine and marijuana which Jack and all his friends had been through. Chandler Brossard had also come out with a novel, *Who Walk in Darkness,* about the Village scene and an alienated writer. Brossard's novel was conventional enough to be considered well-written, but he hadn't been part of Kerouac's crowd, and he had only contempt for the bohemianism which his book described.

Kerouac dismissed the book as completely unserious. He didn't feel Brossard really knew the scene at all. Brossard would have done better to leave Bleeker Street altogether and hang around Times Square instead, where he would have met the real hipsters, and not the literary pretenders downtown. But other readers were impressed. Kenneth Rexroth thought it was the first "Beat" consciousness book.

Holmes' book, *Go*, was, however, a different matter. Kerouac had to confront it, since he was one of its central characters. Holmes, close enough to them to describe their lives, was still different enough from them to have some objectivity about what he thought was their life style, and he'd used them as the people of his novel.

Kerouac was "Gene Pasternak," Allen was "David Stofsky," and Neal, "Hart Kennedy." Holmes himself, the central figure in the novel, was called "Paul Hobbes." He'd wandered into their scene the summer night that he'd gone to Allen's party in 1948, become a close friend of both Jack and Allen and had picked up the story from there.

He didn't try to follow the lines of their comings and goings, as they rushed in and out of the pages, with their raw energy wearing down Hobbes' reservations and hesitancies. A sense of the scene filled the pages, rather than a chronicle of lives and events. He always felt he wasn't really part of the group. As he said in *Go* he had an uneasy sense of "living an instant behind everyone else," unable to watch the hipsters on Times Square listening to bop without seeing them as "these restless youngsters" who heard in the music "something rebel and nameless that spoke for them, and their lives knew a gospel for the first time."

Go was in some ways a strained, nervous book, but it was also a book of sudden vividnesses, containing hard glimpses of reality. Holmes missed whatever it was about their lives that kept them so close as a group, but he did see them in ways they couldn't see themselves. His first description of Neal, when "Hart Kennedy" came to the apartment to borrow ten dollars, was sharp and direct. "Hart" (Neal) seemed to move with "itchy calculation," and gave an impression of "shrewd, masculine ugliness." When he put on a bop record, "Hart" immediately drew himself into the music, bobbing his head up and down and mumbling, "Go! Go!"

Holmes was also free enough of them to have a less romantic view of their involvements with each other. He could see Allen watching Neal with "adoring solemnity," as Jack played up to Neal and imitated him, trying to become "just like him, in a kind of way." He was close enough to Kerouac to know that he was sensitive about his mother working in the shoe factory, and Holmes knew that mémêre didn't like Allen. "Stofsky" said that when he goes to the house, "Pasternak's" mother was "nervously polite," she thought him "unclean." Kerouac had been coming to Holmes with manuscripts and notebooks since they'd first met, and Holmes described Jack's depression over the rejection of his novel by the first publisher: "I decided I wrote it because I wanted fame and money."

In *Go* "Gene Pasternak" (Kerouac) is always working on a new book or scribbling in his journals as he sits in cafeterias waiting for somebody to show up. The cross-country trips were left vague since Holmes didn't share any of them and didn't have a strong impression of how deeply Jack's life centered around them. One of the trips was a "penniless flight across the country in the Cadillac," a "wild week in Frisco," and a "lonely haphazard trek home again on the highways."

Holmes described the scene in New York, the pads, the music, the drinking, the chaos of lives and emotions, and despite the distance he felt from it, he did manage to get the raw feel of the scene into his book. He could keep his own distance from it because he always knew he wasn't part of it. He and his wife Marion (her involvement with Kerouac was one of the book's most emotional moments) tried to keep up with them, but in the novel at the end of "Stofsky's" (Allen's) long party on York Avenue she finally says, "We're *not* like them," and Hobbes doesn't argue with her.

Jack's first response to *Go* had been unconcerned and even generous. In March 1952, Holmes had cleared the title with him, because Robert Giroux had originally used the title for one of Jack's unpublished stories. Jack told Holmes to go ahead and use it. It had been the title for a story about himself and Neal listening to jazz, but he wasn't interested in the story or the title any more. But when he got back to New York and found Holmes suddenly successful he found it difficult to deal with the success, and for the next months their friendship was strained. To Kerouac he'd become an outsider who'd taken advantage of them, and he resented the description of his involvement with Holmes' wife, which he didn't feel was accurate.

Holmes' piece, "This is the Beat Generation," was the first attempt to define the new consciousness that Jack and the others around him shared, but Holmes always credited Kerouac with the term and the definition. What Holmes felt was "the youthful thirst, the restless exuberance, the quality of search, that pulsed in them. I felt it myself. Everyone I knew felt it in one way or another—that bottled eagerness for talk, for joy, for excitement, for sensation, for new truths. Whatever the reason, everyone of my age had a look of impatience and expectation in his eyes that bespoke ungiven love, unreleased ecstasy and the presence of buried worlds within."

Holmes remembered later that he "kept goading Jack to characterize this new attitude, and one evening as he described the way the young hipsters of Times Square walked down the street—watchful, cat-like, inquisitive, close to the building, *in* the street but not *of* it—I interrupted him to say that I thought we *all* walked like that, but what was the peculiar quality of mind behind it?" Jack answered:

It's a sort of furtiveness . . . . Like we were a generation of furtives. You know, with an inner knowledge there's no use flaunting on that level, the level of the 'public,' a kind of beatness—I mean, being right down to it, to ourselves, because we all *really* know where we are—and a weariness with all the forms, all the conventions of the world . . . It's something like that. So I guess you might say we're a *beat* generation.

Chapter Seventeen

Despite the first rattling of what was to become a rain of attention on the beat generation, Jack kept himself apart, even from his close friends. Since he'd first become involved with the others in 1944 Jack had felt himself different. He was to be a great literary artist, while they were always spending their lives with less important things. In him the center was himself, his own vision of himself.

He'd told Allen the year after they'd met that he thought his art was more important to him than anything, that was the difference between him and his friends, and he still persisted in keeping part of himself separate from the comings and goings in Manhattan. His life was still closely tied with his mother. He'd never left her, and their life went on together, despite his frantic trips into the city. She made it possible for him to remain inside his own vision of himself, and she made it possible, with her job, for him to go on writing his legend about this vision. Instead of trying to revise *On The Road* into a more popular book with the new "hipster" image he went on with a new book about his Lowell boyhood, continuing what he now thought of as the "legend" of his life.

He picked up where *Doctor Sax* had ended, just as he was entering high school. As he had written in *Visions of Cody* he thought of what he was doing as a sprawling epic, "my own complete life, an endless contemplation, is so interesting, I love it so, it is vast, goes everywhere." His mother didn't read the books, so they could talk without self-consciousness. He told her that he'd written a new book about Lowell in Mexico City, *Doctor Sax*, but it was in his new writing style and it would be hard for her to understand. But as Allen and Burroughs moved beyond his orbit, and Holmes began to get a popular audience, he felt the distance growing between them. He told himself that they weren't serious. They hadn't, like Jack, accepted the reality that the only true subject of poetry was death.

All of his life Kerouac had felt he had to be a hero, at least to give his life some larger dimension, and the contradictions in the way he was living and the way he viewed it were part of his other confusions. Writing about himself as "Peter Martin" in *The Town and the City*, remembering the excitement of reading *Shadow* magazines

173

when he was a boy, he described how "Peter" walked around the streets of Lowell cursing his life because it wasn't glamorous like Lamont Cranston's, alias the Shadow, a rich, elegantly dressed man about town speeding off in Yellow Cabs "to cope with the 'forces of crime.'"

One of the reasons that he left his first wife Edie was that life with her would have been too comfortable. As he later said, "There's no tragedy in Grosse Pointe." He felt there was tragedy in Lowell, and there was even more tragedy in what he saw as the epic of his own life: the difference between what he'd expected from life and what life was grudgingly giving up to him, the redbrick waiting behind the bright promise of America's neons. His struggle, as he conceived it, to become the best writer of his time, like Proust or Shakespeare, became in his imagination translated into the larger social framework of his disappointment with a visionary America, and finally into the largest framework of all, his obsession with mortality, with death and the end of all human wishes.

The next book went on with the legend, even if it didn't have as overwhelming a sense of the futility of his life. *Doctor Sax* had been his first attempt to use his life as myth. During a visit to the hospital in October 1951, just before beginning to "sketch," he'd read Melville's *Pierre* in the Hendrick's House edition, and he'd been excited by what Melville tried in the book, as the editor described in his introduction, to return to the "basic myth" of his origins in order to discover who he really was.

He told Holmes he'd "pre-written and meditated the plot long before" he moved into Burroughs' toilet with his notebook, so he could write it, even with interruptions, in only three weeks. The new book, the second in what he considered the legend of his life, took a little longer, two months, in January and February 1953. For him one of the most important decisions had been to write the legend of his life in sections, instead of as one book. Proust was strongly in his mind, and Proust's work was divided into separate novels. He later told Holmes,

I have to cut the 'Duluoz Legend' into suitable chronological lengths—I just couldn't pour the whole thing into one mould, if I did it would be a big round ball instead of figures. I suppose Lipschitz thought of this, one final big round ball sitting on a pedestal. But no, he divided his ball. Would Mozart blam all the 86 keys of the piano at once with his 86 fingers? or divide his ball into suitable symphonies, concerti, sonatas, serenatas, masses, dances, oratories . . .

With his mother again, in a quiet apartment where he could work, Kerouac felt he was able to write another book with epic quality based on the years of his life which followed those described in *Doctor Sax*. He had described them before in *The Town and the City*, but he had used the style of Thomas Wolfe and this was the wrong model. This time he was going to trust his instincts and write directly in his own language about his adolescence in Lowell. He began again in the room in Richmond Hill, using benzedrine to keep himself working, and, as he wrote Neal, limiting his life to writing and sleep. The new book was different from *Doctor Sax*, perhaps because he was living with mémère again, and they could talk over the years he was describing, and perhaps because the last two or three years of their life in Lowell, before they'd moved to Long Island, was closer to him.

The new book, originally called *Springtime Mary*, and published as *Maggie Cassidy*, had none of the fantasy of *Doctor Sax*. He may have been stung by Allen's comment that *Doctor Sax* was undigested fantasy and almost incoherent in parts because in the manuscript of *Maggie Cassidy* he followed a straight narrative line, perhaps even thinking of the book in more commercial terms, despite what he'd said about not changing anything for anybody.

Both *Doctor Sax* and *Maggie Cassidy* began with Jack and his boyhood friends out on a Lowell street horsing around. But in *Doctor Sax* the description dissolved into mixed levels of dream, vision and reality, while in *Maggie Cassidy* the boys were moving in a more or less direct line to a New Year's Dance, the dance where young Jackie meets his first love, the high school flirt he calls "Maggie Cassidy," who was actually the girl he'd fallen in love with when he was in high school in Lowell, Mary Carney. It was a romantic novel of love and adolescence, filled with his nostalgia for the innocence of his dreams at that age, a book about love denied; as Ginsberg described it, a novel about Kerouac's "rich adolescence and woetime."

The difference between Jack's story about his senior year in high school and the Lowell memories that had gone into *The Town and the City* was that in the new book he put himself in the center of the scene instead of dividing himself into several characters. In *Maggie Cassidy* the narrative was told in the first person, as he'd done with *On The Road*. Kerouac called himself "Jackie Duluoz." ("Duluoz" means louse in French-Canadian, a sardonic joke of Kerouac's, mocking his own exaggerated view of himself as the hero of his private legend.)

There was a distance between Jack and "Peter Martin," the character he most resembled in *The Town and the City*, a conscious moulding of "Martin" into a conventional figure of other books of the period. But as "Jackie Duluoz" he was closer to his subject, much more personally involved, caught in his wonder over the lost time of his youth.

His whole artistic approach to the book was simply to relive its confused days and long nights, almost as a Method actor would do, pushing himself into a state of heightened emotional intensity that he sustained with benzedrine. *Maggie Cassidy* was also different from *The Town and the City* in its mood of excited joy. He described himself as awkward and embarrassed, but also as happy. He spent much of the book with his friends, "Vinny," "Scotty," "Lousy," "G. J."—all of them French-Canadian like himself, except the Greek, "G.J." Like *The Town and the City* the most vivid moment was an athletic event, this time the spring track meet, where Jack won the 300-yard relay (in the earlier book it was the football game) and the writing was the most excited in the book.

For Jack the fantasy of being a football hero never fully lost its glamour. But everything was wonderful in the book, even the description of Leo Kerouac struggling to find a job in a blizzard in the heartless, redbrick commercial district of Lowell. Leo had been alive then.

Years later Jack and mémêre still mourned his death at home.

Despite the wonder and the joyousness of the prose in *Maggie Cassidy*, Kerouac was also haunted by memories of how awkward and uncomfortable he'd felt as an adolescent. Not the weary, bone-shattered fatigue he felt after hours of track, sprinting after school in late afternoon practice week after week, but instead how thick and clumsy he had felt wearing his heavy letter sweater in the overheated classrooms in high school, and how ineptly he had struggled in his naive lovemaking with Maggie, who broke away from him in one scene and told him:

"I wish you were older."
"Why?"
"You'd know more what to do with me . . . ."
"If . . ."
"No! You don't know how . . ."

He was hardest on himself in the book when he described himself at a surprise birthday party, his arms hanging at his sides in a photograph, hands joined over his fly but with a newspaper caption under the picture reading "LETTER ATHLETE HONORED." When he was at his best he thought of himself as he looked in a second picture, like a "Greek athlete hero with curly black locks, ivory white face, definite clear gray newspaper eyes, noble youth neck, powerful hands locked separate like regardant lions on the hopeless lap," looking as though he had "separate honors" reserved for him "in the dark corridors of this infinity." As he returned to the agony of his adolescence he could glimpse himself again as most adolescents see themselves, at once unable to deal with the immensities of life and at the same time blessed with the feeling of the uniqueness of their own experience.

But there was less confusion about his love for Maggie. It was a hopeless courtship that never could get beyond the simple fact that he was too young. When Jack wrote the book he told his mother there was nothing in it that she couldn't read, and if she wanted she could see the pages he'd written about Papa Leo. Her Jackie, in the book, was a virgin. Despite his prayers after the pain of the hours with Maggie, God never answered his prayers to arrange the success of his love for her. Mémêre had always disapproved of Mary Carney. She told Jack then that Mary was too impatient, wanting to get married before Jack finished his education, but there was nothing in the book that could worry her.

Even when Kerouac came back to Lowell before leaving to join the Navy three years after high school, determined to make love with Mary at last, he was still helpless against the women of his Lowell life. His mother had kept him from spoiling the "purity" of his love for Mary in high school. Mary herself had refused him in 1943 while he was back from Columbia. Then when he struggled with her in the back seat of a car he'd borrowed from a garage, Mary finally laughed in his face and left him to drive back alone, desperately drunk and swearing at himself.

For the rest of his life he wondered what would have happened to him if he'd married her after high school graduation, instead of leaving for New York. He kept trying to imagine himself settled in a little Lowell cottage with Mary, working the railroads, supporting a family of kids. In some essential way it was his most precious dream, even more precious than his memory of her, and since he never came even close to realizing it, it never left him.

After he finished *Maggie Cassidy*, the reality of his life and his frustrated attempts to be a great writer seemed as relentless as Maggie's laughter in the final sentences of his novel. He finished the typing, sure that Carl Solomon would take it for publication as an Ace book, as he'd done with *Junkie*. Under the terms of the option Kerouac had signed with him Solomon had the right of refusal for three manuscripts. He'd already turned down *Visions of Cody* and *On The Road*, and when he turned down *Maggie Cassidy* the terms of the agreement were ended.

Kerouac felt betrayed. He told Allen that the time had come for all "frivolous fools to realize what the subject of poetry is . . . death . . . so die like men . . . and shut up . . . and above all . . . leave me alone." He felt that his

New York friends had been laughing at him all along, and Solomon, with his own emotional problems, hadn't helped the situation. Since 1951 he'd been trying to advise Jack on how to write *On The Road*. At one point he wrote Jack that his "work heralds a renaissance of the American lower middle-class," while at the same time turning down his books. He advised Jack against drugs and offered him contracts for projects like editing an illustrated book on the bop era with Seymour Wyse and Jerry Newman.

None of this interested Jack except possibly the idea of taking a long sexual narrative from *On The Road* and making it into a 160-page twenty-five-cent paperback like *Junkie*, and with a real sales potential. When the last of the three manuscripts was rejected, despite its closeness to the theme and the story that he'd been successful with in *The Town and the City*, he was angry and shaken. He was no closer to success than he'd been when he'd started on the new book.

Since his option with Solomon and Solomon's uncle, A. A. Wynn, was over Jack found himself an agent, Phyllis Jackson, who was with the M. C. A. agency on Madison Avenue. She took the three manuscripts, *On The Road, Doctor Sax* and *Maggie Cassidy,* to try to place with a publisher. At the end of February 1953, just after he'd finished *Maggie Cassidy* and had it turned down by Solomon, Jack wrote Allen a formal letter stiffly informing him that he wouldn't give permission for the use of his name in any advertising for *Junkie* or with any publicity linking him with John Clellon Holmes as an expert on the Beat Generation. Any remarks Jack had made about "William Lee," Burroughs' pseudonym for the book, or the scene were at Ginsberg's disposal only through the proper channels, Jack's literary agency. Jack meant the letter seriously, but it was only a grandstand pose. Phyllis Jackson and M. C. A. couldn't sell *On The Road* or anything else for him, and two months later, in May 1953, he asked Allen, then working a job on the New York *World Telegram* as a forty-dollar-a-week copy boy, to be his agent again. Jack decided to leave once more for San Francisco, taking the bus to California to be a brakeman in San Luis Obispo.

Despite the disappointments about what was happening

to him, he still wasn't defeated. Yet he had to get away and live off by himself. Instead of Shakespeare and Proust, he thought of himself as Melville, worn out and exhausted after writing *Moby Dick* and *Pierre*. It was a ragged and nervous time for him. His mother was beginning to question him, wondering when the struggles would end. He couldn't tell her since he didn't know himself. He no longer felt that people understood what he was trying to do, and even Allen had to be told not to offer an edited excerpt of *Doctor Sax* to *New World Writing*, not understanding that Jack wanted the book published intact. It was time to get away from the East and try the West Coast again, so he got back on the Greyhound, intending to stay away for at least the rest of the year.

Chapter Eighteen

In California Kerouac found there was almost as little for him as there had been in New York. Neal was in the hospital, convalescing from a serious injury to his leg that had happened in March, several weeks before Jack, tired and almost desperate, showed up at the house. Neal had fractured his ankle while shunting boxcars at Millbrae, a small town not far from San Jose. A car-coupler had failed to work and a boxcar had gone rolling down the spur track. Neal had chased it, climbed aboard and had been trying to stop it with the handbrake when the boxcar had stopped suddenly at a bumper, throwing Cassady to the ground.

Jack had never been enthusiastic about the brakeman's job. It had been the only good paying job he could find, and he worked again briefly as a brakeman in San Jose, but Cassady's injury was upsetting. It didn't feel right hanging around the house. Neal later said he felt like Jack had "descended" on him so Jack took a job on a freighter sailing to Panama.

He worked as a waiter in the officers' mess, which he found easier than being a brakeman. He thought he could stay on board, traveling to Europe and the Orient, until he'd built up a large stake. His new plan, now, was to buy mémère a lot and a trailer so she'd have some place to live, while he would go to Paris and starve alone in a garret, writing.

He got enough out of the experience of the officers' mess to write a sketch about it, "Slobs of the Kitchen Sea," later published in *Lonesome Traveler*. But he didn't last long as a seaman. As he admitted himself he was incapable of acting like an ordinary man, never cracking a smile unless it was a superior one, and all because of that angel of loneliness riding on his shoulder.

In August 1953, three months after he'd left, he was back in New York, more unsettled, desperate and confused than ever about what direction to take next. It was a moment in his life when something had to happen, and, suddenly, something did. He found himself drawn into a brief involvement with a girl that was as close to a full love as he had ever come.

In *The Subterraneans*, the book he wrote about their affair, Jack called her "Mardou." She was a black girl he met after coming back to New York in the late summer of 1953, a new face among the new people hanging around Ginsberg's apartment in the East Village. Jack wanted her the moment he saw her. She was beautiful, with high cheekbones that reminded him of an Indian, a girl of such vibrant sexuality that he wanted to kiss her feet in her thronged sandals even before he was introduced to her.

She was a Village "subterranean" who'd been hanging out first with junkies, then musicians, and had just drifted into the circle that Allen knew in his new apartment on East 7th Street. It wasn't Columbia intellectuals now, like the people he'd known on York Avenue. This was a Village crowd, interested in poetry, jazz and drugs. Allen was interested in her, but decided he didn't want to get involved.

She didn't respond to Jack the first night they met.

181

He thought he probably looked like a hoodlum to her, a rough Canuck seaman. They went to a party with Allen and Lucien, smoked a little marijuana and listened to Stan Kenton. She told him later her impression was that he looked like a sad and lonely man, but the first night she went home alone, leaving him with a sullen determination to find her again.

At first he was sure that she was attracted to Allen, "thin ascetic strange intellectuals," instead of "big paranoiac bums of ships and railroads and novels and all that hatefulness which in myself is to myself so evident and so to others too." He saw himself, through all his unhappiness, as "the most conceited bastard who ever lived," and even with Allen telling him to go easy on himself he couldn't stop. The group had changed so completely that he felt himself as an outsider. The feeling had been coming on as he spent more and more time away from them, in California or with his mother, and now his sense of it was a reality.

It was more than just seeing himself as the most talented writer, as the serious one while the rest of them wasted their time. In the vocabulary of jazz he was hot and they were cool. He wore sport-shirts with loud Hawaiian prints or trying to look cool without any instinct for it, light blue shirts with freshly ironed slacks and crepe sole shoes. His mother thought he looked fine when he left the house in Richmond Hill for a night in New York, but at Allen's apartment everybody hung out in grimy undershirts, torn T-shirts and battered sneakers. He was the only one in blue silk shirts and pressed pants. He was the only one still living with his mother.

Jack had lived for so many years with mémère that he could never be part of the East Village scene. He couldn't live with beds that weren't made, sheets that weren't washed or the clutter of books and records that filled most of the apartments he drifted into. In some way he was involved with the details of his life with his mother, proud of taking care of her, escorting her to movies on weekends, mixing her a drink when she got back from work, sitting outside with her on hot summer evenings while she made small talk with the neighbors. He was involved in it, but he couldn't stand it for more than a few days perhaps, at most, a week. He had to break away, get into the Village to smoke marijuana, drink wine and listen to jazz.

When he got into Manhattan he was almost as unhappy. His desperation over his failure to get *On The Road* published, his inability to sell the manuscripts of the other two books, *Doctor Sax* and *Maggie Cassidy*, left him moody and belligerent with Allen as well. He was beginning to drink too much and too often, to badger Allen and Lucien, both of whom had steady jobs and a little money, to buy him drinks when the little money he'd gotten from his mother ran out. They tried to get him to slow down, to stop free-loading, but he wouldn't listen. But Allen was as willing as always to help Jack with whatever he wanted. Jack had a key to the apartment, and Allen finally brought him together again with the black girl, asking Jack to drop by on a night when he knew she'd be coming over for dinner.

This was the second time they saw each other, and after dinner Jack went home with her. They rode an East Side bus back to her apartment in Paradise Alley, a little courtyard on East 11th Street, off Avenue A on the Lower East Side. They danced a little to the radio, then turned out the lights and went to bed. Their affair lasted two months, its storminess and unhappiness matching what was happening to him in every other part of his life, his brooding paranoia finding its mirror image in the girl herself.

"Mardou" was completely adrift in the Village scene, cut off from her family and her background. After living with junkies she had begun to come apart, but when she went back to her family they committed her to a psychiatric hospital. She had come out of it a short time before Jack met her. Drifting in the Village, she stayed with whoever would have her, waiting quietly through all the endless parties until it was decided whom she'd go home with that night, smoking too much marijuana and being stoned too much of the time.

As Kerouac described the scene in the book, "Mardou" passed her time with the hipsters silently, passively waiting in "bohemian mystery, drugs, beards, semi-holiness and . . . insurpassable nastiness." Her story became the hippie trip in the East Village fifteen years later. She described herself as an innocent when she first met Jack and his friends. But she was independent and, though not particularly happy, had great plans about making it.

With his black girl, Jack felt in touch again with what he called "the fellaheen Darkness" in Mexico, sympathizing with her thoughts about the blacks and Indians and America. Her background reminded him of Neal's, with the same rootlessness, the same sad losses, and her beatness had the quality of the redbrick neons, further proof of the price of American life.

She made him think of Indians he'd seen crossing the country. They were the outcasts, going nowhere. Kerouac was moved and saddened by the vanquished Indians and the desperate blacks of America, but he was constitutionally unable to make his black girl happy by spending a full night with her. As soon as he woke up after their lovemaking he hurried home to Richmond Hill to keep his mother company at breakfast, making the coffee for her before she woke up so they could spend a little time together before she went off to the shoe factory. He tried to keep his mother from knowing about "Mardou," and he warned her away from the book he wrote about it afterwards. But she couldn't have missed his painful unhappiness when the affair suddenly ended.

Another of Allen's friends came back into New York in the late summer, the poet Gregory Corso. When Corso came into town in 1953 he was twenty-three, dark-haired, short, with strong eyes and brooding good looks. He was Italian, born on Bleecker Street in the Village in New York, but his mother had died and his father had abandoned him. He'd spent most of his life in institutions or jail. He began writing poetry in prison, and he had been sitting in a Village bar just after his release in 1951 when Allen saw him and began talking with him. Gregory showed Allen some of his writing, and Allen enthusiastically admitted him into their small group. As Gregory described it years later, "One night in a dark empty bar sitting with my prison poems I was graced with a deep-eyed apparition: Allen Ginsberg. Through him I first learned about contemporary poesy . . ."

Corso and Jack also first met in 1951, but they were

uncomfortable with each other. Gregory felt that Jack patronized him and insisted that as an older, more experienced writer he could teach Gregory "some words." Gregory did follow Jack and his girl when he got back to New York in 1953, but as he tells the story he only went over to the girl's apartment to wait for Jack and she insisted they lie on the bed and wrestle. "She was rough and I was just out of jail and she raped me. I told Jack and he cried and I said 'Oh shit.' " Corso was never comfortable about what happened, but looking back at all of it more than twenty years later the woman who was "Mardou" only shrugs. It was a long time ago, and none of it was that important to her.

"Mardou" still hung aroung the group, sitting at the edges of the loose parties Jack still went to, but their affair was over. For him it had been an unhappy two months, leaving him with his self-confidence even more shaken, and he had to get himself over it, to have the last word on what had happened. A few weeks later, in a sudden outburst he wrote his novel about their affair, the entire book finished in three long nights of nearly nonstop typing, his version of what happened.

The writing of *The Subterraneans* was one of Kerouac's most astonishing creative bursts, an emotional surge that almost drowns the pages in its relentless current. He got another long teletype roll from Lucien Carr, stuck it into his typewriter in mémère's kitchen, and "three full moon nights of October" later, keeping at it with benzedrine, he was finished. Later he thought of it as a fantastic athletic feat, because when it was over he was "pale as a sheet and had lost fifteen pounds and looked strange in the mirror." The novel took its emotional toll too. As he explained later to the publisher:

The book is modelled after Dostoyevsky's *Notes from Underground,* a full confession of one's most wretched and hidden agonies after an "affair" of any kind. The prose is what I believe to be the prose of the future, from both the conscious top and the unconscious bottom of the mind, limited only by the limitations of time flying by as our mind flies by with it.

The Subterraneans was closest in its narrative and its sexual detail to a Henry Miller novel, and later Miller wrote an introduction to the book saying that Kerouac's prose was as striking as his confession. When Allen read the manuscript he was astounded at the sound of the prose. Jack had succeeded in taking the way the girl spoke, her syntax and her style, and added his own interpolations and private thoughts which he put down simultaneously with her monologues and their conversations. The sentence structure had broken through to include private thoughts just above the level of consciousness, and yet it had the sound of American actual speech, all welded together by the muscular force of Jack's prose energy.

Both Jack and Allen had been fascinated by the way the black girl spoke. It seemed to them to be the cool sound of bop singers, a distinctive way of phrasing that drew out the syllables strangely. All the time Jack spent with her, he'd listened to the sound of her voice, before rushing back to Richmond Hill and working all morning putting down in his notebook his memory of what she'd said. Kerouac changed the locale of *The Subterraneans* before publication from New York to San Francisco, but otherwise it was as emotionally honest as anything he'd ever written.

When Corso read the novel, he thought Jack had given a true description of what happened, although Gregory persuaded him to cut out the sentences where Jack told how he had tried to kill Corso by picking up a table to throw at him: "Ah Jack, Jack, that isn't you, Jack." But the overall story was true, as Corso saw it, because Kerouac was still loyal to his friends despite the confusions and betrayals. What Jack had done on the first page of the book was to quote Allen, who had said that the subterraneans were intelligent, hip, intellectual but not pretentious and had a Christlike quietude.

Kerouac's pride in tossing *The Subterraneans* off in three nights gave him more lasting satisfaction than anything that happened between him and the girl that summer. Although he'd felt protective toward her, he never got that deeply emotionally involved. In part Jack was put off because of her blackness and her sexual frigidity, but mostly he could never be serious about her because she was not a Catholic. What excited him most was that she reminded him of Neal Cassady. She was a girl who'd suffered in her own life as Neal had, but chauvinistically Jack thought she'd only scratched the surface, she could never come close to the depths of Cassady's madness in her anxieties. He worried more about what his New York friends thought of him than anything the girl ever did, obsessed that the other writers wouldn't think he could live up to his boasts about being the most talented on the basis of his one published novel. *The Subterraneans* was his book to show them he was a genius, even if his emotional vulnerability was never more painfully evident.

He described the night he fought with Ginsberg ("Adam Moorad"), who objected when Jack ("Leo Percepied") got drunk with Gregory ("Yuri Gligoric") and stole a peddlar's wagon off the street. Jack couldn't take Allen's anger, and in a grandstand gesture tried to throw his keys to the apartment at Allen, but they got tangled up with mémère's house keys. The only way to end the fight was to pocket the keys again with a nervous laugh.

Kerouac had been dodging John Clellon Holmes, jealous of his success with *Go*, but he also wanted desperately to impress Holmes, and the resulting confusion was unsparingly described in *The Subterraneans* when Holmes dropped by Ginsberg's apartment one night. Jack was feeling neglected by the publishers and strung out on drugs, and when he heard Holmes in the apartment, he panicked at facing his literary enemy. He felt a little better thinking that Holmes, called "Balliol MacJones" in the novel, wasn't really part of the close-knit clan on East 7th Street which included Ginsberg, Corso and Burroughs, who was staying there and had brought a few *yage* vine cuttings with him from South America.

Jack forced himself into the living room to shake hands with Holmes. Then not quite able to pull it off, he sat down to brood, but as the talk whirled around him and he'd had enough to drink, he saw it as an historic moment, all the old gang together again in Allen's apartment, Holmes in his eighty-five-dollar suit and expensive wristwatch like a rich uptown visitor listening to

Jack's girl as if he were interviewing her for his next book.

The desperate effort to impress "Mac" continued later when the gang trooped out to hear jazz, Jack proud to have Holmes see him with the hip black girl who in some way affirmed his youth and potency. He ended the evening drunk, abandoning Mardou to pay her own cab fare home while he rushed off to see another friend in another bar. "MacJones" had gone home with his wife hours before, but Kerouac never knew when to stop.

When the affair with Mardou was over, there was still Allen's apartment and the old gang. Allen was saving his money for a trip to California via Mexico. Burroughs had talked for hours about the Indians and his experience with their hallucinogenic *yage*, and although he'd brought *yage* back to New York, Allen wanted to see Mexico and perhaps Central America for himself. Burroughs couldn't go back with him. He was pushing on to Tangier, where he thought he might try to live for a while.

There was no sense of permanence to the scene since Allen and Bill would be going separate ways in a few months, but while they were living together Jack hung around too. They were the only two people in the world who understood him and what he was trying to do as a writer. There are many photographs from this time at the apartment, when the friendship between Jack, Allen and Bill was at its most intense. Bill shirtless at the typewriter, Jack sprawling on the sofa while Bill lectured to him with a languid hand, Jack staring into Allen's eyes, involved in telepathic communication with a small primitive statue between them, Jack in a T-shirt and Allen bare chested, their faces only inches away.

After Jack turned out *The Subterraneans* in three nights, his friends insisted he put down exactly the method he had used writing it. They never questioned they were geniuses and that Jack's novels were totally original. Jack said it was all based on "jazz and bop, in the sense of a, say, tenor man drawing a breath, and blowing a phrase on his saxophone, till he runs out of breath, and when he does, his sentence, his statement's been made . . . that's how I therefore separate my sentences, as breath separations of the mind . . . . Then there's the raciness and freedom and humor of jazz instead of all that dreary analysis . . . ." They asked him to try to pin it down a little more closely, so as a favor to Burroughs and Ginsberg, he wrote out his "Essentials of Spontaneous Prose," Kerouac's major aesthetic statement in a lifetime of writing books.

In November 1953, a month before the group at the apartment on East 7th Street broke up, Jack sat down in front of his typewriter in Richmond Hill high on goofballs and wrote his two friends a letter. He just had to tell Allen and Bill he loved them. He knew they were leaving, that their closeness couldn't last long, that when they went off in three different directions something would be over. But when he tried to describe how he felt, he just couldn't do it.

Chapter Nineteen

Kerouac said over and over that life was only sorrow and suffering, and in the low, dark winter at the close of 1953 it was as empty and sorrowful as anything he'd gone through.

The affair with Mardou was over and so was the sudden closeness with Allen and Bill. They'd see each other again, but they'd left their apartment and left him to the cold bleak streets and grimy subways of winter New York. It forced him to begin a final, almost despairing effort to sell the manuscript of *On The Road*. The disappointments, the uncertainties of the struggle left him bitter for the rest of his life.

It was even harder with the relative success of *The Town and the City* behind him. He'd been through the struggle with editors and publishers once, there was no reason to go through it again. If he'd just gone on and written something like his first book he probably would have gotten it published after a minimum of negotiations and editorial assistance, but he'd broken the rules, he'd written a new kind of book, which meant that someone at a publishing house would have to use imagination, instead of old sales figures. It wasn't only that he believed in *On The Road*. He believed just as much in the way he'd written it. To him "spontaneous prose" was the beginning of a new literature. He tried to tell himself that he was too far ahead of his time. He kept remembering Joyce, and that a genius always was forced to struggle, but it didn't do much good as the months dragged past and the book stayed unpublished.

In the six years it took Jack to publish *On The Road* he wrote twelve books, so he didn't exactly spend the years moping. But in 1953 after writing *The Subterraneans*, he entered a different phase of his life, his most melancholy period. The furious energy that had gone into *Visions of Cody, Doctor Sax, October in the Railroad Earth, Maggie Cassidy* and *The Subterraneans* found a new outlet for a time, a new absorption. It was Kerouac's discovery of Buddhism, an enthusiasm that began early in 1954 at a time when he was feeling most lost and alone.

Kerouac was of course born a Catholic, raised a Catholic and died a Catholic. His interest in Buddhism was a discovery of different religious images for his fundamentally constant religious feelings. He always remained a believing Catholic. It was just that, for a time, he was a self-taught student of Buddhism. He read widely and deeply in Buddhist texts, translated sutras from the French, and even wrote a biography of the Buddha. But at the root of his absorption in Buddhism was the fact that he felt it offered him direct philosophical consolation for the disappointments in his life, and, particularly, for the drawn-out agony waiting to place *On The Road* and the refusal of publishers to recognize his genius.

Jack embraced the first law of Buddhism above all others, the statement that "All life is suffering." It seemed to him more succinct, more to the point, truer to his mood than the Biblical rhetoric of Christianity. It was as if the words had been written for him. His Buddhism was a tangled and personal matter, but its most immediate appeal to him was that it served as a defense and as a philosophic way of justifying his suffering to himself.

As always, Allen and Neal were involved in what Jack was doing, although neither of them took up Buddhism as fervently as Kerouac and it wasn't until ten years later that Ginsberg went to India. But in a way, Allen and Neal started Jack off on Buddhism. In the spring of 1953, while pursuing an interest in Chinese painting, Allen had read D. T. Suzuki's essays on Buddhism in the Philosophical Library Series, and had told Jack about them and sent a book of Zen stories to Cassady. Jack wasn't greatly impressed at the time, and it wasn't until the end of January 1954, after Jack had ridden buses and freights into San Jose to live with the Cassadys for the rest of the winter, that he had begun his serious reading in Buddhist texts.

He was hardly in the door the first night when Neal began talking to him about a new enthusiasm for the writing of Edgar Cayce, a California mystic whose books were attracting such wide attention that he'd become the center of a new spiritualist cult. After a hard, early winter in New York, Jack had looked forward to months loafing in the sun with Neal, whose ankle had healed and was waiting for his case for damages against the railroad to come up in March. Jack had saved enough money from a Christmas job at the post office to live easily for a while with the Cassadys, and he didn't expect there'd be anything going on with them in San Jose except the old routine. Neal was working this time at a parking lot and Jack stayed home with Carolyn and the kids, lying in the winter sun in the backyard cactus garden, drawing pictures in Cathy and Jamie Cassady's crayola notebooks, reading and listening to jazz records all afternoon until Neal came home to talk with him, later walking across the street to the store for wine to go with Carolyn's pizza, turning on when the kids were asleep, talking for hours into the tape recorder. This time Cassady was obsessed with his new interest in Edgar Cayce and didn't want to talk about anything else.

Jack began by disagreeing that Cayce was either important or had anything to say. Neal tried to explain

Cayce's "scientific proof" of reincarnation, and Jack scoffed. Cayce's ideas were dreary and second-hand, Jack argued, and if Neal were really interested in that sort of thing, he should throw away Cayce's books and read the original masters, the ancient books on Buddhism, instead of getting so excited about another California religious crackpot.

After Jack had finished *The Subterraneans* a few months before, he'd reread Thoreau, and in his loneliness in Richmond Hill trying to decide what to do with himself after Ginsberg had left for Yucatan and Burroughs had sailed to Tangier, he'd thought the only life for him would be to leave civilization and live like Thoreau. In his books Thoreau had talked about Hindu philosophy, so Jack went back to the library and checked out, purely by chance, *The Life of the Buddha* by Ashvagosa. He remembered it when Cassady started lecturing him about Edgar Cayce. Jack countered with the life of the Buddha, who renounced everything to teach that the cause of suffering is birth and that, as he saw it, the world and the individual soul didn't really exist and that life was a dream. The more he talked to Neal, the more Jack convinced himself that the words of the Buddha made sense.

Cassady was stubborn and wouldn't give way, and to hold his own in their nightly arguments Jack began to spend his afternoons in the San Jose libraries reading all the books on Buddhism he could find. All through February he sat reading in the public library, taking notes on Dwight Goddard's Buddhist Bible, the Baghavad-Gita, the Yoga Precepts, Vedic Hymns, Buddhist Sutras, the writings of Loh-tse and Confucius—a mammoth dose of Eastern Studies. By the end of the month he'd typed a hundred pages of notes from his reading, but arguing with Neal didn't get him anywhere. Cassady was sticking to what he understood, and Jack couldn't convince him that the wisdom of the East was worth a million Edgar Cayces. They mostly argued about immortality, Jack insisting that Cayce had been duped into belief in ego and self-nature, that there was no ego and no individual soul, that Cayce's belief in reincarnation was ignorant superstitution. Neal wouldn't budge, and finally Jack got tired of arguing with him.

By March 1954, even with bennies and goofs at the Cassadys', Jack was beginning to get restless. Allen was still in Mexico, living in Yucatan with a retired movie actress named Karen Shields, staying at her house in Chiapas, going into explorations after Indian ruins and caves. Jack wasn't sure whether he should go down to Mexico to join Allen, or return to his mother in Richmond Hill. Before he'd left New York he'd sent *On The Road* to Little, Brown, but they were taking months to read his manuscript, and the longer it dragged on the more discouraged Jack became.

He tried to lose himself in his library notes about Buddhism, almost as if he'd lost all sense of direction and movement in his own life. Neal was pushing the idea of Jack's staying in San Jose until Allen joined them, although no one was sure at this point when he'd come back. Before leaving for Mexico, Ginsberg had been so excited at the prospect of his trip that Jack had jokingly told Neal that Allen just discovered America had an ancient civilization of its own in Mexico, and you could reach it by second-class bus.

Finally, Jack got bored at Neal's house. He wasn't involved in any big writing projects, unlike his stay early in 1952, when he had *On The Road, Visions of Cody* and *Doctor Sax*. He fantasized about living under a tree by the railroad tracks, or moving into an abandoned adobe hut in Mexico, sitting and letting it all drift past him, but is was just daydreams. He'd decided that Neal was dead, and that they shouldn't just sit around waiting for Allen to show up. Cassady himself was happy with San Jose midget auto races and ball games, into being a calm family man, telling Allen he should come out West where men were men and the women were damn glad of it. His accident had momentarily slowed him down.

Not Kerouac. He was temporarily written out, but he was as restless as ever. The old arguments began again about why Jack didn't get a job. Neal wanted him to take over at the parking lot when he went back to the railroads, but Jack didn't like to drive cars and he wasn't happy as a brakeman. He felt he hadn't learned enough about it. After a near-accident the previous year with a string of boxcars he hadn't braked properly, he wasn't anxious to get back with the Southern Pacific.

Kerouac hung on for two months at the Cassady house until one night near the end of March their tensions exploded in a fight about who was to pay for some marijuana and how it was to be divided. It was a silly quarrel, but Jack felt it was time for a grandstand gesture. He packed his duffel bag and moved into the Cameo Hotel, a skid-row hotel downtown on Third Street in San Francisco.

Once again alone, he started a book, just as he'd done in his hotel in San Francisco in October 1952. This time it was to be a book of poetry he called *San Francisco Blues*, which he wrote sitting in a rocking chair, "looking down on winos and bebop winos and whores and cop cars" out his window onto the street. The poems were freight train blues, marijuana poems marked by nostalgia and weariness. They were very different from the rushing enthusiasm of *October in the Railroad Earth*. The poetic line was unrhymed and unstressed, a gentler and slower version of his sketching in *Visions of Cody* and *Railroad Earth*:

> Rhetorical Third Street
> Grasping at racket
> Groans and stinky
> I've no time
> To dally hassel
> In your heart's house.
> It's too gray
> Im too cold—
> I wanta go to Golden,
> That's my home . . . .

Jack found a drinking buddy in a black writer named Al Sublette, who lived in the Bell Hotel on Columbus Avenue, but mostly Jack just loafed alone with sweet wine and marijuana in his room, scrawling poems as they occurred to him watching out the window onto Third Street as days and nights came and went. The drizzling, damp San Francisco winter entered his bones, despite the bed quilt he pulled over himself on the rocking chair. The rain beading his window was soft and gray, entering into his imagination, drifting soundlessly over the window-pane.

> The taste of worms
> Is soft and salty
> Like the sea,
>   or tears

The poems in *San Francisco Blues* had traces of Jack's reading in Buddhist philosophy in the San Jose library the previous month, but only traces. He'd concentrated all his notes into the hundred-page manuscript *Some of the Dharma*, an account of Buddhism (never published) he thought of as a study guide for Allen when he'd typed it up at the Cassady house. He wrote it on mari-juana, and later he thought some of what he put down was useless because of this, but, nevertheless, he intended the manuscript as a sendoff for Allen into the basic Buddhist texts. It was how he had found the path, and he hoped Ginsberg would follow.

Allen had written he'd arrive at the Cassadys' in June 1954, but, by the middle of April, Jack was back in Richmond Hill, after riding a bus across the country again. He was still upset with Cassady, still arguing with him about Edgar Cayce, telling Neal he didn't believe in karma and that although the world was just a manifesta-tion of mind, he was still living in it.

Neal was into Gurdjieff and Ouspensky as well as Cayce, and Jack felt it all was a dead end. From Cassady's side of it, their quarrel just underlined Kerouac's obstinate unpredictability, with his rushing off after a meaningless argument to live in his three-dollar hotel room, then suddenly phoning to say he was taking off for New York. Neal thought it was because Jack had "drunk himself blotto" with Al Sublette, but he didn't have enough money to live by himself very long at the hotel waiting for Allen.

Back with mémère Jack tried to lead a quiet, meditative life in his room, still waiting for Little, Brown to decide about *On The Road*, which he'd retitled *Beat Generation*. While editors read his manuscript, he took a railroad job on the Brooklyn waterfront to help his mother with the rent. He switched cars off the floats on the docks at $18.35 a day until the physical strain of braking cars was too much for his legs and the phlebitis stopped him again. He'd worked less than a week, but mémêre told him to take it easy, so he stayed home planting a vegetable garden in the backyard with beans and potatoes.

The work reminded him of Thoreau's garden patch at Walden Pond, and he wrote Allen that if his mother asked him to leave, he'd go to El Paso to wash dishes, saving money to live across the river in Mexico for four dollars a month in an adobe hut, reading Buddhist texts and eating bean stews, living the ascetic life. He was very restless, feeling that everything was changing or on the verge of change, but he wasn't at all settled in the new life, nor even sure how to define it.

As summer began Jack spent some of the time typing *San Francisco Blues* and another work called *Book of Dreams* from the notebooks he'd kept over the past two years, still unable to lose himself in his work, telling his mother he just wanted to live a quiet life, yet rushing into Manhattan when she gave him a little money to get drunk in Village bars, talking to old friends like Holmes, Henri Cru, Lucien Carr, John Kingsland, Alan Ansen or whoever wandered into the San Remo on Saturday night. Early Sunday morning he'd stumble onto the subway for the ride to Richmond Hill, falling asleep to nightmares in his own bed, waking up repentant, promising mémêre he'd have a week of abstinence working in the garden and at his typewriter. For a few days he'd feel great, but by the weekend he'd be bored again, wondering what to do with himself.

It was the same as the pattern of the summer before, but there was no intense love affair, no welcoming apartment in the East Village with Allen or Bill waiting to hear what he'd written next. Instead, he saw more of old Horace Mann friends like Henri Cru and Jerry Newman, who had started a record company, Esoteric, and wanted Jack to work for him rounding up jazz musicians and writing album notes.

But the parties wearied him, and at thirty-two he said the young girls made him feel old. Lucien Carr, whom mémêre didn't like, sneaked into the house with bottles of Irish whisky and they drove around Long Island and New Jersey saying hello to old girl friends like Dusty, Alene and Helen Parker. Jack even made a date to read *The Subterraneans* with "Mardou" and left the manuscript with her. When he went back to get it, she was in bed with someone else, and while Jack waited in the hall he could hear the man say that she'd have to publish it herself since nobody else would. Kerouac wanted to break down the door, but finally they opened it and gave his book back to him.

By the middle of the summer, when Allen asked Jack how his Buddhist studies were coming along, he admitted that the philosophy was a little too ascetic for him. He was more into Chinese philosophy and the Tao. Asceticism and yoga were hard for him. While continuing to think of himself as a student of Buddhism, Jack fluctuated constantly in his attitudes toward it. With friends like Lucien Carr or Burroughs, whom he knew were unsympathetic, he tried to be the way he thought they were. Writing to Ginsberg or to Carolyn Cassady, whom he felt sympathized with his religious feelings, Jack insisted that Buddhist and Taoist texts justified his belief that he was too weak to live a normal life.

This was in early May 1954, but a few weeks later Jack was involved in an affair with a junkie so crazy that he admitted to Allen that when he put down sex and women, he was talking through his hat. Through the summer of 1954 he drifted with the parties and the girls, periodically getting disgusted with himself and dipping back into his notes on Buddhism. He only really became deeply involved in trying to practice Buddhism several months later.

The delays and the disappointments with *On The Road* were taking their toll. Little, Brown turned down the manuscript in June, after having kept it nearly six months. Kerouac didn't know where to turn, and in a fit of despair he began working on it again, changing the character of "Ray Smith" (which was then his fictional name in the novel) into a Buddhist, not sure what he was doing anymore. The previous year, with Allen's encouragement, he'd shown the manuscript tc Malcolm

Cowley at Viking Press, who'd been impressed with it but wanted revisions. Although Jack had then contemptuously refused, now he listened halfheartedly to Cowley and agreed to show parts of the novel to Arabelle Porter of *New World Printing*.

Jack didn't want *On The Road* to appear in bits and pieces but Cowley persuaded him that if enough sections were published first in annuals like *New World Writing*, he'd have no trouble getting Viking to accept it. Cowley was also going to mention Kerouac in his new book, *The Literary Situation*, as one of the new writers who called themselves "the beat generation." As Cowley said in his book, "It was John Kerouac who invented the phrase and his unpublished long narrative, *On The Road*, is the best record of their lives." Largely acting on Cowley's enthusiasm for *New World Writing*, Jack worked on an excerpt for Arabelle Porter, trying to combine prose from *On The Road* with *Visions of Cody*, telling Allen he was more excited about seeing sentences from *Visions of Cody* in print than any from *On The Road*, which he was sick of by this time.

When Cowley next suggested that Jack send *Paris Review* the chapter about picking cotton with the Mexican girl in *On The Road*, Jack didn't protest. He'd been paid $120 for the first excerpt, more money than he'd made in years from his writing. After "The Mexican Girl" appeared eighteen months later in *Paris Review*, it was judged one of the best stories of 1955 and included in Martha Foley's yearly collection.

But the recognition came too late. Jack had come a long way from the ecstasy he'd felt writing *On The Road* on the teletype sheets in 1951. The manuscript was revised many times before being excerpted in 1955 and he was to go over it again with Cowley before Viking published it in 1957. The books which Kerouac believed in even more as evidence of his genius—*Visions of Cody*, *Doctor Sax* and *The Subterraneans*—were still without publishers. He told Arabelle Porter not to use his full name as the author of "Jazz of the Beat Generation." It was to appear only under the name "Jean-Louis," almost as if he were publishing it as a spoof, like the poem he'd done with Allen years before in the Columbia *Jester*.

After all the years trying to get *On The Road* published, being proud of himself for not trailing after Holmes' success with *Go* with just another novel about the "beat generation," Jack tried to maintain some shred of what he considered his artistic integrity. He wasn't even sure about what to do with the $120 from the story. Earlier in the summer of 1954 he'd thought of riding a bus back to California to see the Cassadys' new house, bought with the money from the railroad settlement, and having a grand reunion with Ginsberg there.

Jack even imagined Burroughs dropping by from Tangier so the old gang could be together again all night talking with Bill and himself drinking wine, Allen holding up his index finger, lecturing them about the Indians in Yucatan, Neal smoking hash and Carolyn making pizza pies and pouring wine. But when Allen had stayed in the house on his way from Mexico to San Francisco, there'd been a quarrel between him and Carolyn, and Jack knew he couldn't reassemble the East Village scene with Ginsberg and Burroughs in Cassady's suburban house in San Jose. He decided not to spend the $120 on a bus ticket to California, telling Allen if anything he was going nowhere.

Chapter Twenty

Life had never seemed emptier. At the end of the summer of 1954, when the trees in front of his mother's house drooped in the September heat, then turned brown with leaves curling on the sidewalk in the October wind, Kerouac dreamed of the autumn freshness of his old Pawtucket neighborhood in Lowell. Instead of another cross-country trip, he rode a bus upstate to New England to walk the streets of his boyhood, lost in his past. He checked into a cheap hotel near the bus depot and walked twenty miles every day, until he was exhausted.

Revisiting the scenes of his early years reinforced his inspiration. His memory had kept a perfect image of the haunted castle above the house on Lupine Road where he'd been born, although he hadn't seen the castle since he was three years old. He thought of the Duluoz Legend as growing to fill thirty-five volumes, full of detail, but the idea wearied him for the first time, and he wondered if he should bother with so much repetitious detail. It was only in his old church that he really felt rested and momentarily at peace. In his boyhood church, where he'd had his first communion, he sat alone meditating in the silence, and unexpectedly he had an insight that seemed terribly significant to him.

Thinking about how down and out he felt, or as Huncke would have said, how beat, Kerouac suddenly realized that beat had another meaning, a religious interpretation. Beat meant beatitude or beatific.

It seemed like a divine illumination. His mood was no longer down like a Times Square junkie, but seemed to share the wisdom of the vanity of all human wishes, the wisdom of a legendary saint. When he went back to Richmond Hill, he read and meditated on his Buddhist texts more resolutely than ever before, convinced that his religious devotions would lead him down a true path of spiritual wisdom and personal salvation.

After his experience in Lowell, Jack felt that Cassady might be right about reincarnation and he even considered whether Neal might not be his brother Gerard reborn. Desperately he clung to his belief that beat meant beatific. This connection was far more than a verbal pun to Kerouac. He embraced loneliness and humility as though they promised personal salvation, for the first time trying to live out his Buddhism. Like a religious penitent, he even extended the full force of his sympathy to Cassady, trying to subdue his egotism and bury their old quarrels, hoping to come close again.

Jack told Neal that he was the best writer still, and if he could help in any way he'd be glad to do it, especially with the typing, which went so hard for Cassady.

Jack Kerouac at Horace Mann School, 1940.

Jack Kerouac at Lowell High School, 1939.

Kerouac's birthplace, Lowell, Massachusetts.
Photo by Ann Charters.

Jack Kerouac and Lucien Carr, 1944, Columbia University.

(Left) William Burroughs and Jack Kerouac playing a scene from Dashiel Hammett, 1945. Photo Credit: Allen Ginsberg. (Below) Hal Chase, Jack Kerouac, Allen Ginsberg, William Burroughs, Riverside Drive, New York, 1944

Herbert Huncke in Texas, summer 1947. Photo credit: Allen Ginsberg.

Gregory Corso, Allen Ginsberg, New York City, 1951.

Neal Cassady, New York City, 1946.

Neal Cassady, New York City, 1946.

Jack Kerouac and Neal Cassady, California, 1949.

Neal Cassady and Jack Kerouac, San Francisco, 1949.

Jack in California with the Cassadys, 1951.

Neal, John Allen and Carolyn Cassady, 1955.

Jack Kerouac, New York City,
1953. Photo by Allen Ginsberg.

Carolyn Cassady: "Neal in Heaven—an old car and a girl." Photo credit: Allen Ginsberg.

As a teenager, Jack lived with his family in the upstairs apartment. Lowell, Massachusetts. Photo by Ann Charters.

John Clellon Holmes, 1951. Photo by Ann Charters.

William Burroughs, Tangier, 1957. Photo by Allen Ginsberg.

Jack Kerouac, Tangier, 1957. Photo by Allen Ginsberg.

Jack Kerouac, Allen Ginsberg, Peter Orlovsky (standing, left to right), Gregory Corso, Lafcadio Orlovsky (kneeling, left to right), Mexico City, Zocalo, 1956.

Gary Snyder in his Berkeley cottage, 1956. Photo credit: Allen Ginsberg.

Michael McClure, San Francisco, 1955.

Lawrence Ferlinghetti and Gregory Corso in San Francisco, 1969. Photo by Ann Charters.

Shirley Holmes and Jack Kerouac in Old Saybrook, Connecticut, 1960s. Photo by John Clellon Holmes.

The main street of the French-Canadian section of Lowell, Massachusetts. Photo by Sam Charters.

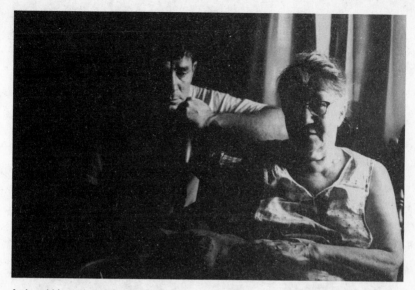

Jack and his mother, Gabrielle Kerouac, 1966. Photo by Ann Charters.

John Clellon Holmes, Allen Ginsberg and Gregory Corso at Kerouac's funeral, Lowell, Massachusetts, 1969. Photo by Ann Charters.

Allen Ginsberg and Ann Charters, New York City, 1967. Photo by Herbert Huncke.

All Neal had to do was scribble his thoughts, send them to Jack, and Jack would type them up and ship them right back.

By December 1954, however, despite his newly discovered beliefs Kerouac felt at the lowest point of his life. At home mémère offered strong resistance to what looked to her like Ti Jean's heretical conversion to Buddhism. She was a believing Catholic, who always wore her religious medal pinned to her dress or apron, and when Jack tried to talk to her about the sutras he was reading or about his efforts to meditate, she was openly contemptuous.

Her anger was stirred also by learning that Jack's second wife was suing him for child support, threatening to put him in jail if he refused. Mémère was still supporting Jack herself, and the idea that he might go to prison if Joan Haverty won her case caused both Jack and his mother alarm. Almost in desperation, he began expanding *Some of the Dharma* into a diary of his moods, including his translations of the Buddhist sutras he was reading in French texts, considering it much more than Buddhist notes for Ginsberg.

After Christmas, mémère decided to stay on with Nin in Rocky Mount, and she persuaded Nin to let Jack live there with the family for the spring. In January and February he stayed alone in Richmond Hill, pulling himself together a little. He had a literary agent called Sterling Lord whom Robert Giroux had sent him to, and although Jack still complained bitterly that all his manuscripts were laying in his agent's drawers, he agreed to retype *On The Road* once more, on the chance that Knopf would buy it. It didn't take them long to turn it down, saying the writing was good but the subject was too limited. Jack's agent sent the book on to Dutton.

In January 1955, Joan Haverty took him to court for child support, as Jack blustered that he couldn't possibly have fathered their daughter. He'd never even seen the child, named Michelle Kerouac, born in February 1952, but one look at her photograph in the courtroom brought him up short. All his life he publically kept denying she could possibly be his daughter, but privately he wrote Allen that the little girl looked like him. Jack's lawyer was Allen's brother Eugene Brooks (he had changed his last name), and they were demanding that Joan Haverty make a paternity test, hoping to show evidence that Kerouac couldn't have been the father of the child.

As it turned out, the test wasn't necessary after Jack showed the judge a letter from a doctor saying that he had an acute condition of phlebitis in his legs and was unfit for regular employment. The judge, who presided in a court filled with indigent black fathers and welfare mothers and children, immediately suspended the matter, telling Eugene Brooks that if the father were disabled, the case would be set aside. After taking a close look at Jack in court, Joan Haverty didn't insist.

He had come to the trial as if it were the prelude to an irrevocable prison sentence, taking along with him a large manila envelope filled with his Buddhist Bible and hundreds of pages of his own notes on the sutras. He showed the envelope to his ex-wife, explaining he was working on another book called *Some of the Dharma*, but Joan didn't take him seriously. So long as he made no attempt to see their daughter, she promised she wouldn't insist on child support, and she even teased him about the idea that he could write a book about Buddhism, implying he was joking but they could each play their own games.

Buddhism wasn't a game to Kerouac at this point. He was still drinking wine and taking bennies to retype *On The Road* in Richmond Hill, taping his legs with long bandages when they began to swell after too much benzedrine. But he was absolutely serious about his religious studies. He wrote Allen that he was on the way to becoming a Bodhisattva, a religious teacher, and that when they met again he would be Allen's teacher. Jack read the Diamond Sutra every day: on Sunday the Dana Charity chapter; on Monday the chapter on Sila Kindness; Tuesday, Kshanti Patience; Wednesday, Virya Zeal; Thursday, Dhyana Tranquility; Friday, Prajna Wisdom; Saturday, the conclusion of the Sutra.

He started memorizing passages to discipline his mind, getting down on his knees to pray in the empty apartment for long hours, reciting the sutras, and reading the

Buddhist Bible (Dwight Goddard's edition of Buddhist texts) in any spare minute. Riding the subways to New York he tried to see through the shabbily dressed people sitting on the hard benches and the cellophane and dust on the dirty subway floors, trying to train himself to perceive the rumpled cellophane with as much love as he felt for the memory of his brother Gerard, since both were intrinsically the same essence.

He described to Ginsberg how he meditated at home in his bedroom, first drinking a small cup of green tea, then locking his door, sitting down on a pillow with folded legs, and breathing gently for twenty minutes to quiet his mind, listening to the sound of silence in the room, trying to relax his cramped muscles and enter samadhi. His legs, already suffering from insufficient blood circulation with phlebitis, pained him excruciatingly in the crossed-leg posture.

Jack tried to stand the pain as long as possible, and then, stoically, sat one minute more, before he allowed himself to scramble to his feet and rub his legs to restore circulation. If he could, he then sat down cross-legged again for another attempt at meditation, trying to do it often every day for as long as he could stand it. He decided that meditation was an athletic accomplishment, and that the muscles he'd developed earlier playing football and running track were only a preparation for sitting cross-legged on the floor, closing his eyes and joining his hands before Buddha. At its best, meditation calmed him into a state of ecstasy, as he described in a poem for Allen, "How to Meditate."

> — lights out —
> fall, hands a-clasped, into instantaneous
> ecstasy like a shot of heroin or morphine,
> the glands inside of my brain discharging
> the good glad fluid (Holy Fluid) as
> I hap-down and hold all my body parts
> down to a deadstop trance—Healing
> all my sickness—erasing all—not
> even the shred of a "I-hope-you" or a
> Loony Balloon left in it, but the mind
> blank, serene, thoughtless. When a thought
> comes a-springing from afar with its held-

forth figure of image, you spoof it out,
you spuff it off, you fake it, and
it fades, and thought never comes—and
with joy you realize for the first time
"Thinking's just like not thinking—
So I don't have to think
    any
    more."

The religious discipline continued in the early spring of 1955, once he moved in with Nin's family outside Rocky Mount. It was a very quiet life. Jack's official position in the family was baby-sitter for his seven-year-old nephew Paul, although for a time he helped his brother-in-law clear some ground to build a new house, cutting trees and burning stumps, digging ditches, sawing and carrying planks. It wasn't until nighttime that he could study Buddhism, waiting up until everybody had gone to bed, sitting at the kitchen table after the dishes had been cleared away and washed, now working on a biography of Buddha titled *Wake Up*, as well as his sutra translations.

There wasn't any privacy with his mother and sister's family around, but as the spring weather grew warmer Jack moved outside to sit by himself for hours, meditating under the clear night stars. Probably his best friend in the house was his brother-in-law's hunting dog, usually tied up in the backyard. Jack would untie him for walks in the pine woods behind the house, skirting the fields of tobacco and cotton.

For a few months he fantasized about living the rest of his life as a religious recluse, studying and meditating and translating sutras, renouncing the world. He sat up until late in the backyard on a lawn chair sipping what he called moonshine cocktails, homemade punch of orange juice, ice, ginger ale and white lightning, whatever he could forage in the pantry to mix with the locally distilled cheap alcohol. After he'd been in Rocky Mount a while, he wrote Allen that he felt happier and more rested than he'd been in years.

He was finding deep satisfaction in his Buddhist studies, relaxing over the compilation of *Some of the Dharma*, by now a large loose-leaf folder of several hundred pages of typewritten sheets. Each page was covered with religious aphorisms, thoughts, quotations from his reading and haikus which he thought of as being like children's poems, but similar to Buddhist koans in their simplicity. He arranged each page in the loose-leaf folder in elaborate patterns, trying for a Mondrian effect with pencil lines drawn in rectangles around the poems, designing the pages separately and with great care as he went along, taking hours at it as a labor of Mahayana Buddhism.

Perhaps Kerouac found his greatest solace in copying out Buddhist precepts for disciplining his mind to accept the long wait, and the daily trips to the mailbox by the side of the country road to find out from his agent if any of his manuscripts had been sold. Kerouac plunged into translating sutras from the French, themselves translations from the Tibetan of the Mahayana Samgraha of Asanga, a great scholar of the first century. He even thought he might make his living as a translator, instead of pinning his hopes on what Sterling Lord could do with the manuscripts of his novels. But translating brought him no money. Sterling Lord, Robert Giroux and Malcolm Cowley read his translations, gathered together under the title *Buddha Tells Us*, and turned down the manuscript. Jack next offered it to the Philosophical Library. They wrote back they would print it if he could guarantee sales of six hundred copies at $3.50 a book. Jack was indignant. He didn't know if he could even guarantee one friend who could come up with $3.50.

By the summer of 1955, Jack's sister and brother-in-law began to ask when he planned to leave. They didn't believe in his writing. "Jazz of the Beat Generation" appeared in *New World Writing* in April 1955, but it didn't seem to them to justify his laziness, and they had nothing but contempt for his belief in Buddhism. His sister lost her temper and said Jack thought he was God. Jack accused her of being jealous and the battle was on.

He went up to New York for as long as he could, borrowing ten dollars from mémêre and hitchhiking both ways. In May, he lunched with Malcolm Cowley, who thought he could help with *Doctor Sax*, but nothing much was accomplished except that Jack got drunk on the martinis. In June, Robert Giroux told him *Doctor Sax*

221

was magnificent but he couldn't publish it. Sterling Lord was doing what he could, sending *The Subterraneans* to Criterion Press, and *Doctor Sax* to Noonday Press, but he got back only rejections. Jack always ended up in the Riviera Bar in the Village, mooching drinks from old friends, boring them with talk of Buddhism, suddenly desperate for company after Rocky Mount, sleeping on Lucien Carr's floor or in the apartment of an old friend, Helen Parker, until he was too flat broke and disgusted to hang around any more, at which point he would hitch-hike back to Rocky Mount.

He was too unhappy, and too undisciplined, to follow the Buddhist precept that drunkenness is as reprehensible as it is productive of bad karma. He still felt himself an apprentice Bodhisattva, but at drinking he was an old hand.

From the solitude of Rocky Mount, he wrote long letters to Ginsberg in San Francisco and Burroughs in Tangier, trying to salve his own loneliness by talking to them through his typewriter. Burroughs, who Jack knew was totally unmoved by Buddhism, didn't get letters with reading lists in the sutras, like those Jack was sending Allen. Instead Kerouac told him about a science fiction story he was writing, later published as the sketch "city City CITY." He suggested to Burroughs that if they could get together in Tangier they could collaborate on a full novel. "city City CITY" was just the short story version, and together they'd produce a hilarious satire. Jack had told Allen that after a *Buddhist Handbook*, he wanted to write *Visions of Bill*, which would consist of spontaneous studies of Burroughs that would be wilder than *Tristram Shandy*.

Even the letters grew thin after a while, and it was obvious to everyone at Rocky Mount that Jack would have to leave. His only income was earning seventy-five cents an hour helping his brother-in-law move television sets, and he told his family he was only waiting until he had saved enough to hitchhike to San Francisco. Once in California he planned to get twenty-five dollars from the blood bank, then try to get a fifteen-dollar-a-night job at the Southern Pacific baggage room. His plans for making a living shifted constantly and his problems were aggravated by the fights he was having with his family about Buddhism. After the months in Rocky Mount, all he could think of was a quiet place of his own, a little hermitage, although he had no idea where. His friend, Al Sublette, had told him in San Francisco that what Jack really wanted at the bottom of his heart was to live like Thoreau in a thatched hut in Lowell, and Jack agreed completely.

The best idea he could come up with himself was to propose to Allen that they live together as hermits in Mexico after Jack got his stake in San Francisco. If Allen could collect California Unemployment they could live in an adobe hut on the border for ten dollars a week and save the rest of Allen's checks for their bus-fare back to New York or even a ship to Tangier. Ginsberg could collect thirty dollars a week, and Kerouac thought that if they tried really hard they could live together on five dollars a week, saving nearly $100 a month.

The plans he wrote Allen had a ring of desperation, but in July 1955 suddenly Jack's fortunes changed. Malcolm Cowley and an editor at Viking Press, Keith Jennison, agreed to accept the manuscript Jack was then calling "Beat Generation." It was published as *On The Road* two years later. Jack was so grateful he even apologized to Cowley for being so difficult over the problem of revisions.

Cowley remembers that he had been greatly impressed with *On the Road*. But he was only an advisor, not an editor, at Viking, and he did not succeed in "infecting others at Viking" with his enthusiasm until Keith Jennison read it too, and their joint enthusiasm carried the day. Cowley and Kerouac began to plan revisions in the manuscript. As Cowley recalls,

I thought there should be some changes to make it more of a continuous narrative. It had swung back and forth between East Coast and West Coast like a huge pendulum. I thought that some of the trips should be telescoped, and Kerouac agreed and did the job . . . All the changes I suggested were big ones, mostly omissions. I said why don't you boil down these to two or three trips and keep the mood of the content.

Kerouac was elated with the Viking contract, and the good news kept coming in. "The Mexican Girl" was sold to the *Paris Review*, and with Cowley's endorsement he was awarded an Academy of Arts and Letters grant of $200 so he could work on a new novel. There was no longer any need to think about living in an adobe hut on the Mexican border on Allen's unemployment checks. Kerouac headed south by himself to Mexico City for a good time. His Buddhist translations, poems and biography were behind him for awhile. With his confidence renewed, he went back to writing about his one central concern, himself.

Chapter Twenty-One

Once back in Mexico City, Kerouac went right to the apartment house at 212 Orizaba where he'd lived before with Burroughs, near the Cine Mexico, the trolley cars and the lush green park with a splendid fountain. Burroughs was no longer living there, but Bill's old New York friend William Maynard Garver (called "Bill Gains" in *Junkie*) had a ground-floor room facing the noisy street.

In no time at all, Jack made himself at home. With *On the Road* sold to Viking, he had a little money. For the first time in years he wasn't up against the prospect of being a brakeman, hustling baggage at the Southern Pacific or selling a pint of blood in San Francisco. As Allen remembered him at the time, Jack was expansive and high, almost triumphant with his sense of his own genius, as Allen said, a "great beautiful open earth-buddy, sweet prince studying Buddha and great prose Melville Jack . . ."

Kerouac rented himself a room for a month on the hard adobe roof of the house, reached by climbing up two flights of stairs past the rapid chatter and music from the crowded apartments of Mexican families, the entire building rundown and falling to ruin, the last flight of thin, metal stairs creaking and cracking against the nails holding it to the crumbling stucco walls. The roof was slippery, flat and full of puddles, with wash flapping on the lines. It was rimmed by a low, two-foot railing that looked totally insubstantial, so that Jack was nervous walking on the roof, afraid he might slip on the slick adobe floor and slide off the building. He hated to watch the kids playing near the soft stone edge of the roof, imagining any minute they'd fall off.

The door of his room was locked by a padlock hooked to loose, rusty nails. He had no electricity, only candles and the brakeman's lantern he carried at the bottom of his duffel bag, along with his clothes and towels, his regular Bible, his Buddhist Bible, his little nickel notebooks, writing paper and airmail envelopes—and all the typescripts of his novels. The room was damp, smelly and far from luxurious, but Kerouac was alone, away from the family arguments in Rocky Mount and free to live as he liked, which meant, to begin with, that he could make up for lost time with marijuana and bourbon, especially driving himself "crazy Miss Greening," his expression for smoking marijuana.

Downstairs in a room with barred windows looking onto Orizaba, was William Garver, who rarely left the building and was ready to sit and talk to Jack all day if he wanted company. Burroughs had said in *Junkie* that Garver took a special pleasure in seeing non-users of heroin start a habit and liked to invite young kids up to his room to give them their first shot.

Jack had known him for years. Three summers before, with Burroughs in Mexico City in 1952, Jack had become good friends with Garver and the dealer, David Tercereo, taking down Tercero's life story in a sketch Jack titled "Dave". Tercereo had died in November 1954, and Bill Garver was the only one left of the old Mexico City crowd. Jack sat in Garver's big easy chair and talked with him through most of the day in a familiar scene of addict paraphernalia. Garver was almost sixty years old, living in Mexico City on a trust fund established by his family. For years in New York, according to Burroughs, he'd supported his junk habit by stealing about thirty dollars every day, usually in the form of coats from large mid-Manhattan department stores. He'd been in jail a few times.

Jack saw him in a romantic light as a great scholar, historian and anthropologist. He was a compulsive talker, and Allen complained that he talked too much, but after a few days listening to Garver, Kerouac hit on an idea for a book. He began to bring his note pad downstairs to sketch poems while Garver talked. It seemed to work fine, and in less than a month he had a book of poems he called *Mexico City Blues*.

Much later, in 1966, Kerouac described his technique:

Old Bill Gaines (Garver) lived downstairs. I'd come every day with my marijuana and my note pad. He'd be high on opium. I had to get the opium in the slums from Tristessa. She was our connection. Bill's sitting in his easy chair in his purple pajamas, mumbling on about Minoan civilization and excavation, I'm sitting on his bed writing poems. And through the whole thing some of his words come in. Like the 52nd Chorus. Just idling all the afternoon. He talked real slow and I could put it all down. He was pleased. I'd show him what I had written and he'd say, "Oh boy, that's good."

Mexico City Blues continued the "sensory meditations" Jack had tried in his *San Francisco Blues* poems the previous year. There he had followed the visual scene out the window of the skid-row hotel. Sitting on Bill Garver's bed at 212 Orizaba, Kerouac let his mind follow his friend's rambling monologue. His method wasn't literal transcription of what was actually being said. Rather, he made his poems out of what he heard, not necessarily what was said, and what he associated in memory with what he heard.

Jack had often told Allen that he identified more with musical geniuses like Bud Powell, Charlie Parker, Billie Holiday, Lester Young, Gerry Mulligan and Thelonius Monk than he did with any established literary scene, and of all the books he ever wrote, *Mexico City Blues* is most directly related to jazz. Bop was to Kerouac a new art form that had broken through to eloquence. His own method of spontaneous composition was meant to do the same thing with words that he heard bop musicians doing with their instruments. When Miles Davis played, Kerouac heard his trumpet sounding long sentences like Marcel Proust.

Following the direction he began with spontaneous prose composition, he improvised freely in *Mexico City Blues*. In fact, he didn't see any significant difference between writing poetry in *Mexico City Blues* and prose in his other books, except that in prose he thought in terms of narrative paragraphs. As Jack later explained his aesthetic theory in the *New American Poetry*, whatever he wrote was spontaneous, pushing the line a little farther than reason dictated, extending it in musical rhythms to the farthest level of his consciousness.

In the haikus Kerouac had written the previous year for his Buddhist book, he had composed the short poems carefully, revising until they seemed structurally perfect. In Garver's room in Mexico City, Jack returned to the approach he'd taken in spontaneous prose, knocking it off fast. He'd found a way to write poetry as fast as he wrote prose. He later told the *Paris Review* interviewer that he used the size of his notebook page for the form and length of the poem, "just as a musician has to get out, a jazz musician, his statement within a certain number of bars, within one chorus, which spills over into the next, but he has to stop where the chorus page *stops*."

The poems in *Mexico City Blues* were bound together less by theme than by Kerouac's internal speech rhythms. At some points, as in the 217th Chorus, they became pure sound. According to Ginsberg, Jack "was writing from the realm of consciousness where it was spontaneous, where it was the realm of sounds." But this type of free association for sound values was in *Mexico City Blues* from the beginning.

Jack wrote *Mexico City Blues* in three weeks, about a dozen choruses a day. At times he incorporated long sections of Garver's talk: subjects ranging from a news account of the Hong Kong to China ferry to his experiences with sodium amytol and heroin (fifty-seventh

227

through fifty-ninth Choruses). Garver's monologue reminded Jack of his own illnesses, the phlebitis in his legs (seventeenth and nineteenth Choruses) and times in the hospital (fifty-fifth and sixth Choruses). Together Garver and Kerouac goofed at the table over bacon and eggs (eighty and eighty-fifth Choruses), then Jack swung into a confession (eighty-seventh Chorus) about all the mad people he'd known since he was four (eighty-eighth Chorus). His memories of his earliest years in Lowell, before he was four years old, occupied nearly twenty choruses.

Most of *Mexico City Blues* was loose sketching, and the choruses were based on what Kerouac saw and heard around him at the moment of writing his poems. Some choruses were more formally structured like a line of recognizable melody in the middle of a free form jazz improvisation. The choruses in *Mexico City Blues* ranged from the freest celebration to the tighter flow of Kerouac's imagination in the 211th Chorus, perhaps the most eloquent poem in the book.

The choruses were marked by Kerouac's melancholy, by his blues, his feeling down and out, lonely and alone in Mexico City. He often referred to Sanskrit terms for states of consciousness, or names of Buddhist teachers, or the philosophy of the Surangama and Lankavatara Sutras, as in the 211th Chorus. According to Ginsberg, Jack was a "Zen lunatic, but with a secret message implied for anyone with gnostic knowledge to pick up" when reading the choruses. But in the poems, Kerouac's imagination and rhythms were his own, and they were what ultimately shaped the book's character.

In the final choruses, 239th to the end, he gave an explanation of Buddha as a bop musician that was about himself too, or Kerouac's image of himself sitting in Bill Garver's room sketching poems. This was Kerouac's image of himself as well as Charlie Parker. He thought of them both as great writer/musicians, pioneers of the New Reality Jam Session.

As the weeks went on in Mexico City, Jack's energy began to run down. The later poems took him longer in *Mexico City Blues*. The 230th Chorus, which he wrote while high on morphine, took hours, because he wrote every line in the poem within an hour of one another. The short nineteen-line poem required almost an entire day for its composition, Kerouac lost in the morphine images and dreams as they floated past in Garver's room, languidly watching the clock and scribbling his thoughts as each hour passed. He luxuriated in his freedom in Mexico City, and put off his plans for joining Allen until September.

Ginsberg was planning to move from his apartment at 1010 Montgomery Street in San Francisco to a small cottage in Berkeley. He was going to enroll at the university for his master's degree, encouraged to think by English Department professors Mark Schorer and Thomas Parkinson that he could get a graduate fellowship. Allen remembers that Jack told him "study Sanskrit, not Latin," and that he'd be happy as a college professor. Jack himself was far from that scene. He was a mad hermit on the adobe roof of 212 Orizaba.

Chapter Twenty-Two

One hot night in August 1955, Kerouac left his friend Garver and went upstairs to try to get some sleep. The kids from a Mexican family downstairs were having a great time on his roof burning a bed to get rid of the bugs. Jack entered into the fun, fanning the fire with his own mattress. They finally went back downstairs, but he couldn't sleep, so he sat up in his room and in the candlelight began a long short story about the Mexican girl who was Garver's connection for morphine in the slums, a story he finished a year later in Mexico City and published as *Tristessa*.

Mexico City Blues was based on his mornings and afternoons with Garver, a book of daydreams, gentle "Miss Green" marijuana and morphine fantasies. *Tristessa*, more dramatically, skirted the edges of nightmare, Kerouac's nighttime adventures in the slums mixing bourbon and morphine, surrounded by people he didn't know well, never really at ease, yet caught in his romantic fantasies about Tristessa, idealizing her as he had Maggie Cassidy and Mardou.

Kerouac first met Tristessa years before, when she'd been in love with her connection, Dave Tercero, nearly forty years her senior. Tristessa kept a picture of Tercereo beside her icon of the Virgin Mary, idolizing his memory as the man who'd taken her off the streets shortly after her addiction at sixteen and "showed her how to live." "Tristessa" wasn't her real name. She'd been born Esperanza Villanueva in Juarez. Jack changed the name when he wrote about her from Esperanza, "hope" in Spanish, to Tristessa, "sadness." Her appeal was like "Mardou's," a tight, black, wasted sexuality. Jack was fascinated with her sexy clothes, her dark glasses and her provocative walk.

But Tristessa was more exotic than "Mardou." Without what was to Jack the tedious intellectuality of Village girls, Tristessa lived the law of the Buddha instinctively, unthinkingly, every action of her life proof to Jack of the Buddhist law that all life was suffering. Most important, Tristessa was a deeply religious Catholic, her religiosity giving her a pervading sadness Jack found irresistible. At last he'd found a girl who reflected his religious feelings, and he felt desperately attracted to her.

Tristessa was, after all, a junkie and a prostitute. She was further removed from the possibility of any close relationship with him by being an Azteca, an Indian girl with black, slick hair hanging in two pigtails, the roll-sod hairdo style of the Cathedral Indians. This just made her more exotic and more desirable. Tristessa was high all the time, always sick, shooting ten grams of morphine a month. But with her lidded eyes and clasped hands, Jack saw her as a Madonna, too far removed from him in her absorption with her own sickness and death to ever love him. This only enchanted her appeal, since it meant she wouldn't be possessive.

Like *Mexico City Blues*, *Tristessa* had a loose, flowing

structure. The first part, titled "Trembling and Chaste," began with Jack and Tristessa riding in a cab to her place in a whore-street district and going into her room. It wasn't until a half dozen pages into the narrative that Jack explained why he went there. The sight of one of Tristessa's friends, El Indio, shooting morphine, reminded Jack of what he'd come for. His mind momentarily flashed back to Garver's room, before the narrative started, when his friend had asked him to score.

By the time Kerouac had set off in the cab with Tristessa he'd had many long sessions with marijuana and morphine in Garver's room writing *Mexico City Blues*, his mind following fantasy after fantasy, starting and dropping the threads of multiple associations. As in *Mexico City Blues,* it was not necessary to explain everything. The description was sometimes as private as a letter to a close friend, or a quick shorthand note to himself.

Entering Tristessa's bedroom, Kerouac was startled at the bizarre surroundings. Inside the room, he was introduced to Tristessa's "sister," Cruz, a little Indian woman with no chin and bright eyes, wearing a battered dress and high-heeled pumps without stockings. There was also Tristessa's friend El Indio, a dealer in morphine, watching Kerouac warily. Many pets ranged free in the room, a cock, a dove who sat on the mantelpiece occasionally flapping his wings, a hen and a noisy rooster, a starving, flea-ridden kitten and a Chihuahua bitch in heat.

Pulling up a chair to the corner of the bed so he could sit between the kitten and the wall icon of the Virgin Mary, Jack stroked the purring kitten and listened to Tristessa talk to El Indio and Cruz, understanding little of their rapid Spanish. Occasionally they translated for him. He watched Tristessa take off her stockings to get under the damp blankets in bed, then quickly looked away.

Sitting in the bedroom drinking his bourbon and Canada Dry, he felt irredeemably an outsider among the three Mexican junkies. When Tristessa offered him a shot, he accepted reluctantly: "I don't want no more morphine after this, I vow." But he was trying to get closer to her and feel less of a clumsy American outsider.

It didn't work. Jack still saw Tristessa, Cruz and El Indio

as a wild group of people. Over the course of the evening the morphine gentled his mistrust of them. He no longer saw El Indio as a thief or Tristessa as a pickpocket, but he still felt uneasy and afraid he'd get robbed or attacked suddenly. He wasn't even sure Tristessa understood the sincerity of his religious belief, afraid that when he reached in at the devotional candle in the icon for a light for his cigarette, she would be offended. The gentle lift of the morphine couldn't altogether erase his mistrust, and finally he yearned to get away.

Kerouac wrote the first part of *Tristessa* a few nights after their evening together. He smoked marijuana writing the story, and later he thought his reverence for the girl's suffering had been expressed in an "ingrown toenail packed mystical style." He told Ginsberg he was very happy with the book, partly because it exemplified more than any of his novels the first law of Buddhism, that all life was suffering, and partly because it was written at a time when he had premonitions of literary success. As he later remembered, Tristessa visited him in his rooftop room:

. . . and saw all my manuscripts on the clay floor and said, "You've got millions of pesos on the floor." I didn't have a cent but she said I had money on the floor. Turned out she was right. *Sax, Cody, On the Road*. I carried all that stuff with me in a big duffle bag, my clothes and manuscripts and my canteen with water in it in case I got trapped in the desert.

Jack was hiding from the girl the fact that he had travelers checks in the duffle bag from the sale of *On The Road*, but he was impressed by her intuition, taking it as a sign of good luck.

Kerouac ended the story about Tristessa by describing her visit to his room, where once again, although he wanted desperately to sleep with her, he told himself to leave her alone, thinking of her as a helpless kitten. He never confessed his love to her that summer, and the story didn't end there. The next summer, before he returned to Mexico City, he wrote her letters telling her he loved her. When he went back to his room at 212 Orizaba in 1956 he wrote Part Two of the book, a sad account of how she had become even sicker than the previous year on goofballs (seconals) and had fallen on the street and hurt her head. Even watching her go to pieces, a purple shawl over her dirty bandage, clutching her kimono to her side, Jack felt he loved her, swearing to Bill Garver that he'd marry her if he thought he could ever become a junkie.

What Jack didn't include in *Tristessa*, because it wouldn't have fitted with the religious reverence he expressed for the girl's suffering, was that the story ended a different way, that he finally, as he later put it to friends, "nailed her."

All I did was suffer with that poor girl and then when she fell on her head and almost killed herself . . . she was all busted up and everything. She was the most gorgeous little Indian chick you ever saw. I say Indian, pure Indian . . . She had bones, man, just bones, skin and bones. And I didn't write in the book how I finally nailed her. You know? I did. I finally nailed her. She said, "Shhhhhhhhhh! Don't let the landlord hear." She said, "Remember, I'm very weak and sick." I said, "I know. I've been writing a book about how you're weak and sick."

But it was not a conquest. She was out like a light. On M. M., that's Morphine. And in fact I made a big run for her from way uptown to downtown to the slum district . . . and I said, here's your stuff. She said, "Shhhhhh!" She gave herself a shot . . . and I said, Ah . . . now's the time. And I got my little nogood piece. But . . it was certainly justification of Mexico!

Early in September 1955, when Jack had finished *Mexico City Blues* and the first part of *Tristessa*, he felt it was time to get moving again, to get back on the road to see Ginsberg. But it was hard to get started. He told Allen that he'd promised himself never to go back to California after fighting with Neal the last time, and that the West Coast didn't offer him anything anymore, but he was curious about Allen's scene in Berkeley.

Ginsberg had sent copies of the poems he'd written that summer while Kerouac had been writing *Mexico City Blues*. Jack read them with Bill Garver and they'd both been impressed. Allen had included a long poem that Jack

233

especially liked. He even inadvertently named it by excitedly writing a letter to Ginsberg saying, "I received your Howl." (Ginsberg later named the poem "Howl.") Jack told Allen that Garver thought there was too much homosexual material in the poems and that Jack should pass the word along to Allen, as Garver said winking, to see what his reaction would be. Jack didn't like the images of "granite phalluses," but he thought "Howl" was genuinely eloquent, having the eloquent rage of the old Jewish prophets. He told Ginsberg that in *Mexico City Blues*, his prophecies were more openly spiritual. Jack was hugely satisfied with what he'd written in Mexico City. If he ever made it to Allen's cottage in Berkeley, there would be a lot of typing to be done.

Finally trying to show some will power, Jack decided to throw whatever marijuana he hadn't smoked down the toilet so he could begin to pack his duffle bag for California. He didn't want to take any marijuana or mescaline for Ginsberg because he was afraid of a border arrest. He took only benzedrine and goofballs for writing. But the marijuana was hard to leave. He didn't get away for another week, trying to smoke up "Miss Green," taking time to wash out his T-shirts and towels in a cold bath of stone on his drizzly roof.

Counting his money before he left, he was very happy with his vacation in Mexico City. He hadn't spent much money and he'd written two books. The only thing that hadn't worked out was a penicillin treatment for the phlebitis in his legs. He'd hoped to get the shots at the Mexican free clinic but he'd decided the penicillin wouldn't be effective with the massive amount he'd been smoking. Even the pain in his legs didn't worry him. After the melancholy depression and loneliness of the past two years in New York City and Rocky Mount, he felt back to his old self again, confident there'd be good times ahead in California with Allen.

Jack didn't have a clear idea what he'd find at Allen's Berkeley cottage. Earlier there'd been plans to make a movie together in San Francisco, a W.C. Fields comic movie of Burroughs on a cable car looking over his shoulder in a raincoat, glinty eyeglasses and a felt hat, of Jack drinking wine with the bums on Howard Street, of Neal in a caboose and Al Sublette digging jazz in North Beach, all of this supposedly a "book-movie" Jack was going to write. Since Allen had written "Howl" he hadn't mentioned the movie idea anymore. Jack might have gotten a sense from the letters that the scene had opened out a little in San Francisco from the Ginsberg-Kerouac-Cassady-Burroughs nucleus of the old days. But Jack was willing to meet whatever was on the way. In a wildly exuberant mood, he wrote Allen just before he left Mexico City that they should prepare for great times ahead. "LET'S SHOUT OUR POEMS IN SAN FRAN-CISCO STREETS—PREDICT EARTHQUAKES!"

Chapter Twenty-Three

In Berkeley Kerouac walked into a scene at Ginsberg's cottage that was different from anything he'd known before in California. In 1955 Berkeley was still a loose university town and most of Allen's new friends were involved in one way or another as graduate students of literature, although casually using the campus library more than they attended classes. Ginsberg's cottage was north of campus at 1624 Milvia Street, an old, wooden frame building, with one large ramshackle room, a small kitchen and bath. It was set back from the street behind more substantial stucco and frame houses, and a long path ran through a tangled, overgrown garden to the sidewalk. There were flowers and fruit trees in the garden, giving it a sense of peace and privacy. After school the neighborhood kids played on the sidewalks or under the old California eucalyptus in the parks.

The first week of September, before Kerouac arrived, Allen wrote a friend, John Allen Ryan, about his cottage, giving an idea of his independence and the easy life style he'd just found in Berkeley:

I have a house here for 35 a month, backyard cottage & private backyard, quite big, filled with vegetables & flowers. Ideal Camden Whitman cottage, I write a lot, depression, solitude, last night a rare half hour of a kind of animistic ecstasy & weeping in the garden, the vines with leaves turned top up in the night as they were left during the hours of day when the gracious sun rayed on them, the father is merciful; I had a vision of that as I havent had in maybe 7 years; a relief, a drop of sweetness. I did some writing & it looks like Chrs. Smart.

The poems Allen mentioned, composed after "Howl," which was written in the Hotel Wentley on Polk Street in San Francisco shortly before he moved to Berkeley, were short lyrics later collected in his books *Howl* and *Reality Sandwiches*, like the poem describing his backyard, "A Strange New Cottage in Berkeley:

> All afternoon cutting bramble blackberries off a tottering brown fence
> under a low branch with its rotten old apricots miscellaneous under the leaves,
> fixing the drip in the intricate gut machinery of a new toilet;
> found a good coffeepot in the vines by the porch, rolled a big tire out of the scarlet bushes, hid my marijuana;
> wet the flowers, playing the sunlit water each to each, returning for godly extra drops for the stringbeans and daisies;
> three times walked round the grass and sighed absently;
> my reward, when the garden fed me its plums from the form of a small tree in the corner,
> an angel thoughtful of my stomach, and my dry and love-lorn tongue.

Ginsberg had been in California over a year before he moved to Berkeley, and he'd gone through many changes. He later said that up to the time he went to San Francisco, he'd been struggling with the question of "finding the Whitman-self-reliance to indulge a celebration of self." He found it in California, where a "radical vision had ripened."

236

In part his struggle had been to resolve his anxieties about his homosexuality and about his literary ambition. Just as Kerouac had wanted publication by Madison Avenue, so Ginsberg had tried to enter the literary "Establishment" as a poet in New York, trying to get help from his old Columbia professors Lionel Trilling and Mark Van Doren. He was never secure in that scene, although his contemporaries at Columbia, whom he'd worked with on the campus literary magazines, like Herbert Gold, Norman Podhoretz and Ted Hoffman, were beginning literary careers. Allen brought his friends' manuscripts around for Van Doren to read. He showed him *The Town and the City* and *Doctor Sax*, and he introduced Gregory Corso to him. Van Doren encouraged Corso to go on writing poetry. But in New York Allen never really felt on strong ground. Once after lunching with Van Doren at the Columbia Faculty Club, Allen told Jack that when he went to the men's room, Van Doren said he'd hold the manuscript of Allen's poems so he wouldn't pee on them. Ginsberg wasn't sure whether or not his old professor was joking.

In San Francisco there was a much looser literary scene. Major publishing was centered in New York, but on the West Coast there was a tradition of small press publishers and a much freer political and social climate. When Allen arrived the previous summer from Mexico he still followed his East Coast patterns. In fact for several months it was almost as if he were determined to try to live as straight as possible. He found himself a girl, wore a suit and worked as a market researcher for Towne, Oller Associates. He even started seeing psychiatrists again. None of them were right for him. As his biographer Jane Kramer described in *Allen Ginsberg in America*, his real breakthrough came only when he found a sympathetic phychiatrist, who advised him to stop trying to be straight and live instead the way he wanted, as a homosexual and a poet.

In the early summer of 1955, Allen met a San Francisco painter called Robert LaVigne who was impressed by his knowledge of Cezanne "and the sophisticated schools in New York around De Kooning." LaVigne took Allen to his Gough Street house to see his paintings. When Allen walked inside, the first picture he saw was a huge nude portrait of a boy sitting on a white blanket thrown over a sofa against a red wall, a portrait of a young friend of LaVigne's named Peter Orlovsky. Allen "looked into its eyes and was shocked by love." A few weeks later, he moved into Gough Street with La-Vigne and Orlovsky, but soon he and Peter left to live by themselves in the Hotel Wentley. Feeling great happiness with Peter and a new sense of self-identity and freedom, Allen began writing the long poem "Howl." The scene in Berkeley liberated him even further.

Jack later remembered his arrival at Allen's cottage for the *Paris Review*:

> . . . I go back to Ginsberg, I go to his cottage, I say, "Hah, we're gonna play the music" . . . he says, "You know what I'm going to do tomorrow? I'm going to throw on Mark Schorer's desk a new theory of prosody! About the dactyllic arrangement of Ovid!"
>
> I said, "Quit, man. Sit under a tree and forget it and drink wine with me . . . and Phil Whalen and Gary Snyder and all the bums of San Francisco. Don't try to be a big Berkeley teacher. Just be a poet under the trees . . . and we'll wrestle and we'll break holds." And he did take my advice. He remembered that. He said, "What are you going to teach . . . you have parched lips!" I said, "Naturally, I just came from Chihuahua. It's very hot down there, phew! you go out and little pigs rub against your legs. Phew!"
>
> So here comes Snyder with a bottle of wine . . . and here comes Whalen, and here comes what's his name . . . Rexroth, and everybody . . . and we had the Poetry Renaissance of San Francisco.

The "Poetry Renaissance of San Francisco" was a later journalist's term. Poetry had no need to be reborn in San Francisco since it had always been alive there. Ginsberg had come to San Francisco with a letter of introduction to Kenneth Rexroth from William Carlos Williams. Rexroth was the center of literary activity in the city, and its biggest name. His books of poetry, essays and translations were all published in New York.

Rexroth had a literary open house one day a week in his home, and gradually Ginsberg met everyone in the scene. Allen was introduced to Robert Duncan, with Jack Spicer the two most active young poets in San Francisco (he met Kenneth Patchen in the City Lights Bookshop), and to the younger poets, Philip Lamantia and Michael McClure, then studying with Duncan. But it wasn't until Allen moved to Berkeley that he found his close friends. On 8 September, 1955, a few days after moving to his cottage on Milvia, he walked over to meet a poet named Gary Snyder whom Rexroth had suggested he look up in Berkeley. Gary remembered that he'd decided to stay home that day instead of going up to Sacramento to see the long-haired Angora goats at the State Fair and was fixing his bicycle in the backyard of his cottage on Hillegass Street when Allen suddenly appeared.

Ginsberg was so impressed with Snyder that the day after their meeting he wrote his friend John Allen Ryan, telling what happened:

. . . a bearded interesting Berkeley cat name of Snyder, I met him yesterday (via Rexroth suggestion) who is studying oriental and leaving in a few months on some privately put up funds to go be a Zen monk (a real one). He's a head, peyotlist, laconist, but warmhearted, nice looking with a little beard, thin, blond, rides a bicycle in Berkeley in red corduroy & levis & hungup on indians (ex-anthropologist student from some indian hometown) and writes well, his sideline besides zen which is apparently calm scholarly & serious with him. Interesting person.

After talking with Snyder, Allen thought again about an idea put to him several months before in San Francisco to organize a poetry reading at a small art gallery called the Six Gallery. At the time he wasn't interested, "not knowing of any poetry around worth hearing," but shortly before Jack arrived at the cottage, Allen was deep into plans for the reading. He told John Allen Ryan that even if it wouldn't be an evening of great poetry, it would be "a great social occasion," and he worked hard on the program.

Rexroth agreed to introduce each poet, and Allen asked Michael McClure, Philip Lamantia, Gary Snyder and Snyder's friend from Reed College, Philip Whalen, to read with him. The plans were in full swing by the time Jack arrived in Berkeley. He went with Allen to a meeting at Rexroth's house to settle the last details of the program. The evening of the reading, Kerouac was there, contributing to the event in his own inimitable way.

Public readings at the Six Gallery, a small art gallery down near the Embarcadero that exhibited the work of young Bay Area painters, had been going on for some time. The first one had featured the poetry of Walter Lowenfels, who came to San Francisco from New York, as Rexroth recalled, in political trouble, charged with being a Communist. Only the Six Gallery would let Lowenfels have a benefit reading, with an introduction from Rexroth. The program just before Ginsberg's in October 1955 was a reading of Robert Duncan's play *Faust Foutu*. As advance publicity for his reading, Allen mimeographed postcards which listed the six poets—McClure, Snyder, Whalen, Lamantia, Ginsberg, Rexroth—and announced:

Six poets at the Six Gallery. Kenneth Rexroth, M.C. Remarkable collection of angels all gathered at once in the same spot. Wine, music, dancing girls, serious poetry, free satori. Small collection for wine and postcards. Charming event.

The advance publicity stirred up a good crowd, and by the time the poets arrived the small gallery was full. Just coming into the room made the poets suddenly conscious they were part of a community. Snyder remembered that they had each felt isolated before, but the sight at the gallery gave them a new feeling. It looked like the reading had called out the entire bohemian community of San Francisco, Marin County and the East Bay. There were left-over gypsies from the Stalinist era, Quaker-Pacifists from World War II, all post-war alienated people, gradually discovering they had friends in the Bay Area. Thinking back, in 1969, to the night of the reading, Snyder said that the poets and the audience that night were living the same life style so popular today, but today "there are more of them. I can remember at one time we thought it was the life style of only three people."

The special quality of the evening, of course, was

sparked by Allen's performance of "Howl for Carl Solomon." Rexroth, dressed up for the occasion in a salvage shop cutaway coat, remembered, "All of a sudden Ginsberg read this thing that he had been keeping to himself all this while, and it just blew things up completely." Allen himself was surprised by the sensation he caused, telling John Ryan that "When I read long poems I get carried away and begin chanting like a cantor, almost to tears, mouthing the worst obscenities." Ruth Witt-Diamant, who had sponsored readings at the Six Gallery and the Poetry Center, "kept sending frantic messages to tone that down, the scandal, etc., but nobody seemed to mind after it was over."

The crowd at the Six Gallery, 100 to 150 people, loved it all, passing gallon jugs of California wine from hand to hand (Kerouac got the wine), greeting friends, cheering on each poet as Rexroth introduced him. The six poets sat on a small stage in large chairs in a semicircle, and as each got up to read his poems, he advanced to the edge of the stage, nodding to acquaintances in the audience, and read with great spirit and intensity. While things were getting started, Kerouac passed a hat, collecting money for the wine, before sitting on the edge of the stage with his own bottle, cheering on the readers. Rexroth thought he carried his gallon of Thunderbird in the same way that F. Scott Fitzgerald carried his silver flask of gin.

Later in his novel *The Dharma Bums*, Jack took three pages to describe the "mad night" of the Six Gallery reading. It was:

. . . the night of the birth of the San Francisco Poetry Renaissance. Everyone was there . . . . by eleven o'clock when Alvah Goldbook was reading his, wailing his poem "Wail" drunk with arms outspread everybody was yelling "Go! Go! Go!" (like a jam session) and old Rheinhold Cacoethes the father of the Frisco poetry scene was wiping his tears in gladness. Japhy himself read his fine poems about Coyote the God of the North American Plateau Indians . . . .

Meanwhile scores of people stood around in the darkened gallery straining to hear every word of the amazing poetry reading as I wandered from group to group, facing them and facing away from the stage, urging them to glug a slug from the jug, or wandered back and sat on the right side of the stage giving out little wows and yesses of approval and even whole sentences of comment with nobody's invitation but in the general gaiety nobody's disapproval either. It was a great night. Delicate Francis DaPavia read, from delicate onionskin yellow pages, or pink, which he kept flipping carefully with long white fingers, the poems of his dead chum Altman who'd eaten too much peyote in Chihuahua (or died of polio, one) . . . . Between poets, Rheinhold Cacoethes, in his bow tie and shabby old coat, would get up and make a little funny speech in his snide funny voice and introduce the next reader; but as I say come eleven-thirty when all the poems were read and everybody was milling around wondering what had happened and what would come next in American poetry, he was wiping his eyes with his handkerchief. And we all got together with him, the poets, and drove in several cars to Chinatown for a big fabulous dinner . . . .

There were many other poetry readings after the Six Gallery, at the Poetry Center at the San Francisco State College, at the Youth Settlement Community Center, where the janitor objected to the drinking in the aisles. Before Jack had come to Berkeley, Allen had thought of having a reading with Kerouac, Ginsberg and Cassady, but it had never materialized. Jack didn't want any part of the spotlight, and Neal begged off too. Kerouac preferred drinking his bottle of wine on the sidelines, cheering on the poets as if he were a spectator at a jazz club.

Even at the parties afterwards, where there was always lots of wine, marijuana and plenty of available girls, Kerouac rarely participated, drinking silently in a chair by the wall. For Allen, the winter became one big party celebrating his success with "Howl," carousing with his friends, taking off his clothes and drinking wine. Jack was a loner. Gary Snyder watched him sit without saying a word for hours at a party, thinking Jack was stoned and totally out of it, but afterwards he was surprised when Kerouac quoted him conversations happening all over the room during the party. Jack was never too drunk to remember, when he wanted to. He used the drunkenness as a defense, a barrier between him and the others. In

242

part, it was because of his shyness. He still felt himself an outsider, a Shadow, different from everybody else. But he complained the other poets were too intellectual and effete to be interesting. He was dedicated to the idea of being different and legendary, even among his closest friends.

Gary Snyder was an exception. Gary had read Jack's story "Jazz of the Beat Generation" when it came out in *New World Writing* that spring, and had been very impressed with the excitement of the prose. He had wanted to talk more about writing with Kerouac, whom he called "Jean-Louis." It all pleased Jack immensely. Allen took him to Snyder's cottage which, compared to Allen's place, was almost monastic, being only twelve by twelve feet square, sparsely furnished with straw mats. But the orange crate bookcases were full of the best collection of Oriental studies Jack had ever seen.

Allen had told Jack that Gary was the only person worth knowing, "with any truly illuminated intelligence, on the West Coast." After meeting Snyder, Jack agreed. He'd had a harder time with Rexroth. When Allen brought Jack over to San Francisco to meet Rexroth, hoping they'd share a common ground in Buddhism and literature, there'd been immediate antagonism between the two men. Jack sensed that Rexroth was more concerned with the esotericism of Buddhism than with personal belief. Rexroth was as much put off by Kerouac. Coming into the living room, Jack announced to everybody at the open house that he was a great Buddhist scholar, but as Rexroth remembered, Jack quickly shut up after realizing everyone in the room spoke at least one Oriental language.

With Snyder, it was much easier for Kerouac. Gary had been studying Japanese for three years, preparing for his trip to a Zen monastery. He was also translating the Chinese poet Han-Shan the fall Jack met him. Modest about his own scholarship, Gary accepted Jack on his own terms as an original. He was sincerely impressed that Kerouac had done all his reading in the sutras on his own. Kerouac, playing up his image as a romantic wanderer, told Snyder he'd found all the books in small town libraries when he was hitchhiking through. The two of them disagreed on most points of Buddhist thought, though their disagreements were primarily differences of emphasis, with Jack a Hinayana Buddhist, hostile to the intellectual effetism, as he called it, of Snyder's Zen Mahayana Buddhism. But the talk was friendly, and it went on for hours, neither convincing the other of anything.

Later in *The Dharma Bums* Jack described the quiet evenings with Snyder, Ginsberg and Whalen often dropping into each other's cottages, sipping tea and reading poems. There were also noisy evenings drinking wine and making athletic love with one of Snyder's girls, whom they called "Princess," actually the wife of a graduate student of English at Berkeley.

Snyder was eight years younger than Kerouac, but Jack couldn't patronize him as he had Allen's younger New York friend, Gregory Corso. This didn't mean he'd let Gary win any arguments about poetry or Buddhism. Kerouac insisted on his theory of spontaneous prose and poetry, telling Allen he should drop any plans to revise "Howl for Carl Solomon." Jack wanted only *spontaneity* or nothing. Snyder and Ginsberg defended revision and craft in poetry, particularly in the work of Ezra Pound, whom Kerouac considered pretentious.

Snyder and Ginsberg had become close friends and Gary began encouraging Allen to give up his idea of doing a graduate degree in English at Berkeley. He wanted Allen to forget all about a "career" and just write poetry without worrying about getting a good job. At a turning point in Ginsberg's life, Snyder helped steer him the way. Jack, who'd been Allen's friend for a much longer time, continued to be a personal influence (his method of spontaneous composition was still basically Allen's poetic guide), but Jack's life style, unlike Snyder's, was of no help to Ginsberg, because Jack was still so closely tied to his mother. Ginsberg's mother Naomi was in a mental hospital, not waiting for him, like mémêre, to come back home for a family Christmas, ready to support him through the rest of the winter. Besides, in Berkeley, Jack was primarily concerned with trying to convince Allen to become a Buddhist, scoffing at the animistic ecstasies he experienced in his backyard. Snyder's advice to Ginsberg, that he could always make a living as a poet if he were willing to work with his hands and live simply, was much more than Allen was ready to hear, much more to the point than Kerouac's long discourses on Buddhism.

Jack argued with Gary about Buddhism, but he agreed immediately when Snyder offered to take him mountain climbing on a weekend trip in the High Sierras. Jack had fantasized for the whole of the previous winter about striking out by himself to unroll his sleeping bag in deserts or river bottoms, and living like a religious hermit. He realized immediately that Gary must have camped out of a rucksack for years and could teach him many practical techniques. Snyder had spent his life in the Pacific Northwest, working summers as a fire lookout in Washington State. He called up another Berkeley friend whom he'd met at Rexroth's named John Montgomery, who Rexroth had suggested would take him to the Sierras. Montgomery remembers that Snyder showed up together with Kerouac at his little cottage on Stewart Street.

John Montgomery (called "Henry Morley" in *The Dharma Bums;* Snyder was "Japhy Ryder") could tell Kerouac had never been in the wilds before by the way Jack romanticized the outing with what Montgomery called "the verve of a Tenderfoot Scout." Kerouac borrowed a sleeping bag and a pair of tennis shoes from Snyder and a knapsack from Ginsberg. Snyder brought the food, bulgar cracked wheat, dried vegetables from the ski shop, chocolate pudding, cheese, dark bread and tea, explaining carefully to Kerouac that when they packed in to sleep overnight on the mountain they had to keep the weight in the rucksacks down as much as possible. Which meant, for Jack, that Gary refused to pack wine. He protested, not believing Snyder's claim that in the high altitude they would be too tired to want to drink, but Gary was planning the trip so Jack gave in.

Montgomery had a car, and they began driving to the mountains on a two-day trip, heading along Route 395, east of Yosemite, to the little town of Bridgeport, California, where they'd leave the car and begin to climb. Montgomery had forgotten his sleeping bag, and then the anti-freeze for the car radiator, so he had to stay behind to drain the water out of his car and didn't start up the mountain with Snyder and Kerouac. Jack soon fell into a rhythm with Gary trudging up the trail.

Snyder was the leader, cautioning Jack about mud in the creek bottoms, clearing rocks off the trail. As they climbed the slope they made up haikus, Jack so impressed with Gary's facility as a poet he scribbled down what Snyder said:

> *Gary Snyder's Haiku* (*Spoken on the Mountain*)
> "Talking about the literary
> life—the yellow
> aspens."

> *Gary Snyder's Second Haiku*
> "I get a hardon from here
> to Connecticut, Goodness,
> 3,000 miles."

At first Jack was proud of not getting tired and of keeping up with Snyder, although he couldn't equal Gary's relaxed practiced stride on the trail. As the climb got steeper and the trail more difficult, Jack began to weaken. They came to a place where they had to jump from boulder to boulder, working their way to where they could pitch camp before tackling the summit, and Jack sat down to change his wet socks and rest while Gary found the right place to leave their packs and cook supper.

They spent the evening in the camp, tired and meditating together in the dusk. Jack's description of the evening in *The Dharma Bums*, as they sat near one another on the big glacial rocks, was of a peaceful happiness, "all completely serious, all completely hallucinated, all completely happy."

Snyder's description, entered later in his journal, echoed Kerouac's response to the mountain in the calm, beautiful starlit night:

Upper Horse Creek Saturday October 22 with Jean-Louis Kerouac, camped under a huge outlaying boulder, a great pitch log burning, John Montgomery camped alone somewhere below. My foolishness, your problem, not mine. My head is being changed. Cold sky the color of Prussian eyes,

246

grey violet in sunset, pale, pale, move Pleides, chocolate pudding.

The next afternoon, Kerouac didn't quite make it to the summit, frightened of the wind and the height. "Now the wind began to howl like the wind in movies about the Shroud of Tibet. The steepness began to be too much for me; I was afraid now to look back any more . . . ." Jack panicked, letting Gary make it to the top alone. Huddled on his belly on a ledge, Jack heard Gary yodel from the summit, but he didn't feel he had any strength left to yodel an answer back. The sight of Snyder a few minutes later running down the mountain reassured Jack —"in that flash I realized *it's impossible to fall off mountains you fool*"—and he got to his feet to run down the mountain after his friend, doing fantastic jumps and runs, cutting his sneakers to pieces, elated to be coming down at last.

The trip earned Jack the nickname of "the Buddha known as the Great Quitter," but it didn't matter to him. He felt he got even with Snyder later on, back on the road, when Gary held back about going into a roadside restaurant. Jack kidded him about being "afraid of spending ten cents more for a good dinner," and said that an old anarchist like Snyder shouldn't be scared of society. Jack quoted Gary in *The Dharma Bums* weakly defending himself, "Well . . . it just looked to me like this place was full of old rich farts and the prices would be too high. I admit it, I'm scared of all this American wealth, I'm just an old bhikku and I got nothin to do with all this high standard of living, goddammit, I've been a poor guy all my life and I can't get used to some things." Kerouac had no trouble. Roadside diners and country liquor stores where he later bought himself a bottle of muscatel and a cigar, bragging to the clerk he'd just climbed the Matterhorn, were Jack's scene. On the mountaintop with Snyder he felt out of his element, but once back in a car on the road he was on familiar ground, and he had the style worked out perfectly.

When they got home from the mountains, Snyder took Kerouac to Goodwill stores, Salvation Army Stores, Army Navy stores and ski shops in downtown Oakland and

Berkeley to outfit him for the bhikku life he'd dreamed about camping out in deserts and river bottoms. It was late October 1955, too cold for any more trips to the Sierras, but Jack was beginning to tire of the Berkeley scene anyway. There were still parties in the cottages and hours of talk over wine about poetry, but Kerouac took to spending more time over in San Francisco, first going back to impress Cassady with his well-packed rucksack, his expensive poncho and his sleeping bag.

Neal was deeply involved with a girl called Natalie Jackson, who was separated from her husband and had a child living back east with her parents. At the Six Gallery reading, Neal and Natalie had seemed very happy together. Neal stood behind her with both arms around her waist, and both of them looked very much in love. There'd been many good times together in their weeks in San Francisco, clowning and drinking beer on the streets, looking over used cars. But when Jack saw her in her apartment the last time, everything had changed.

Neal had persuaded Natalie to forge Carolyn's signature on a check, and he'd lost all the money at the races. Natalie was on amphetamine and she'd become like a skeleton, her eyes huge with terror, lost in a nervous breakdown. Cassady explained that she'd suddenly gone insane, driven wild by thoughts that they were all going to be arrested for their sins. She had tried to slash her wrists, but Cassady had stopped her, and he was very relieved to see Jack show up. He asked Jack to watch her while he went to his brakeman's job, and reluctantly, not at all happy at what he'd gotten into, Kerouac agreed.

Left alone in the apartment with Natalie, Kerouac tried to get her to eat some sandwiches without any success. She was trembling and shuddering and insisted that Jack didn't understand the seriousness of what she was trying to tell him. Instead of being patient, Jack got angry. It was too much for him to handle. As he later remembered his words in *The Dharma Bums*:

"It's nothing but bullshit!" I yelled and suddenly I had the feeling I always got when I tried to explain the Dharma to people, Alvah, my mother, my relatives, girl friends, everybody, they never listened, they always wanted me to listen

248

to them, *they* knew, I didn't know anything, I was just a dumb young kid and impractical fool who didn't understand the serious significance of this very important, very real world.

He kept pleading with her to calm down, to listen to him, to realize that life was a dream, that "God is *you*, you fool!" but none of it did any good. Jack was able to leave when Cassady finally came back to the apartment, but in the early hours of dawn the police came to the door of the apartment. Natalie fled to the fire escape, and trying to jump from one fire escape to another, she fell and was killed.

Kerouac was very upset. The weeks in Berkeley sitting around the cottages arguing about poetry and the Dharma (truth) of religion had come to an end with a "bohemian suicide" splashed over the front pages of the San Francisco newspapers. He told Neal he was going to take his rucksack and hitchhike home, back to his mother in Rocky Mount. Cassady urged him to slow down, to spend a few months living again with Carolyn and the family in the house in San Jose. Jack tried it, but by mid-December 1955, he was too restless to stay.

The sensible thing would have been to wait there, because Malcolm Cowley had written him that they could work together on the manuscript of *On The Road* when Cowley came to Stanford in January. Kerouac told himself that his mother would be too disappointed if he didn't make it back home for Christmas, so one night Cassady dropped him off at the San Jose railroad yards, and Kerouac finally caught a freight down to Los Angeles.

Ever since Snyder had helped him pack his fifty-pound rucksack in Berkeley, Jack had been waiting to camp out on the road. He'd been warned about police patrolling the industrial suburbs of Los Angeles, the open stretches encircled by heavy wire fences, but Jack told himself that if he had just one night in his sleeping bag, he'd push the hitchhiking home to Rocky Mount. After a bus to Riverside, he walked along the highway as trucks and cars roared by him, until he found a place where he thought he might try camping beside the Los Angeles River, gambling on his luck with the highway patrol.

Trucks rushed over Kerouac's head on the river bridge above him, but he ignored the noise, spreading his poncho and sleeping bag down in the "golden sands" of a bamboo grove. When it was dark he scrambled through the thick underbrush for water, spilling most of it on the way back, saving enough for his orange juice concentrate, which he made up to drink along with nutted cream cheese sandwiches. Then he meditated before trying to sleep, sitting cross-legged thinking about the Buddha, his mind returning with the truck growl to thoughts of San Francisco, especially Natalie's death.

Kerouac was deeply sincere about leaving the main highway of American life and turning his back on the stresses of civilization. He wanted to live completely on his own terms with his own soul. He felt he'd gotten nowhere telling his family and friends about his ideas, but in the river bottom that night outside of Riverside, he was content. In the morning he felt exhilarated enough to make up a little prayer, blessing all living things, envisioning himself with his rucksack "a regular Don Quixote of tenderness."

Chapter Twenty-Four

Back on the road, Kerouac hitchhiked short rides from Riverside to Mexicali. A truck driver picked him up, and after Jack led him to off-the-track Mexican saloons, the trucker drove him to Tucson. They'd become good enough friends by this time for Jack to suggest that instead of the truck driver going into a restaurant for a steak, Jack would fry him a big one over a fire in the desert. After the "great protein feast" of steak and milk, the trucker drove him to Springfield, Ohio, where Jack bought himself a bus ticket to Rocky Mount.

It was freezing cold, late in December 1955, when Jack's

bus dropped him on a country road in the North Carolina pine barrens close to his sister's home. After a three-mile walk in the quiet woods, Jack was stomping with his full pack across the yard of the house, where through the lighted window he could see his mother washing up the supper dishes. His first greeting was for the family dog, then he went inside for Christmas.

Jack relaxed over the holiday, admiring the lighted tree in his sister's front window, sitting together with the family in the living room watching the Christmas service from St. Patrick's Cathedral on television, reading St. Paul in the New Testament. He didn't tell them much about Mexico City, but he tried explaining the friends he'd met with Ginsberg in Berkeley without getting very far. His mother wasn't interested in hearing about strange people like Gary Snyder and Philip Whalen. She didn't understand why Jack called them "Zen Lunatics" and "Dharma Bums," or how they could he happy sitting on straw mats in drafty wooden cottages, sipping green tea and translating Chinese poetry.

But one thing the family did understand. Jack's Berkeley friends had told him about a summer job he was applying for as a fire-watcher in the mountains in Washington State. He told his sister he wanted to stay in Rocky Mount through the winter, working on the changes in *On the Road* Malcolm Cowley wanted for Viking Press. He'd definitely be leaving in the spring, bound for the West Coast again, ready to start the job.

The experiences which Jack had in Mexico City and Berkeley had made him much more confident than when he'd lived in Rocky Mount the winter before. He'd written two books he really liked in Mexico City, and meeting Snyder in Berkeley had convinced him that his Buddhist studies were not just a personal idosyncrasy. Snyder had affirmed Kerouac's dream of living a religious life detached from the responsibilities his family was urging on him. Jack wanted to be a wanderer, a bhikku, a "Dharma Bum," and it seemed possible, especially after Snyder had told him that he was "a great hero and noble Buddhist of literature and the road." Kerouac looked forward to unbroken months in Rocky Mount studying Buddhist texts, writing a little poetry, resting for the summer with his friends in California.

Shortly after Christmas, his mother was called to New York for a funeral. Left alone unexpectedly with his sister, his brother-in-law and little nephew, Jack immersed himself in a new novel. As he explained later:

My sister and her husband weren't interested. They went to bed and I took over the kitchen, brewed tea and took benzedrine. It was written by hand on the kitchen table. My sister wouldn't let me light candles so I used the kitchen light. You got to live with your family, you know. Mémêre wasn't there. She went to the funeral of her step-mother in Brooklyn. If she'd been there, I wouldn't have written it. We'd have talked all night. But that funeral reminded me of funerals, my brother's funeral . . . .

The novel was called *Visions of Gerard*, and it was about the death of Jack's older brother Gerard, who died in 1926, only nine years old. It is the earliest book in the Duluoz Legend, Kerouac's earliest memories of childhood. It is also the most religious book in Jack's fictional autobiography. *Visions of Gerard* reflected a much greater peace of mind than Jack's memories in *Doctor Sax*, mostly because he had met Gary Snyder, who helped Jack sort out his religious attitudes more clearly. The memory trips with morphine and marijuana in Mexico the previous summer also helped prepare Kerouac for the book about his earliest childhood. In *Mexico City Blues* he went far back into his memory for the first recollection of childhood, and his preoccupation with his earliest dreams emerged in references in *Tristessa*.

Like *Tristessa*, Kerouac conceived *Visions of Gerard* as a holy book. Allusions to the Buddha and Christ, "my sweet Christ too through all his Paulian tangles and bloody crosses of heathen violence," the Diamond Sutra, the writing of St. Augustine, all the references to Buddhism and Christianity brought Kerouac the same bright truth: "All is Well, practice Kindness, Heaven is Nigh." It was as though having written a biography of the Buddha, *Wake Up*, the previous spring in Rocky Mount, Jack next turned to the life of a Saint, as he conceived of his martyred brother Gerard.

There was sadness and suffering in Gerard's death, but none of the unrelieved misery surrounding Tristessa's sickness. Gerard was born in 1917 with a rheumatic heart. The story of his life was a "pain-tale." He was sick most of the time. The incidents Kerouac remembered about his brother quickly followed one another in the simple narrative, almost like a religious homily. Little Gerard at confession, telling his small sins to the priest; Gerard running uncomplainingly to the drugstore on a freezing winter night to buy aspirin to help relieve his mother's headache; Gerard dozing in the classroom after a bad night's rest, dreaming of the Virgin Mary taking him to Heaven; Gerard's last Christmas in 1926, six months before his death, lying in bed with pains in his legs and chest.

Kerouac turned four years old in March 1925; Gerard died in July. Jack remembered the details of his brother's final illness and funeral less well than he recalled his hundreds of subsequent dreams about them. At the time of Gerard's death, Jack expected some "holy transformation," in which Gerard would be resurrected "huge and all powerful and renewed." Jack had basked in Gerard's love and always missed it afterwards. He could remember the silly affectionate names Gerard called him: "Little Cabbage, Little Wolf, Little Piece of Butter . . . *Ti Jean le gros Pipi*—Little Fatty—you weigh two tons—they'll bring you in a truck—Little Red, Little red mug—Look Mama, the beautiful red cheeks Ti Jean has—he'll be a handsome little boy!—he'll be strong!" The day Gerard died, Jack was gleeful, not understanding why the adults mourned. He had "the dizzy brain of the four-year-old, with its visions and infold mysticisms" that he felt he'd still kept thirty years later, understanding more completely than any adult he'd ever talked to that "life is a dream already a long time ended."

Sitting in his sister's dim kitchen the first weeks of January, scribbling in pencil in his little notebooks about Gerard, Kerouac wrote at his best, his words racing over the pages sustained by the energy and euphoria of the benzedrine he was taking. It was his favorite high, making his language sure and confident, intensifying and clarifying his feelings for his past. Skillfully he combined

253

memories of his mother's stories about Gerard's sickness and funeral with his own fantasies of childhood.

In *Visions of Gerard* dream and reality were blended more smoothly than in any of Kerouac's books. The world of his babyhood in Lowell centered around his mother's kitchen and his playtime with Gerard. Sitting at Nin's kitchen table, it was easy to imagine himself thirty years earlier in Lowell at the family suppers of hamburgers and potatoes and bread dipped in gravy.

At Nin's house in Rocky Mount, Jack spent the afternoons playing with his little nephew and the family dog, and at night he could recall perfectly the vast stretches of his childhood playtime. His memory led him on to the shadowy world of the parochial school and the Catholic church of his childhood. When his sister Nin hung out clothes in the backyard with the wooden pins in her mouth, he remembered his mother looking toward the clothesline one December morning in 1925, and seeing Gerard come home from school early, dragging his feet, after having fainted in front of the nuns in the classroom, too weak to be out of bed again.

Mémère's stories about Gerard were the framework for Jack's narrative, but he combined anecdotes, past dreams and present visions into a fantasy book that seemed to him absolute proof that life was really a "dream already ended." Dream and reality were one in *Visions of Gerard.* The hunger he felt on the night of 16 January, 1956, in his sister's Rocky Mount kitchen, an hour or so before finishing the novel, became an image of a pork chop from 1926, like Bloom's breakfast kidneys in Joyce's *Ulysses,* "a reflection of a pork chop on water" eaten for lunch on the day of Gerard's funeral by Mr. Groscrop in Lowell, a sentence bursting with a flow of free association.

The cat that sat in the Rocky Mount kitchen as Jack wrote came into his vision of mèmère's old Lowell kitchen, and his sensations meditating in the midnight woods before starting to write each evening became his meditations as a baby in his Lowell bedroom: "my mouth's been open in awe an hour you might think the way it's sorta slobbered and run down my cheeks, I look down to discover my hands upturned and loose on my knees, the

254

utter disjointed non-existence of my bliss." Kerouac felt his memory was "limited and mundane," but his sense of the poetry of the event, and his power to recreate his vision in the narrative about Gerard, were never more strongly centered. The world of his experience and the world of his imagination came together in *Visions of Gerard* as in no other book of the Duluoz Legend.

After finishing *Visions of Gerard*, Jack lived another three months with his family. His summer job in the Cascade Mountains was confirmed, but it didn't begin until July. He had no place to stay in California if he arrived too soon before the summer so he tried to stretch out his welcome at his brother-in-law's house. He kept out of the family's way as much as he could, trying to spend most of his time in the woods or playing basketball with his little nephew Paul or sitting on his nylon poncho watching the dog run around the backyard.

As in the previous year, his family began to complain, unimpressed by what he insisted were the necessary solitudes of his serious Buddhist studies. In the evenings on the kitchen table he typed more dreams, adding to his *Book of Dreams* manuscript, and kept up a correspondence with his agent, hoping that Sterling Lord could place more of his books. But after *On The Road* nothing sold.

Jack turned thirty-four years old in March, and his family was worried about him. He had no means of support. *On The Road,* his second book, still hadn't come out, but Jack wasn't discouraged because he was still relieved to have a publisher. All he would talk about with his family were his plans to live alone for two months that summer on a mountaintop in Washington State, proof somehow that he'd turned his dreams for a bhikku life into fact.

His mother and sister argued with him about Buddhism but Jack insisted he was still a Catholic and that both religions taught that life was a dream. He wouldn't admit it to the family, but he liked the life in Rocky Mount. The thrombophlebitis in his legs gave him no more trouble after he started doing yoga head-stands every morning, five minutes a day, as he'd been taught by a railroad bum in Los Angeles the previous December.

Jack added his own particular variation to the exercise, touching his toes to the ground nine times for luck, and his legs never pained him again.

Kerouac even began to feel a certain awe for his own religious powers when he cured his mother of an allergy that was giving her trouble. Jack simply removed some flowers from the house he was sure were bothering her, and the symptoms miraculously cleared up. The trouble was that Jack had put himself into a religious trance to get to the source of mémêre's illness. As he later wrote in *The Dharma Bums*, "This was my first and last miracle because I was afraid of getting too interested in this and becoming vain. I was a little scared, too, of all the responsibility."

It grew increasingly hard for Kerouac's family to be patient with him. A short time after he'd arrived in Rocky Mount, he had felt terribly depressed. After supper he had paced the frosty yard outside the house and thrown himself on the ground, moaning, "I'm gonna die." He had suddenly realized a truth that had the force of a blissful enlightenment, that the "harsh inhospitable earth," as well as himself, was emptiness. He had sat on his poncho under a tree repeating over and over, "I am emptiness, I am not different from emptiness, neither is emptiness different from me; indeed, emptiness is me." The trouble was that Jack was completely alone in his knowledge. His family who were supporting him were totally unimpressed with his Buddhism and what they considered his other childish preoccupations. Jack was unable to convince his brother-in-law of something as simple as that the orange he was eating did not exist. "Well, if that's so, I still don't care." The family hassles were nothing new to Kerouac. He'd had them years before with his father when Jack wanted to stay home to be a writer. Then Jack had complained because he didn't "want to have to work to make a living . . . but'd rather sleep all day and stay up all night scribbling these visions of the world."

Chapter Twenty-Five

In April 1956, Kerouac got word that Snyder had moved into a cottage in Mill Valley that was big enough for him to live in too. Once again Jack packed his rucksack for the road and began hitchhiking to California. The soft life at his sister's house made being back on the road harder than he'd expected, especially when he found himself caught in a freaky April heatwave, walking miles on the highway trying to get rides. He had only sporadic luck in South Carolina, and when it seemed he'd never get out of Georgia, he bought himself a bus ticket to El Paso, Texas, where he hoped he could hop Southern Pacific freights to San Francisco.

In El Paso he walked along the mainline railroad tracks to the outskirts of the city, happy to be in open desert country where he could sleep out on the sand in the arroyo. It was so peaceful he wanted another night, so he spent the afternoon in Juarez and with only eight dollars to get him to Snyder's cottage, he forced himself back on the road the next morning. A Texan offered him a ride to Los Angeles for ten dollars, but accepted the four dollars that Jack said was all he had, and he rode with the Texan and his stories through the night to Los Angeles.

Dodging the railroad police, Jack caught a local freight to Santa Barbara, where he whiled away the afternoon on the beach waiting for the Midnight Ghost, the freight express to San Francisco. Jack settled himself on a flatcar under a truck, held on to his rucksack, stuck his shoes under his balled coat for a pillow and relaxed so completely as the train sped along the tracks that he fell asleep, waking in the glare of the yard office lights in San Luis Obispo, falling back asleep until he was nearly in San Francisco later that morning. He had one dollar when he left the railroad yard, but it was enough for the bus to Snyder's place in Mill Valley, and he didn't have to be back on the road for months.

Snyder's cabin was behind the house of his friend Locke McCorckle, a twenty-two-year-old-carpenter who lived with his wife and two children in the woods outside the town of Mill Valley, on the slopes of Mount Tamalpais. McCorckle lived what Kerouac called "the joyous life in America without much money" in *The Dharma Bums*. Ten years later it was to be the model for his hippie life all over America, but especially California. The man was an ex-college student working a part-time job as a manual laborer, spending lots of time with his family, studying Buddhist sutras on his own. His wife was an expert on managing a house without much money, baking her own brown bread, cooking large pots of vegetable soup. The house was nearly empty of furniture except for straw Japanese mats, lots of books and records and an expensive hi-fi set.

Jack felt at home with the McCorckles and in Snyder's shack halfway up the hill, where the floor was covered with straw mats, the mattress with a paisley cover and the walls lined with burlap. Gary had filled the room with bouquets of mountain flowers and pinned prints of Chinese paintings and area maps of Marin County and northwest Washington to the walls. He was working on a job with McCorckle, but he planned a big wine party to welcome Kerouac. It seemed to Jack that the two months in California before he reported as a fire-watcher would be one long good time. He felt so good in the little cabin that he even sketched a poem about Gary's sink a few days after he arrived.

It was, if anything, an even livelier scene in San Francisco than Jack had found the previous fall. The poet Robert Creeley remembered later that when he came to San Francisco in the spring of 1956, after the closing of Black Mountain College, "for a writer there was really no place that could have been quite like it, just at that time." In May, there was a repeat performance of the Six Gallery reading in a theater in Berkeley which was housed in the converted office of a trucking company filled with old seats from a movie theater. It had been used previously by a small theater company but mostly it had been kept locked and empty. The only other event which took place in the theater about the time of the poetry reading was a concert which a musician just in from New Orleans, Sam Charters, organized with the Traditional Jazz Quartet and the folksinger Barbara Dane. The program for the poetry reading was the same as at the Six Gallery, but since it was a theater stage there were elaborate throne-like wooden chairs taken from an old stage set, and there was a small row of lights that could be turned on in wild flashes of color. Rexroth was down in the front wearing a white turtle neck sweater, introducing the poets and keeping order. Kerouac passed the hat for wine and the gallon bottles went up and down the rows.

Before the reading Allen had people in to his cottage to eat spaghetti. I was brought over to the cottage by Peter Orlovsky. Ginsberg was going through another period of indecision, and he and Peter had stopped living together. I didn't know Peter very well, and the party at the cottage was quiet as people waited for the reading. Everybody ate the spaghetti hurriedly, piled into cars and headed across Berkeley to the theater. Before the audience gathered Peter walked me around the small, dark theater, showing off the drawings tacked on the walls. Most of them were beautiful line drawings LaVigne had made of Allen and Peter making love. It was the first time I was aware of the relationship between them.

Allen read "Howl" under a bright white stage light, gesturing and shouting, a thin, rumpled figure in a raveling dark sweater. There was the same tumult there had been at the Six Gallery. The audience booed and hissed when he shouted "Moloch," and shouted encouragement when he said "Love." Someone backstage threw on all the colored lights when he finished and there was a chaos of flashing colors. The other poets all stood up to shake his hand as everything whirled around them. I remember Kerouac drunkenly embracing his friends on the stage as the house lights were turned on and the audience jammed into the aisles. Everyone seemed excited by the poetry and people sensed that an event had taken place.

Excitement in San Francisco that spring centered also around a publishing venture started the previous summer, in 1955, by the poet Lawrence Ferlinghetti, a "Pocket Poets Series" published by the bookshop City Lights, which Ferlinghetti had started earlier with a friend named Peter Martin. They wanted City Lights to be a place that would serve the function of a Parisian cafe as well as a bookstore, where people could sit around at little tables and read and talk. It stocked mostly paperbacks, opened at ten in the morning and closed at midnight, and was housed in a narrow crowded shop on Columbus Avenue between North Beach and Chinatown. The winding staircase led up to a well-stocked poetry section on the second floor, most of the small press magazines and books in the country collected there.

Within a very short time City Lights was one of the favorite meeting places for poets and bohemians in San Francisco, although for the first two or three years the shop never broke even financially. Ferlinghetti had started to publish the Pocket Poets Series in July 1955, with his own first book of poems, *Pictures of the Gone World*. His idea was to break away from the Bay Area tradition of small presses that published only expensive, if beautiful, limited editions selling to rare book collectors and libraries. Ferlinghetti wanted to bring poetry to everybody's pocket in small and inexpensive paperback books. He followed his first book with Kenneth Rexroth's *Thirty Spanish Poems of Love and Exile* and Kenneth Patchen's *Poems of Humor & Protest*, and these established his series.

Ginsberg agreed to let *Howl for Carl Solomon* appear as Pocket Poets Number Four. When Jack arrived in the spring of 1956, Allen was putting the finishing touches to the book, getting it ready to go to press that summer. Like Ferlinghetti and Snyder, Ginsberg had a more political view of poetry after his years on the West Coast. Ginsberg had first been approached by the San Francisco publisher Berne Porter after he heard "Howl" read at the Six Gallery. Porter wanted to publish the poem as a thirty-dollar volume on beautiful paper, expensively bound as a limited edition, but Ginsberg refused. Snyder thought he did the right thing, turning his back on the earlier tradition of avant-grade small press publishing and the esotericism of the Berkeley poets.

To fill out his Pocket Poets' *Howl* volume, Allen included several of the Berkeley poems he'd written in the fall of 1955—"A Supermarket in California," "Transcription of Organ Music," Sunflower Sutra" (a poem after a walk with Kerouac and Whalen in the Southern Pacific yards), the brilliantly satirical "America" and "In the Baggage Room at Greyhound," where Allen worked until late spring as a baggage clerk: the poem was dated 9 May, 1956.

After Jack arrived at Snyder's cottage in Mill Valley, Allen checked with him for the titles of all the books he'd written since *The Town and the City*, because he dedicated *Howl* to Kerouac, Burroughs and Cassady, his three closest friends. (Lucien Carr's name was also originally included, but it was dropped in the second edition of *Howl*.) The first name on the dedication page was Kerouac's:

DEDICATION
To -

Jack Kerouac, new Buddha of American prose, who spit forth intelligence into eleven books written in half the number of years (1951-1956)—*On The Road, Visions of Neal, Doctor Sax, Springtime Mary, The Subterraneans, San Francisco Blues, Some of the Dharma, Book of Dreams, Wake Up, Mexico City Blues*, and *Visions of Gerard*—creating a spontaneous bop prosody and original classic literature. Several phrases and the title of *HOWL* are taken from him.

It was a period of warm friendship and mutual encouragement. Snyder described the scene in Mill Valley with Kerouac in a poem that was later included in his book, *Myths and Texts*:

White-crowned sparrows
Make tremendous singings in the trees
The rooster down the valley crows and crows,
Jack Kerouac outside, behind my back
Reads the Diamond Sutra in the sun.

The lines were included in *The Dharma Bums* as a poem stuck on a nail of the cabin addressed to Locke McCorkle ("Sean Monahan"). As Snyder later said, when Kerouac wrote his books he sometimes changed little things around for "novelistic purposes." After Jack had lived with Gary a few days in Mill Valley, he wrote his most direct response to Buddhism, *The Scripture of the Golden Eternity*, much more to the point than his reading notes and meditations in *Some of the Dharma* and more personal than his Buddha biography *Wake Up*. Kerouac reported later:

Gary Snyder said, "All right, Kerouac, it's about time for you to write a sutra." That's a thread of discourse, a scripture. He knew I was a Bodhisattva and had lived twelve million years in twelve million directions. You see, they really believe that, those maniacs. I'm a Catholic all along. I was really kidding Gary Snyder. Boy, they're so gullible.
I wrote it in Locke McCorkle's shack in Mill Valley. He's Sean Monahan in *The Dharma Bums*. In pencil, carefully revised and everything, because it was a scripture. I had no right to be spontaneous.

Like traditional Buddhist sutras, Jack's *The Scripture of the Golden Eternity* was a hymn of praise to "One that is what is, the golden eternity, or God, or, Tathagata—the *name*." It had moments of self-definition reminiscent of Ginsberg's Walt Whitman meditations in his Berkeley garden: "I am the golden eternity in mortal animate form," but Jack's sutra was more centrally linked to traditional, ecstatic revelation. The *Scripture* was in sixty-six paragraphs, and the longest one, paragraph sixty-four, was Jack's description of a rapturous vision of the "perfect, the golden solitude, the golden emptiness:"

64   I was smelling flowers in the yard, and
when I stood up I took a deep breath and
the blood all rushed to my brain and I woke up
dead on my back in the grass. I had apparently
fainted, or died, for about sixty seconds. My
neighbor saw me but he thought I had just

suddenly thrown myself on the grass to enjoy
the sun. During that timeless moment of unconsciousness
I saw the golden eternity. I saw
heaven. . . . The "golden" came from the sun in my eyelids,
and the "eternity" from my sudden instant
realization as I woke up that I had just
been where it all came from and where it
was all returning . . . . As I regained
consciousness I felt sorry I had
a body and a mind suddenly realizing I
didn't even have a body and a mind and nothing
had ever happened and everything is alright
forever and forever and forever. O thank you
thank you thank you.

65   This is the first teaching from the
golden eternity.

66   The second teaching from the golden eternity
is that there never was a first teaching
from the golden eternity. So be sure.`

Paragraphs sixty-five and sixty-six were like the verbal
games Kerouac played with Snyder. Once in the Mill
Valley cabin when Gary was busy, he got angry at Jack
for sitting around doing nothing and asked, "Why did
you sit around all day?" Jack reminded him, "I am the
Buddha known as the Quitter." Then, Kerouac wrote:

Japhy's face would crease up in that funny littleboy laugh
of his, like a Chinese boy laughing, crow's tracks appearing
on each side of his eyes and his long mouth cracking open.
He was so pleased with me sometimes.

Kerouac's particular brand of Buddhism, mixed as it
was with his Catholicism, can be found in *The Scripture
of the Golden Eternity*, as well as in the differences he
described in his own Buddhist beliefs and those of Snyder's
in *The Dharma Bums*. At the center of Kerouac's religious
faith was his waiting for death, for heaven and for the
ultimate realization "of why he was there."
   He told Snyder that he "didn't give a goddamn about
the mythology and all the names and national flavors of
Buddhism, but was just interested in the first of Sakya-

muni's four noble truths, *All life is suffering*. " 'Listen Gary,' I said, 'I'm not a Zen Buddhist, I'm a serious Buddhist, I'm an old-fashioned dreamy Hinayana coward of later Mahayanism' . . . my contention being that Zen Buddhism didn't concentrate on kindness so much as on confusing the intellect to make it perceive the illusion of all sources of things."

Snyder also differed from Kerouac in being a political activist, a fervent anarchist, but his political attitudes were not shared by Kerouac. He wrote in *Desolation Angels* that Gary couldn't go back to his lookout job with the Forestry Service because he'd been labeled a Communist. All Jack wanted to do was steer clear of such trouble. To him, living the rest of his life as a Dharma Bum meant he'd be a divinely inspired bhikku, staying away from the politics and problems of American capitalism.

What Jack admired most was Gary's religious discipline, and the intense dedication of his Buddhist activity throughout his waking hours, not his political idealism. Living together with Snyder in Mill Valley, he was most impressed by Gary's meditations, "regular things, by the clock, he'd meditate first thing waking in the morning then he had his mid-afternoon meditation, only about three minutes long, then before going to bed and that was that." Kerouac's Buddhism was "Do-Nothing," Snyder's was "Activity," but in Jack's mind they were both Dharma Bums, "two strange dissimilar monks on the same path."

When Snyder sailed to Japan on 15 May, 1956, planning to be away for some years, Kerouac continued to live in the cabin behind McCorkle's house. He had no trouble finding friends to keep him company for a while. Gary had begun to criticize Jack for the amount of wine he was drinking. The longer he stayed in San Francisco, the more often Jack was drunk. At the parties he'd rather drink than talk or dance. Robert Creeley remembered that Jack, like himself, was too shy to dance, and Michael McClure's wife, Joanna, had a vivid memory of how Jack would enter a room to meet people, coming on strong to give himself social confidence, slapping them on the back clumsily like a high school football player and then subsiding quickly into a dim corner with his own gallon of wine. There was a bad scene at Kenneth Rexroth's house one night when Jack was offensively drunk in front of Rexroth's seven year old daughter Mary and was thrown out. Later at a Mill Valley party, Rexroth made a sweeping gesture to include all the poets present—Ginsberg, Snyder, Whalen—but excluded Kerouac as being unimportant, sneering "He's too drronk all the time."

With Snyder away, Jack turned to his old drinking buddies, Bob Donlin and Al Sublette. Snyder's literary acumen kept Kerouac's self-aggrandizing boasts and grandstand poses in perspective, but drunk with his other friends Jack felt no restraint to his enthusiasm for himself. When he told them he was Shakespeare or Joyce reincarnated, they didn't bring him down by insisting he wasn't. After a particularly drunken binge with Donlin and Sublette in San Francisco on 28 May, 1956, Jack returned to the Mill Valley cabin and tried to prove his boasts by writing a long exercise in spontaneous prose while his friends slept off the wine.

This was a piece titled "Old Angel Midnight." The prose was supposed to be Shakespearean, but Jack coasted on his own personal currents of sweet wine associations and floating perceptions. In the different sections, Jack ranged in his thoughts of friends and places, his form fluid as jello. The predominant mood was one of sweet, alcoholic melancholy. The port wine confirmed his sense of loneliness, and the writing of his spontaneous prose was his only shield in a world where he'd found no place for himself except as his mother's Ti Jean.

On 18 June, 1956, Jack closed up Gary's cabin, said goodbye to the McCorkles and went back on the road, heading north on Highway 101. He was aiming for the Cascade Range in northwest Washington, close to the Canadian border, to report for his summer job at the Forestry Service. Thoughts of Snyder kept coming back to him. In his pack he had the peanuts and raisins left from their last hike together on the slopes of Mount Tamalpais, and it was with Snyder as his example that Kerouac set out to test the bhikku life as it was lived in the West.

Chapter Twenty-Six

It's possible that the summer of 1956 was the only period in Kerouac's life in which he could have tried to live the life of solitude he'd written and talked about so much. It was his absorption in Buddhism that made it possible and though Snyder had first interested him in the bhikku life, his own interest in Buddhism had started long before he'd met Gary. But always before he'd been tied up in the uncertainties of what he was doing. With *On The Road* coming out he could feel sure enough of himself to try it.

Like most of the experiences in Jack's life, the reality of what happened was considerably different from his anticipation. But with almost everything in his books, the description of how important the experience would be is all that's remembered; the flatness, or the discomfort, or the unhappiness of it is forgotten. What happened to him on the mountaintop was that almost nothing happened. His eight weeks on Desolation Peak were just like the eight weeks of all the fire-watchers who spent their summers in the Cascades. It was monotonous, uneventful and boring. By the end of it what he felt most intensely was his own loneliness.

He was sent to a fire-fighting school for a week before he went to his lookout and then the rangers helped him pack his supplies in to the station on Starvation Ridge, in the northern Cascades. Snyder had been a lookout at Crater Mountain on previous summers, and Whalen had been on Sourdough Mountain, and they'd told him a little of what to look for in the terrain—Ross Lake and Mount Baker National Forest nearby, Desolation Peak itself named after a fire in the summer of 1919 that filled the skies of northern Washington and British Columbia with smoke leaving charred snags still visible on Desolation.

On top of Desolation Jack lived in a primitive wooden cabin, the windows of which opened to a view of the surrounding peaks stretching for miles in every direction. There were no other human beings in sight, and his only contact with the outside world was through the Forestry Service radio, which kept the lookouts in daily contact with each other. All he had to do for two months was watch for smoke in the mountains below him and report any fires as soon as he spotted the tell-tale smoke plume.

The days soon settled into a simple routine. There was nothing to do but wait for time to pass, breathe in the thin mountain air, open his canned goods and cook his meals over his woodstove, eat, chop wood, wash his dishes once a day, collect a bucket of snow from the shade on the side of the mountain for washing and cooking, pace along the narrow path in the space around the lookout, report on the forestry radio and watch for fires. No fires threatened Starvation Ridge or Desolation Peak the summer he was there.

He slept on a wooden bunk with a rope mattress in the sleeping bag Snyder helped him pick out in Oakland. To amuse himself he baked rye muffins, played a baseball game with a pack of cards that he'd invented when he was a boy in Lowell, and picked a few sprigs of alpine fir and a wild flower every day to put in a coffee cup on his desk. Jack wrote at the desk facing away from looming Mount Hozomeen on his north, the dark, naked rock of Hozomeen coming to symbolize for him "the Void," with its clouds and thunderstorms, the two sharp peaks of Hozomeen looming in his window as he lay in bed, "the Northern Lights behind it reflecting all the ice of the North Pole from the other side of the world."

During the long afternoons he sat in his canvas chair facing "Void Hozomeen," listening to the silence of his cabin and making up haikus:

Mist before the peak
—the dream
Goes on

> The sound of silence
>> is all the instruction
> You'll get

He'd brought everything with him that he needed to write. Only the benzedrine and marijuana had been left behind. On his desk he had his papers and pencils, Beechnut gum, his tobacco pouch and small pair of aluminum scissors to cut squares out of "Aircraft Flash Message Record" paper to roll his own uneven cigarettes. When he sat at the desk at night and looked at himself in the reflection of the black window, he saw "a rugged faced man in a dirty ragged shirt, need-a-shave, frowny, lipped, eyed, haired, nosed, eared, necked, adamsappled, eyebrowed," then looking down at the papers on the desk with half-closed eyes he saw "the delicate milky litter of papers piled, like some old dream of a picture of papers, like papers piled on a desk in a carton, like a realistic scene from an old Russian film, and the oil lamp shadowing some in half—"

But even with his hours at the desk there wasn't much writing. He scribbled his dreams and his thoughts in his diary, and took two months to write a long letter to his mother, many pages long, assuring her that he would always take care of her.

> Thunder in the mountains—
>> the iron
> Of my mother's love

The days went by in an unending wheel of pale blue skies and floating cloud wisps and dim shrouds of heat filling the lower valleys. He had nothing to associate with, nothing to respond to. Six months before, writing *Visions of Gerard* in Rocky Mount, he had deliberately gone back to his memories of Lowell ". . . to recall childhood, I did eat Ritz and peanut butter and milk at four, and played the baseball game at my desk." But from the windows of his lookout nothing he could see stirred his memory.

In the sixty-three days that he was on Desolation Peak he had enough time to write another eleven books of the

Duluoz Legend, if he'd kept writing at the same speed that he'd written the other narratives of his autobiography. Instead, he just kept a journal, "Desolation In Solitude," that became his book about the "Angels of Desolation," who visited him on the mountain, all the visionary characters who were his only company in the presence of the mountain called Hozomeen Void.

The days on Desolation were occasionally dated—14 August, 22 August—as memory and dream and description of prosaic events in the present intermixed.

As he came closer and closer to the end of his stay at the lookout station Jack began to run out of things to write about: "Enough I've said it all." He tried to convince himself that since nothing really existed in the world then the page he was writing on didn't exist either. This led him to a page of spontaneous muttering, scribbling words as in "Old Angel Midnight," drawing triangles, composing poems from the words "black" and "bling."

Just before he left he tried to write down what he'd learned from the experience, not the vision that he put down later in *The Dharma Bums* when it had become an exciting memory, but what he felt that day, the monotony and boredom of it, his impatience waiting to come down off the mountain.

What did I learn on Gwaddawackamblack? I learned that I hate myself because by myself I am only myself and not even that and how monotonous it is to be monostonos-ponos-purt-pit ariant-hor por por . . . I want to come down RIGHT AWAY because the smell of onions on my hand as I bring blueberries to my lips on the mountainside suddenly reminds me of the smell of hamburgers and raw onions and coffee and dishwater in lunchcarts of the World to which I want to return at once . . . let there be rain on redbrick walls and I got a place to go and poems to write about hearts not just rocks—Desolation Adventure finds me finding at the bottom of myself abysmal nothingness worst than no illusion even—my mind's in rags—

He had gone up on the mountain hoping in the solitude to come face to face with God and instead he came face to face with himself: ". . . no liquor, no drugs, no chance of faking it but face to face with ole Hateful Duluoz Me."

In reality, Kerouac had set himself too hard a test. Two months of sudden enforced solitude was, as Snyder would have said, a "mind-bending experience" for any man, being totally alone and without contracts for the first long stretch of his life, in the midst of a frighteningly vast and impersonal sweep of mountains, crags, boulders, lakes and valleys.

Just down off the mountain, sitting in the forestry motorboat picking up the lookouts along Ross Lake, he felt like a ghost of himself, as though he'd lost touch with human life in the long days of solitude. His ears and his eyes played tricks on him, giving him the eerie sensation that the others in the boat weren't really there: "For just an instant this angel had faded away—Two months in desolation'll do it, no matter what mountain's your name—" It wasn't until he had smoked a few cigarettes, listened to some pop music on the radio at the ranger station, eaten an ice cream cone and caught up on the baseball news that he really felt back with the living, and even then he didn't come totally alive until he was back on the road hitchhiking to Seattle.

In the book he wrote later about this period of his life, *Desolation Angels*, he described everything that happened in the year before *On The Road* was published in more detail than in any of the other books. The second half of the book, "Passing Through," was written in 1961, five years later, but it was as closely detailed a chronology. With this, too, Jack had simply transcribed his daily journal notebooks directly into the manuscript. It's almost a day-by-day account of the restlessness and the moodiness of the year, and at the same time it's almost a blueprint of the way he was living as the year passed. If someone wanted to pattern his life after Kerouac's, *Desolation Angels* would give him the closest look at what Jack's life style was, through the hours and the days. In *The Dharma Bums* Jack had outlined the equipment and attitudes it took to live his way, including both the spiritual equipment as well as ordinary equipment like prosaic tents and Oakland store sleeping bags. In *Desola-*

270

tion Angels was a long and nervous account of how he lived it.

His first days in Seattle, after coming down from Desolation Peak, were typical of Kerouac. He checked into a skid-row hotel, woke up alone, went out early on a gray Saturday morning to empty streets, and, ate, alone, in a restaurant—eggs sunny side up, fried potatoes, a little paper cup of grape jelly and buttered toast with lots of coffee. He walked the streets and watched "all humanity hep and weird wandering on the evening sidewalk," bought cheap wine and drank it lying on the bed in his hotel room, reading magazines, looking at baseball scores and scowling at pictures of Eisenhower in a copy of *Time*.

For someone down from the mountains or just off a ship, Seattle is mostly a string of bars and cheap outfitting stores along First Avenue, a sloping, drab street of dreary brick buildings and jumbled shop windows. There were a couple of dance halls and a burlesque house, but the dance halls had a YMCA feel about them. Jack spent the evening in the burlesque house watching the girls and the comedians. Suddenly he was back in Lowell, "by redbrick neons of the stagedoor," remembering his father's associations with the vaudevillians in Lowell. They were all "just like my father, your father, all fathers, working and making a living in the dark sad earth—" In the smelly, dark rows of seats in a Seattle burlesque house he still wasn't free of Lowell, his father or himself.

A bus got him down to San Francisco, and as in Seattle he slung his pack on his back and walked the streets until he found a room in a cheap hotel. He was elated to be back again: "Wow, an entirely different scene, San Francisco always is, it always gives you the courage of your convictions—" He had friends in town; there was jazz to listen to; it was the only place he knew of where he could drink in the streets without anyone caring. He'd come into town late Sunday afternoon, found himself a room, had a big Chinese dinner and drunk beer until it was late enough to go to the Cellar and hear some jazz.

The club was packed and he had to stand in the outside hall against a wall. The band was playing cool jazz and the audience was mostly black. "They've come from Fillmore in cars, with their girls or without, the cool colored cats of Sunday San Fran in incredibly beautiful neat sports attire, to knock your eyes out, shoes, lapels, ties, no-ties, studs—They've brought their horns in taxis and in their own cars, pouring down into the Cellar to really give it some class and jazz now, the Negro people who will be the salvation of America—" He responded totally to the music, and listening to the beat in the jazz that night, he heard a beat that was even more than the music:

. . . everything is going to the beat—It's the beat generation, its *béat,* it's the beat to keep, it's the beat of the heart, it's being beat and down in the world and like oldtime lowdown and like in ancient civilizations and slave boatmen rowing galleys to a beat and servants spinning pottery to the beat—

Kerouac always wanted to have the first night in San Francisco alone, to do what he wanted to do, to be wildly himself without anyone to watch. But once awake the next day in his shabby hotel it was time to get in touch, make his telephone calls, get people out of bed, get things going. At a coffee shop on Broadway he got back into the old shouting exultations with Allen, Gregory and Neal. "We're all yelling at the same time—We mill around bumping into one another, across streets, down streets, looking for a place to drink coffee—" Neal drove Jack and Gregory to Locke McCorkle's cabin in Mill Valley, and as the car wheeled across Golden Gate Bridge Kerouac felt "wonderful and wild, I've found my friends and a great vibration of living Joy and of Poetry is running thru us—" Corso yelled his new poems, bursting all over with poems; Cassady rapped about his new betting system at the racetrack, an endless monologue in what seemed to Jack amazing rhythms of talk.

Back in San Francisco, Kerouac started drinking wine, a poorboy stuck in his belt, and, as he drank, everything got more confused but more exciting. Allen was back with Peter Orlovsky, then two of the San Francisco poets, Michael McClure and Robert Duncan, drove everybody to Peter's apartment on the south side of San Francisco on lower Third Street, beside the water tanks and industrial railroad tracks, in a black housing project. Peter and Allen lived there with Peter's fifteen-year-old brother Lafcadio. Duncan tried to talk with Jack about his work, but Kerouac couldn't talk seriously. "In fact he's (Duncan) too decent for me—all I can understand is franticness— I wish I could tell him—but he knows I know—"

For the first few days he had to keep up the "franticness," he had to be the one who was different, to have his own way of getting through life. He could even laugh at himself in the wild confusions. At a dinner party that Ruth Witt-Diamont, the director of the San Francisco Poetry Workshop, gave for the poets Jack was drunk, and, as usual, began shouting at the table. "I *always* ride freight trains." Corso, "Raphael" in the novel, shouted back at him,

"Who wants to ride freight trains!"—"I don't dig all this crap where you ride freight trains and have to exchange butts with bums—Why do you go to all that, Duluoz?"— "Really no kiddin!"

"But this is a first-class freight train," and everybody guffaws and I look at Irwin under the laughter and tell him: "It really is, the Midnight Ghost is a first-class train, no stops on the right-o-way," which Irwin knows from knowing about the railroad from Cody and myself—But the laughter is genuine, and I console myself with the reminder, embodied in the Tao of my remembrance. "The Sage who provokes laughter is more valuable than a well." So I well at the wink of that brimming wine welkin glass and pour out decanters of wine (red burgundy) in my glass. It's almost unmannerly the way I wail at that wine . . ."

For a time he was even able to think of himself as a member of the group of poets: Corso, Ginsberg, Snyder, Whalen, Ferlinghetti, Duncan, McClure. It wasn't tightly knit, even coherent in the sense of being together, but for Jack, it was a group, and he could share some of their attitudes and excitements. In *Desolation Angels* there is a sense of identification with the whole group of the "disaffiliated," all of them like himself separate from the mainstream of American life and the Establishment literary scene. Kerouac was different from his friends in being almost apolitical, but in the beginning he was part

273

of their scene as they drifted closer to an anarchist, revolutionary viewpoint.

In September 1956, Allen and Gregory planned how they would run the revolution, deciding they'd "go all the way out! We'll take our clothes off to read our poems!" They had copies of Allen's first book. He'd spent the summer as a seaman off the coast of Alaska, and he'd mimeographed fifty-three copies of a Mexican poem "Siesta in Xalba," to help the time pass before *Howl* came out. Allen definitely thought of *Howl* as a revolutionary document, with the strong political attack of its opening lines, "I saw the best minds of my generation destroyed by madness, starving hysterical naked . . ." Other poems in the *Howl* collection were as specifically political, like "America." "America I've given you all and now I'm nothing . . . . It's true I don't want to join the Army or turn lathes in precision parts factories, I'm nearsighted and psychopathic anyway./America I'm putting my queer shoulder to the wheel."

Ginsberg insisted on confronting the Establishment. He asked Ferlinghetti to mail copies of his City Lights book to established East Coast critics, such as Lionel Trilling, Mark Van Doren, Malcolm Cowley and Joseph Wood Krutch. He was beginning to attract national attention from the "Howl" readings, and he showed Jack an article written about him in the New York *Times* by the poet Richard Eberhart, printed while Jack was coming down from Desolation on 2 September. Kerouac was never comfortable with the political side of Ginsberg, although he described him in *Desolation Angels* as a Jewish prophet, bearded and serious.

Like Kerouac, Ginsberg was aware that the loosely allied group was an exclusive club, but he was unsure of the relationships between them. He brooded that there were plots brewing when the photographer for *Mademoiselle* Magazine came to take pictures of them all but set up private sessions with McClure and Duncan. Allen saw that Duncan would rightly resent exclusive attention on Ginsberg and Kerouac as San Francisco poets presented outside of a larger literary community. Ginsberg often said that he had a vision of everybody hand in hand in paradise and no bullshit: "Hand in *hand* it's got to be."

But there was no way to keep the world from closing in on them eventually, despite the shouting and the nervous running and jumping through San Francisco's foggy streets. Gregory, Peter, Allen, Jack and Robert LaVigne were sitting drunkenly on a curbstone when the police stopped in a cruiser. Neighbors had complained about the noise. Jack was relieved when the police left after a warning. "I wanta instruct my bhikkus to avoid the authorities, it's written in the Tao, it's the only way—It's the only straight line, right through—" The next night everybody got drunk again to be photographed for *Mademoiselle.* As they posed arm in arm, Kerouac, Ginsberg and Corso, Jack saw them inseparably entwined. In his imagination they became the million dollar outfield of an All-Star baseball team. Allen was like "serious Lou Gehrig, who hits long homeruns lefthanded." Gregory was "the fair haired Di-Mag who can play faultless ball without appearing to try or strain," and Jack was "Ty Cobb . . . I'm crazy, nobody's ever liked my personality, I'm no Babe Ruth Beloved."

Everybody finally just got tired. Corso argued with McClure, Peter irritated Jack by pissing on a crowded street, Jack dropped empty beer bottles on the floor at the back of a city bus and the noise they made annoyed the driver. On Friday afternoon Jack shouldered his pack again and took a train down to San Jose with Neal, to stay a few days with Carolyn and the children before going on to Mexico City. Just as in the previous winter he couldn't take the straight life with the Cassadys for more than a little while. There was no separate bedroom for him in their new house, and despite the hashish and the marijuana that was always around, and even though he was sleeping in his sleeping bag in the backyard under the bushes, he became restless with what he thought was a serene family life with the children, the swimming pool, the pizza pies and the never-ending TV quiz shows and advertisements.

However stultifying the domestic scene with mémêre had been, he couldn't stand it with his friends. When he was with them he should be able to let loose himself, and he didn't want them to be tied down to anything. In a few short nights, despite his real affection for Carolyn and the children, it was time to get Neal to drive him down to the Southern Pacific yards. After one last hassle—Cassady was heavily stoned on hashish and insisted on Jack's taking elaborately unnecessary precautions not to get hurt in the railroad yards—Kerouac finally picked up a freight to Los Angeles.

He was still trying to live the wandering life when he crossed the desert on the way to Mexico. Neal had joked once, sitting on a freight with Jack, watching him hang out of the boxcar sniffing the breeze, that in a previous lifetime Kerouac must have spent a lot of time in a dungeon, because he needed so much fresh air. But the police stopped him on the highway outside Tucson and asked what he was doing out. He got off with a warning, but Jack's fears of being jailed ended any further adventures as a bhikku.

In Mexico he tried to pick up the life he'd had there the year before, but that worked out as badly as his attempts to be a lonely Buddhist wanderer on Arizona's interstate highway. He'd planned to rent his rooftop room at 212 Orizaba again, but in the year he'd been away the group he'd known there had fallen apart. Bill Garver was very sick, and Tristessa was so battered he couldn't deal with her. She went into rages on goofballs and tried to beat Jack up. One disaster followed another. Jack told Allen in the last week of September 1956, that Bill himself was ready to leave.

Kerouac tried to shut himself off from the deterioration of his friends by going back to his writing. Using a lot of benzedrine and writing by candlelight he finished his short novel about Tristessa, but he realized that the situation he found himself in had changed the style of the book. With his mood changed after the weeks on Desolation Peak, he thought of *Tristessa* as a sad novel.

But he still had more writing to do. When one book was finished he immediately started another, what he told Allen were the first chapters about his experience on Desolation and then in Seattle and San Francisco, the book that was to be titled *Desolation Angels*. He had already filled in so much of his "legend" in his previous books—*Visions of Gerard, Doctor Sax, Maggie Cassidy, On The Road, Visions of Cody* and *The Subterraneans*—that he felt he was ready to add the chapters about what had happened to him the month before. He originally titled it "The Angels in The World," getting his title from the essay by William Carlos Williams that was to be the introduction to the *Howl* collection. *Howl* wouldn't be published until the end of 1956, but Allen had let Jack read the introduction in manuscript before he'd left San Francisco. Williams had written, "We are blind and live our blind lives out in blindness. Poets are damned but they are not blind, they see with the eyes of angels. This poet sees through and all around the horrors he partakes of . . ."

Jack began to feel more and more depressed. In Mexico City thieves stole a new book of poems he'd been working on and in his anger he wrote Allen, who was planning to come down and stay with him, to hurry up so they could get baseball bats and knives and stones and confront the thieves and recover the poetry. He was feeling vulnerable and a little crazy. Late one night in his little crumbling rooftop room he sat down and wrote a long, hard description of himself by candlelight, almost as if he were taking stock before some turning point on the road:

Take another look at me to get the story better (now I'm getting drunk):—I am a widow's son, at the time she is living with relatives, penniless . . . . I'm 34, regular looking, but in my jeans and eerie outfits people are scared to look at me because I really look like an escaped mental patient with enough physical strength and innate dog-sense to manage outside of an institution to feed myself and go from place to place in a world growing gradually narrower in its views about eccentricity every day—Walking thru towns in the middle of America I got stared at weirdly—I was bound to live my own way . . . I was also a notorious wino who exploded anywhere anytime he got drunk—My friends in San Francisco said I was a Zen Lunatic, at least a Drunken Lunatic, yet sat with me in moonlight fields drinking and singing . . . I was an Ambitious Paranoid—Nothing could stop me from writing big books of prose and poetry for nothing, that is, with no hope of ever having them published . . . Strangely enough, these scribblings were the first of their kind in the world, I was originating (without knowing it, you say?) a new way of writing about life, no fiction, no craft, no revising afterthoughts . . . all of it innocent go-ahead confession, the discipline of making the mind the slave of the tongue with no chance to lie or re-elaborate (in keeping not only with the dictums of Dichtung Warheit Goethe but those of the Catholic Church my childhood) . . . For I was Ti Jean and the difficulty in explaining all this and "Ti Jean" too is that readers who havent read up to this point in the earlier works are not filled in on the background—The background being my brother Gerard who said things to me before he died, though I don't remember a word, or maybe I do remember a few (I was only four)—But said things to me about a *reverence* for life, no, at least a reverence of the *idea* of life, which I translated as meaning that life itself is the Holy Ghost—

That we all wander thru flesh, while the dove cries for us, back to the Dove of Heaven—

So I was writing to honor that . . .

Chapter Twenty-Seven

In October 1956, Ginsberg left San Francisco to meet Kerouac in Mexico City but it took him a while to get there. Allen's trips were already becoming public caravans with crowds of people, like a madcap circus. After spending the night at Neal's, where Gregory had a nightmare about eggs and couldn't face breakfast, the four of them, Allen, Gregory, Peter and Peter's brother Lafcadio, went on to Los Angeles. In nearby Venice they gave the reading that Lawrence Lipton later described in his book *The Holy Barbarians*. Someone in the audience asked Ginsberg what he meant by "naked" values, and Ginsberg demonstrated by taking off his clothes. As Allen told Ferlinghetti, he "disrobed, finally."

Allen, for the first time, was beginning to realize that he could reach audiences, that he could make them respond to his poetry by the force of his stage personality. It was this power that helped to make Ginsberg one of the most important and influential forces in American poetry, and he already had a glimpse of what could happen in the articles that were being written, in the audiences that were jamming into his readings. He wasn't only following Whitman. His "angelic ravings" were in much the same spirit as the poetry of the futurist and Soviet revolutionary Valdimar Mayakovsky, and he had a deep, committed sense of the importance of the writing he and Kerouac were doing. When he arrived in Mexico City at the end of October 1956 he tried to bring Jack out of his depression by insisting they would soon be internationally famous writers, even celebrities. As they sat in Jack's room smoking marijuana, he told Jack: "I want you to listen to my speeches like across Red Square." Their books would raise what Allen called "the Lamb of America," and he made speeches to Jack insisting that "How can the East have any respect for a country that has no prophetic Poets! The Lamb must be raised! Big trembling Oklahomas need poetry and nakedness! Airplanes must fly for a reason from one gentle heart to an open heart . . ."

When Jack rejected Allen's idea of tenderness, Ginsberg asked him what had become of his "old Dostoyevsky curiosity? You've become so *whiney*! You're coming on like an old sick junkey sitting in a room in nowhere."

In San Francisco it had been Jack who wanted to keep going with his wine and his shouts. In Mexico City it was Allen who kept them all moving. He went out to the University to meet Mexican poets, he climbed Teotihuacan, he even dragged Jack to the floating gardens of Xochimilco, where Jack had a good time despite himself.

But Jack was really only interested in sitting around Garver's room, getting high, or watching his friends get high on Garver's morphine, going down into the streets to eat Mexican thin, cheap steak dinners or spending twenty-four cents getting laid by Mexican prostitutes.

Allen couldn't shake him out of his mood, even with his insistence that their lives were going to get better. He finally told Jack he should get a girl. One afternoon, when they were walking through the Alameda, the large park in the center of Mexico City, they all posed together for a sidewalk photographer, standing proudly in a tight group. Allen was in a cowboy hat with his arms around Jack and Peter, with Gregory and Lafcadio kneeling in front of them. They were, as Jack saw them, together, like a team.

The aimless, scattered pattern of Kerouac's life did not change as the weeks passed. It was still only late October, they'd been in Mexico only a few weeks, but the new plan was for everybody to get to New York, save their money and meet Burroughs for a reunion in Tangier later in the winter.

Nobody had much money, although Jack's agent Sterling Lord had written him that an editor at Grove Press named Donald Allen was interested in taking *The Subterraneans* for the first issue of a magazine Grove was starting, *The Evergreen Review*. Jack hoped to get a penny a word for the short novel, about 50,000 words, coming to $500, enough to get him to Tangier. But first they had to find a way to get to New York.

Corso was the first to leave. His first book, *The Vestle Lady On Brattle*, had already been published by students at Harvard, and the poet Randall Jarrell, then the Poetry Consultant at the Library of Congress, was impressed enough with the book to invite Gregory to come stay with him in Washington. Corso was able to fly out of Mexico City, but the rest of them had to pool their money and get in touch with a man who was advertising for passengers to drive with him to New York. Jack jammed everything back in his rucksack and left the room at 212 Orizaba for the last time.

Remembering it later Jack described it as a horrible trip. The man was a boring talker, everyone was sitting crowded with their luggage in the car, three in the front and three in the back, knee to knee for more than three thousand miles. The only good time for Jack was a morning in West Virginia when the driver was too exhausted to continue and made Kerouac take over. Nearly everybody in the car was asleep, and Jack relaxed enough behind the wheel to figure out for the first time in his life how to drive a car. He celebrated that evening with a quart of port wine.

The driver left them on the sidewalk in New York on a freezing November morning. Kerouac felt completely destitute. He didn't have any money, he didn't have any place to stay, he was down to 155 pounds, thinner than he'd ever been in his life, with sunken eyes and hollow cheeks and a hacking cough. Two of his friends, Lucien Carr and Henri Cru, had apartments, but he didn't think he could get away with staying with them for the weeks he had to live in New York before he could use the excuse of a Christmas visit to get back to his mother in North Carolina. Allen was his only hope, and Allen found a couple of girls he knew in the Village. One of them decided she liked Jack, even though he was out of his mind with weariness and hunger, and she let him stay until it was time to go to his brother-in-law's for the holidays.

On the way down to Rocky Mount Jack still had enough of the sense of them all as a team to stop off in Washington and see Gregory, insisting that Corso had to put him up at Jarrell's house. Corso was getting on very well in Washington, explaining his poetic theories to Jarrell. At that time Gregory believed that God was "a beautiful painter who'd painted a beautiful picture of a world that man had painted over." Shelley was Corso's ideal. He was "revolutionary but he spilled no blood," and Jarrell told him his poems were as good as Shelley's.

But Kerouac didn't go over nearly so well. He insisted on boring Jarrell and his family with long monologues about his theory of spontaneous composition, claiming it was the only way to write, until Gregory broke in and told him he sounded like a monomaniac English professor. He was drunk all the time he was in the house, trying to finish Jarrell's supply of Jack Daniels bourbon, and it was easier for everyone after he'd left.

New York had become Ginsberg's scene. He was rushing around to publishers, talking to agents, button-holing editors at parties, trying—as Donald Allen remembered —to "build the big united front." He went with Corso to a party given by the poet who'd written the article about him in the New York *Times*, Richard Eberhart, and spent an hour and a half talking to Arabelle Porter of *New World Writing*, explaining how he and his friends, Corso, Kerouac, Snyder, Whalen and Ferlinghetti, were great poets, soon to be famous. *Howl* had just been published, but you could only buy it then in New York in special bookshops that carried small press books like the Eighth Street Bookshop in the Village. When it first appeared in New York, it didn't really sell very well. In early December 1956, Ginsberg wrote Ferlinghetti to say that nobody he knew in the Village had seen or bought it. Allen questioned why Ferlinghetti wanted to reprint a second edition of 1,500 copies, asking: "Can you sell them?"

Trying to circulate his book, Allen went to the New York *Times* with a copy of *Howl* and did an interview. He hoped that a review in the *Times* or the *Herald Tribune*, or the magazine *Saturday Review*, would "break the ice maybe." By the end of the month the Eighth Street Bookshop had sold out its copies and he began to feel that something was happening. Young Village poets like Dianne Di Prima were writing Ferlinghetti about *Howl*: "Never suspected anybody was writing about now with some degree of honesty. I flipped. Thank him for me." Word was beginning to spread.

While they waited to take off to Tangier, Ginsberg asked his father Louis to drive him, Peter, Jack and Gregory to Paterson, New Jersey, to read their poems to William Carlos Williams, and they had a long "raving and weeping" visit. Williams was most taken with Corso, but he was "worried what he'd be like in forty years." He promised to review Gregory's second book, *Gasoline*, which City Lights was publishing, for the New York *Times*. Ginsberg later wrote a poem about the visit.

To WCW

But I seen you again
in the Fifties "Lotsa bastards

        out there - " pointing thru the window
Kerouac drunk in the kitchen talking with Flossie
        about old Bavarian beer garden
        dances and 1910 medical Europe -

And I lied to you, told you I was never a fairy
        when I was - didn't want to
                shock yr palsied hand

    on mahogany table pizzerria downtown
        Paterson below Market St.

For Kerouac, the break came through Donald Allen, who had decided against including *The Subterraneans* in *Evergreen Review*, Grove Press' magazine, by the time Jack got to New York. He persuaded Grove Press, instead, to publish it as a book. This pleased Jack, and he and Ginsberg went in to Donald Allen's office with all of Jack's manuscripts. Ginsberg also told him that Robert Creeley was planning to use some of their writing in the *Black Mountain Review,* and they showed Don Allen poems of Whalen, Snyder and McClure that he hadn't seen before. Excited by the new work, Don Allen decided that the second issue of *Evergreen* should be devoted completely to the San Francisco scene. He and Barney Rossett, the owner of Grove Press, realized that there were a great many gifted young American writers, although when they'd started publishing they'd been more interested in the European avant-grade.

Don Allen later remembered, "Suddenly all this stuff appeared that I was able to take seriously. I had to change my way of looking to see the new thing that was coming out." By the time Kerouac, Ginsberg and Corso were ready to leave for Tangier, early in 1957, *Evergreen* Number 2 had been planned. It included, among other things, *Howl* and Jack's *October in the Railroad Earth.* Fame wasn't far away. Ginsberg left copies of *Howl* at the *Hudson Review, Partisan Review* and the *New Yorker,* but perhaps the surest sign of their approaching notoriety was a long interview in the *Village Voice* entitled, "Witless Madcaps Come Home To Roost."

Many of the San Francisco poets, among them Kenneth Rexroth, were never able to get over their anger at Corso,

Ginsberg and Kerouac—two New Yorkers and a displaced wanderer from Lowell, Massachusetts—for being called "San Francisco" poets by newspapers like the *Voice*. There had been years of poetry and a strong writers' community in San Francisco, but none of the three had been part of it, and Corso, particularly, was almost a stranger to San Francisco. But because of the early labeling by East Coast journalists and editors, the confusion still continues about San Francisco writing and poetry.

After their "discovery," there was also a little money, and Jack left for Tangier on 15 February, 1957, Gregory left the last week of February and Allen and Peter followed on 8 March. *Howl* was again sold out, both at the Eighth Street Bookshop and at the Gotham Book Mart uptown.

For the first week in Tangier, Kerouac felt completely at home. Burroughs had met him when Jack's freighter, the *S.S. Slovenija*, docked in Tangier and had taken him immediately to the Medina, the old Arab section of the city, where Jack was charmed by the damp alleys, the veiled Arab women, the colorful vegetable stands, the smoke of frying fish and the fun of smoking marijuana openly in the public cafes. Bill had decided to do without drugs for a time and Jack had never seen him looking better. Burroughs had just finished writing *Naked Lunch* and he asked Jack to type it for him. Jack, who was still the champion speed typist of his youth, was happy to help him with it, and he spent most of the first weeks over the typewriter. But Jack was so high continuously either with marijuana or opium, that he began to feel he was suffering from an opium overdose. He even suspected he'd been poisoned by eating hashish that had been sprayed with arsenic. He slid from his first euphoria into a deep depression, and by the time Allen and Peter got there in March 1957, the only thing he wanted to do was get back to America and eat Wheaties by a pine-breeze kitchen window.

They spent a few days horsing around on the beach at Tangier, taking pictures of each other in their wet shorts, enjoying the hot sun after the cold winter in New York, but nothing got through to Jack. He didn't like the new young people hanging around them, and he stayed away from the parties, holing up in his room away from his friends and the hangers-on, drinking his own quart bottles of twenty-eight-cent wine. His favorite pastime was sitting cross-legged on his patio and reading the *Diamond Sutra* facing the Catholic priests at a nearby church who recited their rosaries facing the sea.

As he wrote later it was the time of his life when he lost his "yen for any further outside searching .... At the time I sincerely believed that the only decent activity in the world was to pray for everyone, in solitude." He had waited too many long bitter years for success to come. Before leaving New York he'd spent a week in the Marlton Hotel on 8th Street typing up *The Subterraneans* for Grove Press and going over the final manuscript changes of *On The Road* for Malcolm Cowley, so as he stayed on in Tangier he knew that both books were being typeset for imminent publication, but he told everybody he was already sick of the whole subject. With an almost desperate prescience he sensed that his books would soon become a fad with "the mass of middleclass youth . . ." Sitting at dreary parties in Tangier, listening to the hipsters talk, he groaned, "All this was about to sprout out all over America even down to High School level and be attributed in part to my doing!"

In less than three months he was back in New York. He'd left Allen and Peter behind in Tangier and rushed alone with a rucksack and blue jeans through Paris and London. He was ecstatic getting back home, and he stayed in New York at the apartment of a friend he'd met before leaving for Tangier, Joyce Glassman ("Alice Newman" in *Desolation Angels*). *On the Road* wasn't due to come out until September, but he figured that his advance was enough to rent a cottage for himself and his mother. Since he hadn't stayed in Europe as long as he'd originally planned he had a little money left, and mémère had money from her social security checks.

Kerouac was through with the wandering life. He was no longer a bhikku. All he wanted was a quiet house with his mother, but the only place he could think of where they might be able to live cheaply and where he could be close to his friends was Berkeley. When he went down to Orlando, Florida and told mémère his plans she was doubtful, but he'd come back from Europe months before he'd said he would so he could be with her, and she was willing to try and live in California, if he wanted it.

Mémère was living with Nin in Florida, where the family had moved after Rocky Mount. Jack helped her pack their bags to ride the Greyhound together to California. It was a hard way to travel, but Jack had planned for them to stop over in New Orleans and in El Paso, so he could take her across the Rio Grande River to Juarez, Mexico, and he was excited at the chance to show her things he'd tried to tell her about when he'd gotten back from his trips.

They did have many good moments together, despite the hardship of the long, cramped bus ride. For mémère, the churches in Juarez were a deep religious experience, with their crawling *penitentes* on the cold stone aisles. But once in Berkeley there was no way to make a life. They got in at two on a cold June morning and Jack took his mother straight to the cottage on Milvia where Philip Whalen was then living. Whalen helped get hotel rooms for them both in a cheap hotel not far from the campus. The next night, in the apartment he'd found at 1943 Berkeley Way, Jack got chicken and whisky for a party, and all three of them drank until they passed out. The trip began to sour.

Kerouac tried to get back into the old life in Berkeley, seeing Whalen and Cassady, going over to San Francisco to drink at The Place. On the walls of this favorite haunt hung clippings about *Howl,* local paintings, phone calls and letters that the bartender held for regular customers. Jack had asked Joyce Glassman to meet him in San Francisco, but before she'd had time to leave New York, Kerouac wrote her not to come. San Francisco was land's end and it gave him a lonely feeling. He felt he had to return to New York to live. He was depressed by the dull streets of "flowery" Berkeley and hassled by too many police giving tickets for jay-walking. Besides, there was no way he could reconcile mémère to the new place. She hated the Berkeley fog and missed living close to her daughter Nin. Mémère persuaded Jack to take her back to Florida but before they had a chance to pack up again, a carton of advance copies of *On the Road* arrived at their Berkeley address.

Mémêre had gone to the store and Jack was completely alone in their shabby apartment. Holding the book in his hands for the first time, he looked up as "a golden light" appeared in the porch door. It was Neal, dropping by with his old girl Luanne and two other friends. In *Desolation Angels*, Jack described the scene, a moment in his life that haunted him forever:

We all stare at one another in the golden light. Not a sound. I'm also caught redhanded (as we all grin) with a copy of *Road* in my hands *even before I've looked at it for the first time!* I automatically hand one to Cody who is after all the hero of the poor crazy sad book . . . .

Kerouac felt guilty, almost like a thief, with the book in his hands, but he felt even worse after Cassady looked at it. "When Cody said goodbye to all of us that day he for the first time in our lives failed to look me a goodbye in the eye but looked away shifty-like—I couldn't understand it and still don't—I knew something was bound to be wrong and it turned out very wrong . . ."

Chapter Twenty-Eight

For the first few months after *On The Road* was published in September 1957 it was hard to tell that anything was wrong despite the premonition Kerouac had when he'd handed the first copy to Neal Cassady. When success comes in America it comes in a golden flood, and it seems that whatever you want is there to be taken and that all you have to do is reach out a hand and it's yours. It's only when the wave goes on swirling around you that you begin to feel its dangerous pull.

One night Jack was giving a reading at the Village Vanguard in New York and a reviewer for the *Village Voice*, Howard Smith, dropped around to hear him perform. As Smith was leaving he heard someone standing at the bar in an old Army shirt say, "Well, Kerouac came off the road in high gear . . . I hope he has a good set of snow tires."

Jack needed more than snow tires to survive success. He was elated with the reviews and sales of the novel. Its publication date was 5 September, 1957, and it sold so well that there was a second printing on 20 September and a third printing ordered shortly afterwards. *On The Road* made the best-seller list for five weeks late in 1957. This success went beyond anything he'd dreamed possible after the years of stalling with publishers trying to get any of his books accepted. If he had proven his talent with *The Town and the City* in 1950, it was clear to him in 1957 with *On The Road* that he'd shown the world he was a genius.

The New York *Times* wrote that he'd produced "some of the most original work being done in this country," that the novel marked "an historic occasion . . . the exposure of an authentic work of art." Jack already knew it.

Of all Kerouac's eighteen books, *On The Road* is probably the best, although he preferred *Visions of Cody* and *Doctor Sax* and would have agreed with Ginsberg that this sort of evaulation is meaningless. For most readers, at any rate, he is known as the author of *On The Road*. Fifteen years after its publication it appeared in the Penguin Modern Classics Series in England. It was the book that made Kerouac famous, and deservedly so, because in *On The Road* he captured the spirit of his own generation, their restlessness and confusions in the years immediately following World War II.

Kerouac presented such a compelling portrait of Neal Cassady that his image fashioned the life style of a generation of young readers who came of age in the 1960s and 1970s. In the pages of *On The Road*, Cassady emerged as an archetypal American hero. It's a tribute to Kerouac's literary talent, and the ironic triumph of fiction over fact, that in one sweeping novel he made his best friend a legend, while Jack struggled himself in a lifetime of writing books to create a legend out of his own life.

Kerouac's vision of Neal Cassady ("Dean Moriarty") in *On The Road* centered in one of the most vital fantasies of America, the dream of the cowboy, free and footloose, become a drifter with the crowding and commercialization of modern life. In the novel Jack's intuition made him visualize Neal as a cowboy standing naked in the New York apartment before they were introduced. *On The Road* caught a sense of the American folk hero rebelliousness, the spirit of the wide, western plains in Cassady's colossal restlessness.

When Jack's Berkeley friend John Montgomery met Neal he thought Cassady looked the movie part of a cowboy. But it was Gary Snyder who pinpointed the mythic element in Neal's character. Years later in 1969 Snyder spoke about what gave Jack's portrait of Cassady the appeal that radiates from the pages of *On The Road*:

Neal's a beautiful memory because it's so archetypal. My vision of Cassady is of the 1880s cowboys, the type of person who works the high plains of the 1880s and 1890s—like he is the Denver grandchild of the 1880s cowboys with no range left to work on. Cassady's type is that frontier type, reduced to pool halls and driving back and forth across the country. But he could have been another Jedediah Smith. Smith was one of the great mountain men, a fur trapper for the Rocky Mountain Fur Company, and married to an Indian. An illiterate, violent man. Half for fun, but half for some vision that went beyond that, he took off across Utah— was the first white man to go through Utah—walked along the southern edges of Death Valley, got himself arrested by the Spaniards at the Pueblo de Los Angeles, who had never seen anybody who had come across the plains before, got out of jail, walked over Tehatchepe Pass, was the first American white man to walk through the length of the San Joaquin Valley, walked around in Northern California and ended up in Oregon. Finally he got himself back to the Plains and was killed by the lance of a Cheyenne horseman. But this man was incredible; like, you break with the Bible, and you break with, fight with your father, and you take off.

Cassady was like so many Americans who had inherited

that taste for the limitless, for no limits, which was a unique American experience. You can get hooked on that if you don't know how to translate it into other regions, since when the sheer physical space disappears you go crazy. Which is like the story of America.

The source of this thing is—what do you see when you move across the Plains day after day? That's a mind-bending experience, a wild ecology and an unpopulated terrain. That becomes an archetype immediately for America, literally mythical. It became such a powerful experience that the transmission of that becomes like a phonograph record speeded up faster and faster with less and less space to move in. What was intended to be done was that you should step forth into wild space; what you end up doing a hundred years later is driving back and forth in cars as fast as you can. Initially you were moving very slowly in a totally wild area. What you end up doing is going very fast in a densely populated area. Space becomes translated into speed.

What got Kerouac and Ginsberg about Cassady was the energy of the archetypal west, the energy of the frontier, still coming down. Cassady is the cowboy crashing. The whole thing is of that order . . . .

Cassady was the loner in *On The Road*, the hero left with nothing at the end of the road. He was given epic proportions to live out Kerouac's visions, the sensual ecstatic joy of the road ("we know time, how to slow it up and walk and dig and just old-fashioned spade kicks, what other kicks are there?") and the vision of the despairing, senseless emptiness of the road ("What's your road, man?—holyboy road, madman road, rainbow road, guppy road, any road. It's an anywhere road for anybody anyhow. Where body how?").

Critics hostile to the novel, like *Time* Magazine's, disregarded its archetypal American western hero, attacking its hedonism and "degeneracy," it's manic-depressive pursuit of "dionysian revels," its disregard for established social custom. Kerouac was made the scapegoat, the "Hippie Homer" of a "disjointed segment of society acting out its own neurotic necessity." For all the reviewers who were favorably disposed to the book, there were as many who questioned its values or expressed reserve about what Kerouac was up to.

The New York *Times* review most widely quoted is young Gilbert Millstein's, on Thursday, 5 September, 1957, calling the publication of *On The Road* an "historic occasion . . . an authentic work of art." But when it was reviewed by the regular staff member David Dempsey in the following Sunday's *Book Review* section, while agreeing that the novel was a truly original work, enormously readable and entertaining, Dempsey compared Kerouac unfavorably with Thomas Wolfe, Nelson Algren and Saul Bellow, as having no larger framework within which to develop his characters. *On The Road* was "a stunning achievement. But it is a road, as far as the characters are concerned, that leads nowhere—and which the novelist cannot afford to travel more than once."

But the young people who responded to the book, who read it not as "literature" but as an adventure, recognized that Kerouac was on their side, the side of youth and freedom, riding with Cassady over American highways chasing after the great American adventure—freedom and open spaces, the chance to be yourself, to be free. Kerouac hadn't offered any real alternative to the conformity of twentieth-century industrial America. He ducked the problems of the 1950s such as the Bomb, the pressures of the Organization Man, McCarthy's Un-American Activities Committee. He offered instead a vision of freedom, a return to a solipsistic world of childhood, to an irresponsibility so complete that no other world could ever intrude for long. It he'd started across America too late to join up with the wagon trains, the cowboys roaming the range, the I.W.W. organizers or the Dust Bowl refugees, he'd nevertheless carried on with their uncomprising search for freedom, for the chance to see if a better life couldn't be found by moving on, for the great American dream.

Twenty years after Cassady took Kerouac on the road, a generation of rock stars epitomized their earlier search for a life style beyond the conformity of middle-class America. As Michael McClure said of the singer Jim Morrison after his death from an overdose, he was "turned on to go," like Dean Moriarty. In Kerouac's words in

On The Road, often quoted in rock magazines and repeated in the liner notes of recordings:

. . . the only people for me are the mad ones, the ones who are mad to live, mad to talk, mad to be saved, desirous of everything at the same time, the ones who never yawn or say a commonplace thing, but burn, burn, burn like fabulous yellow roman candles exploding like spiders across the stars and in the middle you see the blue centerlight pop and everybody goes "Awww!"

Kerouac had no idea that he had written a book that would turn on an entire generation. He thought of the book, characteristically, entirely in the personal terms of finding his own "writing soul at last." Being the "Hippie Homer" was the last thing on his mind, even if that was how he was represented after *On The Road*.

Actually, Kerouac's own character of "Sal Paradise" in the novel wasn't completely hedonistic, but most readers didn't distinguish Kerouac all that much from "Dean" because he shared most of the wildness and aimlessness that filled the book. It was largely guilt by association. Jack really had the experiences he described in his books, but when he turned them into picaresque adventure he gave them a sense of excitement by heightening his own emotional response to situations, at the same time as minimizing his own role as participant in the action. By the end of "Sal Paradise's" first day hitchhiking in *On The Road*, trying to go cross-country by first heading north from the subway in the Bronx to the back roads of Route 6, his character was established as being inexperienced to the point of near-ineptitude and idealistic to the edges of absurdity.

The narrator's vulnerability made *On the Road* a comedy, but his humility also pointed to something more. Although "Sal Paradise" had been born too late to open up the West with America's pioneers, his ideals were still romantic and personal. He felt that he was more beat, more lost, more down-and-out, and less prepossessing than any other character in the book, and this underscored his ultimate belief in the total impossibility of ever realizing the promise of his dreams in mid-twentieth-century America.

Kerouac gave himself the same basic character as "Sal Paradise" in the novel he wrote in November 1957, while *On the Road* was on the best-seller list. This was *The Dharma Bums*, which Jack later said he wrote after Malcolm Cowley told him that Viking was interested in buying another book to follow up their success with *On the Road*, just so long as Jack came up with a novel that wasn't obsessively personal like *Visions of Cody* or *Doctor Sax*.

Cowley asked him to keep writing about his friends, so Jack sat down in his sister's kitchen in Orlando, Florida, and in ten sittings (he thought of himself like an athlete, sticking to his typewriter grinding out 15,000 or 20,000 words at a time) he had a story he later called a "pot-boiler." When he inscribed a leather-bound presentation copy of *The Dharma Bums* to his mother, he wrote that it was "A third adventure to pay for the house, the cat food, the brandy and the peaceful sleep."

Just as in *On the Road*, Jack wrote about a friend who had really impressed him, Gary Snyder (named "Japhy Ryder" in *The Dharma Bums*), and just as with Neal Cassady, Jack assumed a character in the novel ("Ray Smith") secondary to his hero, again an initiate into a different life style. Snyder's way was another interpretation of the idealism of the American West, seen—unlike Cassady's—in political terms.

Through "Japhy Ryder" Kerouac again seemed to be speaking for a social minority, not a black subculture of kicks as in *On The Road*, but a more radical social movement that developed into America's counter-culture ten years later. As Jack saw it, Gary's alternative life style was basically a religious way of life in *The Dharma Bums*, "Dharma" referring to the essence or true meaning of life, any noble activities of mind, body and speech. Snyder described the alternative life style in Zen Buddhist terms in the novel:

. . . a vision of a great rucksack revolution, thousands or even millions of young Americans wandering around with rucksacks, going up to the mountains to pray, making children laugh and old men glad, making young girls happy and old girls happier, all of 'em Zen Lunatics who go about writing poems that happen to appear in their heads for no reason and also by being kind and also by strange unexpected acts keep giving visions of eternal freedom to everybody and to all living creatures, . . .

Again Kerouac made himself the spokesman for his friends' ideas, his memory for Snyder's conversations in *The Dharma Bums* as accurate as his transcriptions of Cassady's monologues in *On The Road*. There were broad hints in both novels that "Sal Paradise" and "Ray Smith" weren't really part of the action, were really standing back observing and listening instead of originating the ideas of the books' central characters. But most readers thought Kerouac shared completely the ideas of Cassady and Snyder. Jack never tried hard in the novels to give any other impression, because the only identity he actually had as a young writer struggling to finish *The Town and the City* through the months between the brief times on the road with Cassady, or as the older writer with Snyder in California packing eleven unpublished books in the bottom of his rucksack, wouldn't have fit the fantasy character, vague as it was, which he described himself as being in "Sal Paradise" and "Ray Smith."

If Jack's literary aspiration and industry weren't enough in themselves to make him legendary, then he instinctively attempted to give himself a legendary stature by merging with the central characters in *On the Road* and *The Dharma Bums*:

. . . Japhy and I were kind of outlandish-looking on the campus in our old clothes in fact Japhy was considered an eccentric around the campus, which is the usual thing for campuses and college people to think whenever a real man appears on the scene—colleges being nothing but grooming schools for the middleclass non-identity which usually finds its perfect expression on the outskirts of the campus in rows of well-to-do houses with lawns and television sets in each living room with everybody looking at the same thing and thinking the same thing at the same time while the Japhies of the world go prowling in the wilderness to hear the voice crying in the wilderness, to find the ecstasy of the stars, to find the dark mysterious secret of the origin of faceless wonderless crapulous civilization.

After *On The Road* appeared, Jack's rucksack vanished into the back rooms of his mother's house. There was only a last chaotic California trip still ahead of him. But in the minds of his readers he was forever linked with the "rucksack revolution" he described in his novels. There were three books that really shaped his public image, the three that came out within a year of each other in 1957 and 1958: *On the Road, The Subterraneans* and *The Dharma Bums*. Of the three, *The Subterraneans* was closest in its desperateness and emotional vulnerability to the way Kerouac actually lived his life, but again readers were most taken by the life style of the bohemians in the novel and formed an image of Kerouac as "King of the Beats." He helped it along by saying as publicity for *The Subterraneans* that he spent his time "in skidrow or in jazz joints or with personal poet madmen," passing over his life at home with mémêre.

At the height of Kerouac's success with *On the Road*, Herb Caen, a San Francisco journalist, had coined the word "beatnik" in his column for the San Francisco *Chronicle*. (This was shortly after the Russian Sputnik was launched.) Caen himself didn't mean the word "beatnik" in a pejorative sense (he tried to defend it to Kerouac, without success, in a San Francisco bar one night), but the word caught the public's imagination as a perfect putdown for what they considered the dirty, bearded, sandaled bohemians of North Beach and Greenwich Village, whose spokesman Jack Kerouac had to be, since his novels described "beatnik" life. Jack complained almost in despair to his friend, the painter Hugo Weber, "I'm King of the Beats, but I'm not a Beatnik," but it was too subtle a distinction for most people. When he tried to explain it, he just made it worse.

KEROUAC

Part Three

1957–1969

Chapter Twenty-Nine

From the beginning, Kerouac was typed by the mass media as Dean Moriarty rather than Sal Paradise. His book was "hot" and he was news, and the interviews he gave the press or on television were so candid, so personal, that he became a "personality" as immediately recognizable as a movie star. In interview after interview he insisted that the beat generation *wasn't* "hoodlumism," or "roughneck," or "violent," or "heedless," or "rootless," yet he never could make very clear what it *was*.

As the man who'd thought up the term "beat generation," Kerouac insisted that he alone understood it. It meant "beatific," trying to be in a state of beatitude, like St. Francis, trying to love all life, being utterly sincere and kind and cultivating "joy of heart." The problem, he told a *Pageant* Magazine interviewer, was that after *On The Road* people insisted that "being beat was just a lot of frantic nowhere hysteria." People on TV, on radio, in the newspapers kept asking him what he was searching for so frantically. And, Jack went on, "I answered that I was waiting for God to show his face." When he tried to pin it down more concretely, Jack always referred to the examples of jazz musicians as the essence of beat, nodding their heads over a solo, nodding affirmatively, yes, because "Man, you gotta stay high, that's all." In the next breath he would deny that narcotics had anything to do with it, "The dope thing will die out." He insisted it was only a fad, like bathtub gin. Interviewers would ask him about sex, and he'd say it was "the gateway to paradise," and they'd ask him about visions, and he'd answer, "we're all in Heaven, now, really."

Probably the interview he gave Mike Wallace in the New York *Post* in January 1958 was the most typically laconic. It started, as always, with the meaning of the term "beat generation," went on through the musicians and junkies quickly into mysticism ("What sort of mysticism is it?" "Oh, they believe in love."), brushed once more lightly over jazz and dope ("Have you ever taken dope yourself?" "Sure. A lot. But I never got in the habit because I'm allergic to it."), went back to visions and ended awkwardly on a note of death and unhappiness ("But you *are* in Heaven, Jack. You just said we all were." "Yeah. If I only *knew* it. If I could only hold on to what I *know*.").

The biggest problem was that no matter what Kerouac said and wrote, there was always the public disaster of Jack himself. In order to face the interviews and public appearances he inevitably got drunk, and when he was drunk he was usually a shamble: out of control, maudlin, sentimental and childish. Even among other writers where he could have been taken more seriously, he panicked and turned himself into a clown.

At Hunter College on 6 November, 1958, he was part of a debate with Kingsley Amis, Ashley Montagu and James Wechsler, which centered on the question "Is There a Beat Generation?" Wechsler condemned the anarchy of the beats and saw them as a symbol, a "sort of joke," but Amis and Montagu were prepared to be serious. Montagu saw the "Beat Generation" as "the ultimate expression of a civilization whose moral values have broken down." Amis, speaking as a creative writer, wanted to define the term more exactly: "There is no Angry Young Men movement (in England). There may be a beat generation, but I doubt it."

The press emphasized Kerouac's drunken disorderliness at the Hunter College debate, but according to Ginsberg, there had been a mix-up. Jack had come to Hunter under the impression that he was supposed to read a long paper about the Beat Generation, and he had written his essay "Origins of the Beat Generation" for the occasion. Once at Hunter, he was asked *not* to read the prepared speech but instead to debate extemporaneously the question "Is there a Beat Generation?" As Ginsberg recalls the evening, Jack began to read his essay anyway. Jack was

slightly drunk, but in good humor and funny—
tho' abused by philistines all around, the crowd
confused by the moderator's interruption of Jack,
as if he were *wrong* to rely on the conditions he
was promised at the symposium. He was heroic, in
exactly the situation of an academic hype on his
patience and time that one might have invented in
a novel about the bad manners and insensitivity and
open hostility of smug professors, right wing second
rate novelists (Amis), 1930's moralistic left wing
journalists (Wechsler)—only Ashley Montagu was even
polite, tho' confused. The *Voice,* not knowing the
terms of invitation, blamed Kerouac for talking too
long with his great essay. The climax at Hunter came
when Wechsler shouted "We have to fight for peace"
(eternal quote) and Jack looked at him in exasperation,
said "Wha!? Don't you realize that doesn't make sense?"
or something like; then sat down silent but with
Wechsler's hat on his head. Wechsler got mad and angrily
demanded his hat back! as if Jack were a barbarian just
like he dreamed, *taking his hat!*—An old Zen koan, that
lovely gesture was accounted in *Voice* or otherwhere as
a sign that Jack was "inarticulate," an uncouth drunk!

As the newspapers reported the evening Kerouac ran
down his usual changes about the jazz hipsters and refused
to enter the debate. The press didn't comment on the stuffy
pretentiousness of the other speakers. The reporters went
after Kerouac instead, describing how he dressed in a
checked lumberman's shirt, made faces at the photogra-
phers, swigged from a bottle and acted as if he were a
drunk in a downtown bar, dashing off-stage a dozen times,
shouting, "Live your lives out, they say; nay, love your lives
out, so when they come around and stone you, you won't
be living in any glass house—only glassy flesh. What is
called the 'beat generation' is really a revolution in
manners . . . being a swinging group of new American
boys intent on life." His definition might have been the one
closest to the truth, if anybody even heard it.

As his oldest friends knew from his Lowell days, Jack
was basically a loner, and he used the drinking as a
social defense. Charlie Sampas once said, "Often he pre-
tends he's drunk. It's a lot of hooey. He's really shy."

John Clellon Holmes watched the assault of fame on Kerouac from a closer distance in New York. He knew from his own experience something of what Jack was going through. Confronting the public was next to impossible. Holmes wrote in *Nothing More to Declare*:

They tended to drive their cars recklessly when he was with them, as if he was "Dean Moriarty," and not the Kerouac who hated to drive and whom I had once seen crouching on the floor of a car, in a panic, during a drunken, six-hour dash from New York to Provincetown. They plied him with drinks, they created parties around him, they doubled the disorder in the hopes of catching his eye, and so never glimpsed the Kerouac who once confessed to me, "You know what I'm thinking when I'm in the midst of all *that*—the uproar, the boozing, the wildness? I'm always thinking, What am I doing here? Is this the way I'm *supposed* to feel?"

As Holmes suspected, people looked at Kerouac as if *he* were the Beat Generation.

Yet Jack added to the confusion himself, and the stories about the havoc and disorder swirling around him are as endless as the number of people he brushed against on any one drunken evening. Reading at the Village Vanguard was one of the hardest times. He read well to jazz—and there are two LPs of him with Steve Allen, Al Cohn and Zoot Sims. But the December 1957 gig lasted only a week because he was so drunk he couldn't continue, so drunk that one night onstage he was sick into the piano. When he came into the Village he stayed in a hotel on 8th Street. There were always drunken musicians with him, twelve people piling into cabs, rushing uptown to hear more music, meet more people and stay stoned more of the time.

Despite the drunken times as a celebrity in New York, Kerouac was still making his home in Orlando, Florida with his mother. He found a small two-room apartment for her around the corner from Nin when they came back from Berkeley in July 1957. There was only one brief trip by himself to Mexico City the end of July (again he asked Joyce Glassman to meet him there, his first letters ecstatically describing his eighty-five-cent room with whorehouse mirrors and fancy tiles, his later letters full of loneliness and despair, until he dragged himself sick with fever back to Florida and his mother's care). In late August, he borrowed thirty dollars from Joyce for the bus from Orlando to New York so he'd be in the city when *On The Road* officially came out on 5 September and he was elated that day after Gilbert Millstein's enthusiastic review in the *Times*.

But after the interviews and the champagne parties, sobering up afterwards at Joyce's apartment on his favorite split pea soup and slab bacon, Jack always returned to mémère, to his bedroom next to the room where his mother had a couch in their combined kitchen-living room. In October 1957, he began to work on a play he called *The Beat Generation*, pulling things out of *Visions of Cody* and *Desolation Angels*, living the straight life in Florida, eating his mother's big suppers at eight o'clock and limiting his drinking to rum and coke. Work on the play went slowly. It was too short for a full-length production, and the first week of November he started a novel about his childhood for Viking, *Memory Babe*. Only a few weeks later, he gave up on *Memory Babe* and turned, at Cowley's suggestion, to *The Dharma Bums*.

By the beginning of 1958, Kerouac was thoroughly bored with Florida. He had money now from *On The Road*, and he began coming up to New York frequently to work at Viking over editorial changes on *The Dharma Bums*, riding the buses between New York and Orlando with a bag of his favorite hamburgers from the White Tower. One night in early April 1958, he went to the Kettle of Fish Bar on MacDougal Street in the Village with Gregory Corso, and they antagonized some men in the bar who followed them out into Minetta Lane and beat Kerouac up. Jack got back to Joyce's apartment, his head bleeding so profusely she took him immediately to the hospital. He'd been punched so hard that when he fell on the sidewalk he'd hurt himself badly. Later Jack even suspected brain damage, but it was never medically substantiated. Joyce remembers that in the infirmary he kept saying over and over to the doctors, "Cauterize my wounds, cauterize my wounds."

Soon after the fight, Jack decided he had to find a

better place to live outside New York, but closer to it. He thought of buying a house on Long Island and moving his mother up from Florida to live there with him. Joyce suggested that he look in Northport, a town on the North Shore a short distance beyond Huntington, and her friend, the photographer Robert Frank, drove them out. A realtor showed Jack a picture of a gray house with a backyard running into a high school football field, and Kerouac bought it on first sight.

When mémêre moved up to Northport after Jack's fistfight, she took over totally on her own terms. She told Jack she'd keep house for him, but only if he would take a vow to stay in the house six months and write. Jack promised, convinced it was for his own good. Allen was still in Paris, where Jack wrote him about what was happening. He had withdrawn from the world because he wanted to become his own kind of "simple Ti Jean" again at home with his mother. Outside of a few calm visits with Allen in New York or Paterson at his father's house, Jack didn't want any more mad debauchery with Village or San Francisco types. He just wanted to stay home and work things out. It was partly his mother's influence, but it was also because Kerouac had suddenly himself become afraid of the direction his life seemed to be taking.

In May 1958, Neal Cassady began serving a five-year sentence in San Quentin for possession of marijuana, and Jack and his mother worried that the law might hit them next.

What happened to Cassady was a tragic story, affecting him for the rest of his life. He'd been smoking marijuana for years, but early in 1958 he was suspected by federal narcotics agents of being a dealer. Pretending to be his friends, two agents gave him forty dollars to buy marijuana for them and deliver it. Cassady suspected a frame-up, so he just took the money and went to the racetrack, but a couple of months later the agents came back and arrested him. They had little evidence but were able to produce witnesses. The judge, who found Neal's attitude objectionable, sentenced him on two counts, two years to life. He served two years in San Quentin and three years on parole.

303

After Cassady's arrest, mémère laid down the law that no drugs, not even benzedrine, could ever be brought into her house, but her protectiveness didn't stop there. In July 1958, she wrote Ginsberg in Paris saying that if he came back to New York and bothered her son, she'd tell the FBI about him and Peter. If Ginsberg mentioned Kerouac's name again in his dirty books of poetry, she'd have Allen put in jail, because all Allen had on his mind was dirty sex and dope. She'd raised her Jackie to be a decent boy, and she wanted to keep him that way. Jack let her send off the letter, but privately he complained to Joyce Glassman that his mother's forbidding Allen at the house sounded "strange since I'm buying the house and I'm 36 years old."

Kerouac's house was on Gilbert Street in Northport, Long Island, a $14,000 weathered wooden house with porches in the front and rear. Jack had wanted to buy beat-up old furniture from Delancey Street, old roll-top desks, battered mission tables and easy chairs, but mémère preferred solid maple. So the house was furnished in what Joyce Glassman remembers as "Sears Roebuck American," maple and chintz and a plastic dinette set. Jack contented himself with a new AM-FM radio so he could listen to the all-night Symphony Sid program, and an eighty-five-dollar Webcor four-speed phonograph that played his records "booming deep." He took a bedroom upstairs for his study, moving in a new typewriter and a tape recorder on his desk, filling the room with his stacks of manuscripts, notebooks and books. When things were going well he felt great, eating big meals in the kitchen, drinking beer and watching TV most of the night, exercising and taking walks.

After *The Dharma Bums* he didn't finish another novel for almost four years, although he tried off and on to pick up *Memory Babe*. He felt a little uncomfortable about the lapse of time between completed novels, but he defended himself to Joyce Glassman by saying he was like Melville in the last stretch of his life. Why did people think that the years between *Moby Dick* and *Billy Budd* meant anything to Melville? It was in the "same eternal time" that Melville wrote both.

In Northport Jack turned out a steady stream of magazine articles to cover his taxes and the living expenses. He went back to the *Visions of Cody* manuscript for the articles, using it almost like a writer's notebook, reworking his travel notes into longer pieces for *Holiday* magazine at $2,000 an article and selling also to *Playboy, Esquire, Escapade* and *Nugget.* His agent Sterling Lord was negotiating the sales of *Doctor Sax, Mexico City Blues, Visions of Cody, Tristessa* and *Lonesome Traveler.*

There was enough money to live comfortably for the first time in Kerouac's life, although he never entered the big money or became rich. Jack said his largest book advance was $7,500 from Avon for a paperback original of *Tristessa*, but when *The Subterraneans* became a movie, he only made a few thousand dollars on it. He dreamed of selling *On The Road* to MGM for $110,000, a dream that never came true, although on 30 June, 1958, *Billboard* announced MGM was to begin shooting *On The Road* in San Francisco. The movie would center on the progressive jazz of the Earl (Father) Hines Orchestra and would feature Marlon Brando (as Neal Cassady) and Theodore Bikel (as either Jack or Allen—*Billboard* didn't say).

In Orlando when Kerouac tried to write a play about Neal Cassady, *The Beat Generation*, hoping to follow up his success with *On The Road*, he had found his instincts as a playwright weren't commercial. The play was shown in manuscript to Lillian Hellman, but she said it needed a lot of work before it could be produced, discouraging Kerouac. Two years later he used an act of the play as the basis for a narration he did for a film by Robert Frank called *Pull My Daisy* with Ginsberg, Orlovsky, Corso and Larry Rivers.

Mémêre took care of him in Northport, but living together also resulted in considerable stress for Kerouac. It meant, on its most basic level, that he could never grow up beyond the point of being a son living with his mother and never assume adult responsibility for his own life. He never seemed to worry about anything except the difference in their ages: if his mother died first, who did he have who'd take care of him? On a deeper level, in his dreams, the psychological toll was often present.

In Kerouac's *Book of Dreams*, begun in 1952, his

mother entered his world of fantasy both as his Angel and his Truth, and as a hateful old lady whose grave he dug up to plant marijuana. But he also dreamed of being a child again, lying with mémère arm in arm, Jack crying afraid to die, his mother blissful, with one leg "in pink sexually out between me."

Mémère never let her son forget that she'd supported him by rising at six A.M. to work in the shoe factory for years while he wrote his books. All Jack's income as a writer went into their joint bank account and her signature also had to appear on his checks. Buying the Northport house tied up the first big royalties from *On The Road*, so he never felt financially independent. Mémère managed the money, with just so much for beer and cigarettes. When they first moved to Northport she said there wasn't enough left over to install a phone in the house, and for a while Jack walked a mile to the pay phone to call his friends in New York.

The closest look at his life on Gilbert Street was given by the journalist Alfred Aronowitz, who described it as part of a series of articles on "The Beat Generation" in the New York *Post* in the spring of 1959. Aronowitz spent an afternoon with Ti Jean and mémère, arriving just as Kerouac came home with a huge shopping bag filled with beer for the afternoon. Jack had just turned thirty-seven. He was dressed in a heavy, flannel workshirt, baggy pants and old shoes, his long black hair blowing in the February sunlight. At the door mémère waited "smiling and cheerful, with eyeglasses, an apron, long, woolen stockings and a housewife's bandana tied around her head." She was "a short, not-yet-rotund woman of sixty-four who spoke with that distinct but almost indefinable accent that the French-Canadians have." In the kitchen mémère began to unpack the shopping bag, trying quickly to store its contents in the refrigerator, but Jack adroitly "headed her off and carried what he could to an upstairs bedroom."

The interview started upstairs with Jack saying he didn't sleep in the bed in his study, but in another room. "We have plenty so we use them all." He liked to get up at noon and write before breakfast. As he began to tell Aronowitz about his theory of spontaneous prose, Jack was into his third can of beer. A few minutes later mémêre reappeared to ask if the quiz show on the TV set downstairs was bothering anybody. "No," Jack told her. "Come on in, Ma. You say something, too."

"I don't have much of a story to tell," mémêre said "cheerfully" to Aronowitz, "outside of the fact that I was his benefactor all my life . . . . I'll tell you right now, he always lives with me, outside of when he travels. Well, he wants to write a book, he wants to write something different, so he took off one day and he did. So, anyhow, after they read the book they write an awful lot of things about him that's not so—I know. I'm his mother. Once in a while he takes off, visits his friends, he goes on a ship, but he always comes back."

"But when he did travel," she continued, "there was always money for him. I used to send it any time he needed it, for food, for clothes. I was working in a factory, I was making good money. You know, he's really a nice boy—I mean, as far as I know he's never been a delinquent. Except when he wrote *The Town and the City*, he used to dress up like a bank robber . . ."

Kerouac interrupted, "I only made $2,000, $3,000 on *The Town and the City*."

"Oh, more than that . . . four, anyhow," his mother corrected him. "But let me show you something." She took Aronowitz into the bedroom where Jack slept. "If he was so bad," she said, pointing toward a silver crucifix over the headboard, "would he have that? And that?"— she motioned toward the rosary beads on his night table. "He wore that around his neck, but they broke."

Aronowitz reported that Kerouac looked at his mother "with some degree of reverence" and stood holding his beer can behind him. In his bedroom, Jack proudly showed Aronowitz a bulb attached to the headboard and a sheaf of note paper attached nearby to a wall. "I just fixed this up," Jack said. "I call these bedside sheets. I use them to write down dream thoughts. I hear them in a dream and wake up and turn the light on and write them down."

Jack took the sheets off their hook and read a little: "Death makes a stand in its own darkness . . . Man's will, which is already recorded in Heaven—strange will

307

". . . I can get more grace from a snatnose wart brain . . ."

"Who understands these things?" mémêre asked, "I don't."

"Well," Jack told her, "it means I'm mad. I'm not getting enough grace. I can get more grace from a snatnose wart brain than I can from Heaven—it's a religious thought."

Mémêre told Aronowitz she hadn't read all of Jack's books: "He told me one time that if I read *On The Road* I'd get mad at him, so I read up to page 34 and quit. But I'll read it some day."

When she went out of the room later, Kerouac told the reporter he'd warned his mother never to read *The Subterraneans*, telling her, "you know, it's about a love affair with a Negro girl." But to his mother, in front of Aronowitz, Jack said she ought to read *The Dharma Bums*.

Mémêre continued, "He's a good boy. Once he took me over to his publisher's house, Barney Rosset, because this publisher from France, Claude Gallimard, wanted to meet Jack, and we were all talking French . . ."

"We had a big, screaming dinner," Jack said. "And then we started, my mother and I, started roaming up the street hitting all the bars . . ."

"Gosh," mémêre broke in, "I'll never do that again. Oh, I might as well come out with it—I had too much to drink, but I was having a good time and I was with him . . ."

She glanced at Jack, whom Aronowitz saw sitting erect in a straight-back chair with his face impassive.

"Yes, he drinks a little," mémêre said. "I think a little too much for his health . . . But I like his friends, even Neal—he's a little eccentric. But that other guy, I won't let him in my house."

"She means Allen Ginsberg," Kerouac explained.

"That's right," she said. "And I'm afraid of him. And then one time I read the letter he sent to Jack, and he was insulting priests, Catholic priests that had befriended him . . ."

"He was telling Franciscan monks to take their clothes off," Jack said.

"That's right. And my husband couldn't stand him,

either. Before he died, he made me promise not to let Ginsberg . . . well, I'll go downstairs and make some sandwiches."

Mémère left, her footsteps slowly moving down the stairs, and when she was out of earshot, Jack told Aronowitz, "Awww, she doesn't like my girl friend either. My girl friend, Dodie Müller. Because she has long, long hair and doesn't tie it up. Because she likes to go barefoot. Because she's an Indian. She's ninety-five per cent Indian, and my mother calls her *la sauvage*—the savage. She's a very bohemian painter, you know. She's teaching me how to paint . . . ."

Every fall, mémère would go off for a month or two to stay with Nin in Florida. Left alone in Northport, drinking too much and missing his mother, Jack would think briefly about getting married to his new girl friend Dodie Müller, the widow of the painter Jan Müller, going to Europe with her, maybe writing a book about their trip to Paris. She was teaching Jack how to paint, how to stretch canvasses and make frames, and for a time he was infatuated with her. She was dark haired and lived, he thought, like a bohemian in the Village, just like his dream of the ideal woman.

After buying the house in Northport, Kerouac saw much less of Joyce Glassman. Once he brought her home to meet mémère when the house was full of local kids idolizing him. Jack himself drank steadily through the afternoon. Mémère cooked a festive dinner which everyone ate except Jack, who had his face in his plate. Joyce helped with the dishes, but afterwards Jack told her mémère hadn't liked the way she helped wash up. Joyce was impressed with mémère as a very powerful woman who had a great hold on Jack. He was very much the little boy in her house, with his mother providing a necessary refuge from the outside world. Of course Jack was also held fast by his feelings of responsibility to take care of her. There was no more talk about marriage or trips to Europe. Jack tried to lose himself in his writing, but it didn't work. He had the energy only for typing up old manuscripts like his *Book of Sketches, Tics & Daydreams* and *Pomes All Sizes*. Instead of benzedrine, the doctor put him on dexamyl, but Jack said it didn't have the same effect on his writing.

Ginsberg returned from Paris in August 1959, and despite mémère's protests, Jack continued to visit his apartment on East 2nd Street. Allen had begun *Kaddish* in Europe and was writing at the height of his creative powers, but he always had time to be encouraging. When Jack received a large advance for editing a paperback anthology of Beat writing and then paid the contributors next to nothing, Allen defended him. It wasn't that Jack was stingy, "but he has his mother's native French peasant parsimony."

Ginsberg tried to interest him in a trip to Peru, encouraged him to take mescaline (Kerouac wrote a 5,000-word Mescaline Report about the experience) and comforted him when Jack got angry over a TV parody of himself as "Jack Crackerjack" reading a twisted version of "Howl." Jack didn't have to account to mémère for every minute out of Northport, so long as he came home reasonably intact. Together Allen, Peter and Jack walked around the Village just as in the old San Francisco "Desolation Angels" days, dropping in on friends.

Joseph LeSueur remembers that one Indian summer day near the end of October 1959, they tried to visit the New York poet Frank O'Hara, whom Jack had offended at a poetry reading at the Living Theater earlier that year. Dressed in his heavy lumberjack shirt despite the heat, drinking wine from a pint bottle he carried in his hip pocket, Jack wanted to apologize to O'Hara. Kerouac had interrupted the reading by yelling, "You're ruining American poetry, O'Hara," and Frank had shot back, "That's more than you could ever do." When they found out O'Hara wasn't home, Jack and Allen left him a note, then decided to write him haikus using Joseph LeSueur's typewriter in the apartment.

As the months wore on, Jack became increasingly moody and despondent, and he began drinking harder. Since mémère wouldn't let drugs in the house, he drank instead. As in every place he lived for the rest of his life, he picked up a crowd of local drinking buddies. Besides the apparently endless demands on his time and money, Jack also raged because success wasn't bringing him nearly the satisfactions he'd dreamed of, primarily because he was never taken very seriously as a writer. Reporters kept knocking on his door hoping for a colorful interview, but by 1959 he wasn't fresh news as a literary personality, which made the critical response to his books even more discouraging.

In 1959 and 1960, as the books he'd written finally came out—*Doctor Sax, Maggie Cassidy, Mexico City Blues, Visions of Cody, The Scripture of the Golden Eternity, Tristessa* and *Lonesome Traveler*—there was less and less attention paid to him as a serious writer. Kerouac was used to shrugging off the bad press in *Time* Magazine, which had enjoyed baiting the beatniks in the early days of his success, calling him "a cut-rate Thomas Wolfe" writing "in vivid if not always lucid gushes and rushes, a style he attributes to the rambling reminiscences of his French Canadian mother." Jack thought it was all a conspiracy. He felt the reviewers only liked Philip Roth, Herbert Gold, Bernard Malamud, J.D. Salinger and Saul Bellow, while the best-sellers were in the hands of Michener and Wouk. He complained to his friends that his only readers were kids who stole his books from the stores.

The worst came in 1959, when Jack's favorite *Doctor Sax* was panned as a "largely psychopathic . . . pretentious and unreadable farrago of childhood fantasy-play" by the New York *Times*. Then *Mexico City Blues* was also raked over in the *Times* by Kenneth Rexroth, whose attack on the book could have been motivated by bitter personal anger at Jack's off-handed characterization of him as "Rheinhold Cacoethes" in *The Dharma Bums*. Kerouac had hoped *Mexico City Blues* would establish him as a serious poet, but Rexroth began his review with the ultimate putdown: "Someone once said of Mr. Kerouac that he was a Columbia freshman who went to a party in the Village twenty years ago and got lost. How true. The naive effrontery of this book is more pitiful than ridiculous." With heavy sarcasm, Rexroth quoted "one of the best poems of the book," the lines beginning "I keep falling in love/ with my mother," and then he went on to say, "It's all there, the terrifying skillful use of verse, the broad knowledge of life, the profound judgments, the almost unbearable sense of reality." Jack felt Rexroth wasn't being fair. It was like somebody from the old days had suddenly slammed the door.

Ginsberg did his best. He reviewed *The Dharma Bums* for the *Village Voice* and tried to give "a few facts to clear up a lot of bull." Allen focused on Jack as a creative writer, not as a beat phenomenon. He discussed Kerouac's language, the rhythm of his sentences, his progress in *On The Road, The Subterraneans, The Dharma Bums, Visions of Cody* and *Doctor Sax*, which he called "sketch evidence of the prose pilgrimage he's made."

It was a brilliant review, the best article on Kerouac in those years, but it didn't help lighten Jack's mood because there were too many other fights going on. John Ciardi took him apart in *Saturday Review*, Robert Burstein went after him in "The Cult of Unthink" in *Horizon*, John Updike parodied his style in a short story for the *New Yorker*, Truman Capote attacked him on David Susskind's TV program by saying that what Kerouac did wasn't writing at all, "it's typing." The American College Dictionary asked him for a definition of a new entry, the word "beat generation," but as a writer apart from the "beatniks," Kerouac wasn't taken seriously.

In despair, Jack told Ginsberg that he was going to try to pull himself together and write a book about his last two years of disillusionment with success in America. But somehow he never found time.

Chapter Thirty

By the beginning of the summer of 1960, Kerouac felt he had to break out of his life in Northport. Oppressing him were too many drunken nights in New York bars playing the role of King of the Beats and too many brooding, introspective days hung over in his house on

Long Island, snapping at his mother, sick to death of himself. He'd had eight books published in the past three years, he had over $20,000 in the bank, but he'd never drunk harder or come closer to cracking up.

In June 1960, he wrote Allen Ginsberg a mournful letter longing for time to find himself. Kerouac first dreamed of taking off to Mexico City without telling anybody and renting a quiet apartment for himself with flowers in the window, not his old noisy rooftop room above Bill Garver's place at 212 Orizaba but living alone, walking the streets and lighting candles.

But without some reason strong enough to wrench him out of Northport, he couldn't justify a trip to Mexico. *Holiday* Magazine offered to send him to Europe on a writing assignment, but he was worried that if he met Gregory Corso in Paris, it would be like Greenwich Village all over again. Jack didn't know anyone in Europe he wanted to visit, and there didn't seem to him to be any place that he could flee where he wouldn't eventually attract hangers-on who'd start him drinking again.

So he brooded and sulked in his bedroom at home, writing letters to all his friends complaining that he wouldn't make it through the summer. One of the letters was to Lawrence Ferlinghetti, his publisher at City Lights in San Francisco. Jack had been putting his *Book of Dreams* together for Ferlinghetti, and when he heard how Jack was feeling, he offered his cabin at Bixby Canyon, sixteen miles north of Big Sur, below Point Lobos on the Pacific Coast, for a couple of months. There he could retreat to work on the galleys of the City Lights book and escape from people for a while. The idea excited Kerouac. It seemed like the answer to all his problems, the chance to stop drinking and get back on his feet again. Toward the last week in July 1960, he left his mother in Northport and took the train to Chicago to catch the California Zephyr west. He was unaware of it at the time, but he was heading for what became his last big adventure.

In the three years since the *Howl* obscenity trial Lawrence Ferlinghetti's venture in San Francisco had come a long way. The trial had attracted national attention and helped give City Lights the start it needed.

In 1957 the police had raided the bookshop on Columbus Avenue and charged Ferlinghetti with publishing an "obscene" book, *Howl.* Ferlinghetti and Shig, his partner in the bookstore, went to court and contested the case. Their lawyer, Jake Ehrlich, won it for them with the help of testimonials from noted Bay Area professors and critics. When the trial ended in August 1957, Ferlinghetti and City Lights were both nationally well-known.

By 1960, the Pocket Poets Series was well-established with over a dozen titles. Besides Ferlinghetti himself and Ginsberg, the series included Corso, Patchen, Rexroth and William Carlos Williams. City Lights Bookstore had become a flourishing center for young poets and visiting writers in San Francisco. Ferlinghetti became one of the best-selling poets in the United States with his first book, *Pictures of the Gone World,* which was Number One in the Pocket Poet Series and his second book, *The Coney Island of the Mind,* published by New Directions in 1958, was almost as well-known as *Howl.*

Ferlinghetti and Ginsberg, together, were the leading poets of this new literary underground. Ferlinghetti shared Allen's sense that they and the small number of writers like them formed a special and tightly-knit group, almost like a family. The *Howl* trial in 1957 had first given them their sense of publicly standing together against a common enemy, but afterwards Ferlinghetti had stayed in close touch, as much a friend and fellow poet as a publisher, encouraging Ginsberg through the difficult composition of *Kaddish,* sending advances to Corso to keep him alive in Europe, paying royalties on time and always being there at the bookstore address when the poets needed him. He'd been trying to get a Kerouac book on his list for three years, beginning shortly after the publication of *On The Road.*

In summer 1957, before Jack rode the bus back east with his mother from Berkeley to live in Orlando, Florida, he had offered City Lights the manuscript of *Mexico City Blues,* which Ferlinghetti hadn't liked and had turned down. There was basically a respect between the two writers, but Jack complained that Ferlinghetti didn't appreciate him as a poet. Grove Press took *Mexico City Blues,* and Kerouac next tried City Lights with a 25,000-

word one-line poem called "Lucien Midnight." Ferlinghetti refused it over Kerouac's protest that even if he were to separate the poem into lines, the lines wouldn't make the poem. But Jack wrote him from Orlando at the end of October 1957 that breaking Robert Frost's words into lines didn't make him a better poet than Thoreau.

Ginsberg encouraged him to keep trying Ferlinghetti, because Allen thought that if City Lights published the trinity of Ginsberg, Corso and Kerouac, a revolution would take place in American poetry. A nice sequence of titles, he said, would be *Howl, Gasoline, Blues*. So Jack typed his "San Francisco Blues," the poems he had scribbled in the Cameo Hotel in 1954, describing the bums and commuters he watched out the window on the skid-row corner of Harrison and Third Streets, but the poems were too insubstantial for Ferlinghetti.

By January 1959, Kerouac was relenting a little on his insistence that he wanted City Lights to publish only his poetry. He offered Ferlinghetti a sample of his spontaneous prose called "Old Angel Midnight," which was immediately acceptable. The piece had been widely talked about when it appeared in the magazine *Big Table*, and Jack told Ferlinghetti he could add another section to it to stretch it to book length. Kerouac was very proud of "Old Angel Midnight," thinking of it as a continuation of Joyce's *Finnegan's Wake* and was disgusted when copyright complications interfered with its publication. Irving Rosenthal, editor of *Big Table*, insisted that the material was owned by the magazine. The only other available prose, Kerouac wrote Ferlinghetti, was his bulky *Book of Dreams*, his spontaneous dream diary.

Ferlinghetti still hadn't decided what to do with *Book of Dreams* a year later. For one thing the manuscript was voluminous. He asked if he could publish a shorter piece, Jack's sketch *October in the Railroad Earth*. But Kerouac's agent, Sterling Lord, had been busy in the two years since *On The Road* had made the best-seller list, and all of his manuscripts with any commercial potential were already committed. *October in the Railroad Earth* was going to come out as part of the book, *Lonesome Traveler*, which Lord had sold to McGraw-Hill, and when Ferlinghetti next asked for the transcript of

Jack's narration for the film *Pull My Daisy*, that turned out to have been sold to Grove Press.

In the meantime, Ferlinghetti published a long poem of Kerouac's about Rimbaud as a City Lights broadside, but still he wanted a full book. Jack tried to interest him in the 1000-page manuscript on Buddhist and general religious philosophy, *Some of the Dharma*. He even offered to type parts of it for a small pamphlet like Alan Watts' *Beat Zen, Square Zen, and Zen*, which was doing well for City Lights. Jack had invited Ferlinghetti to visit him in Northport and look over three manuscripts: *Book of Dreams, Book of Sketches* and *Book of Blues*. They finally settled, without the visit, on a selection from *Book of Dreams*. By the end of April 1960, Jack was reworking it for Philip Whalen to read for Ferlinghetti in San Francisco, changing the names of his friends in the dreams to fit with those in his other published books. Whalen's job was to select the best dreams and write the introduction.

Although Kerouac wanted City Lights to bring out his book, he insisted that Ferlinghetti do things his way. When the paragraphing of *Rimbaud* was changed in the galleys, Jack put it back the original way so it would appear on the page just as he had written it when high. In his letters, he lectured Ferlinghetti on his theory of spontaneous prose, emphasizing that he didn't believe in changing a word of a poem or the shape of a paragraph after he'd once written it. Ferlinghetti was amenable with *Rimbaud*, a simple broadside, but he wanted Whalen to edit *Book of Dreams* before it went to the printer. Kerouac agreed since Whalen was a friend whose literary judgment he trusted.

Ferlinghetti had been so easy to work with over the galleys of *Rimbaud* and so generous in offering to lend Jack his cabin, that by mid-summer Jack, in his letters, had nicknamed him "The Smiler," acting as if he were his only true friend in San Francisco and pledging him to secrecy about his proposed trip to the West Coast. He sent Ferlinghetti a stream of letters describing how he had never felt worse in his life, suffering from stomach cramps, diarrhea and insomnia. At home he fought endlessly with his mother, who was very worried about his drinking. In Northport he moved from Gilbert Street to Earl Avenue, but visitors learned his new address and appeared on his doorstep with bottles of Jack Daniels. Even if he didn't know them Jack would let them into the house over his mother's angry protests to drink, talk and play records all night. He'd find out later that the people who'd pretended to be his friends had stolen copies of his books from his bedroom and then gone off to spread the word that he was on the verge of a nervous breakdown, drinking too much and unable to control himself. He had stumbled into a bad life.

Kerouac's proposed stay in Ferlinghetti's cabin in Bixby Canyon was to be his second trip west in a year. During the winter of 1959-60 he'd gone to Los Angeles to appear on the Steve Allen Show and afterwards had run up to San Francisco for a sprawling and chaotic few days drinking followed by a drunken trip back to New York. He wanted to avoid doing the same thing this time so he begged Ferlinghetti not to tell a soul, not even Whalen, he was coming back to correct the *Book of Dreams* galleys. Just in case anyone besides Ferlinghetti was reading the mail at City Lights, Jack signed his postcards with a pseudonym, "Richard Wisp," and warned that when he arrived in San Francisco he was going to phone Ferlinghetti at the bookstore using names like "Adam Yulch" or "Lalaghy Pulvertaft."

The false names were more of a joke than a protective measure and made Kerouac seem like a character in his own *Book of Dreams*, where he had given whimsical names to all his close friends. More than at any other time in his life, he sensed himself during this period as a legendary figure caught in a larger-than-life drama. He had no way of foretelling that the dream of a retreat at Bixby Canyon would turn into a waking nightmare worse than anything he'd described in his *Book of Dreams*.

The trip to San Francisco began with a spirit of escapist fantasy suited to the false names he'd chosen. Jack caught the California Zephyr in Chicago carrying only the rucksack which he'd packed for Ferlinghetti's cabin. A St. Christopher medal had been sewn to the flap by his mother, who'd also reinforced his sewing kit with extra safety pins and special needles so he could keep himself together once he was away from home. She packed a jar of instant coffee and food for sandwiches so he wouldn't have to buy anything on the train. He took her advice and stayed by himself in his roomette for three dreamlike days and nights watching the scenery roll by his window.

The thought entered his mind that the kids reading *On The Road* and *The Dharma Bums* would be surprised at how comfortably he was traveling, if they imagined him twenty-six years old, turning his face to the wind and the rain, forever climbing mountains or out on the road hitchhiking. They wouldn't have believed he was pushing forty, physically and emotionally in a state of near-collapse, but then they couldn't have imagined what he had been through in the past three years.

Later, in the summer of 1961, a year after the trip to San Francisco, when Kerouac wrote about what happened to him in *Big Sur*, he dwelled in the opening pages on the sense of chaos and despair he had carried with him onto the train. He'd come to the end of the line and needed to get away. Since *On The Road* had made him famous, he'd been hounded by reporters, interviewers and fans and had no privacy to write.

Kerouac's dream of a retreat in the woods got off to a shaky start as soon as the train arrived in San Francisco. He'd packed his rucksack for the cabin, but the first place he planted it was on the floor of his favorite skid-row hotel. Instead of phoning Ferlinghetti from the railroad station for directions to Bixby Canyon and going directly there before anyone knew he was in San Francisco, Jack ruined his secret retreat at once by rushing into City Lights Bookstore in North Beach at the height of Saturday night's business. There he met Ferlinghetti and other North Beach friends and they all spent the evening together drinking in Jack's favorite bars. So, despite all his intense precautions, Jack began his holiday with a two-day drunk, sleeping it off in the hotel with Phil Whalen and the painter Robert LaVigne. He woke up late Sunday night, saw the floor littered with empty bottles of wine, and pulled himself together long enough to realize what had happened. Hung over, feeling himself at death's door but still chasing the dream, he dragged himself down to the bus station and at two A.M. arrived

318

bleary-eyed in Monterey, where a cab drove him the fourteen miles further south to Bixby Canyon. Much to Ferlinghetti's surprise, later that morning he found Jack sleeping in the meadow a short way from the cabin.

That afternoon Ferlinghetti drove him back to Monterey in his jeep so Jack could buy groceries. Kerouac was reminded of the time he packed into the Desolation Peak fire station in 1956, and optimistically he imagined another summer like it. But in 1960 he was a different man, physically exhausted from his life as a drunken celebrity, still suffering from the effects of his most recent binge of two days before. Besides, Desolation Peak had been enforced solitude. When he grew bored there he couldn't hike down the mountain by himself; he had to stick it out until the forestry crew came to bring him back at the end of summer. At Bixby Canyon, he could walk out any time he wanted simply by striding through the meadow, crossing the creek and climbing the dirt road of the canyon until he turned up on Highway 1. It would be a difficult test of his will power to wait out the weeks in the canyon so close to San Francisco, but Kerouac was determined to try. In Monterey he bought supplies for three weeks, enough to last him until Ferlinghetti returned with more food for a weekend together before Jack faced a second three-week stretch alone at the cabin. In theory it was a good plan, but like most of his other plans this one didn't work out right either.

To begin with, his first impression of Bixby Canyon terrified him. On his other trips to the West Coast he'd never been to Big Sur, so he was a stranger to the physical scale and rugged solitude of the coastal landscape. Months before when Ferlinghetti had sent him a map of how to get to the cabin, he'd studied it in his Long Island backyard and expected a friendly forest waiting for him in California. But after the cab pulled away the first night, Jack, left alone on the dark, foggy edge of the highway, found himself stumbling blind on the unfamiliar dirt road down to the canyon, hung over and exhausted, the beam of his railroad lantern lost a few inches in front of his feet and the roar of the Pacific Ocean sounding malevolently in his ears. Everything frightened him in the inky blackness. He was caught up short by a cattle crossing imbedded across the road, he heard a rattlesnake in the canyon bushes, he was alarmed by a raging flooded river in the noise of the creek, just waiting for him to slip so it could rush him off to the waiting sea. Even the dark piles of mule dung on the white sand looked sinister to him.

In the light of morning he decided he had some cause for his fears. At the cattle crossing in the road there was a drop down the canyon of what looked like 1,000 feet. Fog poured in from a break in the bluff and somehow the white-capped ocean looked higher than the floor of the canyon where he stood, as though a tidal wave would bring it crashing through the canyon at any minute. Looking up in the sky he was upset to observe the massive aerial bridge that was Highway 1 crossing over the canyon, because right underneath the bridge, in the sand beside the sea cliff, was the wrecked hulk of a car that had crashed through the bridge rail ten years before. Before Kerouac arrived at Bixby Canyon he'd joked to Ferlinghetti that he'd have enough time in three weeks to build a tea-house in the woods if he were Gary Snyder. After seeing the place he felt he would need all of Snyder's composure just to survive there, let alone build anything.

At the other end of the canyon, toward the east beside the wind-blown and stunted trees lurking in the wet fog, there was something that frightened Kerouac and it was particularly unsettling to him because he'd had a premonition about it before leaving Northport. This was a tangled steep cliff with bushes and heather, ferns and conifers, looking strangely Burmese. While he lived at the cabin, Jack stayed resolutely away from that part of the woods. Before he had left for California, he had had a series of drinking nightmares about a mountain, the most horrible one called in *Book of Dreams*, "The Flying Horses of Mien Mo." It had come during a very bad period of dreaming about digging graves in his yard, seeing the end of the world and being exposed "ass naked" like a helpless child on a television program.

His heart sank at the sight of the mountain at Bixby Canyon because he recognized it as an image straight out of the Mien Mo nightmare. In the dream he was riding a bus through Mexico, first with Cassady sleeping beside him, then alone. He was on his way to sign up for a maritime seaman's job, although even in the dream he realized the absurdity of coming "all the way from New York to the landlocked center of Mexico for a sea voyage but there it is. . . ." In the middle of the calm fields of Mexico he dreamt he went into a seaman's hiring hall on the edge of the Mountain of Coyocan, where an obliging official tried to help him, sending letters back to New York trying to straighten out the reason for the trip. While still riding the bus, Jack had his first glimpse of the Mountain of Coyocan, but the glimpse was enough for him to know instinctively that he had come to a legendary place of the gods:

I look up in the sky . . . see that old ten thousand foot or hundred mile high mountain cliff with its enormous hazy blue palaces & temples where they have giant granite benches and tables for Giant Gods bigger than the ones who hugged skyscrapers on Wall Street—and in the air, Ah the silence of that horror, I see flying winged horses with capes furling over their shoulders, the slow majestic pawing of their front hooves as they clam thru the air flight—Griffins they are!

The Mexicans on the bus with Kerouac laughed at him when he tried to explain what he saw: "they laugh not only to hear a stranger talk about it but the ridiculousness of anybody even mentioning or noticing it—" The Mexicans seemed to know a secret about Coyocan they wouldn't tell him because he was a gringo; "They're really laughing at me for my big ideas about the Mountain—"

Waiting in town for his seaman's job, Kerouac watched obsessively the Flying Horses swirl over the mountain, his situation growing "evil and completely sinister" because the Mexicans refused to talk about what he was seeing. When the Horses flew low over the town, they changed into blue and white birds to fool everybody, but he saw them fly higher and revert to Horses, their hooves clawing through the blue sky and crossing the moon, "eerie griffin horror men-horses" with capes unfurling from their shoulders. Kerouac had penetrated the secret of the Coyocan Mountain, like some "Himalayan secret horrors" concealing "the beating heart of the Giant Beast." He was left alone and helpless before the beauty, the mystery and the terror of his vision.

At Bixby Canyon, the mountain he called Mien Mo, the aerial bridge over the beach and the wrecked car in the sand below were living horrors to Kerouac, constant reminders of his vision of death-in-life. The rest of the world went on its way ignoring the signs, but he couldn't get them out of his mind. To make matters worse, he was spending his time at the cabin correcting galleys of the *Book of Dreams*, all the while witnessing some of his nightmares materialize right in front of his eyes outside the door. At the beginning of his retreat he tried to relax and enjoy the solitude of the canyon. He attempted to make friends with the bluejay and the raccoon who hung around for scraps of food.

One night after he'd just settled into the cabin, he closed the board shutters, stoked the fire and sat down in front of the kerosene lamp to read through the night with wide eyes a book Ferlinghetti had left behind, *Doctor Jekyll and Mr. Hyde*. Closing it at dawn, Jack admired the elegance of the novel, but he didn't draw the parallel to his own life in which the nightmares from his *Book of Dreams* revealed his growing inability to push back the forces pressing in on him. The fog which poured into the canyon during the day depressed him and he closed the shutters against it. But the fog actually insured the isolation of his retreat since none of the people who had other cabins nearby were living there while the fog hung on.

After Jack finished the *Book of Dreams* galleys, he immersed himself in a new writing project he had conceived in Northport, the idea of writing a poem called "Sea," the sounds of the ocean first on the shores of the Pacific above Big Sur and then the sounds of the Atlantic on a beach in Brittany. Talking to Ferlinghetti about his plans to begin this new book at Bixby Canyon, Kerouac felt he had come home to something he was particularly suited to write about because of his Breton ancestry as a French Canadian. Half-jokingly he told friends he had to write the poem since James Joyce wasn't about to do it now that he was dead, but the Pacific Ocean nearly overwhelmed him, and was nothing like the Liffey "Riverun" of Joyce's Dublin.

After a few days at the cabin, Jack worked out a

schedule for himself similar to the general pattern of his days on Desolation Peak, with the difference that every night after supper, around eight o'clock, he put on a fisherman coat, took his notebook, pencil and railroad lamp, and walked down the path in the fog under the high bridge to the Pacific Ocean, jumping the beach creek and skirting the piles of dung left by the mule Alf, owned by someone who also had a cabin near Ferlinghetti. At the edge of the shore of Bixby Beach he hunched down in a corner by the cliff not far from one of the caves in the seawall, put out his lantern and in the dark scrawled the sounds the sea made onto the white pages of his secretarial notebook.

It was a writing experiment continuing in the spirit of the composition of *Mexico City Blues* five summers before, when Kerouac had sat through the afternoons with a pad and pencil listening to Bill Garver talking high on morphine in his room in Mexico City, this time transcribing onto his paper the endless, rhythmical cadences of the Pacific Ocean instead of his friend's rambling monologue. But this time, as Ginsberg perceptively understood, it was a "troubling aloneness he entered—troubling for outsider knowing the writing saint's alone with the universe." Sitting alone in the darkness of the beach, with the white breakers swirling around him, Jack was often frightened, yet he felt a strong compulsion to go on with the poem and kept coming back to the beach night after night.

Chapter Thirty-One

After a little over two weeks in Bixby Canyon in August 1960, Kerouac couldn't take any more of the solitude. He scattered the perishable food for the bird and the raccoon, closed up the cabin and left the Canyon. It was a few days before Ferlinghetti was to arrive and Jack thought he'd thumb his way back to San Francisco. It was no problem in the light of morning setting forth on the dirt road to the highway, but when he tried to hitchhike the fourteen miles north to Monterey, he was back into another waking nightmare right out of *Book of Dreams*.

From nine in the morning until four in the afternoon, he had no luck at all. Thousands of people might be reading his books about joyful adventures on the road, but the crowning irony of his trip to California was that nobody was offering him a ride. It had been years since he'd hitchhiked, so he was out of touch. In the summer of 1960 rides were scarce along Highway 1. Throughout the long hot day Jack saw nothing but vacationers driving one of America's most scenic roads, and he needed to take only one close took at them to know they weren't the type of people who would buy his books, let alone offer him a ride.

Cars filled with tourists driving brand-new family station-wagons streamed past him on the highway between Big Sur and Monterey, never even slowing down at the sight of him, totally intent on the postcard views of ocean, cliffs, rocks and beaches. Inside the cars Kerouac saw the henpecked husband at the wheel, silenced by the wife in sunglasses sneering out the window at the probably dangerous hitchhiker lurking beside the road.

In the backseat were the children, endless numbers of them, all fighting over the ice-cream and spilling it on the tartan seatcovers. There was no room inside for a hitchhiker and his shabby rucksack, no place to crouch even on the back platform of the car because it was filled with racks of clothes. Jack was seeing the American dream roll by him on the road in the new car packed with new clothes and a happy family living the blissful life of California.

Trudging down the dirt road back to the foggy canyon was out of the question, so Jack stuck to the highway, limping half the distance to Monterey. The hot tar in the afternoon sun brought blisters to his feet. Finally, a little truck driven by a man with a dog stopped to give him a lift to the bus station. It was the last time he ever hitchhiked. Once in San Francisco, he checked back into his old skid-row hotel for a night's sleep, resting better in the hotel than he had in his sleeping bag at the cabin, unmistakably relieved to be out of the canyon and back to a familiar bed and an old routine in his favorite city.

Despite the weeks without anything to drink, trying to get back into shape, he still wasn't over the previous three years of drunkenness, and his face in the mirror after all the nights listening to the sounds of the sea looked back at him haggard and lost. He had no illusions about why the cars on Highway 1 hadn't picked him up. Looking at his face in the mirror made it obvious why they couldn't fit him into their vacation dream.

The next day at City Lights Bookstore, Ferlinghetti had some bad news waiting for him. The night after Jack had left Northport, his favorite little cat, Tyke, had died. Jack was so touched by his mother's detailed letter about the death and burial of the cat that he included it in *Big Sur*. Ferlinghetti sympathized with him, but Jack knew nobody could understand his feeling for his cats had always been a little crazy, that somehow he identified cats with his brother Gerard, who'd taught him to love them. Even after thirty years Tyke's death brought back painful memories of Gerard's death, but it was also an overwhelming reminder of the loneliness of the life he would return to in Northport. Ferlinghetti guessed that he was headed for another binge so he advised him to go straight back to the cabin for a few more weeks instead of hanging around San Francisco to get drunk again.

At this point in his life Jack wasn't listening to anyone's advice on how to live, and even if he were, he wouldn't take it from Ferlinghetti. Kerouac's increasing paranoia made him feel that although Ferlinghetti wished him well, they weren't really close friends, since in a strange way Jack was jealous of him not only because of his success as a poet, but also because of his success as a publisher. A year later when he wrote *Big Sur* he named Ferlinghetti "Lorenzo Monsanto," the last name suggesting his regard for Ferlinghetti's stability and good sense, but Ferlinghetti was also put off by the gulf between them. When he read *Big Sur* he objected to Jack's description of him: "He made me out a genial businessman, and I don't particularly feel like a genial businessman."

Disregarding Ferlinghetti's advice to get out of town, Kerouac left the City Lights Bookstore with Phil Whalen to go drink at Mike's Place a few doors down the street in North Beach. Unlike Ferlinghetti, Jack felt Whalen took him seriously as a poet, and he respected the intelligent editing job on *Book of Dreams*. They'd been friends five years before in the Dharma Bum days, and the passing years hadn't changed any of Whalen's basic humor and compassion. Jack described him even more affectionately in the pages of *Big Sur* than he had in *The Dharma Bums*. Whalen wasn't a drinker like Kerouac, but he didn't lecture Jack about his drinking. One of Jack's favorite lines from Whalen's poetry was "When I leave town all my friends go back on the sauce." Whalen accepted the drunkenness and even held Kerouac up as a model drinking buddy in "Prose Take-Out, Portland 13:IX:58," published in his book *Memoirs of an Interglacial Age*. Usually when Jack began to drink heavily, Phil just quietly went home. They didn't argue about it, Whalen just left him with another friend, the poet Lew Welch, who drank with Kerouac on this trip.

Whalen, Welch and Gary Snyder had been students together at Reed College, and all three poets became Jack's companions on one or another of his visits to San Francisco after 1955. This time Snyder was studying in Japan, but Jack was no longer so interested in Buddhism. Welch (called "Dave Wain" in *Big Sur*) lived in the same rooming house in San Francisco that Whalen did, and after he joined Kerouac at a bar on Columbus Street, Whalen faded out of the scene—he preferred to stay at home and read while Jack and Lew got drunk. Welch had driven Kerouac back to New York from San Francisco the winter before, after the Steve Allen TV program, a drunken odyssey in Welch's jeepster, stopping for expensive hotels in Las Vegas, exotic dancers in St. Louis and many bottles of scotch along the way. Back in New York, Welch and Kerouac had been photographed composing a poem together with another poet who'd come along with them to Greenwich Village, Albert Saijo. The poem and the pictures (Jack in a baseball cap, his face petulant, touchy) appeared in Fred McDarrah's book *The Beat Scene*.

Lew Welch didn't have Whalen's calm self-possession.

He was, if anything, even more emotionally vulnerable than Kerouac. On this trip he became Jack's driver, taking him around to bars and up and down the East Bay, wherever Jack wanted to go next. With $500 in cashed travelers checks, Jack got back in the role of the drunken King of the Beats, repeating the punishing routine he had fled Northport to avoid. He settled down in a bar over double bourbons and ginger ale with Lew Welch, engrossed with the idea that the American people, who think themselves the cleanest people on earth, really walk around with dirty assholes.

Of the three Reed poets, Snyder, Whalen and Welch, Lew Welch had the most in comon with Kerouac. They were both voluble, emotionally intense men of strong will who had been athletes in high school, star runners, and then gone on to confused stretches of service during World War II. As a poet, Welch was without Kerouac's confidence or facility. Most of his work was unpublished in 1960, but Jack thought he had "that certain something that young hip teenagers probably wanta imitate." Actually Kerouac seemed uncomfortable before the naked intensity of most of Welch's terse poems and much more at ease with Whalen's poetic whimsy. With his thin, brooding face, high arched eyebrows and staring eyes, Welch looked as haunted as Kerouac, and in his drinking he was fleeing some of the same phantoms that pursued Jack: a tangled relationship with his mother, an inability to settle down with a wife for any length of time. Kerouac joked about his sexual sterility, insisting he couldn't have fathered his second wife's child, but Welch was certain of his barrenness, carrying around with him the anguished knowledge that he was "the end of a very strong line."

In a bar on Columbus Street with Lew Welch, Jack began to bury his depression about his cat's death. After enough bourbon and ginger ale he felt exultant being back in San Francisco and even bolstered his courage enough to phone Neal Cassady in Los Gatos, now at home again after spending two years of his sentence for possession of marijuana in San Quentin.

Jack had to be very drunk before he called, because he was very uncertain about whether or not Neal wanted to talk to him. The previous winter he'd been scheduled to read at San Quentin, something Ginsberg and Snyder had done before him, but he had been too cowardly to show up at the prison, getting drunk with Welch in San Francisco instead. It had been partly Jack's fear of jails, but mostly his embarrassment about facing Cassady there, afraid of what Neal might say to him, or whether Neal would be hostile because he had never written much while Neal was in prison. He'd sent money for a typewriter when Ginsberg passed on the word that Cassady wanted one, but Kerouac was entirely unsure of how he stood with his old friend.

It was only by telling Lew Welch that he had to meet the legendary Cassady that Jack got up the courage to make the phone call, and even when Neal called him "old buddy" and insisted he drop everything and hurry down to his house in Los Gatos, Jack was still nervously reluctant to set off at once. He made Welch circle the block with his jeep, with friends from the bar piling in on the mattress in back, picking him up at the curb in front of his favorite Japanese liquor store where he bought a bottle of scotch for the ride. Only then did they drive off down the Bayshore Highway past South San Francisco headed for Los Gatos, a few miles below San Jose.

Although it had been almost three years, Kerouac was still obsessed with the memory of Neal's face when he handed him the first copy of *On The Road* in Berkeley, troubled by the thought that it was the first time that Neal hadn't looked him straight in the eye. He worried how Neal might have been changed by prison, although he knew that Cassady had spent time in reform school when he was a boy. Lew Welch helped him take his mind off the problems by talking nonstop in the jeep as the lights of the suburbs flashed by in the dark night and the white line of the highway rolled under the wheels. Jack's seat beside Lew Welch was broken and he rocked gently back and forth as Welch drove, trying to make himself believe he was not really on the road to Los Gatos but rather swinging on some private back porch back home.

But they couldn't miss the endless housing tracts sprawling alongside the freeway, the mushrooming factories

328

breaking out on the hills all around them. Welch agreed with Kerouac that the population explosion would ultimately blight all America. The bottle of scotch was passed back and forth so often that it ran out before Los Gatos, and Welch pulled off so Kerouac could scramble out for another one. Climbing back into the jeep with drunken bravado, Jack plunked himself down on the front seat feeling like Samuel Johnson.

Kerouac was no longer the impressionable kid who'd followed Cassady across the continent more than ten years before in *On The Road*. He was no longer so dominated by Neal's talking and driving that he felt like Boswell to Neal's Johnson. Now he, not Neal Cassady, was Samuel Johnson, a literary parallel that was much more than a joke to Kerouac. He was fascinated by it, mentioning Boswell's *Life of Johnson* again later in *Big Sur* after he found a copy of the book in Welch's room and although he sensed his friends were bored with it, he insisted upon reading it aloud at breakfast. Somehow Jack felt that Boswell and Johnson vindicated the approach he had taken as a writer, using another man's life for literary material just as Boswell had used Johnson's.

But the result in Kerouac's book was a best-selling novel that made Cassady ashamed to look him straight in the eye. Some people even suggested that Neal had been picked up for possession of marijuana largely because of Jack's description of him using drugs in *On The Road*. By imagining himself as Johnson, Kerouac tried to convince himself that Neal had forgiven him for writing the book, for making money off it, for not writing him letters and for not showing up to read in prison. In other words he hoped that Neal had forgiven him everything.

Long before he met Cassady, while trying to get out of the Navy during World War II, he'd told an examining psychiatrist that he was Samuel Johnson. This literary identification was closely tied to his dream of becoming a great writer, but if it underscored the total seriousness of his literary ambitions, it could also serve as a boast and a brag when necessary, and a humorous reference among friends.

Whatever was running through Kerouac's mind in the

jeep had nothing to do with what the Cassadys were feeling when they opened the door to him in Los Gatos. They were, quite simply, genuinely glad to see him again. Standing beside Neal in his living room, Jack reverted to being Boswell, introducing him to Lew Welch and the others who'd come down in the jeep with them as the fabled Dean Moriarty. The Cassadys had done their best to make Jack feel welcome. Carolyn had lit a fire in the fireplace, something she knew he liked, and Neal insisted they come along with him to his job that night so they wouldn't have to break off the talk. Jack was still uncomfortable with him, expecting Neal would be bitter after the time in San Quentin, but Neal held no grudges and he still gave the place of honor on the bookshelf to the old photograph of him and Kerouac arm in arm in the early days. together as railroad brakemen. If anything, Neal was disappointed when Jack tried to bluster an excuse about not showing up to read in prison. He always suspected it was because he was drinking again and Neal hated to see him drunk.

Everyone piled back in the jeep to follow Cassady to the San Jose highway where he had a job on the night shift as a tire recapper. Watching him yank tires off car wheels, rushing off to throw them on the machine, Jack imagined Neal as a kind of Vulcan at the forge. It was impossible for them to have any time to talk, and even if they could talk, Jack's Long Island paranoia had come with him to the West Coast and was breaking out everywhere.

The next morning Kerouac woke up dead drunk on Phil Whalen's floor in the San Francisco rooming house. He didn't know what he was doing, but he was well into his own private lost weekend. The following day when Jack again woke up, he realized this time he was sliding into an alcoholic depression. He was temporarily saved by a phone call from Cassady asking to borrow $100 to pay the rent; he had been laid off from his job. Rounding up Lew Welch, who had disappeared with his girl, the poet Lenore Kandel, later famous for writing *The Love Book* (she was called "Romona Swartz" in *Big Sur*), Kerouac talked him into driving back to Los Gatos again, which wasn't hard because Welch was just following Kerouac in exactly the same way Jack had so often tailed people himself, waiting for something to happen.

This was the start of the weekend Ferlinghetti had talked about driving down to Bixby Canyon, so Ferlinghetti and his partner at the bookstore, Shig, followed Kerouac and Welch in a second jeep to Cassady's house. Again Jack had the rocking chair next to the driver, but this time he twisted around to talk to Whalen, lounging on the mattress in the back. After Kerouac handed over the money to Cassady, Neal joined the party and the two jeeps continued on their way to Ferlinghetti's cabin.

Surrounded by friends, Kerouac's return to Bixby Canyon was completely different from the way he had limped out of it alone earlier that week, but he was powerless to stop the drinking once he had started again, and all the company of the big poets' weekend at the cabin couldn't wrench him out of his self-destructive mood. Besides Cassady, Ferlinghetti, Kerouac, Whalen and Welch, Michael McClure also drove down from San Francisco with his wife and daughter and stayed in Monterey. Jack saw the group as a major nucleus of San Francisco poets, but in his difficult mood he just went through the motions of going along with them as they heaped wood for a bonfire on the beach, wolfed down steaks and read their poetry.

Later everyone took off for the local hot springs and restaurant at Nephenthe. Kerouac was deep into the wine then, refusing to eat and insisting that he was the one to flick the plastic off the bottle tops with an expert touch from years of wine drinking across the country. When the two jeeps drove back to San Francisco the next afternoon Cassady promised to come back the next day with Carolyn and the children. A young kid, a friend of Lew Welch's, begged Jack to let him stay in the cabin overnight. Jack didn't want anyone around, but he couldn't think of any way to refuse.

Finishing off the last bottle of port wine, Kerouac managed to survive the night, but in the morning there was nothing to drink and he was totally up against it, fighting the onset of delirium tremens. He sweated out his fever, raging while the kid watched. In the afternoon, when he'd somewhat recovered, Jack had the presence of mind to realize he was approaching "the point of adulthood disaster of the soul." But his lowest point at Bixby Canyon was still to come.

Later in the afternoon, more people showed up at the cabin. First Michael McClure returned with his wife and daughter, then Cassady drove back with Carolyn and the children. Cassady was ebullient because he had a car to show off, an old jeep he'd bought, as he told Jack, to celebrate Kerouac's return to California. The jeep was painted grape, the color of the wine they all drank. He drew Jack away from the others to show off the car and to celebrate their first chance to be alone in years with what Jack called the "most perfect of all blackhaired seeded packed tight superbomber joints in the world." Strangely enough, after smoking it, they fell uncomfortably silent. Jack blamed it on his pot paranoia, but being with Cassady had changed. When he wrote *Big Sur* the next summer far away from Cassady, Jack described his friend at the door of the cabin shimmering like an Angel in a burst of sunlight, yet at the time he was annoyed at himself because he could not fully respond anymore to Cassady's rhythm, and delivered a lot of show-off talk in the cabin afterwards in front of everybody to make up for it.

Carolyn later felt that Jack was "always embarrassed and paranoid that he had put Neal in the public eye" as the central character in *On The Road*. Cassady's own impressions of the book depended on whom he was talking to. He acted in public and in front of Kerouac as if he were proud to be the legendary hero of a bestselling novel, and he liked the novel in a literary sense (Neal never doubted Jack's genius as a writer).

But at other times he told people he hated the character who was "Dean Moriarty." As Carolyn remembered, Neal told her that "deep down he was appalled at the guy in the book," at his franticness and his futility. Jack had always envied Neal for being able to express his wildness, and in the novel Jack had looked at it from a literary viewpoint, Cassady as the hero of a novel, an image of Romantic Youth. Neal lived out the archetype of the image, but years later Carolyn was convinced Jack always carried a sense of guilt for creating his image of

Cassady in *On The Road,* convinced he was partly responsible for Neal's decline.

After a day at the cabin, Jack drove with the Cassadys the eighty-five miles back from Bixby Canyon to Los Gatos through the Santa Cruz Mountains, leaving the McClures and the cabin behind him. With Carolyn and the children settled in Los Gatos, Neal headed the jeep toward San Francisco. He had somebody there he was insistent Kerouac had to meet, and it was impossible to argue him out of it. Conversing with Cassady had become difficult, although they did talk about the possibility of *On The Road* being made into a movie. Jack later wrote to Ginsberg that Neal said he would be willing to play Dean Moriarty, since he wasn't that crazy about his job recapping tires. Still, driving with Neal had some of the old magic, and back in the jeep Jack couldn't help comparing him with Lew Welch. With Welch it was all conversation and smooth sailing, with Cassady it was flying wild with the promise of taking off suddenly up to Heaven.

The reason for rushing seventy miles to San Francisco (Carolyn had asked Jack to sleep over in Los Gatos) was that Neal was determined he'd meet his latest girl friend, Jackie. Until he saw her Kerouac was only lukewarm about the idea, thinking Neal was once again asking him to be his stand-in, but at her apartment he was stunned by her resemblance to his New York friend Lucien Carr. And although Jackie was infatuated with Neal, she settled for Jack. He moved into her apartment for a week, and got drunker and drunker, until he was finally unable to pull himself out of a sagging chair in her living room. She wanted to get married, to have him be a father for her four-year-old son, but even lost and adrift as he was, Jack stubbornly resisted. He was fascinated by her resemblance to Lucien Carr, but she bored him.

One afternoon when Kerouac was sprawling numbly in the old chair in the apartment, Phil Whalen dropped by to visit him. He brought wine and his pipe, but one look at Jack made him insist they go outside for some fresh air. Whalen dragged him to a park for an afternoon's exhausted sleep on the grass. Whalen was still

333

sympathetic, but the drinking had gone on so long that he was getting a little worried. The only thing Jack could think of to jar himself out of it was to return to Bixby Canyon, so that night he phoned Lew Welch, to ask him to bring Lenore Kandel and drive him, Jackie and her son down. Even to himself the prospect of bliss seemed remote; much closer to him—it began the next day —was the nightmare of his last days at the canyon.

Continuing to drink steadily, Jack was feeling aggressive enough to bully Welch into detouring past Cassady's house on the way to Bixby Canyon, ostensibly so that he could pick up some clothes he'd left there, but really so that he could watch the fireworks when Carolyn met Jackie. Nothing happened, of course, except silence between them, Kerouac the unhappy witness to everyone being strangers.

His edgy restlessness grew stronger once they reached the cabin later that night to find that although the fog had lifted, a wild August wind blasted off the Mien Mo Mountain and drove the leaves through the meadow and scattered them onto the beach. By four o'clock the next afternoon, Jack's mood matched the wind. He was snarling at Jackie, finding her little boy intolerable, even suspecting that Lew and Lenore were plotting against him. It was worse than the paranoiac fantasies; he had caught up with the grim reality of how little his life was offering him anymore, always passing through.

The road had come full circle. Kerouac's bleak vision of himself turned back to his last sight of Cassady at the end of *On The Road*, beaten and defeated, drifting from one end of the country to the other with no real attachment to life or to love, the end of the dream of life as an adventure with nothing but good times ahead. It looked like the only thing further down the road was the cheap wine that Welch had obligingly raced down to get at the highway store south of the canyon, but as the center of his life the past two weeks, the wine and the whisky had nearly poisoned him. For the first time in his life, Kerouac didn't know where to turn. If he were in Northport his mother might have found a way to calm him down (she would have called him overexcited), but he was thousands of miles away from home with only the sound of the wind and the sea filling his ears at the cabin.

334

The last thirty pages of *Big Sur* are Kerouac's description of his delirium tremens through the long afternoon and night, his friends trying to help him and then finally going to sleep themselves, exhausted, leaving him to his nightmares and hallucinations. For Jack it was an endless night of rigid terror.

At dawn, nearly out of his mind, he finally found relief calling to his dead cat Tyke and hearing sudden screams that rattled through his head. He had the intuitive feeling that he was in a special state of grace if he could just hold out a little longer, and at that moment he was rewarded with a vision of the Cross that broke through his long, anguished nightmare, bringing sweet relief.

With this vision of the Cross, his retreat at Bixby Canyon was ended, his emotions spent. He now realized the emptiness of his earlier romanticizing of suffering and death. At thirty-eight years old in Bixby Canyon, Kerouac had passed the last turn on his road.

Chapter Thirty-Two

The people who had read Kerouac's previous books would have had trouble imagining him, in Cassady's words, as "drunk old Jack," the famous writer with hundreds of dollars to spend on a binge in San Francisco. His optimistic dream of the great American adventure was what made his writing alive, his belief in the essential joyousness of following his own emotions and being excited by the promise of life. In his heart he was always the man leaning forward in his friend's car, peering toward the horizon receding beyond the next stretch of highway. Before returning to California he refused to admit to himself that the frontier had closed, but in *Big Sur* his vision of the American Innocent, the Original Adam, was dramatized so explicitly that it was as though he were seeing it in front of his eyes for the last time.

When Jack first came to the Canyon, he imagined the Indians, the original inhabitants of the Pacific shore, exploring the hidden caves of the Mien Mo Mountain a thousand years ago. Later after a day working on the creek, rearranging the rocks to increase the supply of drinking water at the cabin, he saw himself possessing the innocence of an Indian in the forest. His thoughts moved on to Emerson, whom Jack had read in a little red-leather book. Particularly Emerson's phrase "Infancy conforms to nobody," which Kerouac took as a sanction of his view of himself as a child in the cabin. During one bad moment alone on the beach, taking a deep breath of sea air and getting instead what he imagined as an overdose of iodine, he was unaccountably oppressed by the inevitability of mortality, but he comforted himself with the ideal of Emersonian self-reliance.

The irony was that Kerouac had very little self-reliance. His boredom with himself led him back from Bixby Canyon to San Francisco in two weeks, back to his friends and the bars in North Beach. And if he wanted to think about it, which he didn't, since the thought had no currency in the mind of a believing Catholic, the ultimate evidence of his lack of self-reliance was his vision of the Cross as his salvation at the end of *Big Sur*, the opposite of what Emerson had in mind in his essays.

But Kerouac was a sick man when he came to the cabin, sick of the world as much as himself, far beyond any real test of his own self-reliance. He had done this four years before, anyway, during his summer on Desolation Peak, where he had been forced to be self-reliant through so many painful, empty days that he realized that Emerson's words were just a different phrasing of the Buddhist ideal of withdrawal from the world, and that after six weeks alone on Desolation facing his own void he couldn't wait to return to the world. As he wrote in *Desolation Angels*, he was filled with longing for the "lunchcarts of the World to which I want to return at once . . . . I got a place to go and poems to write about hearts not just rocks."

Kerouac was not troubled by the inconsistencies in his feelings about nature, self-reliance and the Cross. (It was Emerson who also told him that a foolish consistency is the hobgoblin of little minds.) What gives *Big Sur* its power as a novel was not Kerouac's religious vision *per se*. The book was later advertised as the story of the "crack up of the King of the Beats," not as the experience of a deeply religious mystic. Its power stemmed from his control over the story of what happened to him at Bixby Canyon. Kerouac was too often content in his books to string together anecdotes of whatever happened to him, letting his own enthusiasms carry him along, scattering his observations and reactions to events rather than developing any deeper response to them. In *Big Sur* he built his impressions of his experience into a coherently moving whole of richly visualized details all centering in his response to Bixby Canyon.

After Ferlinghetti read the book he insisted that Kerouac's descriptions had nothing to do with his cabin (it was located, for one thing, miles from Big Sur) but that the book was the result of drinking too much sweet wine. Ferlinghetti, Welch and Ginsberg all stayed at the cabin at various times and wrote poems about it, all very different and none like Kerouac's. But Jack's vision of the Cross and his response to the canyon were true for himself, and in *Big Sur* the landscape was powerfully described as an extension of his own uniquely charged frame of mind.

Kerouac had first picked up the literary technique he used in *Big Sur*, what his friend the editor Don Allen recognized as "interior landscape," nearly ten years before, reading Melville's *Pierre*, and he had used it then in his poetic fantasy *Doctor Sax*. At Bixby Canyon, the descriptions of nature do more than suggest Kerouac's vision as an American Innocent. The images of what he sees in his retreat also suggest the idea that nature is the primary reflection of his own mind. At its furthest extension (Kerouac had taken this approach in the first part of *Desolation Angels*) it led to the belief that nature had no existence except in his own perception of it, but in *Big Sur* he was thinking more in terms of Emersonian individualism and man as the measure of all things.

When Kerouac wrote *Big Sur*, the idea that nature was the reflection of his own mind was most fully developed

337

in his description of the creek that ran through Bixby Canyon to the sea. Throughout the novel the creek appeared and reappeared, Jack's relationship with it charting the course of his moods and physical states. Unlike the Pacific Ocean at the end of the canyon, which overwhelmed him, the creek existed on a human scale, almost like an extension of the arteries and veins in his body, its sound at one point even reminding him of Cassady's voice. When Jack stumbled into Bixby Canyon for the first time in the dark, physically sick after the binge in San Francisco, he was afraid of the creek, imagining it, before he had seen it, as a raging river, hearing it crash mysteriously in the night as if it wanted to punish him for entering the canyon so ingloriously. The next morning, after he was refreshed by sleeping in the meadow, the creek was less frightening. When he got to know it better, it didn't only suggest punishment to him, it also offered rewards like a day spent digging out the bed to improve the flow of the water, during which he gained the innocence of an Indian.

Later in the novel Kerouac described the creek as being sensitive to his mood when he returned to the cabin after San Francisco for the weekend with the poets. It seemed to welcome him back. But the next day, horribly hung over, the once friendly creek seemed hostile. The absolute worst was when he returned for the last time to Bixby Canyon with Lew Welch, Lenore Kandel and Jackie and her son, because then he was in such bad shape that when he tasted the water in the creek, he was sure it was poisoned.

The creek at Bixby Canyon symbolized the daytime world of rational consciousness for Kerouac, while the Pacific Ocean, which he only went to at night to write his poetry, was the nighttime world of wild unconscious forces, both in nature and within himself. As he told Ginsberg in a letter in September 1960, he wrote the sea poem with eyes closed pretending he was blind Homer. The sea was mysterious and forbidding like the Mien Mo Mountain of his fantasy, but the mountain itself, blocking the eastern end of the canyon, shrouded in fog, the apparent source of the wind that sent the leaves scuttling along the beach to the sea, was such a terrifying elemental presence that it forced Kerouac to keep his face turned away for fear of seeing prehistoric giant gods of the Mien Mo nightmare. The sea was a less mysteriously active force in the landscape. Its tides came and went while the ocean itself waited for him each night as inexorably as his own death.

At night on Bixby Beach after he'd put out his lantern, Kerouac found himself alone down in the sinister enviroment. Even beside the creek, far from the swirling breakers on the beach, he was overwhelmed by what was waiting for him there. The leaves being blown to sea before the bursts of wind, skittering into the creek, filled him with horror.

In a larger sense, the interior landscape extended to Kerouac's entire experience, not just to his description of Bixby Canyon. Beginning with the opening paragraph of *Big Sur*, in which Jack wakes up abjectly hung over in the dismal skid-row hotel room, he was in a world turned as sour as his own taste for life. The new friends he met in San Francisco were only false parodies of the original hipsters who turned him on. The new "beat dandy" life style offended him, Kerouac's prophetic description of the middle-class kids several years later in beads and beards and ostentatiously worn workshirts and jeans, some of whom might have been youngsters in 1960 in the cars driven by parents who refused Kerouac a lift from Bixby Canyon to Monterey. He exchanged shoes with a boy who told him he'd rather wear Jack's old blue sneakers with the holes in the toes than his own expensive Las Vegas sport shoes, which Jack admired, but Kerouac felt later that the new shoes only brought him bad luck.

His interest in Buddhism, alive and expanding in 1955 with Gary Snyder, had diminished in 1960 to the point where he implied he was sick of the subject. There wasn't even any real joy being back with Neal Cassady, named "Cody" in *Big Sur* and *Book of Dreams*. Their rides in the jeep couldn't compare with the ecstatic "billowy trip in the world" described in *On The Road*. His suspicion of new friends even stretched to Lew Welch, who Jack saw carrying needles for amphetamine in a little box. Women offered him nothing at all, and hearing Jackie talk about the glories of marriage only depressed him further. Jackie and her son were light years from the innocent idyll Kerouac had with the Mexican girl and her child in *On The Road*. When he typed up *Big Sur* in Florida the next summer at Nin's house, his sister made him "leave out the sex part where the girl is blowing me while her son watches. Then she gets him to touch me. That was spooky. I didn't like that."

Just about the only thing left for Kerouac was his writing. In this he was still buoyed up by his own self-esteem and sense of genius. There were hints his self-confidence had its limits, not only when he cut short his nightly sessions on the dark beach transcribing the sounds of the sea, but also more prosaically in his refusal to see Henry Miller on this trip to the West Coast, even after he'd heard how much Miller had admired *The Dharma Bums* and *The Subterraneans*. Ferlinghetti talked him into phoning Miller to arrange a time to have dinner together in Carmel, but Kerouac yielded to his usual response to stress and got drunk in San Francisco instead, phoning Miller every hour to postpone the time he would actually arrive in Carmel until it was too late.

The closest Jack came to a literary talk in *Big Sur* was the afternoon he spent with Michael McClure at Bixby Canyon, when McClure told him he'd been greatly influenced by Jack's poetry in *Mexico City Blues*. Kerouac admired McClure's unpublished book *Dark Brown*, which he read at the cabin, and "The Sounds of The Pacific Ocean at Big Sur" has some elements in it of McClure's approach to language as pure sound phenomena, as well as Kerouac's own method of spontaneous composition in "Old Angel Midnight."

If Kerouac's breakdown at Bixby Canyon was a sign of how desperate his life had become in 1960, at least he was strong enough to rally afterwards and have the last word in his book about it. Forcing himself to transcribe the sounds of the sea was proof that he hadn't been put on earth for nothing. He finished the Pacific Ocean poem to his satisfaction, but he never completed the second half of his projected book *Sea*, the sounds of the Atlantic off a beach in Brittany, despite giving it a try five years later. As if anticipating failure in the larger design of the project, the Pacific Ocean poem concluded *Big Sur*.

Although in the end the Atlantic Ocean eluded him, Kerouac was equal to the waves crashing about him on the Pacific shore.

Back in San Francisco after leaving Bixby Canyon, Jack rested a few days at Ferlinghetti's house on Wisconsin Street before going back to New York. He promised Larry he'd try to switch to wines like burgundy that were healthier for him, since Ferlinghetti was convinced that what happened to Jack at the cabin was only the result of too much skid-row tokay. By the end of the first week of September, Jack felt relaxed enough to be a little more generous with himself. He bought fifty dollars worth of books from City Lights and turned in his return train ticket to spend an extra sixty-nine dollars for a TWA flight to Idlewild, and when he wrote Ferlinghetti from Northport thanking him for the holiday, he said he felt so recovered after their visit that on the plane he ate a dinner of steak and pastries with his champagne and had enough strength to write the stewardess a love note.

New York seemed bitter and hard after carefree San Francisco Jack told Allen Ginsberg in a letter at the end of the month, but he felt like a changed man. He was also doing push-ups and head-stands and losing weight to get back in shape. Best of all, the trip had given him a subject for a new book he was excited to begin. Over a year later the book, *Big Sur*, reached his agent, a much more dramatic, revealing account than his terse description to Ginsberg right after he got back.

Chapter Thirty-Three

The trip to Bixby Canyon was the last major trip for Kerouac. It marked the turning point into his later years. His breakdown at the cabin sealed him off from the affirmations of his earlier life and his earlier books, and

Big Sur was his last major work. He kept on, hoping that "something good will come out of all things yet," but the force was gone, and his life was shadowed and aimless.

Despite what he'd written Ginsberg about starting a new book after California, Jack couldn't really get into it in Northport. There was no burst of writing until July 1961, when he went to Mexico City for a month, after he and his mother had moved from Long Island back to Florida to be with Nin. Mémêre had been saying that his life in Northport was killing him, and his delirium tremens in Bixby Canyon seemed proof she was right.

Jack was in no shape to argue. The best he could do was wangle a month for himself in Mexico City, his first time back in four years. Garver had died, so Jack lived alone in a cheap, dusty street-floor apartment, once more driving himself with marijuana, seconals and benzedrine, trying to finish the book he'd started in Mexico City in 1956, *Desolation Angels*. He wrote 50,000 words by candlelight, continuing the story of his trip across country with Allen and Peter in 1956, their winter in New York and their meeting with Bill Burroughs in Tangier early in 1957.

It felt good being back in Mexico and to be writing again, but he couldn't shake the feeling that there was nothing but hard times ahead. Also without Garver there it was a little lonely. Desperately he made friends with a Mexican clerk who worked in a liquor store who supplied him with seconals and marijuana. One night he invited back to his room five hoodlums who'd promised to give him free marijuana. Once there they brazenly began stealing from his rucksack right in front of him taking his knife, flashlight, even his Noxema. Finally they wanted to walk off with his forty-dollar raincoat, but there Jack drew the line, saying his mother would sock him in the jaw if he came home without it. They went away laughing at him.

When he went back to Florida, he had another manuscript for Sterling Lord, "Passing Through," published in 1965 as Book Two of *Desolation Angels*. There hadn't been a new book in four years, since *The Dharma Bums,* but with the Mexican benzedrine he brought back with him, Jack started another novel in early October 1961, close on the heels of *Desolation Angels*. This was *Big Sur*, which he typed on a roll of shelf-paper in ten nights in his sister's house. After loosening up his memory with "Passing Though," Jack really settled into *Big Sur*.

But for the first time he was a little uncomfortable about what he was doing, using his friends' lives in book after book for his fictional narratives. Writing Carolyn Cassady to ask for news of what happened to "Billy" after he left San Francisco so he could finish the novel, Jack said he felt a little ashamed of himself for writing about people as they were and hoped Carolyn had noticed there was nothing evil or beat about his descriptions of Neal, again comparing their situations with Boswell and Johnson. Thinking back to his good times in California, Jack let some of his loneliness break through in the letter. He insisted to Carolyn that he was very happy living with his mother and the three cats, adding sheepishly, however, that as an adult male it was not always sufficient.

Jack made noble efforts to convince himself everything was all right in Florida. On New Year's Eve he and mémêre lifted martinis to toast each other. Mémêre hoped he'd be happy. His nephew Paul woke up at the midnight whistles, and Jack told himself that with his family he had reached the other shore, there was nothing to yearn after, not even happiness. Only a few months before in *Desolation Angels* he'd written a long, glowing tribute to mémêre's life-long devotion. Without saying a word, he raised a private toast to his mother and himself, wishing them both "the Sweet Dharma Truth instead of a Happy 'New Year.'"

Periodically, the restlessness mounted until Jack felt he had to break away. In September 1962, he told mémêre he wanted to buy land for a cabin in New England as a private retreat. She let him go off for a month, a thirty-day drunken binge that was his worst since the first flush of success after *On The Road*. While he was in Lowell on that trip he met an Iroquois Indian named Paul Bourgeois, supposedly a thirty-four-year-old cousin of Kerouac's, who drove with him back to Florida to meet Jack's family. They weren't impressed with him, saying he was a delinquent (Bourgeois wore a zootsuit and slicked his hair back with fish oil), and they were upset that Jack considered him such a good friend. Jack and the Indian got drunk every night in bars at Jack's expense, exchanging Iroquois war cries with the rebel yells of the Southerners, arm wrestling to test who was strongest. Bourgeois told Kerouac that in two years they could live together on his reservation near the Arctic Circle, and Jack believed him, dreaming of settling down on the reservation with an Iroquois wife. Jack was sure he was part Indian, maybe even as much as eighty per cent although his family laughed and said he was crazy. A year later, when Jack found out that Bourgeois' stories about his tribe and his reservation had been lies, it seemed mémère had been right again.

After *Big Sur* was published in September 1962, there was another flurry of interest in Kerouac, although this was nothing like the success with *On The Road*. But it was enough for him to persuade his mother they'd be better off living closer to New York. *Playboy* Magazine had been interested for a time in giving an entire issue to *Big Sur*, just as *Life* had done with Hemingway's *Old Man and The Sea*. The *Playboy* plan fell through but Sterling Lord sold *Visions of Gerard* to Farrar, Straus and Company (it was excerpted in *Show* Magazine), and an excerpt from *Desolation Angels* appeared in *Holiday* as "On The Road with Mémère."

Back in Northport, Jack found a new house he liked at 7 Judy Ann Court with a lot of trees in the backyard and a six-foot cedar fence that he hoped would guarantee him privacy. He hadn't felt his neighbors in Florida had understood him. He told Allen they thought he was peculiar but in fact he was really a patriot. One of the saddest memories was answering the doorbell in Florida rung by a group of kids with jackets lettered "Dharma Bums" who'd come to see the famous Jack Kerouac. When he came to the door, he later told a New York friend David Markson, the kids' faces dropped a foot and a half. Kerouac said it was one of the saddest experiences of his life. He was so disturbed he couldn't even talk to them.

But in Northport there were more congenial people around. His closest friend was probably the painter

Stanley Twardowicz, who persuaded him to be interviewed by the Northport Public Library, after Jack had refused several previous requests to make the tape-recorded interviews.

At Twardowicz's studio Kerouac met with the assistant director of the library and some friends, and the tapes (published later by *Athanor* Magazine) show him at his most relaxed and informal, comfortable with his friends, not showing off before the press, not too drunk or stoned for coherent conversation.

By the time of the Northport interview, 14 April, 1964, Kerouac felt that he was written out. Jokingly he told Twardowicz he thought he'd become a painter, he was tired of writing, it was just a hobby with him now. Twardowicz reminded him that he'd said the best things he'd written were done in six years, 1951-6. Jack agreed, "When nobody knew me, nobody cared." A friend, Joan Roberts, asked him why those years were so good. Jack replied, "I was a rough and tough customer . . . . Just hackin' across the country, back and forth, with a rucksack on my back, with ten cents in my pocket." He was still writing and he'd be writing up until the last few hours before his death, but he'd slowed down.

As Jack's life became more secluded, his old friends became more famous, but he didn't bother to keep up close ties with them. After the publication of *Naked Lunch*, Burroughs became a widely discussed avant-grade writer. Jack liked *Naked Lunch*, he'd suggested the title and helped type the manuscript in Tangier with Ginsberg; but he didn't like Burroughs' later cut-up method of literary composition, preferring Burroughs to be formal and precise. When Corso came over to collaborate on an article about beat writers for *Playboy*, they got drunk and quarreled instead, Jack telling Gregory that heroin was destroying him. The friendship with Gary Snyder, Philip Whalen and Lew Welch didn't survive the distance between them.

Besides, over the years Kerouac's old friends became increasingly vocal about their ideas of practical anarchism. Snyder, Ginsberg and Whalen were hoping for a spiritual breakthrough for the United States, an alternate plan to Lyndon Johnson's government, a demand for a new

system of social enlightenment that would become a rallying point for the disaffiliated. Jack would have none of it.
He had insisted he was apolitical in the old days,
but as his friends gained widespread recognition as radicals, he raged at them for not being, like him, American
patriots. He would have nothing to do with their politics,
sending Whalen a thousand-word putdown of the New
Left that Philip answered with a gentle reply.

When Allen told him he really ought to get more
politically involved, Kerouac answered that his laziness
was not at all like Ginsberg's great social energy. Allen had
ridden the crest of public appearances, interviews and
poetry readings after his return from Europe, whereas
Jack had just about been sunk by them. He hated making
an ass of himself on some stage at Brandeis. Allen had
a gift for using the press to his own advantage, not only
publicizing his poetry, but over the years spreading his
ideas about social reform. Jack only muddled things,
not even coherent enough to convince the interviewers of
what was to him the first, most basic truth, that he was
being absolutely serious when he said that he considered
himself a storyteller in the great French narrative tradition,
not a spokesman for the masses.

Living with his mother, increasing the distance between
himself and his old friends with his political conservatism,
Jack grew more cut off and lonely, and whenever life at
home became too intolerably narrow, he broke away for
a few drunken days in New York.

Occasionally he dropped by the West 11th Street apartment of his old friend Jerry Newman—it was conveniently
near the White Horse Tavern—and he grew friendly
with Newman's neighbor David Markson, also a writer.
Markson remembers Kerouac as always drunk, always
moody and depressed. "I didn't know where Jack was
coming from, or who he was escaping from." Once Jack
borrowed a T-shirt, disappeared and came back six days
later, the buttons missing from his outer shirt. Markson
stared at him, asking, "You son of a bitch, is that the
same T-shirt you put on six days ago?" It was absolutely
black and filthy. Jack said, sheepishly, "Well, I had a
shower." He'd been bouncing around the Village in the
apartment of some people he called his "disciples."

346

Kerouac told Markson, "They think they're doing what I'd want them to do. They're fucking in front of me, but all I can see is thighs." Often Jack dropped in to see his friend Hugo Weber, the Swiss painter, who had a studio on Greenwich Street. Weber remembers Kerouac ringing his doorbell, stumbling up the stairs with bottles in his arms, settling into the studio to watch him paint. Jack would suddenly grab the brushes, insisting he was a painter too, and compose wildly religious canvases of Madonnas and the Pope.

Weber did his portrait in oils and Kerouac made up a long poem to go with a painting Weber had done of Ulysses S. Grant after both he and Hugo agreed it had somehow gotten out of hand and turned into a portrait of Edgar Allen Poe. Jack often talked wistfully about going to Europe with Hugo, who periodically returned to Switzerland, but the trip didn't come off until June 1965, when Kerouac flew alone to Paris. He and mémère were once again living in Florida. In July 1964, Jack complained to a *Newsday* interviewer that his quiet little side street, Judy Ann Court, had become "too noisy," and mémère again moved him south to be closer to Nin. After nearly a year in Florida, Jack insisted on a little trip for himself. He told his mother he was going to write a book about his adventures in France for Grove Press, and he got away from Florida for ten days to do it.

Jack's first night in Paris he spent $120 on a Montparnasse whore. It embarrassed him to spend so much money, as he described it, trying "to prove something, comma, about my sex," but he was just plain lonely. By his second night in Paris, coming back to the hotel drunk again, this time bleeding (he'd cut his finger with his Swiss Army knife, afraid he was being followed by French thieves), he was so disorderly and disreputable that the manageress asked him when he was going to check out.

Kerouac settled down to business the next day in Paris. He was there to check the history of the de Kerouack family in the Bibliothèque Nationale, but at the library he learned the Nazis burned all this information in 1944 (another librarian later told him this wasn't true, but Jack didn't have time to follow it up). He was the first Lebris de

Kerouack to return to France from the New World in 210 years, but in Paris he spent most of his days being rebuffed by librarians and observing other American tourists being clipped for food and drinks by cynical Frenchmen who made him feel with his French-Canadian accent that he was talking funny French. The last straw came when Jack tried to see his editor at the French publishers, Gallimard. The secretary, haughty and disdainful, wouldn't tell anyone he was in the office or inform Jack that his editor happened to be in New York at the time. Ferlinghetti was in Paris then too, and he later said the people at Gallimard were worried about Kerouac being dangerously inebriated in their office. In disgust, Jack bought an airplane ticket to Brest. He got to the airport on time the next morning only to miss the plane, not hearing the announcement in the men's room.

This comedy of errors continued across France as far as Brittany. He got off the train at Brest late at night, after hours of traveling, and he headed right for the bar to make up for the lost time with cognac and beer. At three A.M., with the help of the police, he found a hotel room, but his luggage was locked up in the airport office. It was a long, hard night for Jack. His estimate of himself was never tougher, almost as if in his pride with his Breton ancestry he found it unbearable to face the reality of his life as he confronted his origins on French soil.

Originally Jack's plan in Brittany was to stay at an inn on the sea in Finisterre and go out at midnight with his raincoat to listen to the ocean and write the second part of the "Sea" poem he'd begun by the Pacific at Bixby Canyon, this time the sounds of the Atlantic off the coast of Brittany. All his gear for the project—pencil and notebook and plastic bag to stick his hand into in case it rained—were locked in his suitcase in the airport office in Brest. He forgot about the project anyway as soon as he arrived. It just seemed much too complicated. The next day he settled for following up a lead about his family name by visiting a man named Ulysse Lebris, who showed Jack his genealogical chart. They drank cognac together and Lebris' daughter, who'd read some of Jack's books in French translations, asked him for an autograph. After three cognacs and an elaborate exchange of compliments, they decided they were all cousins. It was the high point of Kerouac's trip, more like a homecoming than he'd ever imagined.

Returning to Paris and his plane to Florida, Jack remembered to bring mémêre a souvenir ceramic butter-tub from the restaurant of his hotel in Brest. The rest of the trip went by him in a blur, missing one train, sitting up all night on another, until he reached Paris, where he immediately caught a cab for the airport, determined to be on the first plane out. Back in Florida regrouping his memories of the trip (he drank cognac while writing *Satori in Paris* to bring back the flavor of his French experiences), he thought the cab driver who raced him to Orly Airport had given him a satori, a sudden illumination, as Jack defined it in the book. Describing the cabbie, Jack didn't specify what the illumination was, and then he went on to say he thought that the illumination could have come from many different sources during his ten days in France, a taxi driver, a foggy street, a beautiful woman.

Actually just about every encounter with people in France became, in Kerouac's loneliness, a satori. Snyder had told him that the word also meant "seeing your true nature," and perhaps the experience closest to Jack's true nature occurred on the train from Paris to Brest. He shared a first-class compartment with a Catholic priest who was suffering from a miserable cold and a commercial traveler who drank bottle after bottle of wine with Jack in the aisles. Somehow to Kerouac these two men reflected his true nature, the priest and the traveler, and he felt moved enough by the encounter to make a speech about Christ to them. The priest gave him a brief understanding glance when Jack had finished. Later he wondered which one, the priest or the drunken commercial traveler, had been his satori. He could never decide.

Brittany was the last time Kerouac broke out from the dreary pattern into which his life was narrowing so relentlessly. Things were changing at home too. On 19 September, 1964, his sister Nin died of a coronary occlusion. Jack's mother, having now lost two of her children, became very upset. Jack tried to cheer her up by buying her a house in Hyannis, because she'd once told him she always dreamed of living on Cape Cod. There was no real reason to move there, but by the end of March 1966, they packed and shipped everything up north once more to start all over again.

Chapter Thirty-Four

By 1966 there were the first faint stirrings of interest in Kerouac as a serious writer. His books weren't selling well. *Visions of Gerard* and *Desolation Angels* were remaindered in bookstores all over New York. But university libraries were beginning to collect letters and manuscripts of Beat writers and academic critics were including chapters on Kerouac, Ginsberg and Burroughs in their studies of contemporary American literature. The Phoenix Bookshop in New York had begun to issue a series of bibliographies of underground poets, starting with Corso, McClure and Charles Olson, and I offered to compile one on Kerouac.

I wrote mémêre Kerouac that I was working on Jack's bibliography and asked for their help. Jack wrote back that we could arrange a meeting if I were a scholar and a gentlewoman and promised to keep the directions to his house strictly secret. Unwelcome beatniks popping up at midnight looked like ghosts at his mother's door.

He and mémêre were living in Hyannis when I drove there in August 1966, their house a one-storey Cape Cod tract house within walking distance of a blacktop shopping center close to town. The neighborhood surprised me. I'd never imagined that the wild young man in the checkered shirt in the dustwrapper photographs would be living in such quiet, conventional surroundings, lawns neatly clipped, tricycles in the driveways, wash on clotheslines flapping in the backyards.

There was an even bigger surprise when Kerouac opened

the door. Nothing any interviewer had ever described prepared me for the sad figure in the doorway. He was always stocky, about five foot eight, but his muscular frame was soft under the rumpled T-shirt, his face puffy and petulant. He was only forty-four years old, but if anything he looked like the battered, lost father of the young Jack in all the dustwrapper photographs. It was one o'clock, he was just getting up, just beginning to think about drinking his breakfast. Mémère came out of the kitchen in a faded wash dress and apron to shake my hand. She hadn't changed from Aronowitz's description of her in Northport seven years before, still the apparently ageless, cheerful housewife.

She was impressed that I was the Doctor Charters who wanted to work on her son's bibliography. After taking a close look at me, she and Jack began talking rapidly in French-Canadian. They led me through the living room and I caught a little of what they were saying to each other. They were wondering if I was Jewish. Jack broke off and asked me in English, "Charters isn't your real name. What was it before you were married?" I told him Danberg, and that they were right, I was Jewish. He frowned. "Did you understand what we were talking about?" I told him I had, a little. "Okay, we'll talk in English then."

Mémère excused herself to the kitchen, starting to make a plate of baloney and cheese sandwiches, with pickles and potato chips. This Hyannis house was smaller than the Northport houses, and we settled in Jack's bedroom, which had a desk under the window facing the high wooden backyard fence. By the time mémère brought in the sandwiches, Jack had begun to show me his books. He was drinking Johnny Walker Red Label out of a nearly full bottle, and he kept filling his glass as we worked, finishing the bottle before dinnertime, then opening another. I hadn't expected the care he'd taken keeping his books and manuscripts together, thinking that with all the moving about he'd done in his life there'd be chaos, but Jack had always kept his papers, letters and books carefully together, the papers and notebooks in his bureau drawers, the letters filed neatly in a metal cabinet, the books on a shelf in his mother's room. The collection of his first editions had been in the living room first, then in his own bedroom, but they'd been moved out when guests in the house began slipping them into pockets without asking first.

We worked steadily for more than five hours, and while I filled out my note cards for the bibliography, describing the specially bound presentation copies, trying to be accurate with the spelling of the foreign editions—Kerouac had over fifty of them—I asked him questions about the books: When had he written them? Where? How? He was completely open, answering every question seriously and at considerable length, the scotch having no apparent affect on his memory.

As the afternoon light began to fade, he even consented to a dozen photographs, this more reluctantly since he told me he thought he was looking terrible and he hated anyone to photograph him anymore. Hearing us move around in the bedroom while Jack changed to a chair by the window with better light, mémère came in to see what we were doing. She agreed to pose for a picture with him in the living room. They settled themselves without any suggestion from me with Jack's mother in a rocking chair holding the cat, Jack kneeling at her right side. Both faces were sad and downcast, deeply furrowed, the religious medal pinned to mémère's apron glimmering faintly in the dim room filled with colonial chintz and maple furniture. The setting seemed to have no relation to their expressions, or their sad pose.

Mémère went back to the kitchen to fix a chicken pie for dinner. Jack wanted to go for a ride in my car, and she thought of an errand for him at the liquor store. Leaving the house, he palmed a beer into the car so skillfully I never noticed it until we had backed out of the driveway and were headed down the street. We went to the liquor store, then drove to a beach to give my setter pup a run. She'd been in the backyard while we'd been working, a little worried by the cat, but mémère had told me she'd keep an eye on the animals while we worked on the books. At the beach Jack and I walked a little, then sat down while he talked about his patriotism, feeling the alcohol now and not very clear, insisting he was still

352

a Marine and would go off to Vietnam in a moment if they asked him.

We stopped in his favorite Hyannis bar before we went home, where he introduced me to the bartender as the woman who'd come a long way to list all his books for a scholarly bibliography. The bartender, winking at me, told Jack he didn't think he'd written that many books. "Yeah, there's been quite a number," Jack told him. "And how much money do you make from them?" the bartender asked. "About as much as you do," Jack said, moving from the bar to a chair by the piano, "maybe $5,000 a year."

He began a long, rambling story about how he'd gotten into a fight coming home late from the bar, nearly getting arrested, then switched to a fragmented, incoherent anecdote about getting lost in the tall weeds in Florida on a back path home from another bar. The piano made him think of music, which somehow triggered off a memory of living in Michigan with his first wife Edie Parker, and so it went on, until it was past dinnertime and he remembered his mother was waiting for him to come back from the liquor store.

At home we ate chicken pie and drank champagne, Jack sticking to scotch and beer, eating a couple of potato chips and pushing his plate away before his mother could fill it. Mémêre said that champagne was the only thing she could drink anymore, her stomach not what it used to be. Jack insisted she was still young and didn't have to worry about anything but taking care of the house for him.

He wanted to show me the photograph of her when she was a girl, working in the mills. "That's the picture of the girl I want to marry some day," he said to me, dead serious, and mémêre told him to stop being silly. The three of us ate chocolate ice cream and toasted salted almonds for dessert, the nuts a present from a fan in the South, who sent him a big box every Christmas knowing they were Jack's favorite on chocolate ice cream.

It was late after we'd finished, so I thanked mémêre after dinner and said I had to leave to get some sleep at my hotel. Kerouac and I had already agreed I'd come back to finish going through his library the next day.

Suddenly Jack became petulant, refusing to hear I wanted to leave. He scowled at me, "I won't let you back in here tomorrow if you don't spend the night with me." There was no real menace in the threat, his loneliness unmistakable as he desperately tried different ways to get me to stay.

"Okay, you don't have to stay," he finally told me. "I can masturbate. It's just as good."

Next he wanted to phone all his friends in Hyannis to come over to meet me and have a party. Mémère hovered about shaking her head, anxious to get me out of the house.

Jack had been walking out of the room every few minutes to go to the toilet, and the next time he was away I asked her the best way to leave. Instead of telling me, she took my arm and brought me into the living room to show me something. She stopped by the framed drawing of Gerard over the television set in the corner but instead of pointing to this, she turned to the opposite wall, near the kitchen door. Hidden by a calendar there was a gouge in the plaster wall above the chair where she watched television. "He got mad at me last week and threw a knife. You go away like a good girl while he's in there, don't bother to say goodnight."

Jack came back into the room as she dropped the calendar. "What are you showing her that thing for?" he shouted. Her alert bright eyes never left mine. "There's nothing wrong in showing it. It really happened." They began to argue and I grabbed my notes, said goodbye again and made for the front door as Jack disappeared once more into the toilet. Before I got away Jack followed me outside yelling to come back and listen to the Mozart Requiem on his hi-fi. The streets were dark and very quiet. I had the feeling that the neighbors had been through it all many times before.

The next day while I waited for the morning to pass so I could go back to the house, I thought about why meeting Kerouac had turned out so differently from what I expected. The evidence of *Big Sur* and *Satori in Paris* hadn't really changed the image I'd formed of Kerouac from the earlier books. He had still represented the life style of *On The Road* and *Lonesome Traveler* to me, and for the first time I had an insight into his struggle with interviewers, since the image he cast in his books was so different from the reality of the man himself.

Spending the previous day with him I'd learned he *was* the boasts and contradictions of the books, the tone completely candid, the references always personal, ready to say anything in a sudden wild rush of enthusiasm; but he *wasn't* the life style. Through the books he had become a legend in his lifetime, by personifying a fantasy of youth and freedom, racing after the promise and vision of America, not only to me but for a generation of readers whose lives he had touched.

As Ginsberg was to say to me later, Kerouac's picture of himself in his books was always true to his life style at the time, all the changes mirrored from *On The Road* to *Satori in Paris*. I hadn't wanted to accept the changes, caught by his vision of life. There was always a certain amount of glorification in the novels, of course, but in Ginsberg's eyes that was poetry. I realized after meeting Kerouac that the reality of the man was tragic, but the mark of his genius had been to create novels out of the tragedy of his own life. As a literary artist he transformed his own existence full of suffering and enlarged it in his fiction to be greater than life. This constituted the force of his genius, of his originality.

Back at the house there was wash flapping on the clothesline when I parked the car again. I learned later that mémêre had washed and hung out the clothes after midnight while Jack drank with friends he'd phoned when I'd left him. When we started work that afternoon he was quiet and hung over, apparently not remembering anything of the wild shouting scene outside the house before I drove off. His mother didn't refer to it either. The second day we worked a little on the magazines he'd collected with Kerouac contributions, then turned for a longer time to Jack's manuscripts, journals and correspondence, which I was also interested to see. He proudly dug out whatever I asked for, with one exception, the original teletype roll manuscript of *On The Road*. "It's in the safe at my agent's." We parted friends that evening.

Later I learned from Charlie Sampas in Lowell that

I'd been lucky to find Kerouac in such a cooperative mood, because "when he's drinking like that he's usually impossible." We had a friendly correspondence throughout the months I finished compiling the bibliography, Jack sending me new listings as he discovered them, but later on, after the bibliography was published, he became a little less friendly. The trouble came when he couldn't find the cover photograph he wanted me to use, and I used instead one I'd taken in his bedroom in Hyannis. When he saw it he was very angry, accusing me of trying to attack his books by showing him looking old and puffy. "Is there a conspiracy against Kerouac?" he asked. He liked the bibliography itself, taking the time to revise it when I asked him to, but the letters stopped for a while. Later he finally found the photograph he liked, one showing him smiling at his cat, and he sent it on with a friendly note in case I could use it sometime.

Chapter Thirty-Five

In the fall of 1966, life darkened even more for Kerouac. Mémère suffered a stroke that left her an invalid, paralyzed and unable to leave her bed. In November 1966, *Time* Magazine reported that Jack had taken his third wife, Stella Sampas, a sister of his old Lowell friend Charlie Sampas. She was older than Jack, a solid and reliable woman who'd known him since childhood when he went to school with her brothers, and she'd never married, always hoping he'd come back to Lowell and propose to her. Finally Jack did, when he needed a nurse for his mother. Marrying into the Sampas family was also the culmination of a dream for Kerouac. He had used the Sampas family as his model for the idealized family he'd described in his first published novel, *The Town and the City*.

After his marriage, Kerouac moved from Hyannis to Lowell, where he bought a house on Sanders Avenue, across the river from Pawtucketville in the southwest part of town. Mémère was taken for treatments to Boston, and at home Stella patiently nursed her back to partial recovery.

Wearily Kerouac started another novel, hoping to pay some of the medical bills. He picked up a manuscript he'd begun a few years back in Florida called *Vanity of Duluoz*, retelling the story of his years finishing high school and going to New York, a book about football, and war. He was forty-five years old, "in a continual rage," determined to clear up the record of his "suffering in the working world." The book was dedicated to Stella, her Greek name Stavroula, which also meant "From the Cross."

Beginning the book, Jack was reminded of his previous marriage fifteen years before, when he'd started *On The Road* again to tell his new wife about his adventures with Cassady. *Vanity of Duluoz* began, "All right, wifey, maybe I'm a big pain in the you-know-what but after I've given you a recitation of the troubles I had to go through to make good in America between 1935 and more or less now, 1967, and although I also know everybody in the world's had his own troubles, you'll understand that my particular form of anguish came from being too sensitive to all the lunkheads I had to deal with . . . ."

Later Kerouac felt *Vanity of Duluoz* wasn't one of his best works, telling *Paris Review* interviewers:

. . . and finally I decided in my tired middle age to slow down and did *Vanity of Duluoz* in a more moderate style so that, having been so esoteric all these years, some earlier readers would come back and see what ten years had done to my life and thinking . . . which is after all the only thing I've got to offer, the true story of what I saw and how I saw it.

But it was the last book he finished in his Legend of Duluoz. Jack had dreamed of writing the legend of his own life since 1951, and he never said how close he thought he had come. In 1963, still hopeful about his plans for the legend, he envisioned it in its final scope as a giant epic in the tradition of Balzac and Proust.

Before his death, Kerouac worked on what was to be his longest novel, a surrealist study of the last decade of his life, but it was left unfinished. What was published can be read in order as the Legend he intended, even if most readers only encounter the books as separate novels, oblivious of the underlying loose chronology. The Legend of Duluoz begins with *Visions of Gerard*, his earliest years, continues into boyhood with *Doctor Sax* and adolescence with *Maggie Cassidy*, then goes on with *Vanity of Duluoz* into his college years and earliest encounters with Burroughs and Ginsberg. *On The Road* picks up when he met Cassady, mid-way ito the writing of *The Town and the City*. *Visions of Cody* describes the cross-country trips and conversations with Cassady after Jack had discovered spontaneous prose. *Lonesome Traveler* and *The Subterraneans* describe his years working, traveling, and living in New York, filled with the frustration of being unable to sell any manuscripts after his first book. *Tristessa* describes the month in Mexico City before *The Dharma Bums*, while *Desolation Angels* continues after Berkeley to his summer as a fire-watcher and the publication over a year later of *On The Road*. *Big Sur* describes his alcoholic breakdown after the assault of fame and *Satori in Paris* concludes with the loneliness of his final trip to Brittany.

At bottom Kerouac resisted ever completing his Legend. He hadn't the emotional distance in his last years to visualize his life as the tragedy it had become, and his prose had changed, losing its energy and muscle, so that it didn't seem possible he could weld the separate books of his Duluoz chronology into a coherent whole, even if he tried.

His main boast as a writer, what he thought would make him legendary, was that he'd originated a new writing style, spontaneous prose, that he hoped would revolutionize American literature as much as Joyce had influenced English prose. Spontaneous prose, of course, was unrevisable at least in theory, so it meant Kerouac wouldn't go back to change his manuscripts (although he often did before typing them for publication).

By the end of his life, he was beginning to admit he'd been a slave to sounds in the spontaneous prose of "Old

Angel Midnight," where he'd tipped the delicate balance between bombast and babble, but he couldn't come up with any literary technique to help him fit all the volumes of the Duluoz Legend into one continuous tale. All he could think of was to change the names in the various books back to their original forms, hoping that this single stroke would give sufficient unity to the disparate books, magically making them fit more smoothly into their larger context as the Duluoz (Kerouac the Louse) Legend. (He was "Jackie Duluoz" in *The Vanity of Duluoz*, the closest he'd come to giving himself his real name.) Then, when the names had been changed, he wanted the books reissued in a uniform edition to make the larger design unmistakable.

Across the whole range of the Legend, the strongest books centered around characters who were his friends and people other than Kerouac himself. In future years he could be remembered less for spontaneous prose than for his picture of "beat life," especially the literary scene of the group of underground writers in the 1950s, the writers who helped form America's counterculture of social protest and political change. It first emerged as the "San Francisco Renaissance" in 1956 and 1957, and if the proper names were inserted into *The Dharma Bums* and *Desolation Angels*—Kerouac, Ginsberg, Cassady, Snyder, Whalen, McClure, Rexroth, Lamantia, and, later in *Big Sur*, Lew Welch and Lenore Kandel—Jack's narrative could be taken as a brilliant chronicle of the scene. As literary history, the relationships and mutual influence of Kerouac, Ginsberg, Burroughs and Snyder spread into several books: *The Town and the City, On The Road, Vanity of Duluoz, The Subterraneans, The Dharma Bums, Desolation Angels*.

Kerouac was most explicit about Burroughs' influence on him, especially in the years before he began *The Town and the City*. Ginsberg appeared in less depth in the books, mostly as a character Jack couldn't quite trust. In *The Subterraneans* Jack wrote that he could never understand what Allen was saying. Ginsberg later said that he used to be "abashed and bugged" that Jack had portrayed him so superficially, that Jack never transformed him, as he had done Burroughs, Cassady or Snyder into "a major Dostoyevsky romantic character." Allen felt Jack's description of him was a cartoon: "Jack devotes his vision to characters he's baffled by. Burroughs, Cassady, Lucien Carr, Herbert Huncke felt the full force of his sympathy."

Kerouac had proof of Ginsberg's deep feeling for him in the dedication to *Howl,* and Allen was no doubt his most sympathetic friend and strongest literary ally in the last years, but Jack was suspicious of Allen's "omniscient image mania," his politics and his Jewishness, calling him a wolf in sheep's clothing. Usually Kerouac was brusque on the subject. Once when a *Nugget* reporter asked why Ginsberg had never been a prototype for a central figure in the books, Jack shrugged off the question, "Oh, because he's not an interesting character, to me. He doesn't do anything but talk."

Read as historian, Kerouac was a very accurate reporter. His memory and his detailed journal notes kept the record straight. He usually omitted facts rather than invent them. He shaped every page he wrote by his selection of details and emphasis, of course, but he was faithful to his idea of the spirit of what happened, even if some of the minor details were shuffled around a little for libel purposes. The only book which departed significantly from what actually happened was *The Subterraneans,* where Jack placed the action in San Francisco instead of New York. He justified the change by saying he was afraid of a lawsuit, but he was also aware of the widespread interest in San Francisco after the publicity given the scene by journalists writing up the "San Francisco Renaissance," describing the bohemian community in North Beach.

Mostly he inserted only minor changes, like giving Ginsberg a beard in *Desolation Angels,* or made omissions. At the start of *The Dharma Bums,* for example, when he was traveling to Ginsberg's Berkeley cottage, he included the anecdote about his freight train encounter going from Los Angeles to Santa Barbara with the bum who read the prayer from St. Theresa every day, but he only mentioned in passing the story of his being picked up by a blonde in a strapless bathing suit who drove him the final stage of the trip from Santa Barbara to San

Francisco. The ride in the car with the blonde high on Jack's Mexican benzedrine was the basis for a story he later sold to *Playboy*, "Good Blonde." Both encounters happened the same day, but the one with the freight train bum added to the religious tone of *The Dharma Bums*, while the story about the wild ride with the blonde didn't enter into what he later found with Snyder in the book.

Contrary to what Kerouac thought, it was his attitude toward his experience, rather than his spontaneous prose experiments, that made him legendary in his own time. In his books he composed the entire legend of the Beat life before the first installment of it was published in *On The Road*, and his readers came away with the indelible impression that he personified the life style he described. The fact that he violently rejected it, alternately loved and hated his title of "King of the Beats," mirrored his own personal confusion and marked the tragedy of his life, but it didn't detract from the books for his young readers.

As Daniel Talbot perceptively wrote in The New York *Times*, Kerouac "rekindled the Super-Romantic tradition at a time when it needed rekindling . . . . At times he sounds embarrassing, even sloppy. In the end he is more truthful, entertaining and honest than most writers on the American scene." It's an ironic comment on the Kerouac legend that with the sweeping changes in the American consciousness since the 1950s, ushered in partly by Kerouac's books, his particular brand of romanticism was impossible to duplicate by the generation of writers who followed him. His appeal was simplicity itself: "God, man, I rode around this country free as a bee." It was an optimism for a generation who patterned their behavior on what they read in the pages of *On The Road, The Dharma Bums, The Subterraneans*, readers who recognized instinctively that Kerouac was on their side, who loved it when he ended *On The Road* by saying that God was Pooh Bear.

Over and over in every book Kerouac insisted on his innocence. He gave a vision of freedom and spontaneity that entered directly into his young readers' fantasies because it assumed and enforced their idealism too. When he romanticized his trips with Cassady and Snyder, he was writing with his mother looking over his shoulder, minimizing his participation in the action, emphasizing his gullibility, never describing anything he knew she wouldn't forgive.

Kerouac often said his prose method stemmed from his background as a Catholic, confessing his sins to the priest as a boy every week, clearing himself of guilt by a full account of what he had done. He'd stopped going to confession by the time he'd become a writer, but he never stopped thinking like a penitent. Only it was his mother, instead of the priest, who had charge of him.

Chapter Thirty-Six

Kerouac had often dreamed of returning to Lowell, but actually moving there with Stella and his invalid mother didn't bring him much happiness. Even if he'd been able to find the thatched hut in Lowell his friend Al Sublette had jokingly insisted he was looking for all his life, Kerouac wouldn't have been able to live in it. He wasn't Thoreau. People still came looking for the author of *On The Road*, wanting to talk with him, to have him sign books, to ask him out for a drink. He kept refusing interviews, cutting reporters off in mid-question during long distance phone calls, being cagey about giving his address.

There was no special welcome in the house for his old friends either. Ginsberg had been shut out at Hyannis, and he was allowed only one visit in Lowell when he came by with the *New Yorker* reporter Jane Kramer. The only Kerouac in the telephone directory was Hervé Kerouac, a cousin, a workingman who brusquely told everybody who asked for Jack to leave him alone.

Jack's favorite hang-out in Lowell was Nicky's Bar on Gorham Street, owned by Stella's brother Nick Sampas.

Jack was welcome there to sit and drink cheap wine as long as he wanted. The Sampas clan was proud of Jack's fame as a writer and thought he was a good husband to Stella. He'd talk to reporters, but he didn't say much, always careful to tell them he was working on another book, always a little bored by the same questions about the Beats and the Hippies.

Bruce Cook interviewed him at Nicky's Bar for *The Beat Generation*, and watching him drink what looked like port wine, Cook thought he was "beginning to show his drinking." As far as Kerouac was concerned, the whole Beat scene was dead. He gave a good long interview about his writing to the *Paris Review* when Aram Saroyan, Ted Berrigan and Duncan McNaughton came around to the house in Lowell, touched by the memory that Saroyan's father had been an early influence back in the old Columbia days, when Jack was first thinking of becoming a serious writer.

One of the friends from the old days Jack still kept in touch with was Carolyn Cassady. He phoned her several times a year, usually in the middle of the night, and always started off by saying, "Come get a glass of wine and sit down and talk to Jack." He loved reminiscing about their old times in San Francisco and San Jose, talking about their favorite Chinese restaurant on Jackson Street, remembering the parties where they danced and drank wine and ate pizza in front of the fireplace.

The first week of February 1968, Carolyn called to tell Jack that Neal had died by the railroad tracks in Mexico after mixing alcohol and sleeping pills on 4 February, just four days before his forty-second birthday. To keep off amphetamine, Neal had been taking "downers," but he'd mixed the pills with too much alcohol drinking with friends at a Mexican wedding party. Jack hadn't been close to Neal in years, not really comfortable with him in Bixby Canyon, and totally unsympathetic when Neal later became the legendary driver behind the wheel of Ken Kesey's psychedelic acid bus, a wild figure with the Merry Pranksters. Neal had stopped writing Jack after San Quentin, disgusted with Kerouac for drinking so much. On his side, Jack said Ken Kesey and LSD had

ruined Cassady, and the disagreements were never resolved.

Kerouac was never involved with Kesey and tried LSD
only once. This was with Timothy Leary at Harvard in
January 1961. It wasn't a good session for him. Fighting
off constant paranoia, he regressed back to his Navy
discharge, still trying to understand and justify his failure
to take Navy discipline. After this experience with LSD,
Kerouac was sure it had been introduced into America
by the Russians as part of a plot to weaken the country.

The last time he'd seen Neal had been at a party in
New York with Kesey's Merry Pranksters in 1964, when
Ginsberg came up and wrapped an American flag around
Jack. Taking it off, Jack tenderly folded it and put it on
the back of a sofa. But Cassady's death was unthinkable.
Neal had been closer to Jack than anyone, and after they'd
drifted apart no one had taken his place. Kerouac went
on a drunk in Lowell and was arrested, jailed overnight
before his family bailed him out. Life was closing in on
him again, and it seemed best to move on.

At the end of 1968, he paid a friend to drive him,
mémêre and Stella from Lowell to St. Petersburg, where
he hoped the sun and warmth would help mémêre's con-
valescence. During the hundreds of miles to Florida, Jack
sat in the front seat beside the driver, drinking all the
way, while Stella stayed beside mémêre on a mattress in
the back, reminiscent of when Neal drove him from
San Francisco to the Mexican border in 1952 with Carolyn
and the babies on a mattress in the back. This time there
was no anticipation of adventure, no borders to cross.
Jack knew only too well what he faced in Florida.

After the closeness of old Lowell friends and the large
Sampas family, the loneliness and isolation in St. Petersburg were very hard to bear. Sadly enough, even the
phone calls to Carolyn Cassady stopped. Jack called her
from St. Petersburg around Easter 1969, at four in the
morning, after Carolyn had come in late from a party
and was drifting off to sleep. Groggily she picked up the
phone to hear Kerouac's familiar drunken voice, "Hello,
Carolyn, it's old Jack. Pour yourself a glass of wine, pull
up a chair and let's talk a while." She was in no mood
to talk to him and remembers she pretended the long

distance telephone connection was so bad she couldn't understand him. Jack had the operator dial the California number several times, but each time Carolyn said she couldn't hear him. He finally gave up, and it was the last time he ever called her.

Kerouac began to write again, trying to work on the book about the last decade of his life, then dusting off an old manuscript he titled *Pic* (published posthumously). There was very little money from royalties. Trying to support the household, he sold some of his correspondence to university libraries, but he was cautious about the sales, driving hard bargains, saying he might be crazy but he wasn't a fool.

For a large advance, $3,000, he even wrote a syndicated news article defining his position in the Beat/Hippie movement one last time. Almost as if he had a premonition that the end was near, he titled it "After Me, the Deluge," retitled "I'm a Bippie in the Middle" by the press. It was a serious article, one of the most mature he ever wrote, trying to be clear about where he stood politically. His friends had known for years that he was a conservative follower of William Buckley. As Jack said, "I'm pro-American and the radical political involvements seem to tend elsewhere . . . . The country gave my Canadian family a good break, more or less, and we see no reason to demean said country." But some of his old friends were dismayed that he disowned the American counter-culture in one sweeping roll-call. He couldn't understand how Jerry Rubin, Mitchell Goodman and Abbie Hoffman had evolved from his work.

Kerouac couldn't join forces with the anarchist radicals or the Liberal Left, and he wouldn't attend the conservatives' fund-raising dinners or contribute beyond his taxes to the bureaucracy of the paper-shufflers, so he felt himself caught in the middle. There was only one solution, to drop out in the great American tradition of Thoreau, Mark Twain and Daniel Boone.

Death was on his mind, his mother paralyzed in a back room, whispering his name to come sit beside her so she could ask him why God had punished her so mercilessly. Stella moved silently around the house keeping everything going, her voice low and steady, always patient with

Jack's demands, changing the speed on the record player when he pushed Handel's *Messiah* up to 78 rpm so that it sounded silly. In important matters he tried to be responsible, worrying about the money coming in, settling his will with the lawyers, putting the deed to his house in his mother's name so he'd know he'd kept his promise to his father to take care of mémère, even after his death. The house was usually dim, the TV on in the living room, its images flickering without sound, music from the hi-fi coming from speakers in the next room. Jack sipped continuously at half-quart cans of Falstaff, alternating beer with the whisky he kept in a little medicine vial with a white plastic top, snapping off the top to drink, snapping it back on when he pulled at the beer.

The end came on Tuesday, 21 October, 1969. Kerouac was suffering from a hernia and hadn't felt well for weeks. A local writer, Robert Boles, who dropped by the house occasionally to keep him company, remembers that Jack had begun to sit at his typewriter in the darkened bedroom, typing all night for the pleasure of it. Early one morning about fifteen minutes after making an entry in his journal, he disappeared into the bathroom and was gone a long time. Stella listened and heard him vomiting. She'd heard it often before, but this time it sounded "different." Hurriedly she called an ambulance and Jack was rushed to the hospital. There was an emergency operation for massive abdominal hemorrhaging, but Jack didn't survive it. Leaving mémère in St. Petersburg, Stella arranged for the body to be moved to Lowell for the funeral.

It was a traditional Catholic funeral with the open casket on display the night before in the Archambault Funeral Home on Pawtucket Street, the funeral at St. Jean Baptiste Roman Catholic Church the next morning, Friday, 24 October. Kerouac's close friends came from New York—Ginsberg, Orlovsky, Corso, Holmes, Creeley—and some of them mixed with the Sampas relatives and Jack's old Lowell friends at the Funeral Home Thursday night, pausing before Jack's body in its checkered sports jacket and red bow tie, the rosary beads draped over the folded hands.

He looked thinner than most people remembered. Stella,

sitting close by, told everybody that he'd been sick for weeks, and that he'd been "so lonely, so lonely." One of the saddest moments was when I saw Allen, Peter and Gregory, dressed in casual clothes in the midst of the Lowell townspeople in their Sunday best, link arms "like a team" and stand motionless and silent before the stiff figure in the coffin.

The priest at the service at St. Jean Baptiste Church the next day had known Kerouac as a young boy, and his oration was personal and sympathetic. The text was a quotation from Ecclesiastes: " 'They shall rest from their words and take their works with them.' Jack most excitedly felt he had something to tell the world, and he was determined to do it . . . Our hope and our prayer is that Jack has now found complete liberation, sharing the visions of Gerard. Amen. Allelujia."

A long line of cars formed outside the church in the windy October morning to follow the hearse to the Edson Catholic Cemetery, most people from out of town unsure of the way and getting lost as the procession wound through downtown Lowell. I stood with the small group of friends gathered at the grave, and a few reporters mingled with the small crowd. The sun shone on the masses of flowers as Corso filmed the scene with his movie camera. Gregory finished and went over to stand beside the open grave with Ginsberg and Holmes. Before the dirt was piled on the coffin, Allen reached out and dropped a rose into the grave. Slowly I and a few other people did the same.

In Lowell, Kerouac's grave still has no marker. Not that he would have cared. His books are evidence of his presence, the young Jack still alive on his pages to rush on to the next adventure so long as there are people who read the Legend of Duluoz.

KEROUAC

Appendices

Appendix One: Chronology

The Early Years [Section I]

1922   Jean-Louis Lebris de Kerouac born on 12 March in Lowell, Massachusetts

1939   Graduates Lowell High School

1939-40   Attends Horace Mann Prep School, New York City

1940-1   Attends Columbia College

1942-3   Merchant Marine and U.S. Navy

1944   Meets Lucien Carr, William Burroughs and Allen Ginsberg

1946-8   Writes *The Town and the City* in New York City

1946   Meets Neal Cassady

1947-50   First trips across country with Neal Cassady, first attempts to write *On The Road*

1950   *The Town and the City* published

1951   Writes teletype roll manuscript of *On The Road* in three weeks in New York City

The Middle Years [Section II]

1951-2   Writes *Visions of Cody* in New York and San Francisco

1952   Writes *Doctor Sax* in Mexico City, *October in the Railroad Earth* in San Francisco, begins *Book of Dreams* in North Carolina

1953   Writes *Maggie Cassidy* and *The Subterraneans* in New York City

1954   Writes *San Francisco Blues* in San Francisco, *Some of the Dharma* in New York and North Carolina

1955   Writes *Mexico City Blues*, begins *Tristessa* in Mexico City

1956   Writes *Visions of Gerard* in North Carolina, first

370

part of *Desolation Angels* in Washington and Mexico City
1957   *On The Road* published

The Later Years [Section III]

1957   Writes *The Dharma Bums* in Florida
1958-60 Writes sketches in *Lonesome Traveler*
1959   Narrates film *Pull My Daisy* in New York
1961   Writes *Desolation Angels* in Mexico City, *Big Sur* in Florida
1965   Writes *Satori in Paris* in Florida
1966   Marries Stella Sampas and moves back to Lowell, Massachusetts
1967   Writes *Vanity of Duluoz* in Lowell
1968   4 February Neal Cassady dies in Mexico
1969   21 October Jack Kerouac dies in St. Petersburg, Florida

Appendix Two: Notes & Sources

Page numbers of books refer to first editions or reprints from the first edition, unless otherwise stated.

Chapter One
For readers who wish to follow the story of Kerouac's life in his own words, he wrote about his earliest years in Lowell in *Visions of Gerard, Doctor Sax, Vanity of Duluoz* and *The Town and the City* (the early adventures of Mickey Martin, Charley Martin and young Peter Martin). There are also descriptions of his childhood memories in the articles "Home at Christmas" (*Glamour* Magazine, December 1961) and "Not Long Ago Joy Abounded at Christmas" (New York *World Telegram and Sun*, 5 December, 1957—possibly an excerpt from Kerouac's unpublished novel *Memory Babe*). He included an autobiographical summary in *Lonesome*

Traveler, and notes on his earliest childhood in *The New American Poetry* and *The New American Story.*

"Where is this guy, Kerouac, anyway?" is from a letter Neal Cassady wrote to Jack on 1 November, 1948.

In *Mexico City Blues* (95th Chorus) and *Visions of Gerard,* Kerouac said he lived on "Burnaby Street" when he was two years old, but the street isn't on the Lowell city maps. A dream of returning to the 34 Gershom Street house in Pawtucketville with mémêre Jack later called "the happiest dream of my life," *Book of Dreams* (p. 47). And in the same book (p. 89), there are references to the Lilley Street flat and death in Lowell and "the coffin that's never been removed from the parlor of the Kerouacs."

In recent years the name of Moody has been changed to Textile Avenue after it crosses the Merrimack River into Pawtucketville. Kerouac's last home address in Lowell during his high school years and at Horace Mann School was in the tenement above the Textile Lunch at 736 Moody Street, now 16 Textile Avenue. The real names of Jack's friends in high school, described in *Doctor Sax* and *Maggie Cassidy,* were Roland Salvas ("Lousy"), George J. Apostolas ("G.J."), Freddy Bertrand ("Vinny"), and Joseph Beaulieu ("Scotty"). Freddy Bertrand's memory of being in Jack's house the day the letter arrived from Boston College offering the football scholarship was told to me in April 1973 by Jeff Weinberg, a Lowell friend of Freddy Bertrand.

Chapter Two

Jack was deeply interested in tracing the origins of his family and his name. He believed his mother's ancestors had a Bonaparte among them. He mentioned this in the original manuscript of *Satori in Paris,* but decided to drop it from the book because he didn't have sufficient details. In *Vanity of Duluoz* he said that "Kerouac" meant "Language of the House," but a few years earlier he told Fred Jordan, his editor at Grove Press, that he believed his name derived from the Welsh "Caer-a-wach," meaning "Rock or Stone Fortress by the Sea," or "House or Stone Place (Ker) in Field (ouac)." In his *Paris Review* interview the summer of 1968 he told Ted Berrigan and Aram Saroyan that his name in Cornish meant Ker: water and ouac: language of—"language of the water."

Kerouac described his senior year in Lowell High School in *Maggie Cassidy,* and his early years in New York in *Vanity of Duluoz.* In *The Town and the City,* Francis Martin had a high school sweetheart Mary, "an Irish Beauty" like Mary Carney. In *200 Contemporary Authors,* edited by Barbara Harte and Carolyn Riley, Kerouac summarized his education at Horace Mann and Columbia and his odd jobs and wartime service.

Kerouac's Lowell friend Red St. Louis ("Whitey St. Clair" in *Maggie Cassidy*) introduced him to Mary Carney. When we were working on *A Bibliography of Works by Jack Kerouac* compiled by Ann Charters (hereafter referred to as *Biblio.*) Jack told me about his years at Horace Mann School and "all the winning touch-downs." On 1 October, 1941 the Columbia *Spectator* mentioned Jack had left college for Lowell. In a poem "To Lu Libble," printed in *Newsday* 17 December, 1961, Jack described playing on the Columbia Freshman football team. According to the newspaper, when the former coach Lou Little was asked about Kerouac, Lou Little said, "A promising football player and a good boy, though a little headstrong. I wonder whatever became of him."

Leo Kerouac's conversation with Jack in New Haven is from *Vanity of Duluoz;* Jack's service on the *S.S. Dorchester,* his brief return to Columbia football and his six months in the Navy were described in that book also. The drunken incident in Boston before he shipped out aboard the *Dorchester* is in *On The Road* (p. 202).

On 13 January, 1961, while trying the psilocybin mushroom with Allen Ginsberg and Timothy Leary, Kerouac relived his 1943 experience in the hospital with the Navy psychiatrist Doctor Rosenberger. Jack described meeting his psychiatrist in the hospital elevator. The doctor asked, "Where are you going, Jack?" Jack answered, "I'm going out to kick the gong around." It was shortly after this exchange that Kerouac was given what he called an "indifferent character discharge." See also *Book of Dreams* (p. 45), for "old Navy bootcamp madhouse dreams of regimented life I hated so much." In another dream (pp. 47-50), he summarized what he did during the war and said, "Somewhere there I took the wrong road."

Chapter Three
Most of the material in this chapter, including the direct quotes, can be found in *Vanity of Duluoz* (pp. 177-257). A fictionalized account of Jack's falling in love with Edie

Parker and mémêre's arguments against his living with her are in *The Town and the City* (pp. 406-7).

In a letter to Fred Jordan on 23 October, 1967 Kerouac described raising his bail bond after the Kammerer homicide and his parents' visit with him in jail. On 1 September, 1944 the Columbia *Spectator* reported his marriage. *Book of Dreams* (p. 36) mentions the benzedrine scene in New York. Burroughs' interview in the *Paris Review* summarized his background before meeting Kerouac.

Manuscripts and letters concerned with Ginsberg and Carr's "New Vision" as young writers are on deposit at the Ginsberg Archives at the Columbia University Library. The description of Kerouac and Ginsberg in the Union Theological Seminary and Allen's recognition of the special affinity between them, are from my interview with Ginsberg at his farm in Cherry Valley, New York on 20 August, 1970. Ginsberg also mentioned the moment with Kerouac in his *Indian Journals* in Calcutta, 1963.

Chapter Four

Kerouac described staying with Ginsberg at Columbia and Burroughs in New York City in *Vanity of Duluoz*. The last pages of that book also chronicle Leo Kerouac's death and Jack's efforts to write *The Town and the City*. A fictionalized account of his brief football career and his quarrels with his family about his New York friends is in *The Town and the City* (pp. 407-13, 418-24). In his *Paris Review* interview Jack gave more details about his "Self-ultimate" period in Livingston Hall, Ginsberg's questions about changing his name to "Allen Renard," his Dashiell Hammett collaboration with Burroughs and his determination to be a great writer like Thomas Wolfe. The story about Leo Kerouac and the New York rabbi is also in the *Paris Review*. In the *Biblio*. Charles Sampas let me quote Kerouac's letter to him about *The Town and the City*, 29 December, 1949 and Jack told me that his first novel was "fiction."

On deposit at the Ginsberg Archives at Columbia are the Ginsberg-Kerouac notes on Kammerer's homicide and Ginsberg's detailed descriptions of Burroughs' West Side apartment. There are also letters from Dean MacKnight to Louis Ginsberg about Allen's suspension from the College (17 February, 1945) and Allen's letters to his brother Eugene in October 1944 about Kerouac and about consulting a physician. On 31 July, 1946 Dr. Hans Wassing wrote Dean MacKnight advising Ginsberg's readmission to the College. Allen was "psychologically pretty much as sound as they come." The Columbia Archives also has Ginsberg's notes for the unpublished story about "Bill Ducasse" and "Leon Bliestein," and "A Vision of the Apocalypse," Allen's story about the Times Square Pokerino. (Compare with Kerouac's description of the Nickel-O in *The Town and the City*.) Ginsberg's Columbia Woodberry Prize poem, "The Happy Warrior or Death in Violence," written in August 1945, was another early literary work using Huncke's conversation; the poem was dedicated to William Burroughs. Allen told me about Jack's wanting to write about "mortal companions."

Junkie is the most detailed account of the narcotics scene in New York with Huncke ("Herman") and Bill Garver ("Bill Gains"). Burroughs himself was "William Lee." In *Naked Lunch* Burroughs included more on "Bill Gains" (p. 219). *Junkie* (Ace Books, 1953 reprint, p. 43) describes Burroughs' use of newspapers on the New York subway; compare with *The Town and the City* (pp. 376-8). Also in *Junkie* (p. 106) Burroughs says when on morphine he will listen but not talk much; see *Vanity of Duluoz* (p. 268) for the conversation between Burroughs and Kerouac in New York.

In an interview at Cherry Valley on 20 August, 1970 Ginsberg told me about Kerouac's benzedrine high and his own theory relating benzedrine addiction to the ecological disturbance of the atomic bomb. Lucien Carr reminded me of Kerouac's pride in his childhood nickname "Memory Babe" in an interview in New York in November 1970. See also the early pages of *Maggie Cassidy*.

Chapter Five

Most of the questions in this chapter are from *On The Road*. Kerouac's account of meeting Neal Cassady in the opening pages of *On The Road* was repeated, with variations, to Carl Solomon in a 7 March, 1952 letter. In the original teletype-roll manuscript, which Robert Giroux so kindly let me see, the meeting occurred not after he split with his wife but after his father died. Neal came into his life at a time when he felt death pervaded everything and with that meeting life once again had begun.

The "legend" of Neal's boyhood is told in *Visions of Cody*. Cassady's *The First Third* contains his autobiography, including his description of his brother Jack in Denver, his "autobiographical fragment" about meeting Ginsberg in the

West End in 1946, smoking pot with Vicki Russell for the first time and his "great sex letter" of 7 March, 1947.

Kerouac quoted Cassady in *Visions of Cody* as having only been convicted three times of stealing cars, but on 3 July, 1949 Neal wrote Jack saying he had a record of ten arrests for various misdemeanors and had served fifteen months on six convictions. Cassady's report to Justin Brierly about his reading in the reformatory was reprinted in *Mano-Mano*, summer 1971. His letter to Kerouac about the "bowery beef-stew" in Denver was written 27 March, 1947.

Charles Olson spoke to me about Cassady's interest in cars and girls in an interview in Gloucester, Mass. on 26 July, 1968. On 13 June, 1969 I interviewed Donald Allen in San Francisco, who was impressed with Cassady's obsession with cars. Once Neal had asked Donald Allen to drive him someplace in San Francisco, and when Allen said he'd like to but couldn't because he didn't own a car, Cassady didn't believe him. It was inconceivable to him that somebody would not own a car.

Ginsberg gave me his impressions of Luanne Cassady in an interview at the West End Bar on 18 September, 1969. In New York on 12 October, 1972 he told me about making love for the first time with Burroughs and Kerouac at the Everard Baths. When contacted in Bolinas, California on 1 October, 1972 Hal Chase remembered he introduced Jack to Neal shortly before Christmas 1946. In Los Gatos, 8 October, 1972 Cassady's son John described Neal's characteristic mannerisms of nodding his head and shrugging his shoulders when talking. That day Carolyn Cassady showed me the family's home movies of Neal, Ken Kesey and Allen Ginsberg. She also played me tapes of Jack and Neal reading and talking. Her account of Neal's "rapping" was printed in *Rolling Stone* on 12 October, 1972. See also Kerouac in *On The Road* (p. 250) on Cassady talking to his women, "making logics where there was nothing but inestimable sorrowful sweats."

Chapter Six

Kerouac's first cross-country trip was described in Part One of *On The Road*. *Transatlantic Review,* winter 1969, contained transcriptions of a conversation between Kerouac and Cassady in San Francisco in 1952 about Burroughs' Texas farm. Neal also described the farm to Jack in letters in September 1947, including a long account of his last night in Texas with Huncke and Ginsberg in the hotel room. According to Kerouac, Malcolm Cowley later made him edit out the episode in *On The Road*.

Ginsberg's handwritten manuscript of "Last Stanzas in Denver" is on deposit at the Columbia Library. Jack's naiveté with Henri Cru in California in 1947 was echoed by Ginsberg's description of Kerouac as "a type of simpleton" in a letter to Mark Van Doren on 1 June, 1948.

Chapter Seven

Holmes' *Go* has extended descriptions of Ginsberg's apartment at 1401 York Avenue, his poetry and his visions during the summer of 1948. Holmes centered his novel around his own apartment at 56th and Lexington Avenue in New York.

Ginsberg wrote Mark Van Doren in 1 June, 1948 about *The Town and the City* as "the Great American Novel." Kerouac wrote Ginsberg on 18 May, 1948 saying he'd sent a recommendation for Cassady as a brakeman with the Southern Pacific. Cassady described his suicidal impulses and his training as a brakeman in a letter to Kerouac on 16 June, 1948.

Holmes' *Nothing More to Declare* included Ginsberg's speech at a party on York Avenue, Holmes' first meeting with Kerouac, his reading of *The Town and the City* notebooks and Kerouac's first efforts to write *On The Road* in "Melvillian sentences."

Jack told me about writing the "great Sax dream" when we were compiling the *Biblio*. At that time he also showed me the notebook called "A Novella of Children and Evil."

Herbert Gold's *My Last Two Thousand Years* (pp. 83-6) has the incident with the wine glass at Ginsberg's party, but Gold remembers the story as occurring shortly before Allen's departure for Africa for the first time, whereas he'd actually been to Dakar the previous fall, 1947. (See *On The Road*, p. 98).

Kerouac's journal notes for his first version of *On The Road* (27 November, 1948) were printed in *A Creative Century* (Humanities Research Center, University of Texas). Jack wrote Allen on 17 November, 1948 about what "Levinsky" does in his new novel. Burroughs' letter to Ginsberg on Factualism was written on 9 November, 1948 and Kerouac's letter to Ginsberg about same on 10 December, 1948.

Chapter Eight

Part Two of *On The Road* narrates the story of Kerouac's trips with Cassady from Christmas 1948 to February 1949. In "The Great Western Bus Ride" (*Esquire*, March 1970), Kerouac told about his first bus trip from San Francisco north to the Pacific Northwest and on to New York, probably in February 1949.

Compare *On The Road* (pp. 102-7) with *Go* (*pp. 95-106*) on the scene when Neal and Luanne come to New York after Christmas. Burroughs described his life in New Orleans the winter of 1949 in *Junkie*, omitting Kerouac and Cassady's visit. *On The Road* also contains the "Shrouded Traveler" dream and Jack's snapping his fingers, no longer "Memory Babe."

Burroughs wrote Ginsberg on 5 June, 1948 about Kerouac's getting away from "ma" in Ozone Park. Kerouac repeated Cassady's phone conversation about driving the Hudson to New York to Ginsberg. On 11 January, 1949 Neal wrote Carolyn he couldn't sell the Hudson in New York.

Carolyn Cassady is "Camille" in *On The Road*, Helen Hinckle "Galatea Dunkel."

Burroughs complained to Ginsberg about Cassady's behavior in New Orleans in letters written 30 January and 7 February, 1949.

Chapter Nine

Part Three of *On The Road* describes Kerouac in Denver in 1949 and the drive from San Francisco to Denver, Chicago and New York with Cassady. His mother (referred to as his "aunt" in the novel), not a "rich girl" in Denver, gave him the money to pay for his ride to Cassady's house in San Francisco when all his "bridges were gone."

"Jazz of the Beat Generation" in *New World Writing* (1955) has a more extended account of the jazz Jack and Neal heard in San Francisco and Chicago. Comparing this early sketch with parallel passages in *On The Road* gives some idea of the editorial cuts and revisions in the novel before its publication in 1957. In August 1954 Jack told Allen that he wanted to sneak sentences from *Visions of Cody* into the "Jazz of the Beat Generation" sketch, sentences like "Lester is like the river, it starts in near Butte, Montana at a place called Three Forks . . . ."

Kerouac's letter on 29 March, 1949 to Ed White about selling *The Town and the City* was printed in *Mano-Mano*,

378

summer 1971. Robert Giroux told me about his experience as Kerouac's editor in a telephone interview in New York on 18 October, 1972. Giroux even went home with Jack to meet mémêre. She had distrusted all of Jack's New York friends, but she apparently liked Giroux on sight. His father had been French Canadian, and Giroux found mémêre "very funny, very salty" when they talked together. In front of him she told Jack, "This man is like a banker. Stick with him. Stay away from those other bums." Giroux answered, "I'm not a banker, I'm an editor."

David Diamond very kindly wrote me on 9 April and 3 May, 1973 about Bill Cannister's death and told me about showing *The Town and the City* manuscript to Alfred Kazin, a literary consultant at Harcourt, Brace, who passed it on to Robert Giroux. At the time Kazin was teaching a course on Melville at the New School which Kerouac had joined. Among the many people who had read the completed, black hard cover bound voluminous manuscript of *The Town and the City* was the composer David Diamond, who'd met Jack and Lucien Carr a couple of years before. They'd come down to the Village to hear his music and went out together to listen to bop at Birdland. Diamond was so enthusiastic about the novel that he tried to help Jack find a publisher by showing it to his close friend Kazin, who liked it and told Giroux about it also.

Book of Dreams (pp. 115-6) includes Kerouac's dream of being the "young genius writer (like the me of 1949)."

Kerouac wrote Ginsberg on 23 May, 10 June, and 5 July, 1949, about his summer in Denver. The lines "Down in Denver" are in *On The Road*. Jack also wrote Allen about his slow progress with the novel and quoted extensively from the manuscript. The hero in that early version was a man called "Red" who traveled to California with his friends "Smitty" and "Vern," looking for a lost father, listening to jazz and running into a "Mystic Tenorman." Ginsberg remembers that Jack wanted to write about his generation and put it on the map.

Eldridge Cleaver in *Soul on Ice* found Kerouac's identification with the Denver blacks and Mexicans in *On The Road* remarkable social criticism, the first stage of white American youth's rejection of racial conformity. Cleaver wrote (p. 71), "The disaffected youth were refusing to participate in the system, having discovered that America, far from helping the underdog, was up to its ears in the mud trying to hold the dog down."

Sterling A. Brown, however, thought that Kerouac's views were merely "A Greenwich Village refurbishing of old stereotypes" about the idyllic happiness of the blacks in the Denver slums. By 1960, in *Big Sur*, Kerouac was much less romantic in his references to black people. See also *Athanor* 2 (1971).

Burroughs warned Ginsberg about Huncke in a letter on 23 August, 1948. Cassady wrote Kerouac about being "blood brothers" on 25 December, 1947, about "listening good" on 1 November, 1948, about getting on the road in August, 1949. Compare Cassady's description of himself as "jazz hounded Cassady" in his August 1949 letter with *On The Road* (p. 153). Neal's letter to Jack on 3 July, 1949 about setting his broken thumb became the paragraph on page 153 about "a setting of the bones that was difficult."

Carolyn Cassady was interviewed about the San Francisco scene in 1949 in *Rolling Stone*, 12 October, 1972. There is some discrepancy about her daughter Cathy's age in the interview; she must have been nearly a year old at the time, not four months. Neal had three children with his second wife Carolyn; two daughters, Cathy (born September 1948) and Jamie (January 1950) and a son John Allen Cassady (September 1951) named after John Kerouac and Allen Ginsberg. His initials spell J-A-C.

Chapter Ten

On The Road Part Four describes Kerouac's meeting with Cassady in New York in the spring of 1950, Jack's trip to Denver, Neal's drive with him to Mexico and the return to New York City. "A Billowy Trip in the World," their Mexican experience, was published in *New Directions* 16 (1957) shortly before *On The Road*.

Kerouac's letter to Cassady 14 December, 1950 reminisced about their adventures in Mexico, material that went into *On The Road*. Neal went to Mexico for a quick divorce to legitimize his son Curtis, born to Diana Hansen in November 1950. Diana Hansen told me on 20 October, 1972 that Curtis was named after Cassady's favorite "Curtis Street" in Denver.

Kerouac wrote Ginsberg on 28 February, 1950 about not seeing Cassady anymore, about autobiographical materials being the source of fiction and about the early form of *On The Road* with the Denver realtor. On 29 October, 1950 he wrote Allen about being in God after the heavy sessions with drugs in Mexico City. Burroughs warned Kerouac about going too far with his interior searching on 18 September, 1950.

The New York *Times* reviewed *The Town and the City* on 5 March, 1950. Holmes wrote Cassady on 18 November, 1950 about Joan and Jack's wedding. In his *Paris Review* interview, Kerouac told about the bathroom peephole in Cannister's loft. Their collaboration in bed mentioned in Alfred Aronowitz's "Jack Kerouac: Beyond the Road," the New York *Post*, 22 October, 1969.

Chapter Eleven

In a letter on 30 December, 1950 Cassady told Kerouac about the three things he wanted in his life.

Kerouac's search for "deep form, poetic form" and writing *On The Road* on a roll of "shelf paper" were mentioned in Holmes' *Nothing More To Declare*.

Cassady's letter about hitchhiking to Los Angeles is in *The First Third*. On 17 March, 1951 Cassady told Kerouac he wrote with a "sense of careless freedom." In Ginsberg's *Paris Review* interview, 1966 he said that Jack wanted to use the kind of things Neal talked about in his own writing. Burroughs wrote Ginsberg about "Factualism" on 9 November, 1948. Kerouac told Hugo Weber about formulating his "legend" in the hospital in a letter on 12 April, 1962.

In *Athanor*, Fall 1971, Kerouac told his interviewer how he started *On The Road* with his first meeting with Cassady. Jack told me in his *Biblio.* how he wrote the novel for his second wife. Years before he gave the same story to the *Saturday Review*, 28 September, 1957.

In Bruce Cook's *The Beat Generation*, Lucien Carr described living in the loft while Kerouac wrote *On The Road*. Robert Giroux was apparently misquoted in *The Beat Generation*. Giroux told me in New York on 20 October, 1972 that he never said Kerouac wasn't Shakespeare or that Shakespeare never revised.

On 15 May, 1951 Cassady wrote Ginsberg asking what he'd meant by saying Jack had gone back to the woman who wanted him the most.

Chapter Twelve

Kerouac described his attempts to get a seaman's job with Henri Cru and his bus trip from New York to San Francisco in *Visions of Cody*. See also the sketch "Piers of the Homeless Night" in *Lonesome Traveler*.

"Pic" is mentioned in *Visions of Cody*, a book Jack started shortly after returning to New York after the summer in Rocky Mount. In a *Newsday* article on 17 February, 1961, "Playing Baseball with Jack Kerouac," Jack told about a fictional "Pic" Jackson, a hard hitting pitcher, whose name was short for "Pictorial Review," which suggests that he might have intended to include "Pic" growing up to be a baseball player in *Visions of Cody*. As the novel was published in 1971, "Pic" is set in 1948 and the story is told by a ten-year-old black boy, "Pictorial Review Jackson," in the black dialect indigenous to the North Carolina farm country around Rocky Mount.

In *Visions of Cody*, Kerouac boasted that he'd dodge the great black bird "by sheer animalism" and detailed how he packed his sea bag. On 9 April, 1973 David Diamond told me that Kerouac attended Alfred Kazin's classes on Melville at the New School for Social Research in New York, although the New School has no record of him as a credited student. See his reference in *Visions of Cody* to feeling cheated over the exchange of textbooks on Fourth Avenue. In his Introduction to *Lonesome Traveler* Kerouac said he was at the New School in 1948 and 1949.

The anecdote about Henri Cru and the gun at Christmas in San Pedro is in "Piers of the Homeless Night."

Ginsberg, who made love with both Cassady and Kerouac, said that both were passive lovers and therefore never sexually attracted to each other. But the artist Robert LaVigne, who slept with Cassady, said that Neal was a fantastic lover. Diane DiPrima described making love with Kerouac (unsatisfactory) in her novel *Memoirs of a Beatnik*. Since the number of men and women with whom Cassady and Kerouac were involved sexually is so large, a consensus is clearly necessary to elucidate conjecture. In a letter on 25 August, 1954 Jack told Carolyn Cassady, who'd been angry at Allen for making love with Neal, that she needn't worry about it and that he personally wasn't interested in such a liaison.

In the *Biblio.* Kerouac explained that Cassady's house in San Francisco was an ideal set-up for writing. In her *Rolling Stone* interview Carolyn told about making love with both Jack and Neal.

Quotations in this chapter from *Visions of Cody* include Jack on living in the clutter of Neal's clothes in the attic, the "bumclothes that put bums to shame" and the discovery of "his writing soul at last."

Carl Solomon clarified the Myshkin-Kirilov anecdote, which had been variously reported, in a telephone interview in New York on 18 October, 1972.

Kerouac wrote Ginsberg on 18 May, 1952 about how the idea of sketching came suddenly to him in the Chinese restaurant with Ed White on 25 October, 1951, which made him want to revise the conventional narrative of *On The Road*.

Ginsberg told me on 27 September, 1972 that spontaneous prose, the belief that poets must improvise, was evidence of Kerouac's early intuitive knowledge of Buddhism as expressed in *Milarepa*: "First thought is best thought." See also Ginsberg's *Indian Journals*, "The very act of writing creates emotion . . ." and "lonely handiwork of self keeping record of self's consciousness—the old Yoga of Poesy."

In June 1963 Kerouac told Holmes about standing in front of the bakery window and sketching, and about Lee Konitz and the courage to go ahead with spontaneous prose. In the *Paris Review* (1966), Allen said that sketching had a single elastic rhythm. This *Paris Review* interview and the one with Burroughs were reprinted in *Writers at Work*.

Chapter Thirteen

Kerouac referred to his "in-depth" book about Cassady as *Visions of Neal*, *Visions of Enal* and *Visions of Cody*. Throughout the manuscript he wrote the name Neal, then changed it to Cody when he submitted the typescript for publication. Ginsberg told me *Visions of Cody* was an "in-depth" version of *On The Road* in an interview on East 10th Street on 1 June, 1966.

Quotations in this chapter from *Visions of Cody* include Jack's description of Neal, his thoughts of "mad valuable me," "this record is my job," "a great rememberer," Cassady's roach kit, the tape conversation about Neal's breaking his nose and the description of Cassady in the kitchen with his family.

David Meltzer's interviews with Lew Welch in *The San Francisco Poets* has the line about language being a way of moving too.

For the early uses of the redbrick image in Kerouac's work, see *The Town and the City* (pp. 343, 413). See also *Visions of Cody* (pp. 34-5). Carl Solomon was impressed by the redbrick image in Kerouac's prose. Solomon wrote him on 13 December, 1951, "I am equally fascinated by your flair for concrete detail and by the dreams they contain (the red brick)." Early in 1952, Ace Books advanced Kerouac $500 to complete *Visions of Cody* after Jack showed them the chapter describing Neal playing football in Denver. Kerouac wrote Solomon on 27 December, 1951 right after he got back to Cassady's house from San Pedro, that what he'd been writing about Neal was really about himself.

Kerouac said in his *Paris Review* interview that he became discouraged trying to finish *Visions of Cody* with a tape recorder. He wrote to Solomon on 27 December, 1951 about publishing Cassady and described the hour tape of *Doctor Sax* in Neal's attic.

Solomon advised Cassady early in 1952 (undated letter) about how to become a writer in the "great confession vogue." Kerouac asked Ginsberg if Solomon thought Cassady was an idiot. On 15 May, 1951 Neal told Allen about his problems writing his life story and suggested that *On The Road* was too trivial for Jack, who should start a book about his early life. Later in 1954 Kerouac told Cassady that when he wrote *On The Road* in 1951 he had not yet learned the "looseness of talking-speech" and was imitating Dashiell Hammett's style.

Kerouac complained to Ginsberg on 10 May, 1952 about Cassady's strict household economy and described their visit with Lamantia and the drive to Nogales with the family. In Cassady's letter to Ginsberg on 10 July, 1952 he spoke of Kerouac being "with the Indians permanent."

Chapter Fourteen

"Mexican Fellaheen" in *Lonesome Traveler* describes Kerouac's bus trip to Mexico City in 1952, including his meeting with Enrique. *Junkie* describes Burroughs' experience in Mexico.

In an interview in Stockholm in July 1971, Bill Sanders said he had been in Mexico City when Burroughs accidentally shot his wife through the head while playing "William Tell." Sanders called Burroughs a "connoisseur of drugs" and told me about the ex-G.I.'s scene in the Bounty Cantina.

I also spoke to Burroughs about the accident (London, 29 November, 1972) and during our conversation he clarified the story.

Kerouac wrote Ginsberg about the Mexican bus ride in a letter on 10 May, 1952 and asked about subtitling *On The*

Road "A Modern Novel." He also mentioned *Queer* and said that Joan's death had been entirely accidental. On 18 May, 1952 he asked Allen to be his agent for *On The Road* and said he was going to start *Doctor Sax* as well as a book about Burroughs and a novel about the Civil War.

Burroughs wrote Ginsberg on 26 March and 8 April, about his situation with the Mexican police and his plans to move to Panama. Burroughs wrote Kerouac on 3 April, 1952 about breaking a morphine habit with codeine. See *Junkie* about being supplied with drugs in Mexico City for thirty dollars a month.

Allen told me Jack considered *Doctor Sax* "a myth of puberty." In the *Biblio.* Kerouac explained about writing *Doctor Sax* in the toilet of Burroughs' apartment. For more details, see the *Paris Review* interview, including the fact that the book was "hallucinated."

Book of Dreams (pp. 101-2) has another link between Burroughs and the fantasy character Doctor Sax. Ginsberg told me on 12 October, 1972 that the original Sax had been Jack's imaginary companion in Lowell modelled after The Shadow.

Walter Gibson was interviewed at his home in Putnam Valley in May 1967, about his years writing *The Shadow* pulps and the mysterioso atmosphere of the stories. Mallay Charters at age four told me that during the night children are afraid to go outside because they don't know who the shadows are.

Chapter Fifteen

In our London interview of 29 November, 1972 Burroughs remembered that although Kerouac spent a lot of time with Cassady, they didn't always get on very well. In Mexico City the summer of 1952 there was considerable acrimony between them about money—arguments about who paid for the gasoline on their trips together. Cassady complained to Burroughs about Kerouac's stinginess at that time.

In the last pages of *Junkie* Burroughs mentioned leaving Mexico City for a trip alone after *yage* in Central America since "my wife and I are separated."

See "The Railroad Earth" in *Lonesome Traveler* for Kerouac's life as a brakeman with the Southern Pacific the last months of 1952. On 22 August, 1952 Cassady wrote Kerouac a long letter about how to become a brakeman.

Kerouac began his "History of the Hip Generation" in Rocky Mount in August 1952.

In her *Rolling Stone* interview, Carolyn Cassady remembered living with Neal and Jack in the big old house at 1047 East Santa Clara Street in San Jose. Cassady wrote Ginsberg on 4 October, 1952 about the tensions with Kerouac in the house. Although Neal had a "whole closet full of weed," Jack wouldn't smoke with him.

Kerouac complained to Ginsberg on 15 March, 1952 that Cassady didn't seem to like him anymore. He told Allen how Neal had hung up on him after their quarrel in San Jose and later came to the railroad yards and asked him to come back home. In an undated earlier letter Kerouac mentioned the strange types he'd met working on the railroad. See also "The Railroad Earth" for descriptions of his railroad work.

Kerouac's method of sketching like a "talky caboose," "the thinking during swift writing" and "the secret of LINGO" were mentioned in his *Paris Review* interview. Jack's mind being "attacked by words" is in *Visions of Cody*.

Ginsberg asked Kerouac on 15 March, 1952, "What will you care if you faced your responsibilities?" In a letter to John Ryan on 28 August, 1955 Ginsberg described Kerouac as being "at the height of his romantic sense of himself."

Chapter Sixteen

Kerouac wrote Cassady on 10 January, 1953 about his wary response to his old New York friends and his envy of Holmes' success with *Go*. Earlier from San Francisco (8 November, 1952) Jack told Allen that he wished Holmes the best of luck. He complained to Allen that he hadn't asked for Marion Holmes' attentions in an undated letter. John and Marion Holmes were later divorced.

Ginsberg wrote Cassady that Kerouac was "all hung up on noise" and "flitting from soul to soul" in an undated letter in late 1952 or early 1953. Ginsberg told me in Cherry Valley that the "window-looking scene" in *Doctor Sax* was a "freeze frame" realization of "visionary tenderness" and that Jack believed that love "animated" their writing.

Holmes wrote "This is the Beat Generation" for the New York *Times* in 1952 and it later appeared as a chapter in *Nothing More to Declare*. He credited Kerouac with defining the beat style for him in November 1948. Earlier, in *The Town and the City* (p. 402), Kerouac had Huncke ("Junkey") use the word "beat." Jack and Allen always said that Huncke had first told them the meaning of the word, but Jack insisted that he was the first person to say "beat generation." On 23 August, 1954 Kerouac wrote Ginsberg that "beat" belonged to him as the title of a book—he'd just changed the title of *On The Road to Beat Generation*, hoping this might help sell the novel. He also told Allen that he saw the word "beatitude" in "beat", a broader implication which could be understood in all Romance languages.

Chapter Seventeen

Kerouac insisted to Ginsberg in a letter on 13 November, 1945 that there were essential differences between them, and on 6 September, 1946 he repeated to Allen that art was the most important thing in the world to him.

I learned about Kerouac's idea to cut the Duluoz Legend into suitable chronological lengths in my interview with Holmes in Old Saybrook, Conn. in February 1967.

Kerouac wrote Cassady on 10 Jaunary, 1953 that while working on *Springtime Mary* he was limiting his life to writing and sleep. Ginsberg described the novel as a story about Kerouac's "rich adolescence and woetime" in an undated letter to Cassady early in 1953. For the names of Jack's boyhood friends in Lowell, see notes to Chapter One. The scene making love with "Maggie" is in the novel.

Kerouac inscribed his presentation copy of *Maggie Cassidy*, lettered in gold on the spine, "To mémêre from Ti Jean. Read in here on page 80 and 84 about Papa Leo."

Solomon wrote Kerouac on 13 December, 1951 that his work heralded a renaissance of the American middle class, and suggested a book on bop on 31 January, 1952.

Kerouac told Ginsberg about his agent Phyllis Jackson and asked Allen to try to get *Doctor Sax* published, in early 1953.

Chapter Eighteen

"Slobs of the Kitchen Sea" in *Lonesome Traveler* describes Kerouac's work in the officers' mess shortly before his affair with "Mardou." *The Subterraneans* is about his life in New York City later in the summer of 1953.

Ginsberg wrote me in June 1972 about the black girl's pad on the Lower East Side. Corso's description of meeting Ginsberg in New York in 1951 and a photo of him and Allen at that time are in *Scenes Along the Road*. Corso told me in a tape interview in San Francisco on 16 June, 1969 that

Jack had tried to teach him "some words" in 1952. Corso also gave his version of how Jack's affair with the black girl broke up: "She was rough and I was just out of jail." "Mardou" shrugged off the affair when I talked to her about it one night in New York in 1970.

Kerouac didn't let his feelings about Corso keep him from writing a blurb for *Gasoline* on 15 October, 1957 for Ferlinghetti, praising Corso as one of the two best American poets. Ginsberg was the other.

In *Partisan Review* (vii; 1; 1970), Gore Vidal mentioned that Kerouac left out of *The Subterraneans* the time the two of them went to bed together at the Chelsea Hotel after an evening with Burroughs. Vidal is called "Arial Lavalina" in *The Subterraneans*.

Kerouac explained in the *Biblio.* how he wrote *The Subterraneans* in three long nights; see also his *Paris Review* interview where he went on to say that his writing was all based on jazz and bop. A few early critics responded to his attempt to write with "the raciness and freedom and humor of jazz." See Ralph J. Gleason in the *Saturday Review*, 11 January, 1959: Kerouac's voice in *On The Road* is "the explicit, vivid vocabulary of jazz." Also Warren Tallman's long analysis, "Kerouac's Sound."

Kerouac tried to make a speech on goofballs about his love for Ginsberg and Burroughs on 21 November, 1953.

Chapter Nineteen

Poems from "San Francisco Blues" in Kerouac's *Scattered Poems* edited by Ann Charters (City Lights, 1971). On 26 October, 1954 Kerouac told Ginsberg that his poems in San Francisco had been written spontaneously and complained that some of the images were thin. He told Allen that he wrote them sitting in a rocking chair in his San Francisco hotel and titled them "San Francisco Blues/Written in a Rocking Chair."

Kerouac described his arrival in San Jose in a letter to Carolyn Cassady on 17 May, 1954. He wrote Neal on 3 December, 1953 that Allen had discovered America's classical heritage in Mexico. On 29 June, 1953 Cassady asked Ginsberg to come out West.

In an article in *Escapade*, "The Yen for Zen," Kerouac told about reading *The Life of the Buddha* and deciding that the only life for him was to live like Thoreau. He wrote Ginsberg in May 1954 about "Some of the Dharma." At this time Jack was also reading Buddhist texts in the New York Public Library. (Ginsberg told me Jack had found Dwight Goddard's *Buddhist Bible* in the San Jose Library.) In the same letter he mentioned living in Mexico for four dollars a month. On 17 May, 1954 he wrote Allen about his New York drunken times and his life in Richmond Hill. Allen remembers Jack telling him he showed "Mardou" the manuscript of *The Subterraneans* and complained that yoga was hard on him. On 7 December, 1954 he warned Allen that Buddhist teachings would be appropriated by intelligent but insincere poseurs who'd use it for their own ends.

Kerouac's statements to Ginsberg about Buddhism having no attraction for Burroughs and Cassady are in letters from May 1954 and 26 October, 1954. In May 1954 he also said that Buddhist texts assured him that life was a dream. See also Kerouac letter to Carolyn Cassady on 17 May, 1954. On 25 August, 1954 Jack told her that he was working again on *On The Road* and that both she and Neal would be in it.

Kerouac put down Malcolm Cowley and *New World Writing* in a letter to Ginsberg on 21 November, 1953 but on 23 August, 1954, after Little, Brown had rejected *On The Road,* he told Allen that he admired Cowley for championing him and that the $120 from *New World Writing* was his first pay since 1953. He wrote Allen about going to San Francisco and making a "bookmovie" with him, Burroughs and Cassady on 26 October, 1954.

Chapter Twenty

Kerouac wrote Ginsberg on 26 October, 1954 and 21 November, 1954 about his return to Lowell, on "beatific," and on the idea that Cassady might be his brother Gerard reborn. See also Aronowitz interview with Kerouac in "The Beat Generation," New York *Post,* and *Book of Dreams* (p. 159) for a dream in a Lowell skid-row hotel.

Compare Kerouac's weariness in Lowell at the end of 1954 with his boundless enthusiasm for writing about his "own complete life" earlier in *Visions of Cody*.

In a letter to Carolyn Cassady on 2 July, 1954 Jack praised the *Diamond Sutra* for helping him get over his horror of the railroads. He also spoke against Christianity, an indication of how deeply he was beginning to become involved with his Buddhist studies.

Kerouac wrote Ginsberg about his manuscripts laying in

his agent's drawer in an undated letter, possibly late in 1954. On 20 May, 1955 he complained to Ginsberg that Sterling Lord wouldn't write him. Publically he always spoke highly of Lord's management but Sterling Lord's letters from Kerouac, on deposit at the New York University Library, have many requests from Jack for more frequent communication.

The poem "How to Meditate" is from *Scattered Poems*.

On 20 May, 1955 Jack wrote Allen about "cityCityCITY" and said he'd apologized to Cowley for refusing to publish *On The Road* with him in 1953. On 2 September, 1955 he told Allen that the Philosophical Library would publish *Buddha Tells Us* if he could guarantee 600 copies sold at $3.50. On 4 March, 1955 he wrote Ginsberg about "Visions of Bill."

Kerouac wrote Ginsberg on 1 June, 1955 about borrowing ten dollars from his mother. On 14 July, 1955 he mentioned the quarrel with his sister in which he accused her of being jealous. Letters on 27 May and 27 June, 1955 described his efforts to get *Doctor Sax* and *The Subterraneans* published and his sale of "cityCityCITY" to the *New American Reader* for $50. On 29 June, 1955 he told Allen about drinking in the Riviera Bar with Lucien Carr and getting drunk on martinis with Malcolm Cowley. His plans to live on Ginsberg's California Unemployment checks in Mexico were detailed in a letter on 4 July, 1955; on 14 July, 1955 he told Allen about Al Sublette's comment about a hut in Lowell.

I had a letter from Malcolm Cowley and a telephone interview with him in October 1972 about his suggestions for the revisions of *On The Road*. When he and Keith Jennison accepted the novel for Viking, it was still titled *Beat Generation*.

Chapter Twenty-One

Tristessa describes Kerouac's life at 212 Orizaba with Bill Garver.

Kerouac wrote Ginsberg on 14 July, 1955 about selling blood in San Francisco or hustling baggage. Ginsberg wrote John Allen Ryan on 28 August, 1955 about Kerouac as "great prose Melville Jack."

See *Biblio.* for "Old Bill Gaines lived downstairs."

Ginsberg told me about Kerouac's writing "from the realm of consciousness" and that *Mexico City Blues* was a "grass book" and Kerouac a "Zen Lunatic" in an interview in

New York in December 1970. See the *Paris Review* interview with Jack for the morphine composition of the 230th Chorus of *Mexico City Blues*. On 7 August, 1955 shortly after his arrival at 212 Orizaba, Kerouac told Ginsberg that morphine had made him sick the first day he tried it.

Chapter Twenty-Two

In *Tristessa* Kerouac described the girl's morphine habit, her room in the whorehouse district, her lack of possessiveness, her friends El Indio and Cruz, Jack's scoring for Garver and his own experiment with morphine.

In the *Biblio.* Jack explained how he wrote *Tristessa* after fanning a fire on the roof with his mattress and the girl's telling him "You've got millions of pesos on the floor." The *Paris Review* interview reveals Tristessa's real name and how Jack finally "nailed" her and about the "ingrown toenail packed mystical style" of the novel.

Kerouac wrote Ginsberg in August 1955 saying that the West Coast didn't offer him anything, but that he had a lot of typing to do. On 7 August, 1955 he mentioned the penicillin treatments for his leg; on 2 September he said he was packing for California; and on 6 September he gave Allen Garver's response to "Howl" and described his own prophecies. On 20 April, 1973, Ginsberg told me how Jack named his poem "Howl." In our Cherry Valley interview, Allen recalled Jack's invitation to shout their poems in the streets.

Chapter Twenty-Three

The Dharma Bums describes Kerouac's life from September 1955 to August 1956. Tom Parkinson kindly wrote me on 23 March, 1973 giving a fuller account of Ginsberg as a graduate student at Berkeley:

> You also say that Mark Schorer and I encouraged Allen to think that he could get a graduate fellowship at Berkeley. I don't know about Mark; what I said to Allen was the normal encouragement that one gives any talented person who wants to go to graduate school at a time when money was more available than now. As a matter of fact, I remember vividly the night that I told Allen that getting a doctorate was clearly not the route for him. We were on the freeway passing Aquatic Park at the moment, and he had been complaining that his mind simply didn't function any longer in the way required by courses in biblio-

graphy and Anglo-Saxon. He was very miserable but didn't want to drop out because people had been kind to him and he didn't want to betray their trust. (Tom Parkinson)

Ginsberg's letter to John Allen Ryan (9 September, 1955) included this early version of "A Strange New Cottage in Berkeley." A later version appears in *Reality Sandwiches* (City Lights Books). In the same letter he also told of meeting Snyder and organizing the poetry reading at the Six Gallery. On 8 December, 1955 he told Ryan that he read his long poems in public like a cantor but "nobody seemed to mind after it was over." Ginsberg wrote Kerouac in June 1952 about Mark Van Doren and the Columbia Faculty Club. In the notes for a San Francisco exhibit of Robert LaVigne's paintings, Allen wrote about his knowledge of Cezanne and DeKooning and how he fell in love with Peter Orlovsky.

In our interview in San Francisco on 12 June, 1969 Gary Snyder told me how he met Ginsberg on Hillegass Street and about the Six Gallery reading with the bohemian community in the audience being the "life style of only three people." Snyder also described Kerouac at the Berkeley parties quoting conversations verbatim after they were over. Snyder's interview in Stockholm in June 1972 by Gunnar Harding contained the information that he read "Jazz of the Beat Generation" before he met Kerouac, and that, much to Kerouac's delight, he called Jack "Ti Jean."

Snyder's haikus spoken on the mountain are in *The Dharma Bums*. He read his journal entry for October, 1955 to me in San Francisco. The rest of the description of the Sierra trip is from *The Dharma Bums*, as is Kerouac's night sleeping out in Riverside as a "Don Quixote of tenderness." On 20 February, 1973, John Montgomery told me about the cause of Natalie Jackson's death in San Francisco and described the Sierra trip he made with Kerouac and Snyder:

The California Matterhorn is just an easy walk with a rock top with broad ledges hardly requiring the use of hands. I could see the last pitch. As I didn't sleep the night before, I was too tired to want to reach the top in the time it would have taken; we were late, mainly my fault, and I didn't want to have Jack hiking back to the road after dark. The fear that Jack had is common to people who haven't known hills or mountains. God knows there are enough hills in Western Massachusetts but Jack hadn't tried them . . . . Jack was quite impressed with my hiking on the way back and I guess it's because I rested while they went on a few feet higher; anyway he had been overextended. Yet we drove all night and when I walked to the cottage with him about 6:30 a.m. he amazed me by inviting me in to have coffee as *I* was on my *last* legs. I declined. (John Montgomery)

Kerouac wrote Ginsberg on 14 July and 6 September, 1955 about Ezra Pound. See also *The Dharma Bums* (p. 23).

John Montgomery described Kerouac as having the "verve of a Tenderfoot Scout" in *Jack Kerouac: A Memoir* (Fresno, The Giligia Press, 1970).

In Los Gatos on 8 October, 1972 Carolyn Cassady told me that Natalie Jackson had forged her signature on a check and that Neal had lost all the money at the races.

See *Book of Dreams* (pp. 167-8) on Kerouac's annual return home to spend Christmas with mémêre.

Chapter Twenty-Four
Kerouac wrote about his trip from Los Angeles to Rocky Mount, the long drive with the trucker, the Christmas of 1955 with his family and his meditations in the woods in *The Dharma Bums.*

In the *Biblio.* he explained how he wrote *Visions of Gerard* in his sister's kitchen. The remaining quotations in this chapter are from *Visions of Gerard.*

Chapter Twenty-Five
The second half of *The Dharma Bums* relates the story of Kerouac's life in Snyder's cabin in Mill Valley, including Snyder's response to Kerouac as the "Buddha known as the Quitter" and their discussions of their different approaches to Buddhism.

Robert Creeley told me the details of the San Francisco scene in 1956 in our interview on 7 July, 1969 in Annisquam, Mass.

In the *Biblio.*, Jack told me about Gary telling him it was time to write a Sutra. The verbal challenges Kerouac and Snyder exchanged were also a traditional Zen Buddhist exercise.

In my interview with Gary Snyder on 12 June, 1969 he

mentioned that Berne Porter had wanted to publish *Howl*. On 7 June, 1973, Lawrence Ferlinghetti wrote that Berne Porter's offer "must have come *after* my original offer to Allen which came in the form of a telegram I sent him the night of the infamed Six Gallery reading in SF and which he would have received the next morning in Berkeley. This telegram ended with the following words: 'I greet you at the beginning of a great career.' (Emerson to Whitman?) Actually Allen and I had talked about a City Lights edition a week or two earlier at CL bookstore, and it had been agreed then to do it, though the Six reading fired me up to do it faster than I had originally planned. Now, it seems to me that the Berne Porter offer was for a fine press or deluxe edition at a higher price, not a popular paperback . . . ."

In June, 1972 in Stockholm he mentioned the small factual changes that Kerouac made in his books for "novelistic purposes." I had asked Snyder specifically about the Mill Valley poem Jack included in *The Dharma Bums* written about "Sean Monahan" reading the *Diamond Sutra* in the sun. Snyder had actually written it about Kerouac. In Stockholm that same afternoon in June 1972 Joanna McClure told me about Jack's shyness at parties and his habit of slapping people on the back when he first met them.

Lawrence Ferlinghetti was interviewed on 4 June, 1969 in San Francisco about starting the City Lights Bookstore and the Pocket Poets Series. Earlier in New York I interviewed his partner Peter Martin about the founding of City Lights.

Chapter Twenty-Six

Book One of *Desolation Angels* chronicles Kerouac's weeks on the mountain and experiences in Seattle, San Francisco and Los Gatos in the summer of 1956. Compare the different descriptions of the fire station in the last pages of *The Dharma Bums* and the opening chapters of *Desolation Angels*. See also "Alone on a Mountain Top" and "The Vanishing American Hobo" in *Lonesome Traveler*. The quotations in this chapter are from *Desolation Angels* unless otherwise indicated.

In San Francisco in 1969 Kerouac identified with his friends as poets separate from the mainstream of American life, but his political attitudes, when he occasionally spoke out, leaned to the right even at that early date. On 23 August, 1954 he wrote Ginsberg not to encourage a friend's Communist bent. To encourage Communism, according to Kerouac, was to be a foolish Liberal, like Burroughs, and Allen's feeling that Leftism was in the American tradition of dissent was equally misguided. Kerouac insisted that such dissent was treasonous.

Although Kerouac was restless with Cassady's family in Los Gatos, he also felt guilty about interfering with their home life when he stayed with them. See *Book of Dreams* (pp. 114-5).

Kerouac's description of Part Two of *Tristessa* as "choppy and terse" is in the *Paris Review* interview. His long description of himself as a "widow's son" is from *Desolation Angels*.

The William Carlos Williams quote is from the introduction to *Howl*.

Chapter Twenty-Seven

Book Two of *Desolation Angels* chronicles Kerouac's experiences "passing through" Mexico, New York, Tangier and Berkeley. See also *Escapade,* August 1960, "The Last Word" for more anecdotes about Tangier; "Big Trip to Europe" in *Lonesome Traveler*; and "On the Road with Mémère" in *Holiday*, May 1965. Ginsberg's conversation with Kerouac in Mexico City is from *Desolation Angels*.

In a letter on 2 June, 1955 from Rocky Mount, Kerouac told Ginsberg that Malcolm Cowley had asked him if he knew Corso, and that Gregory was apparently making a big hit with *The Vestle Lady on Brattle*.

I interviewed Corso in San Francisco on 16 June, 1969 for his views of Shelley and God as "a beautiful painter." See also *Desolation Angels* (pp. 284-7).

Donald Allen told me of his experiences editing *Evergreen Review* Number Two and about Ginsberg in New York trying to "build the big united front" in our San Francisco interview.

Ginsberg wrote Ferlinghetti on 15 January, 1957 about visiting Williams with Kerouac and Corso. See *Indian Journals* for Ginsberg's poem to Williams.

Kerouac described living in Tangier and the hashish sprayed with arsenic in a letter to Joyce Glassman on 22 February, 1957. Apparently Burroughs originally titled his novel "Naked Lust," but Ginsberg misread it as "Naked Lunch" and Kerouac was the only one to catch it (Kerouac letter to Ginsberg, 20 June, 1960). Jack was interviewed in Northport in 1964 about his return from Tangier to New York in 1957, his experiences in Paris and London without any money, and crossing the Atlantic third class on the *S.S. New Amsterdam;* see *Athanor* 3 (1972).

See *Desolation Angels* for Kerouac's belief in Tangier that he must pray for everyone in solitude, for his books becoming a fad with youth and for Cassady's looking away "shifty-like" after seeing his first copy of *On The Road* in Berkeley.

Chapter Twenty-Eight

The Village Voice Reader reprinted Howard Smith's report of Kerouac at the Vanguard, "Off the Road, Into the Vanguard, and Out." Snyder told me in San Francisco on 12 June, 1969 that "Neal's a beautiful memory."

A cross-section of the reviews of *On The Road* gives some idea of the impact of the book and the controversy it sparked:

Saturday Review: "A dizzy travelogue that gives the reader little chance but to gobble a few verbal goofballs and thumb a ride to the next town."

Washington *Post*: "The frantic fringe."

Cincinnati *Enquirer*: "Really mad."

Louisville *Courier-Journal*: "The Romantic Novel's last Whimper."

Savannah *Morning News*: "The narrow dialogue of the hipster is tiring, a little too far out."

Omaha *Morning World Herald*: "Uncouth."

Houston *Post*: "This is a book for the dispossessed, for young Bohemia, for those whose lives so far have led nowhere."

San Francisco *Chronicle*: "It's about something everybody talks about and nobody does anything about, the delinquent younger generation."

After Gilbert Millstein's sympathetic review of *On The Road* in the New York *Times*, the review in the *Village Voice* on 18 September, 1957 was perhaps the most favorable. There Arthur Oesterreicher described the popularity of the book in the Village, people carrying it in the streets, leafing through it in bookstores, hugging it under their arms as they rode the subway to work. Kerouac was compared favorably with Wolfe, Whitman, Twain and Henry Miller, and *On The Road* was said to offer "a rallying point for the elusive spirit of the rebellion of these times, that silent scornful sit-down strike of the disaffiliated." Oesterreicher concluded, "The ugliness of American life appears on every page of *On The Road* but does not fill it . . . Beneath the beatness on the surface of everything, Kerouac finds beatitude."

Michael McClure wrote about Jim Morrison in the San Francisco *Chronicle* on 14 July, 1971.

See the *Biblio.* for details of how Kerouac wrote *The Dharma Bums* and his inscription of the book for mémêre.

Grove Press' publicity release for *The Subterraneans* quoted Kerouac that he spent his time "in skid row or jazz joints." For Viking Press advance review copies of *On The Road,* the dustwrapper announcement dwelled on the mad hedonism of the book:

On The Road is about Sal Paradise, Dean Moriarty and their friends—one moment savagely irresponsible and the next touchingly responsive and gentle. The narrative of life among these wild bohemians carries us back and forth across the continent and down to New Orleans and Mexico. The characters buy cars and wreck them, steal cars and leave them standing in fields, undertake to drive cars from one city to another, sharing the gas; and then for variety they go hitch-hiking or sometimes ride a bus. In cities they go on wild parties or sit in joints listening to hot trumpets. They seem a little like machines themselves—machines gone haywire, always wound to the last pitch, always nervously moving, drinking, making love, determined to say Yes to any new experience. The writing at its best is deeply felt, poetic and extremely moving. Again at its best this book is a celebration of the American scene in a manner of a latter-day Wolfe or Sandburg. The story itself has a steady, fast, unflagging movement that carries the reader along with it, always into new towns and madder adventures. (Viking)

Hugo Weber repeated Kerouac's statement, "I'm King of the Beats, but I'm not a Beatnik" to me in New York in November 1968. Patricia MacManus described meeting Kerouac soon after the publication of *On the Road.* He took out of his tattered wallet a worn, much handled "holy picture" of the Virgin of Guadalupe and gave it to her. On the back was a printed prayer with these lines underscored in ink: "My son, do not be troubled nor disturbed by anything; do not fear illness nor any other distressing occurrence . . . . Have I not placed you on my lap and made you my responsibility? Do you need anything else?" (Patricia MacMannus in *The Progressive,* June 1973)

Chapter Twenty-Nine

Kerouac never published a novel about his years as a famous writer after *On The Road* was published. But on 16 December, 1958 he wrote Ginsberg that he was planning to end *Desolation Angels* with a fictionalized celebration of the publication of *On The Road* and the fame that followed. Kerouac intended to show how he began as a hitchhiking bum and had gone on to become famous.

In a sketch "New York Scenes" in *Lonesome Traveler,* Kerouac described his years roaming around the city with his friends, but he omitted his feelings about becoming a celebrity after *On The Road.*

Kerouac was interviewed in *Pageant* Magazine, February 1958, "Lamb, No Lion." See also *Esquire,* March 1958 for Kerouac's "The Philosophy of the Beat Generation" and *Playboy,* June 1959 for "The Origins of the Beat Generation." On 6 November the *Village Voice* reported the Hunter College debate between Kerouac, Amis, Montagu and Wechsler.

See *Book of Dreams* (pp. 173-4) for Kerouac's dream on the day after the publication of *On The Road.* Charles Sampas was interviewed in Lowell in October 1966 and told me about Kerouac's pretending to be drunk.

Memory Babe, the book Kerouac started in October 1957, was never published. In a letter to Joyce Glassman in the late summer of 1958 Kerouac said he was still trying to finish it but he was bored with the story and significant details escaped him. It was also hard for him to write on dexamyls, he said, and asked her to buy him some benzedrine.

For about a year he had been toying with the form of the book and finally decided to shape it by piling up a series of typical events on a Christmas weekend in Lowell in 1933 when he was seven years old. At the center was a flashback to the Heavenly Vision of Memory Babe. In the Vision Jack was a shepherd boy with his Lowell school friends, St. Joseph was Leo but he couldn't identify the Virgin. When he woke up Christmas morning after the Vision, he went to church and celebrated the holiday with his family in Lowell. Perhaps an idea of what Kerouac intended in *Memory Babe* is suggested by his sketch "Not Long Ago Joy Abounded at Christmas," printed in the New York *World Telegram and Sun* on 5 December, 1957, a few months after he first began work on the novel.

In our interview in New York on 18 October, 1972 Joyce Glassman remembered Kerouac's saying "Cauterize my wounds" and that it was strange to have his mother forbid his friends to visit. She also recalled his comparing himself to Melville.

On 24 March, 1959 Kerouac wrote Ginsberg wondering if his belligerent drunkenness wasn't the result of brain damage. He also told Ginsberg that he planned to stay in Northport with mémêre. Mémêre wrote Ginsberg in Paris on 13 July, 1958.

Carolyn Cassady was interviewed on 6 October, 1972 about Neal's arrest and conviction in 1958. On 12 June, 1959, 430 days after going to San Quentin, Neal wrote Jack a sad and ironic postcard saying that giving those "offbrand cigarettes" to the federal agents had freed him from his responsibilities to job and family and permitted him to concentrate on really important things like which wall to stare at in the tiny cell he shared with a gunman.

Kerouac's film script for *Pull My Daisy* was published in 1961 by Grove Press. *Pull My Daisy* has become a classic underground film, and there are extended accounts of how it was produced at Alfred Leslie's studio in David Amram's book *Vibrations* and in Leslie's article about the film in the *Village Voice*, " 'Daisy': 10 Years Later."

The idea for the scenario of the film was suggested to Kerouac, according to Carolyn Cassady, by an incident that happened in their house in Los Gatos. She told me on 8 October, 1972 that she and Neal had met a young Swiss Bishop at the Liberal Catholic Church in 1956 and wanted Jack to hear him. Neal asked the Bishop to come to the house, and he showed up with his mother and his aunt. Kerouac, Ginsberg, Peter Orlovsky and Pat Donovan were in Neal's living room drinking wine while they waited to talk to him. As Carolyn remembered, they didn't have much furniture in the new house so Jack sat on the floor by the Bishop's feet, turning to look up at him and say "I love you." The two little old ladies sat on the couch. Allen made room for himself between them and put his head on the ladies' knees, insisting "Let's talk about sex." The Bishop was steadfastly "mystical" through all the shenanigans, according to Carolyn, but she was embarrassed. Neal, as always, just went on talking.

Years later in New York, Kerouac told the story of the Bishop to Alfred Leslie, who immediately recognized its possibilities as a film script. Copies of Jack's story were circulated as a scenario for the film, and the shooting was done in Leslie's studio with Ginsberg, Orlovsky, Corso, Larry Rivers, Mooney Peebles, David Amram and others in January-March 1959. According to Leslie's friend, the poet James Tate, Kerouac was barred from the studio after the first sessions because he'd show up drunk "with real bums from the Bowery" and cause a commotion. After Robert Frank had filmed about thirty hours of the scenario, it was edited down to twenty-eight minutes and Kerouac was brought in to overdub his narrative. Leslie remembered that "Kerouac's dialogue was used as voice-over rather than lip-sync" because Leslie wouldn't accept anyone reading Jack's lines except himself. "His taking all of the voice parts paralleled his literary style where all of the characters were aspects of himself. Kerouac's narration was a triumph." Jack objected to the narration because it was recorded four times, once at his home in Long Island and three times in a sound studio, and the tapes were cut, edited and rewoven into one track. Jack wanted his spoken dialogue to be used intact.

Alfred Aronowitz's "The Beat Generation" in the New York *Post*, 10 March, 1959 is the source for the quotations about Kerouac's life on Gilbert Street in Northport.

Ginsberg wrote his brother Eugene Brooks on 23 January, 1957 about Kerouac's having his mother's "native French Peasant parsimony." Jack described the "Jack Crackerjack" TV parody by the actor Louis Nye to Allen in a letter on 6 October, 1959. *Clothesline* 2 (1970) had an account of Kerouac, Ginsberg and Orlovsky trying to visit Frank O'Hara in New York City in October, 1959. The account was written by Joseph LeSueur.

The New York *Times* reviewed *Doctor Sax* on 3 May, 1959 and *Mexico City Blues* on 29 November, 1959. *Time* Magazine called Kerouac a "cut-rate Thomas Wolfe" on 24 February, 1958. On the David Susskind TV show in September, 1959 Norman Mailer protested when Truman Capote said Kerouac's work was typing, not writing. Mailer tried to defend the spontaneity and intuitive approach of the beats and the hipsters and said that modern man was drifting too far from his senses. But Kerouac cared little for Mailer's defense. He put Mailer down for saying God was dead and suspected Mailer was associating himself with hipsters only to further his own career. In the last years of Kerouac's life he liked to get drunk and tell a favorite story about finding Mailer in a men's room pissing on another author (Larry

Vickers on "Jack Kerouac: The End of the Road" in *Father Joe's Handy Homilies*, June 1970).

In a letter to Allen Ginsberg on 24 March, 1959 Kerouac said he sent the American College Dictionary a definition of "beat generation," and connected the disaffection of the "beats" with the Cold War. On 20 April, 1973 Ginsberg explained what he saw happen to Kerouac at the Hunter College debate. Tom Parkinson wrote me on 23 March, 1973 that *Kaddish* was well along in the winter of 1957-8 when Allen visited him in London.

Chapter Thirty

Big Sur describes Kerouac's summer in San Francisco and Bixby Canyon in 1960.

Most of the quotations in this chapter are from *Book of Dreams*, unless otherwise specified. Ginsberg wrote me about the composition of "Sea"—"the writing saint's alone with the universe" on 20 April, 1973.

Chapter Thirty-One

In our interview in San Francisco on 4 June, 1960, Ferlinghetti told me he objected to his description as a "genial businessman" in *Big Sur*. Welch's knowledge that he was "the end of a very strong line" is in his interview with David Meltzer in *The San Francisco Poets*.

Carolyn Cassady was interviewed in San Francisco on 6 October, 1972 about Neal's impressions of *On The Road*.

Chapter Thirty-Two

Kerouac told his *Paris Review* interviewers that his prose in *Big Sur* was the perfection of his three styles: the speedwriting of *The Railroad Earth*, the mystical style of *Tristessa* and the confessional madness of *The Subterraneans*. *Big Sur* told a "plain tale in a smooth buttery literate run."

In the *Biblio*. Kerouac stated that his sister had objected to the sex passages in *Big Sur*.

Kerouac wrote to Ferlinghetti in September 1960 thanking him for the cabin at Bixby Canyon and told of his flight back to New York.

Chapter Thirty-Three

Satori in Paris describes Kerouac's trip in June 1965. Kerouac asked Carolyn Cassady on 17 October, 1961 about what happened to "Billy" after he left San Francisco.

In "The Last Word" in *Escapade*, Kerouac wrote about toasting in the New Year with mémère.

Snyder told Ginsberg on 22 November, 1962 that "Another name for Satori is kensho, which means seeing your true nature. This ain't a vision."

Keruoac wrote Ginsberg on 18 January, 1955 saying that he thought Burroughs would become a great writer. Ten years later Kerouac said he disliked Burroughs' literary experiments.

Whalen wrote Ginsberg on 20 November, 1968 about Kerouac's "1000 word put-down of the New Left and all his other paranoias."

David Markson was interviewed about Kerouac on 19 October, 1972; Hugo Weber in October and December 1968.

In a letter on 1 December, 1965 to Fred Jordan, his editor at Grove Press, Kerouac said he wanted to be certain that readers connected the name of Raymond Baillet with the taxi driver at the beginning of the book and therefore not miss the meaning of the title, *Satori In Paris*.

Chapter Thirty-Four

Kerouac wrote me in August 1966 saying that beatniks looked like spooks in his mother's door.

When I spoke with Sterling Lord in New York City about Kerouac on 18 October, 1972, Lord shook his head over Jack's naiveté about how much the Hyannis bartender was earning. Lord estimated the bartender probably made about $20,000 a year to Kerouac's $5,000. Certainly Kerouac was earning very little income from his writing at the time I visited him. His sales were very low, for example $600 for the three part serialization of *Satori in Paris* in *Evergreen Review* (1965) and $400 for the excerpt "The Death of Swinburne" from *Vanity of Duluoz* (1967).

Burroughs told me in London on 29 November, 1972 that in his opinion, Kerouac's personality never changed. "He was always primarily a writer and not a person. He felt that everything he was doing as a person he was pretending to do."

Chapter Thirty-Five

See *Vanity of Duluoz* for Kerouac's being "in a continual rage" about his "suffering in the working world." Stella and Jack Kerouac were married on 18 November, 1966.

Kerouac's being a slave re "Old Angel Midnight" is from

his *Escapade* article in April 1961, "Jack Kerouac Takes a Fresh Look at Jack Kerouac." Evidence that he rewrote his books, despite his public denials to interviewers, can be found by comparing his manuscripts with the published versions. He often described to his friends the revisions as they were in progress, as in a letter on 28 October, 1958 to Carolyn Cassady about working over *Visions of Gerard*.

Ginsberg was interviewed at the West End on 18 September, 1969 about Kerouac's devoting his vision to characters he's baffled by. Kerouac said in *Nugget* in October 1960 that Ginsberg didn't do anything but talk.

Kerouac wrote Carolyn Cassady on 17 October, 1961 apologizing for telling the truth about everybody in his books, adding that he always made an effort to play down the sordid aspects. In the *Paris Review* interview he said, "Notoriety and public confession is a frazzler of the heart you were born with, believe me." The interview also included, "I rode around this country free as a bee."

See Daniel Talbot's review of *Tristessa* in the New York *Times* on 19 June, 1960 for Kerouac's rekindling of the "Super-Romantic Tradition."

In Hyannis in August 1966 Kerouac told me, "I hear Tennessee Williams won't let his mother read everything he publishes. Why should I?"

Chapter Thirty-Six

In Carolyn Cassady's 6 October, 1972 interview in San Francisco she told me about her last phone calls with Kerouac.

Kerouac's statement "I'm pro-American . . . . The country gave my Canadian family a good break" is from the *Paris Review* interview. His comments about Abbie Hoffman and other New Leftists are from a wire service story which appeared in October 1969 and was variously called "Man Am I the Grand Daddio of the Hippies" and "Kerouac: The Last Word from the Father of the Beats."

Descriptions of Kerouac's last months in St. Petersburg are from articles by Jack McClintock in *Esquire* (March 1970), Robert Boles in *Falcon* (summer 1970) and Larry Vickers in *Father Joe's Handy Homilies* (June 1970).

Appendix Three:
Bibliographical Chronology

Books	Written	Published	Period in Duluoz Chronology
Visions of Gerard	Jan. 1956	1963	1922-6 Lowell
Doctor Sax	July 1952	1959	1930-6 Lowell
Maggie Cassidy (Springtime Mary)	early 1953	1959	1938-9 Lowell
The Town and the City	1946-9	1950	1935-46 Lowell, N.Y.
Vanity of Duluoz	1968	1968	1939-46 Lowell, N.Y.
On The Road	1948-56	1957	1946-50 Cross-country
Visions of Cody (Visions of Neal)	1951-2	1959	1946-52 Cross-country
The Subterraneans	Oct. 1953	1958	Summer 1953 N.Y.
Tristessa	1955-6	1960	1955-6 Mexico City
The Dharma Bums	Nov. 1957	1958	1955-6 West Coast
Desolation Angels	1956, 1961	1965	1956-7 West Coast, Mexico, Tangier, N.Y.
Big Sur	Oct. 1961	1962	Summer 1960 California
Satori in Paris	1965	1966	June 1965 Paris
Mexico City Blues	Aug. 1955	1959	
The Scripture of the Golden Eternity	May 1956	1960	
Pull My Daisy	March 1959	1961	
Book of Dreams	1952-60	1960	
Lonesome Traveler	1960 (compiled)	1960	
Pic	1969	1971	
San Francisco Blues	April 1954		
Some of the Dharma (Buddha Tells Us)	1954-5		
Wake Up	1955		
Pomes All Sizes	1960s		

Appendix Four: Identity Key

Name	The Town and the City	Vanity of Duluoz	On The Road	The Subterraneans	The Dharma Bums	Desolation Angels	Big Sur	Book of Dreams
Jack Kerouac	Peter Martin et al.	Jack Duluoz	Sal Paradise	Leo Percepied	Ray Smith	Jack Duluoz	Jack Duluoz	Jack
Allen Ginsberg	Leon Levinsky	Irwin Garden	Carlo Marx	Adam Moorad	Alvah Goldbook	Irwin Garden	Irwin Garden	Irwin Garden
Neal Cassady			Dean Moriarty		Cody Pomeray	Cody Pomeray	Cody Pomeray	Cody Pomeray
William Burroughs	Will Dennison	Will Hubbard	Old Bull Lee	Frank Carmody		Bull Hubbard		Bull Hubbard
Gary Snyder					Japhy Ryder		Jarry Wagner	
Gregory Corso				Yuri Gligoric		Raphael Urso		Raphael Urso
Philip Whalen					Warren Coughlin		Ben Fagin	
Michael McClure					Ike O'Shay	Patrick McLear	Pat McLear	Danny Richman
Lawrence Ferlinghetti				Larry O'Hara			Lorenzo Monsanto	James Watson
John Clellon Holmes			Tom Saybrook	Balliol MacJones				
Kenneth Rexroth					Rheinhold Cacoethes			
Herbert Huncke	Junky		Elmo Hassel					Huck
Philip Lamantia					Francis DaPavia	David D'Angeli		
Lew Welch							David Wain	
Lenore Kandel							Romona Swartz	
John Montgomery					Henry Morley	Alex Fairbrother		
Randall Jarrell						Varnum Random		
Gore Vidal				Arial Lavalina	George			
Peter Orlovsky						Simon Darlovsky		Simon Darlovsky
Robert Duncan						Geoffrey Donald		

Appendix Five: Index